Venus and Virtue

Venus *and* Virtue

Celebrating Sex and Seeking Sanctification

EDITED BY
Jerry L. Walls, Jeremy Neill,
AND David Baggett

CASCADE *Books* · Eugene, Oregon

VENUS AND VIRTUE
Celebrating Sex and Seeking Sanctification

Copyright © 2018 Wipf and Stock Publishers. All rights reserved. Except for brief quotations in critical publications or reviews, no part of this book may be reproduced in any manner without prior written permission from the publisher. Write: Permissions, Wipf and Stock Publishers, 199 W. 8th Ave., Suite 3, Eugene, OR 97401.

Cascade Books
An Imprint of Wipf and Stock Publishers
199 W. 8th Ave., Suite 3
Eugene, OR 97401

www.wipfandstock.com

PAPERBACK ISBN: 978-1-4982-9634-2
HARDCOVER ISBN: 978-1-4982-9636-6
EBOOK ISBN: 978-1-4982-9635-9

Cataloguing-in-Publication data:

Names: Walls, Jerry L. | Neill, Jeremy | Baggett, David

Title: Venus and Virtue : Celebrating Sex and Seeking Sanctification / Jerry L. Walls, Jeremy Neill, and David Baggett.

Description: Eugene, OR: Cascade Books, 2018 | Includes bibliographical references and index.

Identifiers: ISBN 978-1-4982-9634-2 (paperback) | ISBN 978-1-4982-9636-6 (hardcover) | ISBN 978-1-4982-9635-9 (ebook)

Subjects: LCSH: Sexual ethics | Sex—Religious aspects—Christianity | Chastity | Homosexuality—Religious aspects—Christianity | Christian ethics

Classification: BT708 W35 2018 (print) | BT708 (ebook)

Manufactured in the U.S.A.   01/11/18

Permission was obtained to reprint and expand upon the following works:

Hiestand, Gerald. "A Biblical-Theological Approach to Premarital Sexual Ethics, or What Saint Paul Would Say about 'Making Out.'" *Bulletin of Ecclesial Theology* 1.1 (2014) 13–34.

Broadway, Anna. "Practicing Trust," *Books and Culture,* January–February 2012.

The following Bible translations are used in this book:

New International Version, copyright © 1984 by Biblica, Inc.™ Used by permission. All rights reserved worldwide.

English Standard Version, copyright © 2001 by Crossway, a publishing ministry of Good News Publishers. All rights reserved.

New American Standard Bible, copyright © 1995 by The Lockman Foundation. Used by permission.

New English Translation (NET) Bible, copyright © 1996–2016 by Biblical Studies Press, LLC. All rights reserved.

Lexham English Bible, copyright © 2010 Logos Bible Software. Lexham is a registered trademark of Logos Bible Software.

King James Version

For Heather, a brown-haired, brown-eyed beauty who knows well the ways of both Venus and Virtue.

—J. N.

Contents

Contributors List | xi
Acknowledgments | xvii
Introduction by Jerry L. Walls | xix

Part 1: Biblical and Theological Foundations for Human Sexuality

CHAPTER 1
Garden of Delights and Dilemmas: The Old Testament on Sex | 3
—*Lawson G. Stone*

CHAPTER 2
Premarital Sex for Christians: Yes, No, or Maybe? | 18
—*Joseph R. Dongell*

CHAPTER 3
Three in One and Two Become One: A Christian Theology of Sex | 34
—*A. Chadwick Thornhill*

CHAPTER 4
Biological Transformation: Does Marriage Change Your Relational DNA? | 49
—*Jeremy Neill*

Part 2: Christian Sexuality for Singles

CHAPTER 5
Why Young Christians Wince at Old-School Sexual Ethics | 65
—Brett McCracken

CHAPTER 6
How to Trust God with Your Body | 79
—Anna Broadway

Chapter 7
From Lizards to Stallions: Exercising Moral Faith | 92
—David Baggett with Marybeth Baggett

CHAPTER 8
What Would St. Paul Say about "Making Out"? | 106
—Gerald Hiestand

CHAPTER 9
What About Sex? Habits of Heart for a Fulfilling Sexual Relationship and a Happy Marriage | 121
—Mary Rice Hasson

CHAPTER 10
Continence, Character, and the Morality of Masturbation | 140
—Matthew Dugandzic

CHAPTER 11
Chastity's Helping Hand? How Masturbation Can Serve Virtue | 151
—Erin Dufault-Hunter

Part 3: Christian Sexuality for Persons with Same-Sex Attraction

CHAPTER 12
A Christian Response to the "Born This Way" Theology of Homosexuality | 175
—Raymond Phinney

CHAPTER 13
Same-Sex Attraction and the Calling of God | 195
—*Ron Belgau*

CHAPTER 14
The Sexual Pluralist Revolution: Reasons to Be Skeptical | 211
—*James S. Spiegel*

Part 4: Pastoral Wisdom for Christian Sexuality

CHAPTER 15
The Place of Forgiveness in the Marriage Bed | 227
—*Stephanie Ellis*

CHAPTER 16
Leavening the Dough of Sexual Purity . . . by the Spirit | 240
—*Jay Thomas*

Index | 253

Contributors List

David Baggett is a professor of philosophy in the Rawlings School of Divinity at Liberty University in Lynchburg, Virginia. Author or editor of over a dozen books, he is coauthor (with Jerry Walls) of *Good God: The Theistic Foundations of Morality* (Oxford University Press, 2011) and *God and Cosmos: Moral Truth and Human Meaning* (Oxford University Press, 2016), and the executive editor at MoralApologetics.com.

Marybeth Baggett is an associate professor of English at Liberty University. She is the coauthor of two books (with her husband David): *At the Bend of the River Grand* (Emeth, 2016) and *The Morals of the Story: Good News about a Good God* (IVP Academic, 2017). She has written a handful of academic articles on subjects as diverse as Thomas More and Nella Larsen. Her research and teaching interests include literary theory, contemporary American literature, science fiction, and dystopian literature, with particular concern for the work of Kurt Vonnegut.

Ron Belgau is the cofounder, with Dr. Wesley Hill, of the *Spiritual Friendship* blog (spiritualfriendship.org), and was invited to speak at the World Meeting of Families, as part of Pope Francis's 2015 visit to Philadelphia. He studied philosophy at St. Louis University, where he taught ethics, medical ethics, philosophy of the human person, and philosophy of religion. His work has appeared in the *New Oxford Review*, *First Things*, and *Notre Dame Magazine*, where one of his essays shared first place for "Best Investigative Writing or Analysis" in the Catholic Press Association's 2005 Press Awards. He has spoken about sexuality and prolife issues in churches and at universities in the United States, Canada, and the United Kingdom.

Anna Broadway is a writer and editor living near San Francisco. The author of *Sexless in the City: A Memoir of Reluctant Chastity* (Doubleday/WaterBrook, 2008), she is also a contributor to the anthologies *Faith at the Edge* (Ave Maria, 2008), *Talking Taboo* (White Cloud, 2013), and *Disquiet Time* (Hachette/Jericho, 2014). She holds an MA in religious studies from Arizona State University and has written for the *Washington Post*, *The Atlantic* online, *Books and Culture*, *Christianity Today*, *Journal of the History of Sexuality*, *Paste*, Beliefnet, *Relevant*, and other publications. She also contributes regularly to the the Women section of *Christianity Today* online (www.christianitytoday.com/women). Find her on Twitter @annabroadway or visit sexlessinthecity.net.

Joseph R. Dongell (Joe) and Regina (his wife of thirty-five years) reside in Wilmore, Kentucky, and have two adult children. He earned an MDiv from Asbury Seminary, an MA in classical literature from the University of Kentucky, and his PhD from Union Theological Seminary in Virginia. He serves as a professor of biblical studies at Asbury Theological Seminary, having joined the faculty in 1988. His research includes a book coauthored with Jerry Walls called *Why I Am Not a Calvinist* (InterVarsity, 2004). Joe enjoys coffee, brisk walks, gardening, old machinery, and long conversations with people who do not (yet) embrace the Jesus of the Bible.

Erin Dufault-Hunter has been since 2006 an assistant professor of Christian ethics at Fuller Theological Seminary. She completed her undergraduate degree at Occidental College and her PhD at the University of Southern California. Erin has published in Christian ethics and Christian sexual ethics in particular. Her publications include the following: *The Transformative Power of Faith: A Narrative Approach to Conversion* (Lexington Books, 2012); "The Downside of Getting It Up: How Viagra Reveals the Persistence of Patriarchy and the Need for Sexual Character" (*Journal of the Society of Christian Ethics*, Spring–Summer 2012); and the following entries in *The Dictionary of Scripture and Ethics* (Baker Academic, 2011): "Individualism," "Orphan," "Pornography," "Sex and Sexuality," "Sexual Ethics," "Sociology of Religion," and "Spousal Abuse."

Matthew Dugandzic is a PhD student in Christian ethics at the Catholic University of America. He serves as the web editor of *Fare Forward* (farefwd.com) and his writing has appeared in the publication *First Things* and on the blogs *Ethika Politika* (ethikapolitika.org).

Stephanie Ellis has a PhD in counseling psychology and an MA in counseling and guidance. She has worked as a psychotherapist for nearly a decade with individuals, couples, and families; she also trains counselors in her work at Houston Baptist University and teaches courses on couples, marriage, and family counseling. She lives and works in Houston with her husband and two daughters.

Mary Rice Hasson, JD, is a fellow at the Ethics and Public Policy Center in Washington, DC, and the director of the Catholic Women's Forum at EPPC. She is the editor of *Promise and Challenge: Catholic Women Reflect on Feminism, Complementarity, and the Church*. Mary writes and speaks frequently on issues related to women, sexuality, marriage, faith, and gender. She and her husband Seamus have been married for 34 years and are the parents of five sons and two daughters.

Gerald Hiestand, a PhD candidate in classics at the University of Reading, is the senior associate pastor at Calvary Memorial Church, and the director and cofounder of the Center for Pastor Theologians. Gerald is the author of numerous articles and books, including *Sex, Dating, and Relationships: A Fresh Approach* (Crossway, 2012), and is coeditor of *Beauty, Order, and Mystery: A Christian Vision of Sexuality* (IVP Academic, 2017). Gerald and his wife have four children. They live in the village of Oak Park, just outside of Chicago.

Brett McCracken is a senior editor for The Gospel Coalition. He is the author of *Uncomfortable: The Awkward and Essential Challenge of Christian Community* (Crossway, 2017), *Hipster Christianity: When Cool and Church Collide* (Baker, 2010) and *Gray Matters: Navigating the Space between Legalism and Liberty* (Baker, 2013). He also writes regularly for *Christianity Today* and his website, BrettMcCracken.com. He lives with his wife in Southern California where he serves as an elder at Southlands Church. Follow him on Twitter @brettmccracken.

Jeremy Neill is an assistant professor of philosophy at Houston Baptist University, where he has taught since 2011. He is a graduate of Wheaton College. He has published over twenty articles and reviews with journals such as *Faith and Philosophy*, *Philosophy and Social Criticism*, *Review of Metaphysics*, *Social Theory and Practice*, *Political Theology*, *Res Publica*, and *Public Reason*.

Raymond Phinney has a doctorate in experimental psychology from Washington State University. He has studied perception, attention, and cognition for twenty years using behavioral methods, single-unit electrophysiology and optical imaging in monkeys, and functional MRI in humans. After postdoctoral work at Rutgers University's Center for Molecular and Behavioral Neuroscience and at the Medical College of Wisconsin, he took a position in the psychology department at Wheaton College in 2004. He has served as the chair of the undergraduate psychology program at Wheaton since 2011.

James S. Spiegel is a professor of philosophy and Religion at Taylor University, where he has taught since 1993. He has published ten books and over eighty articles and book chapters. His publications, which primarily explore issues in ethics and philosophy of religion, have appeared in such scholarly journals as *Sophia, Faith and Philosophy, Toronto Journal of Theology, Theory and Research in Education*, and the *International Journal of Philosophy and Theology*, as well as popular periodicals such as *Christianity Today, Books and Culture, Salvo,* and *Touchstone*. Jim's books include *The Benefits of Providence: A New Look at Divine Providence* (Crossway, 2005); *Faith, Film, and Philosophy* (coedited with R. Douglas Geivett; InterVarsity, 2007); and the two-volume Idealism and Christianity series (as general editor; Bloomsbury, 2016). Jim and his wife, Amy, blog together at *Wisdom and Folly* (wisdomandfollyblog.com). They have four children and live in Upland, Indiana.

Lawson Stone has taught at Asbury Theological Seminary since 1987. After graduating from Asbury College, he served as a missionary in Kenya. Dr. Stone served as a translator for the New Living Translation and has contributed scholarly articles to the *Journal of Biblical Literature, Catholic Biblical Quarterly, Dictionary of the Old Testament: Historical Books* (InterVarsity, 2005), *Dictionary of Major Biblical Interpreters* (InterVarsity, 2007), *The New Interpreter's Dictionary of the Bible* (Abingdon, 2009), and *Biblica: The Bible Atlas: A Social and Historical Journey Through the Lands of the Bible* (Global, 2006).

Jay Thomas is the lead pastor at Chapel Hill Bible Church in Chapel Hill, North Carolina. He is married to Rebecca and they have four children. Jay is a graduate of Wheaton College (BA) and Gordon-Conwell Theological Seminary (MDiv and ThM). He is a fellow of the Center for Pastor Theologians and an instructor for the Charles Simeon Trust, a ministry that equips pastors with the convictions and competencies to preach expository sermons. His church is committed to gospel-centered, biblically driven, multicultural, and multigenerational ministry with a heart to be a church for the good of the Raleigh, Durham, and Chapel Hill region of North Carolina.

A. Chadwick Thornhill is the chair of theological studies and an associate professor of apologetics and biblical studies for the Liberty University School of Divinity. He is the author of a number of articles and essays and the books *The Chosen People: Election, Paul, and Second Temple Judaism* (IVP Academic, 2015) and *Greek for Everyone: Introductory Greek for Bible Study and Application* (Baker, 2016).

Jerry L. Walls is Scholar in Residence and a professor of philosophy at Houston Baptist University, where he has taught since 2011. He has published numerous articles and several books, including *Hell: The Logic of Damnation* (University of Notre Dame Press, 1992); *Heaven: The Logic of Eternal Joy* (Oxford University Press, 2002); *The Oxford Handbook of Eschatology* (as editor; Oxford University Press, 2008); and *Purgatory: The Logic of Total Transformation* (Oxford University Press, 2012).

Acknowledgments

The inspiration for this book grew out of a spirited discussion about Christian sexual ethics on Facebook. Both the nature of the discussion and the energy it elicited led me to think a book like this would be a valuable resource for many contemporary Christians. Thanks to the several participants in that discussion, especially my former student Chris Attaway, who raised a number of questions that sparked that original debate.

As always, I am grateful to my family for their love and support, which adds meaning to everything I do. Thanks to Tim and Angela Amos, Madelyn Rose, Mackenzie Grace, and Abigail Joy; and to Jonny and Emily Walls.

—Jerry L. Walls

This book has been a long time in the making and I am grateful to a number of people for their patience and encouragement throughout the process. First, I am grateful to Jerry Walls for raising the idea of this book and helping me see it through. Jerry's passion for everything he does is incredibly infectious. I am grateful also for David Baggett's encouragement throughout the book's editing phase. Dave's work ethic is an inspiration! My beautiful and brilliant wife, Heather, has, I think, heard most of the arguments in this book at least a half dozen times. She urged me not to give up on several occasions when the book encountered obstacles. Finally, I am grateful for the support of my family: Max, Cherry, Christopher, and Micah Neill; and Gordon, Niki, and Mark Elliott. They have been wonderful cheerleaders along the way.

—Jeremy Neill

INTRODUCTION

Christian Sexual Ethics

Castration or Celebration?

JERRY L. WALLS

In 1956, Elvis Presley performed his hit song "Hound Dog" on the Milton Berle television show, and it set off a national controversy. The problem was not because English teachers and grammarians everywhere rose up to protest his use of the word "ain't," nor was it because the song was deemed offensive to women by referring to them as hound dogs. No, the firestorm was ignited because Elvis famously gyrated his hips in such a way that earned him the name "Elvis the Pelvis."

The criticism was both immediate and sharp. His performance was repudiated for its "vulgarity" and "animalism" and many saw it as an attack on morality. Reaction among religious leaders was especially intense, epitomized by an article entitled "Beware Elvis Presley," which appeared in the weekly publication of the Roman Catholic Church.[1]

This episode illustrates just how radically sexual attitudes have shifted in a remarkably short period of time. The sexual revolution of the sixties and seventies was swift and decisive. Pop culture, which both drove the revolution as well as reflected it, has dramatically changed since the days when Elvis caused a national uproar with his pelvic gyrations. For at least a couple generations now, we have been schooled by numerous sitcoms and popular songs in which various forms of non-marital and non-traditional sex have been depicted as perfectly normal, harmless, and even charming. Sexual expressions of every variety have become so commonplace that the

---

1. For all the claims in this paragraph, see https://en.wikipedia.org/wiki/Hound_Dog_(song).

reaction to Elvis in 1956 is simply incomprehensible to most of us, except as a quaint bit of cultural history. There has been a sea change in our moral attitudes that runs so deep we can hardly see it.

This dramatic change has generated tremendous confusion about sex among Christians as well as the rest of the culture. Most traditional boundaries have broken down, and many of us have no idea where the boundaries are to be located these days, or even whether they are still in force. The deepest reason for this is because we no longer have a clear idea why things are right or wrong, or what makes them so.

In his chapter on "Sexual Morality" in *Mere Christianity*, C. S. Lewis drew a distinction between the Christian rule of chastity (sexual morality) and the rule of modesty or propriety. The former, he argued, remains the same in all times and places, but the latter varies from culture to culture, and from one generation to another. Lewis wrote during a period when standards were changing, and he offered this opinion:

> I do not think that a very strict or fussy standard of propriety is any proof of chastity or any help to it, and I therefore regard the great relaxation and simplifying of the rule which has taken place in my own lifetime as a good thing. At its present stage, however, it has this inconvenience, that people of different ages and different types do not all acknowledge the same standard, and we hardly know where we are.[2]

Lewis's description of his own time as one in which "we hardly know where we are" applies to our time as well. And part of the reason is that many people do not believe the rule of chastity is any more certain or definite than the rule of propriety. Most people might agree that the Elvis episode shows that we have a "less fussy standard of propriety" or modesty, and agree with Lewis that a more relaxed standard on that score is a good thing.

But what is far more telling is that we have also become "relaxed" about the rules of sexual behavior and practice. Our culture no longer recognizes any difference between rules of chastity and rules of modesty and propriety. All such rules, we tend to think, are relative and completely open to change from generation to generation. To raise objections to premarital sex, or homosexual behavior, or divorce on demand is for many people today as preposterous as expressing outrage at Elvis's "Hound Dog" performance. Indeed, "we hardly know where we are."

If we had some idea how we got here, it might give us a clue about where we are. Consider a passage from one of the most noted critics of Christian morality in the history of thought, Friedrich Nietzsche, whom I

---

2. Lewis, *Mere Christianity*, 95.

fondly call "my favorite atheist." Nietzsche is my favorite because he pulled no punches, and ruthlessly forced his readers to face the implications of atheism. He believed that many of his contemporaries who had rejected Christianity still wanted to hold on to at least some parts of Christian morality. Nietzsche believed they were dishonest, and had not fully come to terms with the consequences of their atheism.

> When one gives up Christian belief one thereby deprives oneself of the *right* to Christian morality. For the latter [traditional Christian morality] is absolutely *not* self-evident: one must make this point clear again and again.... Christianity is a system, a consistently thought out and *complete* view of things. If one breaks out of it a fundamental idea, the belief in God, one thereby breaks the whole thing in pieces: one has nothing of any consequence left in one's hands.[3]

Notice Nietzsche's point that traditional Christian morality is not self-evident. It depends on God for its warrant and binding authority. Deny God, Nietzsche insists, and you undermine Christian morality. And this, I think, goes a long way in explaining our moral confusion. God has largely dropped out of sight in the "public square" of our culture, and this is even more the case with respect to the specific beliefs of Christianity. Many people still want to promote morality, even traditional morality, but they have lost the traditional reasons for doing so, and it is far from clear why they still hold such views. The connection between God and morality that Nietzsche insisted upon is no longer recognized. We should hardly be surprised if Christian morality founders and loses credibility when that happens.[4]

Nietzsche welcomed these developments and cheered the decline of Christian morality. In his view, Christian morality is completely at odds with our natural instincts and consequently it leads to hypocrisy and unhappiness. While it purports to improve people, in reality it only tames and weakens them and drains them of their vitality for life, like animals in a cage. In a similar vein, and more colorfully, he charged that Christianity is a morality of "castration."[5]

I believe Nietzsche was partly right in one way, but profoundly wrong otherwise. He was right that Christian morality only fully makes sense when connected to the larger body of Christian belief, starting with belief in the Christian view of God. He failed, however, to truly appreciate the Christian

---

3. Nietzsche, *Twilight of the Idols; and, The Anti-Christ*, 80–81.

4. For extended argument that God best explains morality, see Baggett and Walls, *God and Cosmos*; Baggett and Walls, *Good God*.

5. See Nietzsche, *Twilight of the Idols; and, The Anti-Christ*, 52–55, 66–67.

vision of reality, and as a result, he completely misrepresented Christian morality and its view of sexuality.

Indeed, his notion that Christianity represents a "castration" morality epitomizes a common misconception about the Christian view of sex. Many people believe that Christians are negative about sex or only tolerate it as a biological necessity. Too often Christians are only heard from when they are telling us what they are against, and as a result our positive account of sexuality falls out of sight in the broader culture. This often leaves the unfortunate impression that a positive view of sexuality and its pleasures is a discovery of secularism. Or worse, the proponents of a reckless lifestyle claim it as their prize possession, the lead item in the hedonist trinity of "sex, drugs, and rock 'n roll."

In this book we will argue (as will be apparent from our title) that Christianity promotes a morality of celebration, not one of castration. To appreciate the meaning of Christian morality, it must be understood as an integral part of the cosmic drama that animates Christian theology. The story starts with creation and the pleasure of God in his work, which he declares to be good; indeed, very good. Without a robust theology of creation, we will have a shriveled theology of salvation. We will see the call to holiness or sanctification as a call to deny or suppress our sexuality. In short, we will fail to see that salvation is the redemption and healing of the entirety of God's good creation, which includes our sexuality. So, properly understood, celebrating sex is not at odds with seeking sanctification. Quite to the contrary, the two go hand in hand, like lovers enjoying a walk in the park.

To show this, it is essential that we recover the biblical and theological foundations of morality. It is only when we appreciate the beauty and goodness of the Christian story that we can fully see the truth of Christian morality. The truth of the Christian story will not come into focus for us if it is not seen in light of its magnificent beauty and goodness.

This book begins with biblical and theological considerations, but it does not stop there. It ranges widely over a number of disciplines as we seek to address the diverse questions and issues surrounding sexuality that Christians wrestle with today. Our collection of authors includes not only experts in biblical studies and theology, but also experts in philosophy, psychology, pastoral ministry, pop culture, and women's issues. We hope to provide a resource that is not only theologically grounded, but practical in the best sense of the term. We aim to speak to the real concerns of Christians in the twenty-first century who aspire to follow Christ faithfully in all areas of their lives, including their sexuality, but who struggle to know how to do so in contemporary culture. This book is intended to help pastors, youth leaders, and others in Christian ministry as well as the persons under their care. We also commend it to those outside the church who may be curious about the Christian view of sex, or the Christian worldview in general.

In addition to the diversity of disciplines and areas of expertise that our authors represent, we also want to highlight the fact that this book is an intergenerational project. Our contributors include several younger authors as well as senior scholars. Moreover, this book is an ecumenical project with representatives not only of several Protestant traditions, but Roman Catholicism as well. Obviously, each of us speaks for himself or herself, and we differ among ourselves on some important issues, including positions taken by other contributors in this book. For instance, while all of us reject premarital sex, some of our authors differ about what kinds of physical affection are acceptable before marriage, ranging from very strict views to views that are more relaxed. Likewise, some of us believe masturbation is always sinful, but some of us believe it can be an aid to persons committed to a life of Christian virtue. We are united, however, in our conviction that Christians need to recover the rich resources of Scripture and orthodox moral theology in order to make sense of a Christian view of sexuality.

Any book dealing with contemporary sexual issues can hardly ignore the hard, and often painful, questions surrounding homosexuality and the LGBT movement, and we have not ducked these questions. Unfortunately, this issue has become one of the most volatile in the so-called culture wars, and it stirs intense feelings and emotional reactions on all sides. The matter is exacerbated by the fact that this is the issue about which many conservative Christians speak loudest, and the one where they insist on drawing a line in the sand. By striking contrast, unfortunately, heterosexual sins have been winked at for generations in many of these same communities. In such circumstances, homosexuals may understandably be skeptical of what is really going on when homosexuality has become the rallying cry to speak out about moral decline and decadence, and they may rightly wonder what is motivating this sudden outbreak of moral concern.[6]

Given these realities, it is difficult even to address these issues from a traditional Christian viewpoint without being accused of prejudice, ignorance, and even hatred. We have no choice but to address them, however, and we emphasize that we aim to speak respectfully as well as forthrightly, even as we recognize that any attempt to do so will likely be controversial. Our message, however, is one of grace rather than condemnation. Relatively few persons in contemporary culture have escaped altogether from sexual

---

6. See my essay "Homosexual Behavior and Fornication."

sins and scars of one sort or another, and we aspire to offer words of hope and healing for all of us.

In any case, we offer these essays to any who want to understand and wrestle with the hard issues of sexuality that polarize our culture. We especially commend them to Christians who are seeking sanctification as they rightly desire to celebrate the gift of sexuality. We hope readers of this book will come to see ever more clearly that these are not only compatible goals, but goals that are mutually enriching, precisely because it is God himself who has joined them together. Venus and Virtue are truly a match made in heaven.

Bibliography

Baggett, David, and Jerry L. Walls. *God and Cosmos: Moral Truth and Human Meaning.* New York: Oxford University Press, 2016.

———. *Good God: The Theistic Foundations of Morality.* New York: Oxford University Press, 2011.

Lewis, C. S. *Mere Christianity.* Grand Rapids: Zondervan, 2001.

Nietzsche, Friedrich. *Twilight of the Idols; and, The Anti-Christ.* Edited by Michael Tanner. Translated by R. J. Hollingdale. New York: Penguin Classics, 1990.

Walls, Jerry. "Homosexual Behavior and Fornication: Intimate Bedfellows." *School of Christian Thought* (blog), June 28, 2013. https://christianthought.hbu.edu/2013/06/28/homosexual-behavior-and-fornication-intimate-bedfellows.

Part 1

Biblical and Theological Foundations for Human Sexuality

1

Garden of Delights and Dilemmas

The Old Testament on Sex

Lawson G. Stone

Turning to the Old Testament for guidance on sex can be a daunting experience. Stereotypes about the OT being all absolute, simplistic legalism quickly collapse before a long, symphonic, complex epic of national identity played out on the world stage from Egypt to Turkey to Iran, stretching over thousands of years, weaving through four world-class empires, embracing three languages, many cultural upheavals, and even two total civilizational collapses! Then again, nobody actually "wrote" the OT the way an author or editor creates a book, imparting a uniform, single theme and viewpoint. The OT is an eclectic anthology accumulating over the entire period in which ancient Israel lived.

This diversity can create the false impression that the OT lacks a consistent ethical understanding of human sexual intimacy. After all, its characters practice polygamy, prostitutes are spared after battles for having hosted spies, adulteresses whose husbands are murdered become queen mothers, and a Jewish princess who scores with the emperor saves her people from annihilation.[1] To complicate things even further, most Christians have been taught that the OT is at best only second-rank scripture, a legalistic

---

1. Polygamous patriarchs include Abraham (Gen 12–26), Jacob (Gen 29–30), Joseph (Gen 41:45), although polygamy typically gets portrayed as an over-complicated and generally unhappy situation. On Rahab the harlot and the spies, see Josh 2; 6:17, 22–25. 2 Sam 10–12 and 1 Kgs 1–2 detail how Bath Sheba goes from one-night stand to queen mother, and Esther makes a saving sexual impression on the king of Persia (Esth 2).

document either transcended or utterly negated by the grace and love revealed in the New Testament.

And yet the three major monotheistic world religions find in this book the wellsprings for their worldview, theology, and moral vision, confessing it to be inspired by God to convey his truth, his will, to his people. For Christians, the OT remains a vital voice in our Bible. Jesus loved it, quoted it, alluded to it, and declared not a jot or tittle would pass away until all things are fulfilled. He chided the Pharisees for thinking they could find eternal life in the OT when they ignored its principle subject matter, namely, Jesus Christ himself. The words of Jesus and NT authors are saturated in the OT; and in his very last epistle the very mature St. Paul declared that "all scripture," by which he meant the OT, was inspired by God and, more importantly, profitable on every level: for doctrine, reproof, correction, and training in righteousness, thus equipping God's servants for any task they might engage (2 Tim 3:16–17). Before there was a recognizable NT, the apostolic fathers of the late first and early second centuries taught extensively from the OT; and the first heretic expelled from the church universal, Marcion, among other departures from the gospel, denied the OT its place in Christian scripture. Clearly Christian reflection on any important topic, such as sex, cannot afford to ignore the voice of the OT.

To study the OT responsibly, we must dive into the languages, literary forms, and cultural contexts of its writing. Good interpretation arises from a lively engagement with the text, in the framework of the event horizons that shaped it, in a quest for the truth of God that was its fountainhead and is its ultimate reason for existence. All of this must be pursued with a will to know and do the will of God, whatever that turns out to be, and we must humbly seek and depend on the grace of the Holy Spirit to give us honest hearts, clear minds, and diligence to persevere on the path of study.

We also need a place to start, and a direction. Actually the Bible helps us here. The opening chapters of the Bible present narratives of creation and human sin. All ancient cultures used such stories to articulate their core values, their essential worldview, and the justification for their institutions and behavior in the world, offering a rationale for everything from their imperial aspirations and choices for capital cities to a prayer for healing a toothache! Other stories, featuring humans offending the gods and the coming of great floods, charted why things currently are not as they were at the creation, how the original ideal slipped away. Ancient cultures understood the human condition in some way to be at odds with the original creation and strove for a glimpse of how that original wholeness might be recovered.

Genesis 1–3 therefore provides a frame sketching the OT approach to sex.[2] These chapters cast a moral vision; they articulate a worldview, a set of core values that undergird all the diverse treatments of sex that we find in the OT. Obviously, I am not the first to address this topic. My discussion here will depend on the broadest consensus of competent scholarly interpreters, as found in many commentaries and standard reference works. Nothing I say here is unique to me, though I confess I have followed my own instincts and not any one scholarly treatment in detail. Therefore the scarcity of footnotes here should not be taken to mean I have not relied heavily on other interpreters. Rather, I am offering a summary that results from having taught these chapters in the classroom and in church settings for thirty-five years. What I offer here is the synthesis of a career of study and teaching, finding my own way through the OT.[3]

Genesis 1: Sex and Human Identity

The story of the seven days of creation found in Genesis 1:1—2:4a makes the creation of humanity, in the image of God, as male and female, the climax of God's creative work.[4] Repeatedly, God declares his creative acts to be "good." But following the creation of humanity, we hear "*very* good!" None can doubt that this story celebrates humanity as the apex of creation, especially humanity as male and female. The key passage is 1:26–31 (my translation):

> Then God said, "Let us make humanity in our image, according to our likeness, so they can rule over the fish of the sea and over the birds of the sky and over the cattle and over all the earth, even over every creeping thing that creeps on the earth." So God created humanity in his image: in the image of God he created him; male and female he created them. Then God blessed them; and God said to them, "Be fruitful and multiply, and fill the earth, and subdue it; and rule over the fish of the sea and over the birds of the sky and over every living thing that moves on the earth." Then God said, "I now give you every plant bearing seed that is on the face of all the earth, and every tree which has

---

2. My "go to" commentaries on the creation stories remain von Rad, *Genesis*; Hamilton, *Book of Genesis*; Arnold, *Genesis*.

3. For an encyclopedic compilation of all the relevant passages, interpretive issues, information and bibliography it is hard to beat the 850-page treatment of Davidson, *Flame of Yahweh*.

4. A very helpful treatment of the general interpretation of these stories is found in Blocher, *In the Beginning*.

fruit bearing seed; it shall be food for you; and to every animal on earth and to every bird in the sky and to every thing that moves on the earth that has the breath of life, I have given every green plant for food"; and that's how it happened. Then God saw all that He had made, and indeed, it was very good. Evening came, then morning, the sixth day.

The most prominent part of this description is not actually sex, but humanity's commission to have dominion over the rest of creation. Ancient religions understood creation as a temporary order forcibly imposed upon a fundamentally disordered ultimate reality. The default for the universe was chaos, depicted typically as the dark, stormy sea, sometimes portrayed as a dragon or sea monster. As order emerges, the forces of chaos try to destroy it, and one god arises to vanquish the chaos monster and institute an ordered world. In ancient cultures, this victory was reenacted every New Year, stressing the fragility of order and the constant pressure of disorder. Genesis 1, however, takes a different approach. The sea is present, but not as a threat. It is the backdrop of creation and, along with the earth, will participate with God in bringing about an orderly, beautiful world. All the creatures of the land, sea, and sky form part of God's order, which emerges step by step with each "day" of creation. No force rivals God or threatens to overturn his order. Nevertheless, the text seems to think there are some possibilities of the creation going awry and requiring guidance, so humans are created and commissioned. First, they will be God's representatives in the creation, hence, they are his "image," taking the same word used for the images, or "idols," of pagan gods. Second, as God's appointed representatives, their dominion should guarantee that creation continues to flourish according to God's plan. So, while there is no cosmic chaos with which battle is joined, this creation is still no wind-up toy that will only behave as God foreordained. It has within it an open-endedness and many possibilities for good, but possibly also a potential for disorder. Humans, as the agents of God, preside over the creation with the same gracious good will that was exhibited by the Creator himself.

In the context of fostering the orderly flourishing of creation, the story's statements about human sexuality sound several vital notes. First of all, human sexuality is strictly *binary*, male and female. Ancient religions often blurred the male/female boundary, as legends of shape-shifting and gods disguised as males or females show. One of the speakers in Plato's *Symposium*, for example, expounds the original existence of four genders in the form of two binary beings that were separated, resulting in four sexual orientations, namely, homosexual and heterosexual males and females. So the ancients and the authors of the OT were well aware of alternative views of sex difference. Therefore, the OT's very clear statement that there is only male and female, each oriented only to the other, is notable.

In addition, Genesis 1 frankly describes sex difference as *biological*. The Hebrew terms used for female and male persons identify physiological differences. The female is "the pierced one" and the male is "the one with a monument." Recalling that ancient monuments were tall obelisks clarifies the latter reference. Likewise, the call to be fruitful and multiply connects the male/female difference with reproduction. In a world in which fluidity of identity was quite conceivable and often portrayed in myths and legends, the OT writers strongly link sexual identity with the body and its reproductive powers. The idea of being a woman in the body of a man, for example, though familiar enough in ancient cultures, is never affirmed in the OT and clearly excluded by the way the OT can happily correlate physical, biological features with overall sex identity.

Curiously, sex difference is *basic* to creation, but is *not basic* to the nature of the Creator. The Genesis story stands out with its absence of any hint that creation occurs by means of divine procreation. The creator God has neither male nor female consort. In Egypt, even the one creation story beginning with a single deity still featured him as sexual, conceiving the other gods via his own semen landing on his own flesh. But in Genesis 1 God strangely lacks any sex-related detail, creating strictly by speaking the world and its features into existence. We conclude from this that sexuality, seen as divine all over the ancient world, is seen as strictly a feature of the created order in the Bible. God, while portrayed by male social roles in the OT, is never portrayed as an actual man, with male body parts and sexual drives.

That being the case, paradoxically, the male/female difference is basic to humanity being created in God's image. The closest explanation in Genesis 1 for the meaning of humanity being "in the image of God" comes from humanity being "male and female." The key statement, in 1:27, is a little poetic couplet shaped via Hebrew parallelism in which two lines are composed so that they explicitly link together, but with the second line expanding, refining, and defining the first. So the statement, "in the image of God he created him [humanity]," is expanded by "male and female he created them." The parallel structure elaborates "image of God" with the "male and female." Since God is not portrayed as a sexual being, evidently there is a richness in the divine person that could not be adequately expressed in a monolithic humanity, but could only be approximated by humanity as male and female. The critical point is that human identity as male and female rests at the core of our existence as created in the image of God. Of course, the animals in creation also possessed the differentiation between male and female, but in them this difference is not linked to any likeness to God or to a commission to preside over creation. For humans, sexuality points to God's own rich personhood, which is far more than can be grasped by male, or female, or even both.

Genesis 1 portrays male and female as fully equal. They jointly receive the commission "Let *them* rule . . ." Presiding over creation's thriving is the joint calling of man and woman together. This passage underscores the partnership of men and women, clearly signaling that the manifestation of the image of God cannot be complete unless both men and women together carry out the divine commission.

The vital role of human identity as fundamentally sexual explains a peculiar feature of the Bible, especially the OT. The OT singles out sexual sin especially because of the harm and damage it can cause. By identifying sexuality with the image of God in humans, Genesis 1 makes clear that sins in the domain of sexuality corrupt the very image of God in us, drive a wedge in the male-female partnership in God's image, and undermine the divine commission to rule creation.

Among all the sins noted in the OT—murder, theft, lying, etc.—it is sexual sin alone that stands as the most persistent metaphor for utter apostasy from God. Violation of the first two commandments of the Decalogue, the prohibition on acknowledging any other God than Yahweh and the prohibition against religious veneration of any image in the entire creation, shatters Yahweh's covenant with his people. Monotheism and the exaltation of God's nature beyond any visual image are the hallmark contributions of the OT to later civilization. The violation of these form for the OT the essence of sin itself. Repeatedly in the OT, the violation of these two commandments are depicted under the imagery of sexual sin. In the book of Judges, which portrays the collapse of Israel after its entry into Canaan, the author declares in a sweeping indictment (Judg 2:6—3:6) that the Israelites "played the harlot" and abandoned Yahweh for other gods (Judg 2:17). Again, in the story of Gideon, which sits in the very center of the book of Judges, the hero Gideon creates a religious icon for the people—evidently to serve Yahweh. But the people, in the words of Judges 8:27, "whored after it." The most poignant use of this image appears in the prophecy of Hosea, whose personal life, marriage to a harlot, her subsequent betrayal of him, and the aftermath of these events (Hosea 1–3) became the overarching image for God's relationship with Israel. More examples could be cited, but the crucial point here is not merely that sexual sin stands as a large image for the violation of the essential charter of Israel's faith; it is also *the only such sin that functions this way*. The OT hates the exploitation of the poor, but this evil never becomes an archetype for apostasy. Even murder, the ultimate crime against the sanctity of human life, does not become such an archetype. Sexual sin holds center stage pointing to the essence of apostasy, and sexual integrity stands as the image of faithfulness. The dominance of this imagery does not point to some twisted obsession with sex, nor does it point to a denigration of sex. Far from it. It in fact arises from the high importance of sex in understanding human nature.

Moving to the laws in the OT reinforces the centrality of sexual integrity and sexual sin in the moral vision of the Bible. The book of Leviticus, for example, presents a section known to interpreters as the "Holiness Code." In this block of material, Leviticus 18–20, Yahweh invites Israel to "be holy, as I am holy." Here we find the second part of the greatest commandment, "you shall love your neighbor as yourself" (Lev 19:18). Much of Western culture's vision of a just society actually comes from Leviticus 19, with its calls to exercise kindness and mercy, to leave fields partially harvested to allow the poor to glean food for themselves, and to show respect for all. But this chapter stands in a larger structure, a "bracket" that frames it. That bracket presents not one, but two long lists of prohibited sexual relations (Lev 18:1–23; 20:10–21). Both lists are addressed to the Israelite male head of household, the most powerful person in the ordinary Israelite community. This male, who possessed extreme authority to dispose of the affairs—and the persons—in his extended family, is strictly charged to avoid any sexual exploitation of others. The list of prohibited sexual targets, which is detailed, would be unthinkable in many cultures, where the power of the male head of household permits many abuses and leaves him all but untouchable. Here, the Israelite male is warned not to imitate the sexually exploitative behavior that characterized the Canaanites, who preceded them in the land. The result of crossing this line of protection against sexually victimizing members of the community is striking: the land itself will "vomit you out" (Lev 18:24–30; 20:22–27). Again, the unusual prominence and detailed description of these sexual boundaries does not suggest an unwholesome obsession with sex, nor is it a puritanical attempt to prevent anyone from having fun. It arises from seeing the capacity for sexual intimacy as central to human nature, sacred, a pointer to our being in God's image. A sin here strikes at our very personhood before God. Sexual predation is the ultimate interpersonal abuse of power.

So Genesis 1 places human sexuality in a paradoxical position. On the one hand, God himself is a being utterly beyond all categories of gender or sexuality. God is not a male or a female, has neither spouse nor consort, does not create by sexual generation, and lacks nothing in the unbounded richness of his own life. On the other hand, he has imparted, gifted, to creation the generative power of sexuality, constituting human beings in his image, a richness of personhood in God only approximated in finite human life by the totality of humans as male and female together. Our identity as either male or female, and as together sharing in God's commission to rule creation, means that sins in this domain carry a destructive force greater than other sins. Partaking as it does of this sacredness, the OT rightly emphasizes boundaries on human sexual behavior.

Christians today, as heirs of a shallow, "cheap grace" piety, have trouble with the idea of a scale of moral offense. We often hear the claim that some sin, usually not sexual, is "just as bad" as some sexual sin, and conversely, that sexual sin must be no worse than, say, breaking the speed limit or cheating on taxes. They assert a false moral equivalence among things thought to be sin. Thus, the church's emphasis on sexual sin appears selective, obsessively harsh, and hypocritical. Theologically, of course, there are no degrees of "lostness." Scripture clearly divides between life and death, following Christ and not following Christ. That fact, however, does not in any way imply that there are therefore no degrees of moral offensiveness or harm in different sins. Scripture and plain reason show that different sinful actions cause differing levels of harm. Sexuality clearly appears in Genesis 1 (and elsewhere) as something highly valued, and therefore safeguarded with strong moral boundaries.

Genesis 2: Sex and Human Intimacy

Genesis 2:4b begins a new story, one quite different from 1:1—2:4a. The tape rolls back to the pre-creation state and the story unfolds quite differently. Some find it disturbing that the OT offers us two distinct narratives about creation, but the ancient world would not have found this surprising. For example, the ancient Egyptians had at least four different creation stories. The author of Genesis evidently had no problem seeing 1:1—2:4a and 2:4b—25, which are quite different, as bearing joint witness to God's vision for human life. Our job is to allow each to have its own voice while exploring how they vitally interact to create a rich picture of how God intended life to be.

Genesis 2 is, from beginning to end, about the origins and meaning of human sexual desire and bonding. While Genesis 1 seemed to suggest humanity was made male and female right from the start, Genesis 2 weaves a tale in which first God creates a male, a "dirt creature," into which he breathes the breath of life, which for the OT is vital for any sentient existence, after which Adam becomes a "living being," traditionally translated "living soul." This statement is not about Adam's spiritual nature, though. The Hebrew expression translated "living soul" or "living being" is the standard term for any animal life, as is the possession of the "breath of life." As of Genesis 2:7, Adam is alive, but we are not told much more about his nature. God then plants a beautiful garden called Eden, which means "ecstasy," typically of an erotic kind! He places Adam into this pleasure garden and we learn Adam has a specific job: he must "tend and keep" this garden. Apparently, this perfect garden has a potential it cannot realize fully unless it is helped along, so Adam is placed in this garden to "till" it. The Hebrew term used is the common word for working or serving. This garden of delight also evidently faces a threat of some kind, for Adam is also commissioned to "protect" this garden. The Hebrew term denotes guarding, carefully protecting something. The story then comes to a screeching halt. One can almost smell burning literary rubber as the story slams on the brakes! God says, "*It is not good* that the man be alone." Coming after seven "goods" in Genesis 1, this is an abrupt reversal. This remarkable statement flies in the face of the fact that all that has happened so far has been the direct work of Yahweh himself! A perfect God, a perfect man, a perfect garden; sin has not yet intervened . . . but something is still not right: Adam is alone. God resolves to fix this by making "a helper suitable for him." The Hebrew term for "helper" is not so much a subordinate assistant as a vital presence, life support, not merely a crutch. This helper is also "suitable." The Hebrew expression used is intriguing, composed of three different elements. The last is the pronoun suffix meaning "him." The body of the word, though, is unique to this one story in the OT. It combines the preposition meaning "like" with another preposition that means "opposite, across from." By combining the ideas of likeness and opposition in one word, the Hebrew text has adroitly defined the interplay of likeness and unlikeness that energizes relationships between men and women. Adam's aloneness, his "not good" condition, can only be relieved by one who is both like him and yet opposite him.

To solve this problem, God is depicted going back to the drawing board. As he made Adam, God creates *from the earth* all manner of animals, all called, like Adam, "living beings." He presents them to Adam, the text says, "to see what he [Adam] would say about them." It is as if God, in some suspense, presents his latest labors to Adam for approval! We are then told that whatever Adam said became the name of that animal. Since the text then sadly notes that, among all these animals, not one was found that was a "helper like-opposite him," we can conclude that each animal's name amounts to a way to say, "Wrong again, God!" The story now hits a brick wall. After all, this is God. God has made this man, has seen a problem, and his efforts at solving it have failed! They failed because none of the animals fulfilled the "like-opposite" test. They were different, to be sure (alligators?), but they failed at being the same. On the other hand, God could not simply make another Adam, another man, because then the constitutional opposition, the vital "viva la difference," would be missing. The crisis is resolved by God casting Adam into a kind of coma. He then pulls tissue directly out of Adam, which he "builds" into a woman. Note that God had "molded" Adam out of dirt—pottery language. But the woman is "built"—the term is architectural—not from the earth, like Adam and the animals, but from living human tissue. She is made from him, but she is constitutionally quite a different being, perhaps Humanity 2.0!

The question now is what Adam will say when he awakens and beholds this utterly novel creature: one like him, not one of the animals; but also one very much not like him, made not from the soil but from Adam's own humanity. The suspense in the narrative is palpable. Adam awakes, and his cry of amazement brings the story to an emotional climax. The Hebrew for Adam's exclamation employs an onomatopoeic term associated with a sharp blow or impact, or a single, definite occurrence of something. The term, pronounced "PAH-ahm," exactly corresponds to the English "boom!" or "bam!" Adam cries out, colloquially, "BOOM!" *He celebrates immediately her intrinsic tie to himself—"bone of my bones, flesh of my flesh"—and yet also grasps that she is different.* If he is, in Hebrew, 'ish ("man"), her likeness and difference from him is captured in his naming her 'isshah, the common Hebrew term for "woman," thus ending the story with a wry grammatical pun!

The crucial statement of the story follows. A voice, either the narrator or God, declares three things about this new relationship. First, "this is why a man leaves his father and mother . . ." The creation of the woman sets up a relationship that trumps that of the man's own family of origin. In the ancient world a man incorporated his new wife into his own extended family, presided over by his own father. In such a world, this is a radical word. She is not to be annexed to his existing family, but represents a compelling reason for him to leave them behind.

Second, ". . . and cling to his wife . . ." The man now forms a radical and profound attachment to the woman. The Hebrew term translated "cleave" (KJV) or "hold fast" (ESV), when used of material things, refers to a tight joint, glued, soldered, or welded. It generally has the idea of sticking, adhering. Jeremiah 13:11 uses the term to describe how a man's underwear clings to his body! The term is also used of humans devoting themselves to deities, whether Yahweh, the God of Israel (Josh 23:8), or idols (Josh 23:12), and implies a formal pact followed by faithful allegiance. Used in human relationships, the term describes two persons who are not blood-kin who forge an alliance, a pact of loyalty, as in the story of Ruth (Ruth 1:14–18). The result of this pact is the two parties becoming bound together as if they were, in fact, blood-kin.

This bond between the man and woman brings us to the third term in Genesis 2:24, "... they shall become one flesh." In the Hebrew scriptures, the term "flesh," especially when paired with "bone," points not so much to a mystical union of souls, but to the solidarity of kinship and the obligations it imposes (see Gen 29:14; 37:27; Judg 9:2; 2 Sam 19:13). The result of the joining of Adam to his wife is not merely, or even mainly, some merging of soulmates into one common spirit, but the creation of a bond as binding, durable, and obligatory as kinship. "One flesh" points to an absolute mutual belonging; "My beloved is mine, and I am his!" (Song 2:16).

The typical term used in the Bible for a personal, social bond that creates kinship among persons not previously related is "covenant." These were always sealed with a public oath and declaration. The nature of marriage as a covenant in the OT uniting a man and woman, in the context of family, community, and God, calls for public recognition. Unlike the privatistic piety of contemporary life, biblical faith was communal and public. A covenant in the Bible, whether with God or between human parties, always assumes a prior history among the parties, a clear set of expectations in the relationship to be consecrated, and always culminates in a vow that is witnessed by the community. Just as the OT sees marriage between a man and woman as analogous to the relationship between Yahweh and Israel, the NT enlarges this vision to Christ and the church. Therefore, abruptly withdrawing sex and marriage from the realm of public covenant and making them primarily a matter of private feeling and personal gratification rips up the fabric of the biblical revelation.

The sexual dimension of our Genesis 2 story becomes evident in the next verse, though it is expressed in a delicate, indirect manner, which I'll translate quite literally here: "And the two of them were naked, Adam and his woman, and they were not ashamed of each other." The stress on "the two of them" in Hebrew focuses sharply not on them as individuals, but as a new unit, a pair. The quality they share between them is "naked." This Hebrew term occurs in several forms and bears a wide and intriguing range of senses. Far from meaning simply "nude," in some forms it actually means "clever, shrewd" (Prov 12:16, 23; 13:16), while it also can refer to various states of undress. In this case, the nakedness of the man and woman is not a naive or virginally innocent thing, but full of shrewdness and cunning, aware of precisely how to act and what to do. This impression is born out by the next phase, "they were not ashamed." The grammatical construction used makes the absence of shame mutual; they were not ashamed of or for each other. But more importantly, "shame" here is not mere embarrassment. Ancient cultures wove their values around more than right and wrong; they also focused on honor and shame. Honor came from doing exactly the right thing effectively, while shame involved being in a position in which one simply could not act. Shame in its extreme form could end, as it does in some societies today, in ritual suicide. "[T]hey were not ashamed of each other" would freely translate as "they knew exactly what to do." In the context of nakedness as acute, shrewd awareness, this shamelessness adroitly signals their immediate, even skilled sexual union, effectively obliterating the "not good" that hung over the solitary Adam. Even God seems to retire to a discreet remove.

Most surprising, we hardly even notice that there is not a word in Genesis 2 about childbearing. Sex in Genesis 2 is not how humans "be fruitful and multiply," but about wiping out that "not good . . . alone" with a good dose of "naked and not ashamed." There is another place in the OT that distinctively celebrates the sheer delight of sexual intimacy between a man and woman without regard for childbearing, and that is the Song of Solomon.[5] Karl Barth observed that, in concert with Genesis 2, the Song of Solomon revels in ". . . the rapture, the unquenchable yearning and the restless willingness and readiness, with which both partners in this covenant hasten toward an encounter."[6] This "terrifyingly strong" celebration of sex in the Song of Solomon makes absolutely no reference to conception or procreation, but sings solely of intimacy. Barth even suggested that from Genesis 2 through the Song of Solomon we can project a line through history to the climax of the ages, the Marriage Supper of the Lamb, the final joyful union of Christ with his Bride. Therefore, with its affirmation of the delight of the man and woman in their knowing nakedness, and all that it involves and anticipates, Genesis 2 proves that our pleasure garden was named very aptly.

The sexual delight between the man and woman in Genesis 2, though embodied in a somewhat quaint narrative, functioned in the OT world as a portrayal of Israel's core values regarding intimacy between men and women. Such stories, called by scholars "etiologies," embed vital beliefs and moral claims in superficially quaint stories. So the key point in our story is the fact that sexual intimacy exists in a total weave of life, relationships, economics, and community. Marriage recognizes this. Moderns, however, only think of sex individualistically as an act of pleasurable intimacy between the man and woman. They have no notion of sex as an act embedded in the social matrix, economic life, and transgenerational history of their community, to which they are accountable for all their actions. The idea that extramarital sex, as an act of autonomous gratification, is acceptable is only

---

5. I owe my first awareness of this insight to the late Dr. Dennis F. Kinlaw.

6. Barth, *Doctrine of Creation*, 312–13. The whole discussion, 312–29, is worth savoring.

imaginable in the post-sexual revolution world of not just easy contraception and abortion, but a world in which no particular significance for society as a whole attaches to sex. In modern life, we don't really have "intercourse" in the full sense of that word—we just copulate. Thus, despite being a sexually saturated society, modern or postmodern life remains starkly devoid of sexual satisfaction.

Genesis 3: Eros under the Shadow

Just one verse after declaring the shameless naked intimacy of the man and woman, a shadow falls over the story. "Now the serpent was more crafty than any beast of the field which the LORD God had made." The narrator tells us two things about the tempter, the serpent. First, the serpent was "crafty" or "shrewd." The term translated "crafty" is actually the *same word* that is used in the immediately preceding verse to describe the naked intimacy of Adam and Eve. The serpent possesses the identical quality that characterizes the man and the woman in the unashamed bliss of their nakedness. Thus he shares with them a vital, and unnerving, quality.

The second comment made about the serpent contains a bombshell. He is more crafty ". . . than any beast of the field which the LORD God had made." This expression explicitly tags Genesis 2:18–20, where God creates "every beast of the field." The linkage tells us *the serpent was one of those beasts*. But recall, these animals were all created as candidates for Adam's companion, the "helper suitable for him." So the serpent belongs to that class, and was *created as a potential companion to Adam*. More importantly, the serpent, as the most "knowingly naked" of the animals thus created, was the best candidate of them all for the role of companion to Adam! Most importantly, like all the other animals, *the serpent was rejected by Adam* as his consort. As a result of the failure of any of the animals, including the serpent, to be Adam's companion, the story took its sharp turn in the "building" of the woman and the subsequent cry of delight, devotion, and naked intimacy.

The significance of the description of the serpent best lies in the fact that, as such, he would have been the most suitable of all the animals to serve as Adam's partner, since he possessed in the highest degree that quality that later characterized the man and woman in their shame-free union. This explains in the narrative why the serpent can speak, reason, and interact. He would have been the most capable of providing an approximation of the companionship that is celebrated between the man and the woman. If the serpent's speech and reasoning with the woman indicate a degree of personality, then the reason for his hostility specifically against the woman becomes clear. The serpent hated her most because she fulfilled exactly the role for which he had been rejected.

The point of this little digression is to note that just as sexual intimacy uniquely characterizes the union of the man and the woman, it is therefore also the target of their enemy's ferocious assault. Authentic, shameless, knowing, naked intimacy will be attacked and undermined by a lesser, guilt-laden, bogus claim to knowing that will lead not to nakedness, but to a desperate covering and to guilt and shame before God. The entire focus of the serpent's ire is on that one point: their bond of intimacy. Sadly, the attack succeeds, and human sexuality suffers. Without treating the rest of the narrative in detail, we can only say that in their need to hide, their shame before God, in the curse of Adam's work now becoming fraught with anxiety and pain, in Eve's conception and pain being multiplied, and in the appearance of a twisting of desire into a power relationship between the man and the woman . . . the serpent's attack has done frightful harm to human sexual intimacy. The rest of the biblical narrative will be a journey for humanity and God. Not only will humans need to find their way back into a relationship with God, their utter helplessness to do so will compel increasingly dramatic actions of divine grace as he seeks to rescue and restore his creation. Redemption will also involve men and women not only finding a way back to God, but finding a way back to each other as well. The Bible's teaching and guidance on sexuality serve that redemptive journey. To the extent that God redeems and transforms a lost and corrupt humanity, he will also redeem and transform human sexuality.

Do You Think I'm Sexy?

In an online discussion about these matters, when I presented some of the information I've shared here, one commenter protested that this was the "least sexy" conversation about sex that they had ever participated in. I thought this remark emblematic of the whole problem. Sex has been divorced from every other reality than the most obvious ones of raw attraction and short-term pleasure. "Sexy" in our culture is a sad, pale cartoon, mainly of women, made up of too much cleavage, too little self-respect, too much butt crack, too many tramp stamps, and overtight clothes. "Sexy" has cheapened women far too soon, kept men adolescents far too long, and reduced us all to commodities. "Sexy" testifies to our emptiness, a hunger, but not to real desire. Lots of energy, but is it really passion? Lots of smoke, but not a fire to light our lives, warm our souls, and nourish our hearts. The eyes of the goddess are painted, but the eyeholes are empty.

The Bible teaches us that intimacy between men and women is about so much more than "sexy." Sex—intimacy—is about helping your wife recover for months from a very difficult delivery of a baby you sort of had something to do with. Real sex is about loving a spouse's wrinkles and grey or thinning hair . . . or no hair because of the chemo. Sexual intimacy is about sitting by the bed wishing you could be the one suffering instead of them. Sexual intimacy—"one flesh"—is an eighty-something-year-old man snuggling in the hospital bed next to his dying wife, holding her in his arms, softly singing hymns to her through the night as she crosses over. Sex is feeling off balance when you have to go without your wedding band for some reason. It's about staying together through times when you don't feel in love, don't feel dedicated, and don't feel committed, but you remember that before God and his church you made a promise, a covenant, and you'll honor it—and discovering that those who keep faith with that formal, so-called legalistic boundary inhabit a garden of satisfaction and joy known only to those who surrender to its secret.

Bibliography

Arnold, Bill T. *Genesis*. New Cambridge Bible Commentary. Cambridge: Cambridge University Press, 2009.

Barth, Karl. *The Doctrine of Creation*. Church Dogmatics III/1. Edinburgh: T. & T. Clark, 1958.

Blocher, Henri. *In the Beginning: The Opening Chapters of Genesis*. Downers Grove, IL: InterVarsity, 1984.

Davidson, Richard M. *Flame of Yahweh: Sexuality in the Old Testament*. Peabody, MA: Hendrickson, 2007.

Hamilton, Victor P. *The Book of Genesis: Chapters 1–17*. New International Commentary on the New Testament. Grand Rapids: Eerdmans, 1990.

Rad, Gerhard von. *Genesis: A Commentary*. Translated by John H. Marks. Rev. ed. Old Testament Library. Louisville: Westminster, 1972.

2

Premarital Sex for Christians

Yes, No, or Maybe?

Joseph R. Dongell

Common Stories

Three times in the last few months I've bumped into the question of whether premarital sex is appropriate for Christians. Scrolling through Facebook, my wife happened upon a selfie posted by a distant relative. There she was, standing arm-in-arm with her boyfriend, beaming with obvious joy. In the background one sees a church with people streaming all around. The caption read something like this: "We've been at this church for over a year now, and we love it!" But the good news of this posting is clouded by the fact that the couple has also been living together (unmarried) for at least the same length of time.

A pastor friend of mine from the rural Midwest passed through town and stopped in for coffee. I was interested in hearing about the ups and downs of pastoral ministry from his perspective. One thing led to another, and we found ourselves discussing a challenge he was facing with the contemporary worship team, a situation he had inherited from the previous pastor. As it turns out, the lead vocalists (a man and a woman) were living together and unmarried. To complicate matters, no one was quite clear about the nature of their faith commitment to Jesus. It seems that the previous pastor had envisioned the worship band as a tool for reaching the lost, hoping that unbelieving musicians would end up being drawn to Jesus over the course of their "ministry activity" within this Christian worship.

A few days ago I learned of a crisis that had developed within a large evangelical student fellowship at a major Southern university. The executive leadership had learned that numbers of their unmarried student leaders were living together and sexually active. When the issue was raised, many of the students in question were quite certain that their behavior was above reproach and not at all unchristian, mainly because their sexual activity was noncoercive, mutually respectful, and tastefully private. In the end, the executive leadership insisted that anyone exercising leadership at any level must refrain from premarital sex. Numbers of students left their posts in leadership, if not the fellowship altogether.

These three scenarios illustrate what most people sense: that our current culture (North America) has been steadily moving away from traditional Christian sexual ethics. Even if some might argue that the actual sexual behavior of unmarried folk has not shifted as dramatically as we might think, surely the popular perception has. Most television shows and movies now presume that "dating" means that a couple is having sex regularly, if not also living together. Men and women who are still virgins after, say, the age of eighteen are portrayed as dysfunctional, abnormal, and emotionally deprived. So routine are these assumptions that sex between unmarried characters is no longer part of a movie's cutting edge, no longer part of an agenda (explicit or implicit) that a progressive writer may be pushing. It just is.

Given the pervasive pressure of popular culture upon the church, it should not be surprising that many people who identify as Christian and attend church are either transitioning away from traditional sexual mores toward progressive ones or are simply remaining within the progressive vision they have already inherited from our larger culture. We can be sure that scenarios like those I've described above will only increase in number and intensity if our culture continues on its current trajectory.

The Long-Running Consensus

But the questions about contemporary trends in sexual behavior, or projections about how many people (whether inside or outside the church) consider premarital sex to be a sin, are beside the primary point I want to deal with in this chapter. Here I want to ask about the Bible's own perspective on the matter.

Down through twenty centuries of church history (until very recently), there has been unanimity across the entire Christian fellowship on what the Bible teaches about premarital sex: it is wrong. Catholic,

Orthodox, Protestant, Pentecostal, and all brands of Christianity between and beyond these have taught without hesitation that premarital sex is not acceptable for followers of Jesus. Typical of all traditions is the wording of the Catechism of the Catholic Church: "Fornication is carnal union between an unmarried man and an unmarried woman. It is gravely contrary to the dignity of persons . . . ."[1]

It is amazing to realize that Christians who have disagreed fervently with one another across the ages over such matters as the papacy, the nature of the Lord's Supper, the nature of the clergy, the number of sacraments, predestination, prayers to the saints, and the canon of biblical books were of one mind when it came to the question of premarital sex. It was not only a sin, but a serious sin at that.

This common conviction did not arise by accident or coercion. It arose from the rather obvious teaching of Scripture on the matter as gathered from both the Old and New Testaments. Out of the many passages we could cite, we'll content ourselves with brief comments on four primary texts that should illustrate well enough the drift of the whole.

(1) The creation story depicts the union of man and woman along these lines: "Therefore a man leaves his father and his mother and cleaves to his wife, and they become one flesh" (Gen 2:24). These lines are penned by the narrator of the story, who is generalizing beyond the individual characters of Adam and Eve to set in place God's plan for humanity. In this vision of sexual union, the sequence is crucial: *first* comes the leaving of father and mother, and only *then* comes the cleaving with its various forms of intimacy. This "leaving" surely depicts something public, something objectively established, something socially recognized.

It is too shallow a reading to imagine that this "leaving" can be merely private and internal, or that marriage is "just a piece of paper" required by the arbitrary authority of church or state. The Genesis vision for all humanity is that sexual union be protected as a privilege for those who have been openly and publicly identified as set apart from parents for each other. In other words, sex is a social act, not merely a private activity between two secluded individuals. In following Jesus, believers step away from the individualizing of sex (i.e., "it's just something between you and me"), and step into a vision defined by God's original intentions for human beings as social creatures.

Sometimes Exodus 22:16–17 is imagined to establish the principle that sex between two unmarried people converts them into married people

---

1. Catholic Church, *Catechism of the Catholic Church*, 624.

simply by virtue of the act of intercourse itself. One might say, "If we had sex, that's OK. We just married ourselves in God's sight."

But any fair reader of this passage must admit that the entire context deals with all sorts of violations, all sorts of infractions against God's will (see all of Exod 22:1—23:19). Just a few verses after 22:16-17 we find a prohibition against oppressing strangers, orphan, and widows (22:21-24), and against abusing the poor (22:25-27). Here in 22:16-17 we are not being given a pathway for how a couple may *appropriately* fuse themselves together in marriage, but how a *violator* must rectify the sin of not having secured the blessing of marriage before sexual intercourse. The sequence described in this scenario of intercourse-then-marriage is surely not endorsed as God's holy preference. The marriage described here is a divine requirement laid upon one who has been identified as a violator.

Sometimes it is claimed that the entire Old Testament must be set aside as irrelevant for Christian ethics. Such an approach is profoundly confused, to put it mildly. It is true that certain features of life and piety in the Old Testament are not carried into the New Testament as incumbent upon Christians. We no longer offer animal sacrifice, or return property to family lines every fifty years, or refrain from eating pork products. Most matters related to the sacrificial system, to food, to farming and property, etc., have been discontinued in their literal senses. Christians must indeed read the Old Testament through the lens of the New Testament, since the new covenant is "better" than the old covenant (Heb 8:6).

But Jesus himself also made it clear that the very core of his vision stands in full harmony with the core vision of the Old Testament. If we agree that Jesus's ethic of love lies at the heart of the Christian message, then we must acknowledge that Jesus merely quoted from Deuteronomy 6:4-5 and Leviticus 19:18 when commanding that we love God and neighbor (see Matt 22:34-40; Mark 12:28-34; Luke 10:25-28). And when asked about sexual ethics (marriage and divorce in particular), Jesus immediately seized upon Genesis 2:24 as the clearest window into the purest will of God (Matt 19:1-12; Mark 10:1-12). If we want to stand with Jesus, we must also stand with the core message of the Old Testament, as Jesus envisioned it. There is no New Testament sexual ethic apart from Old Testament sexual ethics underpinning it, just as Jesus insisted.

(2) The story of Joseph and Mary points to the same marriage-before-intercourse sequence we've just mentioned. Mary and Joseph were engaged to be married, but were apparently abstaining altogether from sexual intimacy. How can we gather this? Because Joseph knew *with absolute certainty* that the child was *not* his when he discovered that Mary was pregnant. The reason he never imagined that he could be the father, knowing that

someone else had impregnated her, must have been that he himself was not having sex with her . . . at all. Joseph was a godly man not only because he wanted to protect Mary's reputation as much as possible, but also because he had already been protecting her sexual purity throughout their relationship. Surely this sexual purity as unmarried people speaks directly to their greater moral fitness for parenting Jesus, the incarnate Son of God.

(3) In Matthew 19:1–10 we find Jesus teaching sternly against divorce, warning that marriages can be dissolved only under strict conditions. Hearing this, his disciples suggested that the safer approach for all concerned would simply be to abstain from marriage altogether. But Jesus rejected their proposal, explaining that the state of celibacy (i.e., life without sexual intimacy) is a gift, and that no one should be forced into such a state as a matter of course. In other words, the state of marriage should be considered the regular expectation for Jesus's disciples, with celibacy treated as an exception made possible by a special dispensation of God's grace.

In the complementary passage of 1 Corinthians 7:1–9 (especially v. 1) we learn that some Corinthian Christians were likewise considering abstaining from marriage. Perhaps they imagined that they would be freer to devote themselves to serving others in the name of Jesus (as Paul himself suggested a few verses later in 7:32–35). But Paul would not endorse their suggestion as a blanket policy for believers. His concern was that, as unmarried persons, they would find it difficult to remain sexually inactive, sexually pure. Marriage, in the limited sense he treats it here, is an alternative to the completely unacceptable option of sexual immorality (that is, to sex outside marriage). "But because of the temptation to immorality, each man should have his own wife, and each wife her own husband" (7:2).

Viewing these two passages together, we see that Jesus and Paul both envision marriage as the only legitimate venue for sexual intimacy. In other words, marriage and sexual abstinence are the only two options from which disciples of Jesus are free to choose. And when we examine both passages in light of each other, we discover that neither fidelity in marriage nor purity in celibacy will be easy! Each will require large measures of God's sustaining grace, grace that is promised elsewhere in Scripture to all who look to God in faith.

(4) A great many passages in the Bible identify "immorality" (*porneia*) as something particularly sinful, something the Christian individual (and the Christian community) must guard against with special vigilance (e.g., Acts 15:20, 29; 1 Cor 6:13, 18; 10:8; 2 Cor 12:21; Gal 5:19; Eph 5:3; Col 3:5; 1 Thess 4:3; Heb 13:4; Rev 2:21; 9:21). Paul explains that sexual sin is peculiarly serious because of the harm it inflicts on its several victims. On the one hand, the Holy Spirit (who inhabits the Christian) is profoundly grieved if

ever the sacred temple of the believer's body is sexually stained. On the other hand, Christians who engage in sexual sin violate *their own persons* when surrendering their bodies to impurity (1 Cor 6:18–20). In this we learn that our bodies are not just billions of cells collected into merely material entities. Our bodies are not somehow detachable from "who we really are." Rather, my body is part of the integrated whole of who I really am. I don't merely *have* a body. I *am* an embodied person. This is why rape, for example, is so profoundly damaging and cannot be recovered from as simply as one will heal from a kick in the shins. The very core of the person is touched through sexual intercourse, whether forced or consensual. For good reason the apostle urges Christians to "run" (*feugo*) from sexual immorality (1 Cor 6:18), given the damage it inflicts on the core of a person.

Some people claim that the Bible does not condemn premarital sex because they can find no single Greek word referring exclusively to premarital sex. Technically, it is true that no single Greek word exclusively denotes the particular sexual sin of premarital sex. The Greek term *porneia* is a general term, covering all the varieties of sexual activity outside marriage.[2] In one context a writer may use this term to refer specifically to incest, in another context to prostitution, in other to homosexuality, or in another to adultery. In general contexts where no particular sexual sin is under discussion, the term quite naturally and normally has in view all sexual activity outside of heterosexual marriage, including premarital sex.

Imagine that I have warned my staff that I will fire anyone who engages in "theft." Weeks later I fire Bob, who was guilty of theft by deception. Later I fire Wanda, who stole funds by unauthorized electronic transfer. Later I fire Jim, who stole by literally taking all the money in the tip jar. Each incident is a different kind of theft as defined by law. I can refer to any one of them as "theft" or to all of them together as "theft," though every type of theft is technically different. The lack of a single English word corresponding exclusively, say, to theft by deception, in no way proves that this is not a theft, or that we have no concept of such theft. Similarly, *porneia* may in a given passage have reference to premarital sex (as the logic of 1 Cor 7:1–2 demands), even if elsewhere *porneia* may refer to other kinds of sexual sin (as in 1 Cor 5:1ff.) or to all sexual activity outside of marriage considered together (Col 3:5). There is nothing puzzling, tricky, or dishonest about this kind of linguistic flexibility normally at work in human discourse.

To summarize, the long-running consensus through the ages and across all Christian traditions that premarital sex is contrary to God's will

---

2. Bauer et al., *Greek-English Lexicon of the New Testament and Other Early Christian Literature*, 854.

arises not from narrow-mindedness, or fear, or rejection of sexuality *per se*, or various kinds of repression. It arises from the Bible itself, read as a whole, and read in light of its grammatical, literary, and historical contexts.

A Religion of "No"?

A great many Christians would agree with everything I've laid out to this point. With regard to popular culture, they also see a large-scale swing towards accepting, affirming, and even promoting all sorts of sexual activity outside the framework of heterosexual, monogamous marriage. They also see with me a clear moral code allowing sexual intercourse only within heterosexual, monogamous marriage. They would also acknowledge the truthfulness of the Bible, and affirm the importance of following the Bible's teachings. But at the same time, they have come to feel that Christian sexual ethics is primarily a thundering "no" that constantly denies pleasure. The negative tone of it all is felt by some especially in the Ten Commandments, nine of which are cast as prohibitions: "Thou shalt not . . ." (Exod 20:1–17). Many who grow up in Christian homes or schools emerge with the deeply ingrained suspicion that everybody outside the church is having a blast, free to enjoy life and all its pleasures without the constant shaming and negativity of parents, teachers, and pastors. In my experience, it is precisely these kids who are most likely to bolt entirely from the faith, seeking those bold colors and sensual pleasures long denied to them.

In large measure this is understandable, and has played itself out repeatedly across the generations. It is often a manifestation of people coming of age and trying to establish their own identities as distinct from that of their parents. One way of saying "I am not you" is to reject the mores held by one's parents. We commonly hear of young adults "sowing wild oats," and then hear of their return (months, years, or decades later) to a lifestyle closely matching what they had earlier abandoned.

And yet there are deeper dynamics at work in all of this, larger wheels turning beneath the surface. On one hand, the perception that the Bible, or Christianity, or "the church" is all about suppressing pleasure and happiness may be blamed in part on the messengers. Sadly, I must report what everybody already knows: far too many Christians down through the ages have been narrow-hearted, legalistic, sour, colorless, and angry. Out of their own pain they have inflicted pain. They themselves tragically envision God as an angry, never-satisfied Ogre always spewing "noes" even before he hears our questions. This God stamps out pleasure wherever it is found, preferring to fill our lives with suffering. Only when human beings are bent over in pain, bereft of pleasure, and filled with sorrow will this God be happy.

The crushing irony in all of this is that these messengers are merely channeling the voice of the serpent in the garden of Eden, which in the course of the Bible's larger narrative essentially matches the voice of Satan! It all works like this: The Bible begins with the story of God creating humanity and setting them in the garden of Eden. We should not miss that the word "Eden" is etymologically related to Hebrew words for "pleasure," "delight," and "delicacies."[3] Right from the start, then, we meet God as the author of pleasure, as one who has created a fabulous park, planting it full of trees laden with all every kind of fruit and nuts imaginable, "every tree that is pleasant to the sight and good for food."

Now, out of this forest of trees God identified *only one* tree as forbidden. To put it another way, God's single "no" was vastly outweighed by a thousand "yeses." The God we meet in the garden, then, is overwhelmingly the God of "yes," the God lavishly ordering his "very good" new world toward pleasure for humanity.

But it was exactly this truth that the serpent attacked in his first words to Eve, "So, God has forbidden you to eat of *any* of the trees in the garden?" To grasp the force of the question, we must hear the character assassination buried within it: "What! This Ogre is shutting you out from the pleasure of *all* these trees? How horrid of him! How mean and insensitive!" And this fundamental lie about God's character distorts everything that follows, and is always on the lips of God's enemies. All the forces of darkness across the ages seek to portray God as the God of "no," the God of anti-pleasure. Their complementary lie, obviously, is that our greatest happiness can be found only by cutting loose from the God of the garden and setting out on our own (unique, designer) pathway towards self-fulfillment.

But those who truly walk with God have experienced for themselves what the psalmist reports: "Therefore my heart is glad, and my soul rejoices; my body also dwells secure. . . . Thou dost show me the path of life; in thy presence is fullness of joy, in thy right hand are pleasures for evermore" (Ps 16:9, 11). "How precious is thy steadfast love, O God! The children of men take refuge in the shadow of thy wings. They feast on the abundance of thy house, and thou givest them drink from the river of thy delights. For with thee is the fountain of life; in thy light do we see light" (Ps 36:7–9).

Beyond these references to joy and pleasure in general, we find that the Bible celebrates the more particular delight of human sexuality in its fertility (Gen 1:26–28), in its intimacy (Gen 2:21–25), and in its sheer

---

3. Holladay, *Concise Hebrew and Aramaic Lexicon of the Old Testament*, 266.

erotic pleasure (Song of Solomon). So wonderful is this wide-ranging intimacy in marriage that it becomes a prized metaphor for depicting the love of God for Israel, even the love of Christ for the church. Here again we meet the God whose first and last will is for pleasure, for recapturing Eden and its beauty for the whole world in an irreversible way. One day, the trees of the garden in all their healing potency will again be available for feasting upon, and the highest pleasure imaginable, that of seeing God's face, will become reality (Rev 22:1–5).

But what of God's "no"? Even if there were a thousand "yeses" in the Garden of Eden, there was still one emphatic "no!" So how can we square the image of an affirming God with the image of a God who withholds even *one* form of pleasure from us? The answer is obvious, requiring no particular religious or moral commitment to discern it. The athlete, striving for the larger good of victory, says "no" to foods that would diminish the body's performance. The law student says "no" to social invitations that would threaten the focus needed to pass the bar exam. The good parent will say "no" to things endangering the child, though the child may beg for them at length. A great many of our "noes" actually demonstrate a strong love and protective care for ourselves and others. Put another way, we all set boundaries against temporary and partial pleasures in order to attain greatest pleasure. If we intend to achieve the highest satisfaction in any area of life, we must learn to say "no" clearly, firmly, and often.

What we know instinctively about life now helps us make sense of God's "no" to premarital sex. All around this "no" is God's much larger "yes" to our thriving, "yes" to our true happiness, and "yes" to our deepest fulfillment. So it will not be enough for us to believe that God says "no" to this particular pleasure (or to any other forbidden pleasure for that matter). Armed only with God's "no," we will ultimately be driven to bitterness, despair, or sadness, or else to abandoning the faith altogether, unless . . . we catch a vision of the kind intention of God's will, and become inwardly convinced that God is *for* us, not against us. It all has to do with getting behind the lie of the serpent to recover a vision of the loving God who designed pleasure for us in the first place. Then we will see God's "noes" as the pathway we must walk if we are to travel on through to God's overwhelmingly wonderful "yeses" (1 Cor 2:9). For many Christians, this breakthrough into a deeper experience of God as loving Father, of entering into the full confidence that God is fundamentally *for* us, is the missing piece in their spiritual journey towards obedience. It's difficult to obey an Ogre, especially when sacrifice is involved.

So How Far Is Too Far?

Having grown up in church and having attended a Christian college, I've often discussed with friends what lines Christians should draw regarding sexual intimacy before marriage. Many people do accept the "no" of premarital sex as a clear line they will not cross. But the terrain leading up that line is more challenging to map out.

In recent years, I've become aware of a movement among some Christians who have boldly determined to avoid nearly all physical contact before marriage. For some of them, their kiss at their wedding will be their first kiss. I have no argument with them, so long as they have not fallen prey to the view that sex itself (even after marriage) is somehow dirty. But it could be that for some folks this approach makes perfect sense and is spiritually laudable, especially if they are trying to emerge from earlier habits of promiscuity. But I myself do not recommend this approach as a matter of course.

On the other hand, years ago a Christian friend of mine explained his sexual relationship with his fiancé. "We're 'dry f*cking.'" He was quite proud of his discovery, believing it to be the best of all worlds. As he saw it, they were preserving their virginity, they were removing no articles of clothing (and therefore were not naked), and were not even putting their hands under their clothing. But they were, to put it bluntly, grinding on each other's bodies in full simulation of intercourse and achieving orgasm in the process. "No premarital sex here," he insisted. Some others would join him in this logic, claiming to preserve virginity by engaging only in oral sex.

Reflecting on this now, I remember a recent visit of mine to a venerable hotel in San Antonio, the Menger. Stepping into the lobby is an experience all its own, with antique furniture tastefully stationed all around. I noticed an old piano off to the side, carefully protected from curious guests by velvet roping. A folded cardboard sign had been placed on it: "Do not play the piano; Do not lean on the piano."

For some reason I shifted mentally into the literalistic humor of a twelve-year-old. "Well, the sign doesn't prohibit jumping on the piano, or banging on the piano keys, or spray painting the piano, or bouncing a basketball on it." Indeed, we must admit that none of these escapades I had imagined was technically prohibited by the sign.

And yet we know that the manager would have disapproved of every one of these pranks. We also know that it would be impossible for any manager to think of (and explicitly prohibit) every form of harm a person could inflict on the piano. Most guests understand that a certain *cooperative imagination* is required for complying with the wishes of the management to preserve the beauty of the old hotel and its furnishings. If we are willing both to *discern the underlying concern* implied by the sign, and then actually to *embrace that concern*, we will naturally refrain from all sorts of actions (even unstated) that would endanger the old piano.

So it is with the Bible's "no" to premarital sex. We betray ourselves as moral twelve-year-olds if we imagine that "no premarital sex" means precisely, exactly, and without remainder, "no penis in vagina." Somehow we are ignoring the real issue at stake. We are refusing to develop the cooperative imagination necessary to protect the "piano" of sexual intimacy, so as to receive God's full blessing for our full thriving. Unmarried couples who truly want to follow Jesus will not be satisfied with "technical virginity." They will talk and pray together, learning how to express their physical affection in ways that honor the spirit, and not merely the letter, of God's Word.

Is This Legalism?

When some Christians begin taking obedience seriously and announce their intention of avoiding a given sin (like premarital sex), certain other Christians quickly accuse them of "legalism." At least as I have heard it, this charge begins with the claim that "we're all sinners," and then insists that any anxiety about committing sin somehow constitutes a denial God's grace, a denial convicting one as a "legalist." In this view, "accepting God's grace" means that we have finally come to hear God essentially saying to us, "You're sinners, but that's OK. No worries! That's reality!"

Though I'm tempted to launch a full-scale rebuttal of this logic, I'll address only its distorted understanding of legalism. In Scripture, we find these three varieties of it: (1) legalism as adding humanly created rules to God's law (Mark 7:1–8); (2) legalism as obeying the letter of the law while violating its spirit (Mark 7:9–13); and (3) legalism as substituting the knowledge of God's law for the doing of it (Rom 2:17–29). In other words, "legalism" always involves minimizing, subverting, or evading God's law. Equating moral seriousness with legalism gets things exactly backwards, since legalism at its core is *a flight from moral seriousness* (read again the passages cited above).

Whenever we appeal to "grace" to minimize moral seriousness about sin, we are mocking the gospel and making nonsense of countless Scripture passages (e.g., Rom 8:12–13; Gal 5:21; 6:7–10; Eph 4:30; 5:3–5; 1 Thess 4:1–8; 1 Pet 1:13–16; 2 Pet 1:3–11; Rev 2:12—3:22). Warnings throughout the *New* Testament issued to *Christians* must be drained of their urgency if we insist on creating a theology of grace that allows us to "chill out" about

God's call to holiness. If I am feeling uneasy about the Bible's call to sexual purity, feeling guilty about my own carelessness in these matters, feeling troubled when thinking about God's holiness, I must not imagine this to be the voice of Satan, or of legalistic Christianity, or of the last remnants of a puritanical American culture. It is nothing less than the voice of the Holy Spirit of God bringing conviction (John 16:7–11; 1 Thess 1:4–5), drawing me towards God's grace that can actually transform me into the kind of person I need to become.

What If I Never Get Married?

For many people, saying "no" to sex outside of marriage essentially means saying "no" to sex entirely. For a variety of reasons, marriage will never happen for them.

This is a painful reality to face. I have seen many single friends struggle through every Christmas, every Valentine's Day, every wedding, and every baby shower. Each of these events seems to scream out, "You're alone! You're a misfit! You'll never be happy!" Their prayers have not been answered. They constantly battle temptations towards bitterness, anger, and despair. They often wonder if God really loves them. "Life isn't fair! God isn't fair!"

I've learned some of my greatest lessons from my students. Many years ago, a class moved onto the turf of same-sex attraction. In the discussion that followed, a student asked, "Isn't the Bible preventing gay and lesbian people from ever having their desires fulfilled? Is that really fair?"

We fumbled that question around for a while, until a thirty-something student raised her hand from the back of the room. Anita (I'll call her) laid out her story like this: "I have no same-sex attraction, but concluded several years ago that I would never be married though I very much want to be. My desire to have a husband and children will never be satisfied. More than that, my faithfulness to Jesus requires that I not share in sexual intimacy with anyone else."

She went on to explain that her emotional downward spiral didn't stop until she began seeing how many other people found themselves in painful situations they never asked for, their dreams and aspirations permanently blocked. She noticed people with diseased or distorted bodies, people born into oppressive and violent families, people locked into poverty or debt, people trapped in war-torn countries or crime infested neighborhoods. She met people who once had a spouse and children only to have lost them in unspeakably tragic deaths.

On the other hand, she then realized that for many millions of people marriage (and/or sex) did not bring the happiness or deep satisfaction they had sought. People who are fundamentally unhappy and dissatisfied before they marry will inevitably carry this disposition right into their marriage, likely dooming it in time. It was clear that "having sex," even a lot of it, would not lift them out of loneliness.

She finally concluded that her happiness in life must not (and cannot) be determined by her marriage status or level of sexual activity. Of course losing these is a real loss, a loss that cannot be papered over as if it were nothing. Anita was not playing a shallow mind game with herself of "misery enjoys company." But she was seeing the larger truth in not allowing her sense of value or her experience of deeper joy to be finally determined by these things. She had made the transition. She knew she was person of infinite value, beloved of God, despite it all. I found myself agreeing entirely with her.

What If I've Failed?

Whatever the percentages are, surely millions of people wanting to follow Jesus find themselves facing the fact that they have already failed regarding sexual purity. Too often the messages they get from Christian leaders gravitate into one of two extremes: either the sin of premarital sex is minimized in a "pastorally sensitive" move to ease their anxiety, or it is treated as if it were the unpardonable sin, permanently ruining those who have fallen into it.

The Bible endorses neither of these approaches. On the one hand, sexual sin is frequently named in the Bible as particularly serious, partly because it so deeply touches our person, the depth of our identity. So this concern is as old as the Bible itself, and was not the invention of a sexually repressed Victorian England of a century and a half ago.

On the other hand, the good news of the gospel is precisely addressed to *all of us* as sinners against God's wise will, and especially to folks whose sins may be more obvious and overtly destructive. Paul actually names some of the more notorious lifestyles in view: "Do not be deceived; neither the immoral, nor idolaters, nor adulterers nor the sexually perverse, nor thieves, nor the greedy, nor drunkards, nor revilers, nor robbers will inherit the kingdom of God." He then adds this remarkable note: "And such *were* some of you. But you were washed, you were sanctified, you were justified in the name of the Lord Jesus Christ and in the Spirit of our God" (1 Cor 6:9b–11; emphasis added). Though the facts of our past cannot change, our identities can. Once we *were* such people; now we're *not*. God always meets full and heartfelt confession with full and thorough forgiveness (1 John 1:9). Really good news!

The Deeper Question

I've waited until now to comment on several books that have recently splashed onto the scene. Put simply, their authors are proposing that premarital sex is not necessarily wrong for Christians, despite the widely-held consensus across the centuries that the Bible forbids it. The title of one book puts these cards on the table: *Good Christian Sex: Why Chastity Isn't the Only Option*.[4] Another book promises in its subtitle, *New Perspectives on Christian Purity*.[5] In one endorsement on its back cover, we are told that the author "lights a path forward" regarding sexual ethics in ways that "make sense in everyday life." In another endorsement, a reader welcomes this "corrective to punitive sexual teachings that harm the lives of many well-meaning Christians."

In an earlier draft, I devoted the first third of this chapter to evaluating these new perspectives, point by point. But soon I reconsidered. At issue isn't really how one interprets a particular verse of the Bible, or what exact meaning a Greek or Hebrew word should bear. The real issue has to do with the Bible itself: whether or not it reliably reveals God's will for Christians. I answer "yes" to this, while these authors essentially answer "no."

These authors participate in a movement found largely within mainline churches today. "Progressives," as they call themselves, focus strongly on justice (or better put, the absence of justice) in all dimensions of society. They see the church (throughout the ages) and the Bible (throughout its pages) as hopelessly infected with racism, sexism, homophobia, classism, misogyny, patriarchy, and so on. They believe that only recently have oppressed peoples begun emerging from silence to challenge the structures (especially the church and its religious teachings) that have been harming people with impunity for centuries on end. A key goal of the new liberation is freedom from traditional sexual mores, particularly from heterosexual, monogamous marriage as the central sexual norm. In place of that norm they urge an approach that in their view is more reasonable, more affirming of all varieties of human experience, more humane, and more loving: that all sex that is freely chosen and mutually pleasurable (between consenting adults) is holy, just, and good. Marriage is irrelevant to this equation. It's that simple.

4. McCleneghan, *Good Christian Sex*.
5. Anderson, *Damaged Goods*.

And so, while progressive Christians will mention the Bible (always being careful to lift up the "love commands" as mandatory) and identify the Bible as a valuable "resource," they show very little interest in allowing the rest of the Bible to speak with authority and clarity for defining with particularity just what love does or doesn't mean. In other words, the progressive movement happily harvests "love" from the Bible as a slogan, and then quickly moves on to define love according to prevailing (popular) cultural conventions or personal preference. When we are told, "Only you can define your sexuality," or, "Virginity is a social construct," or, "Gender is a staged performance,"[6] it is clear that sexual ethics is now something being improvised in a never-settled journey of discovery within each individual, rather than a vision received from a good and loving Creator. The two approaches are worlds apart, even if they both happen to be speaking about the same Bible from time to time. For progressives, the Bible is not the final word, but something to take into account as one tries to arrive at one's own final word on other bases.

Some readers may now be realizing that this indeed is the deeper question: Can I trust the Bible, or . . . should I finally be trusting my own feelings and instincts? Can I reliably and meaningfully hear the voice of God in the Bible, or is the Bible a chaotic echo chamber of competing and corrupted human voices? To put it in terms of premarital sex, what if the Bible clearly names this as unacceptable for followers of Jesus? Will I then say, "Well, that settles it for me," or, "I'll need to evaluate that in light other voices"? This is the deeper question we all must face.

Progressives often challenge us to question all things. I receive this as good advice, if we want to avoid swallowing errors and confusions of all kinds. In my (literally) hundreds of hours of intense conversation with my atheist, agnostic, and progressive friends over the last fifteen years, I have often heard this advice given, but almost always aimed in a *restricted* way toward what they view to be *traditional* views. What I have rarely heard (as I have often pointed out to them) is a willingness to question *their own* views. Why should we not question, for example, what seems to be the unquestioned dogma of progressives: that "truth" is something subjectively determined by each person? How can that claim constantly be asserted without any supporting argument, without any proof that this, in fact, is how "truth" is to be discovered? I would be happy if *all* us would reflect more honestly on how and why we know what we claim to know. And I have a measure of confidence that a *truly radical willingness to question everything* (including

---

6. Ibid., 171–78.

one's own doubts) has had a strange way of leading many people ultimately to Jesus of Nazareth as revealed in Scripture.

How Love Wins

I am glad that a great many have already arrived where I too have arrived: that it really is all about *love*. A loving Creator has lovingly made us, and knows better than we ourselves know just what will make for our deepest happiness for the ages to come. It is *in love*, then, that we find our Father telling us "no," actually an intense and passionate "no," to anything and everything that would harm us. And when I, by God's grace through the Spirit, break through to understand, and see, and feel his love for me; when I become inwardly convinced by his loving voice that I am cherished and beloved; when I hear the comprehensive "yes" he speaks over my whole life and for my whole thriving, then (and only then) will I be able to embrace his "noes" for what they actually are: his deeper way of saying, "I love you!" Insanity? Maybe. But maybe not.

Bibliography

Anderson, Dianna. *Damaged Goods: New Perspectives on Christian Purity*. New York: FaithWords, 2015.

Bauer, Walter, Frederick W. Danker, William F. Arndt, and F. W. Gingrich. *A Greek-English Lexicon of the New Testament and Other Early Christian Literature*. 3rd ed. Chicago: University of Chicago Press, 2000.

Catholic Church. *Catechism of the Catholic Church: With Modifications from the Editio Typica*. 2nd ed. New York: Doubleday, 2003.

Holladay, William Lee, editor. *A Concise Hebrew and Aramaic Lexicon of the Old Testament: Based upon the Lexical Work of Ludwig Koehler and Walter Baumgartner*. Grand Rapids: Eerdmans, 1971.

McCleneghan, Bromleigh. *Good Christian Sex: Why Chastity Isn't the Only Option—and Other Things the Bible Says about Sex*. New York: HarperCollins, 2016.

3

Three in One and Two Become One
A Christian Theology of Sex

A. Chadwick Thornhill

When most in Western culture think about how the Bible addresses sex, the predominant image likely conjured is one of a prudish religious text that has lots of rules to follow to take the fun and freedom out of sexual experiences. This may even be accompanied by the attitude that Christians must be embarrassed about sex and keep discussions about such things at a minimum. I will admit freely, as one raised in a Christian home in the Bible Belt, that I felt a bit red-faced at our university library as I was checking out thirty or so books on sex, religion, and theology in preparing for this chapter.

Somewhere along the way, shame became closely associated with sexuality in much of Western Christianity. Those raised in a conservative Christian context, in America in particular, likely also encountered some form of Christian purity culture along the way, which places emphasis on waiting to engage in sexual intercourse until marriage and condemning those kinds of sexual enterprises (sex outside of marriage, same-sex sexual acts, etc.) the Bible prohibits. While these matters form some of the basic tenets of a Christian view of sexuality, they focus primarily on the prohibitive side of the matter and fail to equip Christian young people with a positive vision of where sex and sexuality fit within a Christian worldview. The church needs to seriously consider how to frame a positive and compelling view of sexuality and to articulate that vision which grows out of the biblical texts and the best of the Christian theological tradition.

The strategy that has failed much of the church in the West often attempts to scare young people into not having sex (e.g., warning against unplanned pregnancies, STDs, ruining your future marriage, etc.). This reveals that Western Christians often operate with an ethic grounded in pragmatism or consequentialism (i.e., the consequences or effects of the action determine its right or wrongness). This type of articulation of putting sex in its proper place lacks any positive vision, other than occasionally that, "Sex will be better if you wait until you're married." What it fails to articulate is that sex will "feel good" whether married or not. We certainly face an uphill battle to teach and live out a Christian view of sex. Commercials selling everything from cars to hamburgers now come loaded with sexual imagery. Pornographic images can be found readily all over every digital medium available. Sexual imagery is literally everywhere. Even cartoons aimed at children frequently have sexual innuendos present. To truly embrace a biblical and Christian view of sexuality, we need more than dos and don'ts and more than a list of possible negative outcomes. We need a compelling vision of how sex fits within the story of the Bible, and how followers of Jesus live out that story in our messy world today.

Redeeming the Body

Christians have a complicated history as it relates to the physical body. The body is often viewed as something that needs to be repressed, if not escaped. This attitude, however, sits uneasily with two bookends of the Christian story: the creation of the body by God, and the future resurrection of the body into eternity. If bodies were made "good" and will be perfected, why the negativity and shame about bodies, and particularly about sex, widespread among many Christians today? A short-sighted theology of the body has all sorts of implications for how we view life and godliness today.[1]

While Augustine cannot be blamed for all of these shortcomings of Western Christian thought, he played a significant role in the largely negative and prudish view of sexuality that has often dominated in Christian history.[2] Behind Augustine laid several centuries of philosophical thought influenced heavily by Plato. As Middleton traces this history, Plato's thought tended toward dualism, heightening the value of the soul and diminishing

---

1. For a helpful modern conversation partner, see John Paul II, *Man and Woman He Created Them*.

2. Whether this was Augustine's intent or not, it is certainly often how he is read and how his influence is perceived.

or extinguishing the value of the body.³ Though Platonism took various forms and phases between Plato and Augustine, it is not hard to find dualistic and Platonic aspects of Augustine's thought (especially as articulated by Plotinus), along with other church fathers. Augustine, for example, argued that sexual intercourse was what passed the sin nature from parent to child, stating that "those who are born from the union of bodies are under the power of the devil . . . because they are born through that concupiscence by which the flesh has desires opposed to the spirit."⁴ Sexual desire was thus sin itself and responsible for transferring the sinful nature. Of course, there is much of great value to be learned from Augustine and the other church fathers, but we must read them thoughtfully and carefully with a constant eye toward the text of Scripture.

Middleton suggests that Augustine's turbulent sociopolitical context and his neoplatonic framework were factors that led him toward understanding the Christian eschatological hope as a journey away from the physical world. This means, according to Middleton, "there is simply no redemption of the cosmos in Augustine's eschatology."⁵ Through the centuries, the theology of the church experienced "a shift of expectation from earth to heaven, accompanying a shift from the resurrection of the body to the immortality of the soul."⁶ Such a vision sits uneasily with the Christian (and largely Jewish) view of the resurrection of the body to an incorruptible state in the "age to come." Middleton notes that in the twenty-first century, largely due to rediscovering the Jewish context of the New Testament, many theologians have recovered an emphasis on the embodied and physical (though transformed) nature of the renewal of the created order.⁷ Though differing in their eschatological frameworks, this renewed emphasis on the importance of the material world, and of the human body in particular, is welcome.

Given that evangelical theology heavily emphasizes conversion and salvation, misunderstanding the future eschatological state likewise results in misunderstanding our present earthly reality. A disembodied future state or a primarily spiritual existence "in heaven" overlooks the God-givenness of our bodies. This then often leads, pragmatically, to a lack of concern for the body, other than to fight against its carnal inclinations. As it relates to a Christian theology of sex, Winner notes that these theological confusions

---

3. Middleton, *New Heaven and a New Earth*, 31–34, 283–312.
4. *C. Jul.* IV.4.34, quoted in Couenhoven, *Stricken by Sin, Cured by Christ*, 44.
5. Middleton, *New Heaven and a New Earth*, 292.
6. Ibid., 294.
7. Ibid., 303–12.

mean, "We are not sure whether bodies are good or bad; it follows that we are not sure whether sex is good or bad."[8] Are our bodies a gift or a curse? Is sex a joy to be celebrated or a temptation to overcome?

In deeming our bodies as a gift that has been tainted rather than an obstacle to be overcome, we can embrace the blessing of an immortal, incorruptible, embodied existence in God's future renewed and restored world. As Wright summarizes, "According to the early Christians, the purpose of this new body will be to rule wisely over God's new world. . . . There will be work to do and we shall relish doing it . . . the garden will need to be tended once more."[9] In pragmatic terms, this means we live in the time between the times. The kingdom of God is both "here" and "near" (Mark 1:15; Luke 17:21), but not fully consummated, what New Testament scholars often refer to as an "inaugurated eschatology." Followers of Jesus are new creatures, but not yet fully what they will be (1 Cor 15:20–28; 2 Cor 5:17). We do not yet see him as he is (1 John 3:2). Christians thus both already possess and still await the possession of their future glorified state.

If all this is so, how much more should we understand that sex is both a created and redeemed good through the work of the triune God, even as we recognize that there are still thorns and thistles present in our beautiful but fallen world. To be sure, there is good, bad, and ugly throughout the Bible on these matters, from the institution of marriage and the celebration of sexual passions; to the depiction of polygamy, incest, rape, adultery, and other forms of deviant or abusive behavior; to varied tones on singleness, celibacy, marriage, family, and the church. It is all part of the Bible's story of sex.

God, Love, and Sex: Beginning at the Beginning

The story of sex in the Bible begins with the creation of man and woman. In the two accounts of creation in Genesis 1 and 2, we learn both male and female are created (1) in God's image, (2) to be fruitful and multiply, and (3) to fill, subdue, and rule over creation. They were to be mediators of God to his world. From Genesis 2 we learn that the woman is created to eliminate the loneliness of the man, and the two are joined together as husband and wife and become one flesh. His state of loneliness was "not good," an anomaly in the creation narrative overrunning with goodness.[10] Adam needed an embodied "other" who shared in his likeness to bring relational goodness to

8. Winner, *Real Sex*, 33.
9. Wright, *Surprised by Hope*, 161.
10. Jones, *Faithful*, 29–30.

his existence. God's creation—male and female, human relation, sex, bodies, procreation—was thus good, indeed, very good.

Part of the intent for this union of others was for the sake of procreation. Husband and wife are here tasked with the charge to both fill the earth (i.e., have children) and subdue it (care for and rule over creation). Within the original plan for marriage, bearing children, filling the earth, was the Creator's design. Family and fellowship are thus uniquely embedded in the divine arrangement for union of husband and wife.[11] In fact, it is not hard to imagine that filling the earth and subduing it go hand in hand. How could only two care for the expanse of God's created order? Certainly other humans were needed for this enterprise.[12] And so God invites male and female into both the act of ruling his world and the act of creating within it by both the creativity of their labors and the creation of other image-bearers through their becoming one flesh. Ruling and creating are divine prerogatives gifted to those who bear the image of the divine.

While the Genesis narrative does not tell us how much time passes before things go awry, within the narrative itself it happens rather quickly. After the pronouncement of the union of husband and wife, and the recognition that there was no shame in their nudity, the serpent deceives Eve, and subsequently Adam, and sin, death, corruption, and destruction enter God's good world. As a result, the relation of husband and wife finds new tensions. The wife will desire to control her husband and the husband will seek to control his wife (Gen 3:16). In a world marred by sin, the cooperative intention of created husband-wife relations devolves into a power struggle.[13] Thus, "In place of openness comes shame; joy and love are marred by pain, lust, and domination (Gen 3:7, 16)."[14] Though the result of sin here on husband-wife relations likely does not focus on the sexual dimension of the relationship, clearly the sexual enterprise possesses the danger, most often expressed by men, to possess and control another and reduce their humanity to the status

---

11. The *Book of Common Prayer* summarizes, "The union of husband and wife in heart, body, and mind is intended by God for their mutual joy; for the help and comfort given one another in prosperity and adversity; and, when it is God's will, for the procreation of children and their nurture in the knowledge and love of the Lord." Church of England, *Book of Common Prayer*, 423.

12. Augustine states, "[Nuptial blessing] was given before they sinned, for its purpose was to make it clear that the procreation of children is a part of the glory of marriage and not of the punishment of sin." Augustine, *City of God* 14.21, quoted in Louth and Conti, eds., *Genesis 1–11*, 39.

13. Longman, *Genesis*, 67–68. See ibid. and Grenz, "Theological Approaches to Male-Female Relationships," 98.

14. Sprinkle, *Biblical Law and Its Relevance*, 156.

of an object.¹⁵ Sin damages both the relationship and the joining of flesh to flesh, both pronounced as created goods just a chapter earlier.

While Genesis 1–2 provides a vital lens for Christian theology into the intent of marriage and sex, and Genesis 3 shows us what *is* (power-seeking) instead of *what should be* (mutuality), there is another theological dimension that is crucial to understanding sexuality. Prior to the creation of male and female and the establishment of marital union, we find another, truer kind of love and desire. Following Lewis, "We begin at the real beginning, with love as the Divine energy. This primal love is Gift-love. In God there is no hunger that needs to be filled, only plenteousness that desires to give."¹⁶ If God is love (1 John 4:8), and humans are made in the image of God, when we ask questions about sex, we ask questions fundamentally about love and desire. In a Christian theological framework, our reference point for answering those questions must be God.

So how do we work toward a Christian definition of love? What are the theological resources available to redeem sexuality? The answer starts, perhaps surprisingly, with the Trinity. The doctrine of the Trinity has a long, rich history for aiding in questions of love and human relations. More specifically, the doctrine of *perichoresis*, the mutual indwelling and interpenetration of the three persons of the Trinity, provides a deep theological grounding for the way in which humans open up to one another in interpersonal relationships, and more concretely within sexual union. Though the doctrine of *perichoresis* did not attain creedal status, it holds an important place in Christian thought in articulating the intra-Trinitarian relations of Father, Son, and Spirit.¹⁷

So what is meant by this "mutual indwelling and interpenetration" of the Trinitarian persons? Keller writes, "The life of the Trinity is characterized not by self-centeredness but by mutually self-giving love. . . . Each of the divine persons centers upon the others. None demands that the others revolve around him."¹⁸ Eternally before human relations existed, divine relations existed. Torrance states, "*Perichoresis* is not a static but a dynamic concept, for it refers to an eternal movement in the Love of the Father, the Son and the Holy Spirit for one another, which flows outward unceasingly toward us."¹⁹

15. See Grenz, "Theological Approaches to Male-Female Relationships," 83–85.

16. Lewis, *Four Loves*, 126.

17. Though the term itself was not used concerning the Trinity until later, the concept is clearly rooted in the writings of Athanasius and the Cappadocian fathers. See Crisp, "Problems with Perichoresis." See also Torrance, *Christian Doctrine of God*, 168ff.

18. Keller, *Reason for God*, 215.

19. Torrance, *Christian Doctrine of God*, 172.

God's love for us first and eternally existed within the godhead, and overflows to us, but also likewise grounds the love that humans should express toward one another: an other-seeking, other-serving kind of love. Leithart draws this out in writing, "The Father-Son-Spirit relation is the archetype of all human relationships, including sexual and romantic relationships."[20] Likewise, Lewis describes the relations between the persons of the Trinity, stating, "in Christianity God is not a static thing—not even a person—but a dynamic, pulsating activity, a life, almost a kind of drama. Almost, if you will not think me irreverent, a kind of dance."[21]

Theologians have thus spoken of this love at times as *eros*, as longing and desire for another. Those words—longing and desire—for many Westerners have primarily sexual connotations. The *eros* in mind here, however, is not one seeking the fulfillment of one's own desires (i.e., for copulation), but rather a desire *for* another. There is, no doubt, a connection between *eros* and sex, as Plantinga observes when he writes, "*sexual* desire and longing . . . is a sign of something deeper: it is a sign of this longing, yearning for God. . . . It is love for God that is fundamental or basic, and sexual eros that is the sign or symbol or pointer to something else."[22] Lewis likewise notes both the intensity and the relational nature inherent in *eros*. He writes, "The *thing* [sexual intercourse] is a sensory pleasure; that is, an event occurring within one's own body. . . . Eros makes a man really want, not a woman, but one particular woman. In some mysterious but quite indisputable fashion the lover desires the Beloved herself, not the pleasure she can give."[23] This *eros*, longing and desire, then exists in sexual activity but cannot be reduced to it, and in particular cannot be reduced toward selfish lust. *Eros* desires the other for the good of the other, not simply the good of the self.

The more we understand and embrace the love of God, and allow that love to transform us, the more will we be empowered to express true love, in all of its dimensions. Sexual intercourse, then, acts as an image of the combination of this perichoretic union within the Trinity and the other-serving and other-desiring love found within the character of God. As Grenz describes, it represents "the relationality within the eternal divine life."[24] Though this type of perichoretic, *eros*-oriented love involves feelings, it cannot be reduced to feelings. It contains the posture and practice of seeking another. The reason sex is often described in our culture as such a

20. Leithart, *Traces of the Trinity*, 136.
21. Lewis, *Mere Christianity*, 175.
22. Plantinga, *Warranted Christian Belief*, 316.
23. Lewis, *Four Loves*, 94.
24. Grenz, "Theological Approaches to Male-Female Relationships," 93.

transcendent experience is very simply that the goodness of sex is grounded in something—or better, someone—transcendent. And so, as Hirsch insightfully recognizes, "Sex . . . isn't just about sex. And maybe this *is* one of the reasons our culture is so fixated with sex—because in it they are also looking for "something else."[25]

God, Sex, and Covenant Fidelity

We cannot limit the expression of divine *eros* and love in sex to the act of sex itself. Within Christian thought, this longing and physical oneness must be accompanied with a further characteristic that is grounded in the divine life, that of fidelity. When Christians speak of marriage as a covenant, they rightly insist that the proper context within which sex should occur is a covenantally committed one. As Leithart describes, "Sex involves the union of two into one, and this union is a union of mutual envelopment and mutual indwelling. . . . The physical indwelling points to a personal entanglement and intertwining that persist beyond the bedroom."[26] Sex without covenantal commitment is sex without love, Christianly defined. Sex outside of a covenantal commitment always has too few "strings attached." Even if it occurs within a committed relationship, the lack of formal commitment, the lack of a covenantal bond, provides a thin, incomplete context for sex, and thus the Bible insists that, as it was from the beginning, sexual intercourse should occur within the context of a covenantally committed, other-serving, other-desiring relationship.[27]

One need not look far in the biblical text to find this covenantal commitment rooted in the character of God. Perhaps the best expression, however, of this reality exists in the book of Hosea. Hosea's marriage to the prostitute Gomer was a visible portrait of the unfaithfulness of Israel to her covenant with YHWH. Just as covenant faithfulness was required between husband and wife, but absent in reality for Hosea and Gomer, so faithfulness was required for Israel but absent in reality. In spite of this,

25. Hirsch, *Redeeming Sex*, 25–26.

26. Leithart, *Traces of the Trinity*, 42.

27. Grenz rightly highlights the covenantal nature of marriage, which distinguishes it from other human relationships and sets the context in which sexual intercourse is intended. This, in turn, emphasizes the necessity of fidelity (especially since covenantal fidelity is a major theme throughout the Bible), the embrace of the other (not just "another" person, but one who is a true different, i.e., male and female), and ultimately, because of these realities, serves as a metaphor both for intra-Trinitarian love and for the bond between Christ and the church. See Grenz, "Homosexuality and the Christian Sex Ethic," esp. 127–38.

Hosea remained faithful to Gomer and extended to her forgiveness so their relationship could be reconciled. Hosea's life in the book serves as a picture of the enduring faithfulness of God, who, in spite of Israel's unfaithfulness, extends forgiveness to her and seeks reconciliation with humanity in general. At stake, then, in Christian marriage is not just personal piety, but embodying the faithfulness of God. Faithful marriage points to a faithful God, and so marriage "figuratively foreshadows, even in the ambiguities of the present time, God's unbreakable covenant faithfulness which will finally bring healing to the world."[28]

If marriage, as a covenant, signifies a committed, other-serving, other-desiring relationship, sex symbolically enacts what the relationship signifies. This view of marriage and sex finds expression in Jesus's teachings about divorce in Mark 10:2–12.[29] For Jesus, marital unions must be viewed as unbreakable, since God has ratified the covenantal union of husband and wife, and the two, in marriage and in sex, have become one flesh. The connection that sexual intercourse provides is both symbolic and actual. It is the physical and spiritual bonding of husband and wife.[30]

Certainly the biblical crescendo as it relates to sex emerges within the pages of the Song of Solomon. The book opens, "May he kiss me passionately with his lips, for your love is better than wine" (1:2, LEB). The lovers describe their desire for one another. "Look! You are beautiful; your eyes are doves" (1:15, LEB). They delight in the body of the other. "His fruit is sweet to my taste" (2:3, NIV). "His left hand caresses my head, and his right hand stimulates me" (2:6, NET). They long for the presence of each other. "All night long on my bed I longed for my lover" (3:1, NET). The groom relishes the body of his bride. "Your lips are like a scarlet thread; your mouth is lovely" (4:3, NET). "Your breasts are like two fawns, like twin fawns of a gazelle that browse among the lilies" (4:5, NIV). The bride invites her groom to join to her. "Blow on my garden, that its fragrance may spread everywhere. Let my beloved come into his garden and taste its choice fruits" (4:16, NIV).

---

28. Hays, *Moral Vision of the New Testament*, 366.

29. Commenting on Mal 2:10–16, which Jesus therein references, Block outlines that divorce in ancient Israelite culture signaled a lack of reverence and fear toward Yahweh, an act of treachery against one's companion, a breach of covenant commitment, an act of treachery against the community, the disruption of a stable environment for raising children, covenantal rejection by God, and moral deficiency in the character of the (typically male) initiator. Block, "Marriage and Family in Ancient Israel," 51–52. See also Sprinkle, *Biblical Law and Its Relevance*, 170.

30. See Hays, *Moral Vision of the New Testament*, 351.

There's nothing prudish about the Song of Solomon. It delights in the bringing together of bodies. In nudity. In sexual play. In erotic sex.[31] But this is not sex for sex's sake. This is sex rooted in *eros*, in desire not just for the body of another, but for the other. This is marital union, of bride and groom, committed to the other. And this is mutuality.[32] There is no machismo conquering. There is mutual delight. Sex is grace. A gift from God as a means, yes, of procreation, but also, as in the Song of Solomon, of physical intimacy and pleasure.[33] And in sex, husband and wife give their bodies as gifts to one another, reflecting the nature of the true and perfect Giver.

Sex, the Church, and Christosis

I have thus far argued the Bible contextualizes sex within marriage because it is an activity that demands a covenantally committed, other-desiring, other-serving kind of love. Any other context is too thin, and ultimately makes sexual activity a self-serving or unfaithful enterprise that does not produce human flourishing. The divine program does not, of course, limit this other-focused relationality to the marital bond. Though this is uniquely embodied within the marital relationship and uniquely pictured within the act of sexual union, the New Testament expects this communal mutuality embodied in the life of the church as well.

This necessarily recontextualizes the place in which we understand marriage. Kingdom allegiance is primary, and familial bonds must not threaten or take priority over allegiance to Jesus. So Stanley Grenz notes that, according to Jesus, "the primary human bond is not marriage and family, as important as these are, but the company of disciples."[34] Likewise, Joseph Hellerman, commenting on 1 Corinthians 7, notes that marriage is "a secondary priority in view of what God is doing to grow his eternal family in the world."[35] Marriage is important, beautiful, and a wonderful part

---

31. So Jensen comments, "Given the relative explicitness of its cadences, it is no surprise that most Christian traditions have tended toward allegory.... Otherwise the pomegranates appear too juicy." Jensen, *God, Desire, and a Theology of Human Sexuality*, 12.

32. On the mutuality of Song of Solomon, see ibid. For the same theme in Paul, see Westfall, *Paul and Gender*, 196, which includes fresh perspectives on the most controverted texts. See also Hays, *Moral Vision of the New Testament*, 49–50. It is noteworthy that the woman's voice occupies far more space than the man's in the book.

33. Indeed, it is striking that in this, the most sexually explicit book in the Bible, there is no mention of children or procreation.

34. Grenz, "Homosexuality and the Christian Sex Ethic," 130.

35. Hellerman, *When the Church Was a Family*, 90.

of part of God's created vision, but we must not idolize it. It is the church which is essential and is the means by which the reality of the kingdom of God is made manifest in God's world today, through union with Christ and Spirit-filled participation in the very life of God as revealed in the life, death, and resurrection of the Son of God.

This is an important reminder for Christians who are single or celibate, either by choice or otherwise, and so Hays comments, "Within the church we need to shatter the power of the myth that only married people are normal and that only marriage offers the conditions necessary for human fulfillment."[36] The members of the body must embody the same kind of other-serving, familial, committed love that is intended for marriage, because this love is God's love. True love. A Christian marriage that neglects the priority of the kingdom misarranges its values and thus operates with a dysfunctional agenda. Kingdom life must frame all else, not vice versa.

This is a far cry from the rampant individualism prevalent in the mindset of most Westerners (including Christians) today. Returning to Hellerman: "Our culture has powerfully socialized us to believe that personal happiness and fulfillment should take precedence over the connections we have with others in both our families and our churches. . . . The tune of radical individualism has been playing in our ears at full volume for decades."[37] If there is a value most Westerners share across different worldviews, it is the importance and primacy of the individual and their rights and freedom to choose their path in life and express their self-identity.

In view of this, it is not surprising that Western culture also treats sexuality as a matter that defines identity. To be true to one's self is to embrace whatever sexual inclinations and orientations one feels drawn toward. This means heterosexual, lesbian, gay, bisexual, asexual, intergender, intersexual, transgender, etc. identities all should be affirmed and cultivated. Sexual identity for the Christian, however, can never be one's primary identity. If we take Paul at his word that in Christ there is no male or female, Jew or Gentile, slave or free, this means that cultural, social, and biological identities are necessarily secondary to Christian identity.[38]

---

36. Hays, *Moral Vision of the New Testament*, 373. Jones writes, "A good theology of sex needs to reclaim and proclaim the good of both marriage and singleness. In both marriage and singleness, Christian bodies are testimony to the faithfulness of God." Jones, *Faithful*, 68.

37. Hellerman, *When the Church Was a Family*, 4.

38. Jones recognizes that gender identities are, to some extent, socially constructed realities. Jones, *Faithful*, 31ff. For example, pink and blue have no inherent qualities of masculinity and femininity, yet are strongly associated in the West with particular gender identities. For Christians, discerning biblical marks of gender identity versus cultural ones is a challenge, but one that needs to be taken with care and seriousness.

While our culture today frequently answers the question "Who am I?" with various categories of sexual orientation, the Christian response must be, "I am in Christ, a participator of the people of God, a member of the body of Christ."[39] Our true existence, our true humanity, is found through identification with and participation in the work of Christ. God's "wonderful plan" for our lives is conformity to the image of Christ—Christosis—which requires cruciformity, embodying the sacrificial pattern of the life of Jesus.[40] This is true for husband and wife, married believer and unmarried believer. Sex and sexuality can sanctify us, both in teaching us restraint and abstinence when necessary and for revealing to us a relational God who has created relational creatures and given to them sex as *one* means of expressing nearness, other-serving love, intimacy, and vulnerability.

Though sex within the confines of male-female marriages may be the divine ideal, this does not entail that virtuous, God-honoring sex will automatically take place in such marriages. Husbands may abuse their wives. Wives may spitefully withhold themselves from their husbands. Only a Spirit-filled, cruciform marriage in which each spouse is committed to the good of the other will provide the context in which sexual intimacy can flourish and relational nearness can flourish as well. So, as Hays writes, "Christians set free from the power of sin through Christ's death must continue to *struggle* to live faithfully in the present time."[41]

Writing to his son Michael, J. R. R. Tolkien once penned,

> The essence of a fallen world is that the best cannot be attained by free enjoyment, or by what is called 'self-realization' (usually a nice name for self-indulgence, wholly inimical to the realization of other selves); but by denial, by suffering. . . . No man, however truly he loved his betrothed and bride as a young man, has lived faithful to her as a wife in mind and body without deliberate conscious exercise of the will, without self-denial. Too few are told that—even those brought up 'in the Church.' Those outside seem seldom to have heard it.[42]

---

39. Hays argues, "Never within the canonical perspective does sexuality become the basis for defining a persons' identity or for finding meaning and fulfillment in life. The things that matter are justice, mercy, and faith (Matt. 23:23). The love of God is far more important than any human love. Sexual fulfillment finds its place, at best, as a subsidiary good within this larger picture." Hays, *Moral Vision of the New Testament*, 390.

40. Gorman, *Becoming the Gospel*, 98–99.

41. Hays, *Moral Vision of the New Testament*, 393.

42. Tolkien, *Letters of J. R. R. Tolkien*, 51.

New Creatures

The ethical question for the Christian concerning sex (and indeed all ethical matters) is: Will we live within the symbolic world of the Bible, or in a delusional world of our choosing? Will we embrace our "in Christ" identity by choosing, each day, Spirit-enabled conformity to the image of the crucified and risen Son? Will we accept the calling to take up our cross and die to sin daily? Will we prioritize the good of others over only seeking the good of our self? The powerful deception of postmodernism is that the world is ours to create. But this sin of creating our own world and our own identity within it is simply idolatry, taking the title of Creator for ourselves. The temptation to define our own identity takes root in the same temptation that deceived the first man and woman: to create for ourselves and become like gods. But those "in Christ" are already on their way to becoming like God, but only through conformity to the self-sacrificial, other-loving, other-seeking image of the Son, the firstborn among many siblings.

God's plan for the world and for our bodies is redemption. It is resurrection: bringing life from death. This means Christians, though living with an awareness of the good restraints necessary when it comes to sex, have profoundly beautiful reasons to celebrate sex as God's gift to husbands and wives. Sex, rightly configured in a covenantally bonded, other-serving, other-desiring marriage, is good not because God arbitrarily decided so, but because it reflects the realities of the kind of love we find within the godhead. Sex acts as a sign of the redemptive love of God, the love that is restoring the goodness of God's created order. Accordingly, Christians have the best of reasons to embrace the joy of sex with grateful hearts. It is fitting, then, that we conclude with one of the most famous celebrations of erotic love in the English language, by the Christian poet John Donne.

> Come, madam, come, all rest my powers defy;
> Until I labour, I in labour lie.
> The foe ofttimes, having the foe in sight,
> Is tired with standing, though he never fight.
> Off with that girdle, like heaven's zone glittering,
> But a far fairer world encompassing.
> Unpin that spangled breast-plate, which you wear,
> That th' eyes of busy fools may be stopp'd there.
> Unlace yourself, for that harmonious chime
> Tells me from you that now it is bed-time.
> Off with that happy busk, which I envy,

That still can be, and still can stand so nigh.
Your gown going off such beauteous state reveals,
As when from flowery meads th' hill's shadow steals.
Off with your wiry coronet, and show
The hairy diadems which on you do grow.
Off with your hose and shoes; then softly tread
In this love's hallow'd temple, this soft bed.
In such white robes heaven's angels used to be
Revealed to men; thou, angel, bring'st with thee
A heaven-like Mahomet's paradise; and though
Ill spirits walk in white, we easily know
By this these angels from an evil sprite;
Those set our hairs, but these our flesh upright.
Licence my roving hands, and let them go
Before, behind, between, above, below.
Oh, my America, my Newfoundland,
My kingdom, safest when with one man mann'd,
My mine of precious stones, my empery;
How am I blest in thus discovering thee!
To enter in these bonds, is to be free;
Then, where my hand is set, my soul shall be.[43]

Bibliography

Block, Daniel. "Marriage and Family in Ancient Israel." In *Marriage and Family in the Biblical World*, edited by Ken M. Campbell, 33–102. Downers Grove, IL: InterVarsity, 2003.

Crisp, Oliver. "Problems with Perichoresis." *Tyndale Bulletin* 56.1 (2005) 119–40.

Donne, John. "To His Mistress Going to Bed." In *The Poems of John Donne*, edited by Edmund Kerchever Chambers. London: Lawrence & Bullen, 1896; Bartleby.com, 2012. http://www.bartleby.com/357/81.html#1-32.

Episcopal Church. *The Book of Common Prayer: And Administration of the Sacraments and Other Rites and Ceremonies of the Church.* New York: Oxford University Press, 1979.

Gorman, Michael J. *Becoming the Gospel: Paul, Participation, and Mission.* Grand Rapids: Eerdmans, 2015.

---

43. Donne, "To His Mistress Going to Bed."

Grenz, Stanley. "Homosexuality and the Biblical Sex Ethic." In *Christian Perspectives on Gender, Sexuality, and Community*, edited by Maxine Hancock, 127–50. Vancouver: Regent College Publishing, 2003.

———. "Theological Approaches to Male-Female Relationships." In *Christian Perspectives on Gender, Sexuality, and Community*, edited by Maxine Hancock, 83–102. Vancouver: Regent College Publishing, 2003.

Hays, Richard. *The Moral Vision of the New Testament: Community, Cross, New Creation: A Contemporary Introduction to New Testament Ethic*. New York: Harper Collins, 2013.

Hellerman, Joseph H. *When the Church Was a Family: Recapturing Jesus' Vision for Authentic Christian Community*. Nashville: B & H Academic, 2009.

Hirsch, Debra. *Redeeming Sex: Naked Conversations about Sexuality and Spirituality*. Downers Grove, IL: InterVarsity, 2015.

Jensen, David H. *God, Desire, and a Theology of Human Sexuality*. Louisville: Westminster John Knox, 2013.

John Paul II, Pope. *Man and Woman He Created Them: A Theology of the Body*. Translated by Michael Waldstein. Boston: Pauline, 2006.

Jones, Beth Felker. *Faithful: A Theology of Sex*. Grand Rapids: Zondervan, 2015.

Keller, Timothy J. *The Reason for God: Belief in an Age of Skepticism*. New York: Penguin, 2008.

Leithart, Peter J. *Traces of the Trinity: Signs of God in Creation and Human Experience*. Grand Rapids: Brazos, 2015.

Lewis, C. S. *The Four Loves*. San Diego, CA: Harcourt Brace & Company, 1960.

———. *Mere Christianity*. Grand Rapids: Zondervan, 2001.

Longman, Tremper. *Genesis*. Story of God Bible Commentary. New York: Harper Collins, 2016.

Louth, Andrew, and Marco Conti, editors. *Genesis 1–11*. Ancient Christian Commentary on Scripture, Old Testament 1. Downers Grove, IL: InterVarsity, 2001.

Middleton, J. Richard. *A New Heaven and a New Earth: Reclaiming Biblical Eschatology*. Grand Rapids: Baker Academic, 2014.

Plantinga, Alvin. *Warranted Christian Belief*. Oxford: Oxford University Press, 2000.

Sprinkle, Joe M. *Biblical Law and Its Relevance: A Christian Understanding and Ethical Application for Today of the Mosaic Regulations*. Lanham, MD: University Press of America, 2006.

Tolkien, J. R. R. *The Letters of J. R. R. Tolkien*. Edited by Humphrey Carpenter and Christopher Tolkien. Boston: Houghton Mifflin Harcourt, 2014.

Torrance, Thomas F. *The Christian Doctrine of God, One Being Three Persons*. London: Bloomsbury, 2016.

Westfall, Cynthia Long. *Paul and Gender: Reclaiming the Apostle's Vision for Men and Women in Christ*. Grand Rapids: Baker Academic, 2016.

Winner, Lauren F. *Real Sex*. Grand Rapids: Baker, 2006.

Wright, N. T. *Surprised by Hope: Rethinking Heaven, the Resurrection, and the Mission of the Church*. Grand Rapids: Zondervan, 2008.

4

Biological Transformation

Does Marriage Change Your Relational DNA?

Jeremy Neill

Are married persons the same as unmarried ones who live together and love each other? Is the wedding ceremony a mere procedural formality, or does it mark a relational change? Is the purpose of marriage just the governmental tax break, or is it something more? In this chapter I will argue that marriage is a special relationship and that a married couple differs from an unmarried, cohabiting couple in crucial ways. The relational status of the married couple is ontologically different from that of the unmarried couple, no matter how long the unmarried couple has been together, and whether or not the unmarried couple is living together. The change that marriage brings about is meaningful, permanent, and fundamentally different than cohabitation—and it's an awesome thing!

Now Something We Once Were Not

> O gracious and everliving God, look mercifully upon this man and this woman who come to you seeking your blessing. (*Book of Common Prayer*, hereafter *BCP*)

To say that the married couple is ontologically different from the unmarried couple is to say that the very essence or nature of the relationship has changed. The married couple—in the eyes of the community and also in the eyes of God—is different *in kind* (or ontology) from the unmarried couple.

The fact of their marriage is what makes the difference: the married couple is another sort of relational species, made out of different interpersonal DNA, and on a life trajectory that is different from an unmarried couple. At the heart of the ontological difference between the married and the unmarried couple are the special ties of the former, celebrated on their wedding day. The husband and wife, unlike their unmarried counterparts, are united on their wedding day in a covenant of commitment. Their marriage is grounded in their oaths and it is formally acknowledged by their community. Their vows are emotionally and physically binding in a way that is foreign to the unmarried couple. Their covenant distinguishes them from unmarried couples by virtue of its forthrightness: in pledging their fidelity to each other, the marrying partners are making their intentions known in a way that unmarried couples are not. It takes work for a marrying couple to live up to the permanence and exclusivity promises of their wedding day. But their lives of emotional and sexual fidelity offer immense payoffs—both inside and outside of the marriage bed!

Another reason why a married couple is different from an unmarried one is because marriage, as a relational species, was invented by God. Way back in the book of Genesis, God instituted marriage for the whole human race: "That is why a man leaves his father and mother and is united to his wife, and they become one flesh" (Gen 2:24, NIV). Marriage was not intended to be solely for Christians, Jews, or any other people group. The marriages of non-Christians, Gentiles, and many others were also intended to partake in the real, ontological change.

Because of its divine origins, there are some Christians—my Catholic brothers and sisters—who consider marriage to be sacramental. They view marriage as an external and visible sign, accompanied by a promise of Christ, that imparts to the couple an inner and spiritual grace. The power of the marriage sacrament, for Catholics, lies in the promise of Christ and in the fact that marriage, like the sacraments of baptism and Holy Communion, is marked by a visible sign. Catholics are right to say that marriage is a wonderful institution, and a true gift of God. But as a Protestant I do not think that marriage is a sacrament. The Bible does not represent marriage as being devised by Christ or laid down in the New Testament. In fact, as a relational species, marriage appears to have been created from the beginning in Genesis as soon as humans were gendered. The view that Catholics and Protestants hold in common is that marriage involves a real metaphysical change. This is what Jesus is referencing when he says in the New Testament that "they are no longer two, but one flesh. Therefore what God has joined together, let no one separate" (Matt 19:6, NIV). The use by Jesus of the "one flesh" formula is a metaphorical acknowledgement of the real change that God instituted way back in Genesis!

The Ceremony Is Temporary But the Values Are Eternal

> Marriage is not to be entered into unadvisedly or lightly, but reverently, deliberately, and in accordance with the purposes for which it was instituted by God. (*BCP*)

The wedding ceremony is an important marker of the change in the marrying couple. A ceremony is a microcosm of values, encapsulating in ritual and artistry the reasons for getting married. It also offers an account of the differences between married and unmarried couples. Its values and oaths are exclusive to married couples, and cannot be similarly realized by others. To be sure, marriages sometimes take place in the absence of ceremony. The momentous day does not even have to be celebrated at all in order to be legitimate. But a formal affirmation of some kind—before God and usually before witnesses as well—is fitting as a marker of the status change for the marrying couple. In practice, of course, most marrying couples do want to hold a ceremony to mark their relational change. People like parties and we also want to invoke our cultural heritages on our happy day. In the Judeo-Christian tradition, and in many other traditions as well, there is every reason for couples to be confident in the ceremonial possibilities that their heritage offers: the rituals that have been passed down from our ancestors are some of the most meaningful ways that we can celebrate marriage and the role of God in our intertwined lives.

What does the wedding ceremony do, though, vis-à-vis the marriage and the change that the couple undergoes? Why should the couple, even if they are convinced of the importance of getting married, trouble themselves to hold a public and time-consuming event? One purpose of the ceremony is to celebrate the values of the couple's union. The idea is for formal rituals to equip the couple to affirm alongside their family and friends their reasons for marriage and the principles of marriage. I will call the wedding ceremony that (I think) does best at celebrating the values of marriage the "classical style." By the classical style I mean a way of doing weddings that has arisen out of a Judeo-Christian heritage, that incorporates many different rituals, and that today has become venerable and cherished throughout the Western democracies. One reason why the classical style is so treasured is because it has captured the hopes and dreams of so many marrying couples down through the centuries! Its elegance and reverence are compelling markers of the relational change that occurs whenever couples pledge their faithfulness to each other. The classical style makes marrying couples both inheritors and creators: they are the inheritors of a tradition that treasures the values of marriage, and their ceremonial choices also at the same time offer their own contributions to that tradition!

What makes the classical rituals so expressive of the values of marriage? In part, the rituals are important because, as markers of the couple's new status, they offer a school of relationships. By upholding the rituals of the tradition on their happy day, it is possible for marrying couples to learn a lot about the promises and possibilities of their union. The classical ceremony is intended to honor the past and to mark the change in the couple's relationship. It visibly ties their real change in status to the many other couples who have married down through the centuries. At the same time, and in another sense, the classical ceremony is intended to anticipate the couple's future. Its customs are grand and old, and, having been refined over the centuries, it equips the marrying partners to acknowledge their continuity with past generations. The details of the classical ceremony are, of course, familiar. It uses long-standing rituals of dress and speech, and its attendants are groomsmen and bridesmaids. It relies on established musical pieces and its steps are preplanned. Its bride enters to music, and is accompanied by parents. Its minister blesses the union and offers reflections on the nature of marriage. Central to the classical ceremony is the solemn (but joyful) vow exchange.

In part, the reason why ceremonies are valuable is that they highlight so many of our hopes and dreams. Think, as examples, of the ceremonies that we prefer on our grandest and most formal occasions. Every once in a while one of those splendid British royal weddings takes place. When it does, the pageantry and tradition of the classical ceremony is celebrated around the world. Persons once again are able—en masse—to share in the values of marriage and to recall to their minds their reasons for marriage. The reverence and majesty of our wedding ceremonies, royal or otherwise, are often remembered for years after they occur. Occasionally our wedding ceremonies are big and bold. At other times they are small and intimate. In nearly all of their forms they are special occasions because they celebrate the values of marriage—in a way that is inspirational and that is not available to the unmarried couple. At the end of the day there is perhaps no more graceful and gracious way than a ceremony for a couple to start their life together.

What precisely is it about a wedding ceremony that makes it such a poignant microcosm of values? How are the values that it celebrates better than the values of other relational arrangements—like cohabitation, or friends with benefits, or hookups? Here I want to speak from the experience of my 2014 wedding. The ceremony on that hot day in June was an exhilarating adventure. My wife and I had dated for about sixteen months before we took the plunge. The four-month engagement and planning process, though joyous, was also tiring because it was so work intensive. For my wife it was sometimes exhausting. My role was not as creative as hers, but I did assist her in her labors. Our ceremony had a distinctive message about the relationship we were entering. Its emotional message was that humans do best in long-term relationships. Its sexual message was that marital unions are, on balance, more emotionally prosperous than nonmarital ones. That message also marked a crucial distinction between married sexuality and unmarried sexuality: the sexual fidelity that the classical ceremony highlights is for the marrying couple a source of stability and trust that is not similarly available to unmarried persons. Unlike unmarried persons, the husband and wife are pledging—explicitly and publicly—their sexual loyalty. The emotional and sexual commitments of the ceremony are values that have, down through the centuries, produced numerous happy marriages. Their message, in contrast to the message of cohabitation, friends with benefits, or hookups, is that the emotional and sexual fidelity that has worked in the past, producing so much personal fulfillment, will work similarly well in the future for the marrying couple. Speaking personally, I think I can say with confidence that knowing that one's lifetime partner is sexually faithful is an incredibly empowering thing!

By highlighting the values of marriage, the classical ceremony simultaneously does two things: it celebrates the couple's relational transformation and prepares them for their life together. So the reason why a ceremony is important for marrying couples is not just that the values they are celebrating have worked in the past across different cultures. The rituals are valuable also because they offer couples the emotional and relational tools of a prosperous life. By celebrating their status change through a public occasion, the couples are making it known to their community that they intend to build their marriage on the fidelity, care, and honesty that have worked for generations.

In part, the reason why ritual is important is because marriage is a momentous status change. Most wedding ceremonies—classical or not—greet marriage with both seriousness and joy: their customs are supposed to be sober and reflective, and their happiness is an opportunity for the couple and their friends to rejoice. Ceremonies are ways of acknowledging that the marrying couple is now something that they once were not. Through word and deed, and before God and man, the couple is announcing a change in their status. One of the main messages of the classical ceremony is that marriage is permanent—truly, a new and beautiful relational creation! At the center of the classical ceremony is its vow exchange. The momentous status change that this exchange celebrates is a more lasting thing than a gym visit, or a haircut, or the purchase of a phone or computer. In commemorating their happy day in a formal and public way, the marrying couple is asserting that they intend for their union to be lasting.

A Moment of Silence, Please: The *BCP* Ceremony

> O God, grant that by your Holy Spirit, this man and woman, now joined in holy marriage, may become one in heart and soul, and live in fidelity and peace. (*BCP*)

For our own wedding my wife and I chose the ceremony in the *Book of Common Prayer*. The *BCP* wedding is an eloquent and stately occasion. Its proceedings explain the differences between married couples and unmarried ones. It cites Bible verses, offers prayers, and is reverential throughout. The ceremony proceeds slowly. First the minister lays out reasons for the couple to get married. Then he cautions the couple against frivolous commitments: "The union of husband and wife in heart, body, and mind is intended by God for their mutual joy; for the help and comfort given one another in prosperity and adversity; and, when it is God's will, for the procreation of children and their nurture in the knowledge and love of the Lord. Therefore marriage is not to be entered into unadvisedly or lightly, but reverently, deliberately, and in accordance with the purposes for which it was instituted by God."

In part we chose the *BCP* ceremony because, as Christians, we felt that it explains God's role in the couple's relationship. There are numerous moments in the *BCP* ceremony when the minister thanks God for life's blessings. On a couple of occasions he also praises God for husband-wife relationships. Hardly anything occurs in the *BCP* ceremony without a Scripture or a blessing. A number of people in the years since our wedding have told us how reverent they felt at our service. In our view this is no accident. It stems directly from the Christian emphasis of the *BCP* ceremony and the way that the ceremony highlights the unique qualities of marriage. The rituals of the *BCP* ceremony are gracious and graceful as instructions about the role of God in marriages. They also are exhilarating experiences for the persons who are seeking to live out their values!

In the *BCP* service the vows are prescribed for the couple. The bride and groom do not write their own vows. The reason why my wife and I wanted to use classical vows was that we wanted to acknowledge, in front of our community, our participation in something that was bigger than ourselves: a covenantal union into which generations before us had entered. By submitting ourselves to the *BCP* vows, we were recognizing the wisdom of our ancestors about the ways in which couples ought to enter that union. We likewise were underscoring how our relationship was changing—from impermanence and uncertainty to stability and confidence. The *BCP* vows are binding unto death: "In the Name of God, I take you to be my wife (husband), to have and to hold from this day forward, for better for worse, for richer for poorer, in sickness and in health, to love and to cherish, until we are parted by death. This is my solemn vow." Our marriage has not yet undergone many difficulties. When it does, we know that our vows will have helped prepare us for the test.

In the *BCP* ceremony, and in other Christian ceremonies as well, the vows are said in the presence of God. God is both a witness and an instrument of the real change that the couple undergoes on their happy day. Their vows are a reminder that, before God, they are no longer unmarried. The husband and wife are now in a covenantal relationship in which they have each promised to play a part. God will hold them accountable for their vows. Does this standard of divine accountability apply also to non-Christian couples? In the Scriptures God appears to be a witness as well, if only implicitly, to the marital promises of non-Christian couples—couples who are not celebrating a Christian ceremony and whose weddings do not acknowledge God's place in their marriage. The Scriptures suggest that they too are accountable for their promises, though perhaps not in the same way.[1]

Fidelity is the central value in the *BCP* vows, and this does more than anything else to separate the married couple from the unmarried couple. What the liturgy of the *BCP* ceremony is saying is that commitment is possible for the marrying couple in a way that it is not for unmarried couples. The way in which the marrying couple's fidelity is acknowledged in the *BCP* ceremony is through their oath—before God and others—of faithfulness unto death. For centuries, the fidelity that the *BCP* ceremony celebrates has been foundational to successful marriages. A wife can rely on a husband who is sexually faithful. A husband can rely on a wife who is emotionally committed. The fidelity oaths of the couple are indicators of their real change and are central to their mutual flourishing. It's all very powerful stuff! The practical impact of the oaths is to assure the husband and wife that their spouse will be there, through life's ups and downs. We humans are able to function more successfully when our loved ones are reliable and

---

1. In none of the main marriage passages in the Old and New Testaments is it suggested that marriage is exclusively for God's people.

trustworthy. The message of the classical ceremony is that a conscientious vow observance is a game plan for a healthy union, in a way that an unmarried couple or a cohabiting couple cannot similarly experience.

Sexuality, Community, and Humility: Choose One, Two, or Three

> Most gracious God, pour out the abundance of your blessing upon this man and this woman. (*BCP*)

Marriage is a comprehensive union of two souls: spiritual, emotional, mental, sexual, and physical. Its sexual connection is one of its most vital components. What the ceremonial vows illustrate is that the sexuality of the married couple is now qualitatively different from that of the unmarried couple. The married couple's sexuality, predicated on a pledge of emotional fidelity and physical exclusivity, is different—in kind—from the sexual activity of unmarried persons. The ceremony, as an external and communal sign of the marrying couple's internal and relational change, renders the couple's sexual exchanges forthright and transparent in a way that the sexual exchanges of unmarried persons are not. The ceremony celebrates transparent sex, with no secrets—an exhilarating concept in our modern world!

Another way that a wedding ceremony marks the marrying couple's status change, thereby indicating the importance of their new life together, is by involving the community. At our own wedding my wife and I were only a small part of the goings-on. While in one sense we were celebrating *our* marriage, nevertheless, at the same time our community was also celebrating itself. The labors of the parents, teachers, friends, and relatives in our community that led up to that happy day had equipped two of its own to navigate the first stage of their lives together. A ceremony is an appropriate way of marking the couple's status change in part because a marriage, by nature, is a public occasion. The bride and groom are the members of a community and are not the marriage's only contributors. Others are the preacher, the groomsmen and bridesmaids, the Scripture readers, the singers, and the musicians. The *BCP* wedding does a good job of involving the congregation in the proceedings. At several junctures it asks the congregation to respond to the minister's questions and to bless the couple's marriage. At our wedding my wife and I wanted to be accountable to our community for our promises and our status change. In the call-and-response of the *BCP* ceremony the community is asked to support the husband and wife, to provide them with relational sustenance, and witness to their sexual commitments. The community is urged also to promote the couple's emotional success.

The presence of witnesses is central to the couple's status change. It shapes the acknowledgment of that change by their community, and it equips their community to keep the couple accountable for their vows. The charge of sexual fidelity that it highlights is something that the community recognizes and that the members of the community can subsequently use to demarcate the marriage from the couple's previous, unmarried relationship. Presumably, in the audience there are other husbands and wives who have been true to each other down through the years. For the marrying couple, they are examples of the sexual "yes" for which the couple has waited! The exclusivity that the marrying couple is promising is, or ought usually to be, inspired by the couples who have preceded them. When the dating couple harnesses their desires and waits until their marriage to say "yes" to each other they are doing much to secure their future happiness together. Abstaining from sex until marriage is a decision that my wife and I made in our own relationship; both of us were virgins on our wedding night. Such abstention enables marrying couples to look expectantly to a future of healthy sexuality: a "yes" that is worth the wait. It's not that there isn't grace for those who have fallen short of the ideal, but doing it as God intended remains the optimal choice. God's directives here are not arbitrary impositions, but rather a beautiful and successful blueprint for our sexual flourishing.

Another reason why it is important for couples to involve their community in their marriage is that doing so expresses their humility. When a couple chooses marriage and celebrates via ceremony they are submitting themselves to values that are larger than themselves. In including their friends and family members in their happy day, they are acknowledging that the day is not their own. Instead of trying to construct the values of their marriage from the ground up, and instead of choosing cohabitation over marriage, they are connecting their lives to a grand social background. The ceremony enables them simultaneously, through ritual and artistry, to recognize their debt to others and to acknowledge their own limitations. They are starting their marriage with honesty and realism because they are announcing to their friends and family their need for community support. The humility of such an acknowledgement is for the marrying couple a pathway toward emotional and sexual togetherness because it subverts their selfishness and self-reliance, while promoting their selflessness and dependence.

Still another reason for couples to marry and to celebrate via ceremony is that doing so uplifts others. The marrying couple has on their wedding day a unique opportunity: by word, deed, and example to strengthen the marriages in their community. At our own wedding we wanted to share with our guests the special values of marriage and also, at the same time, to inspire their own relationship efforts. We did not just want to celebrate the values of marriage by ourselves: the fidelity, care, exclusivity, love, and honesty of marriage, in our view, needed to be sources of community inspiration. Usually, marrying couples are the representatives of a new generation. Their ceremony is a sign that the cultural baton is now theirs. The wedding rituals are an acknowledgment of the responsibilities that they are taking up via their relational transformation. On their special day they are witnesses to their community: they are telling their community that the relationship they are entering into will require special sacrifices, including a sacrifice of permanence, which unmarried couples, who are not similarly bound by oaths, do not undertake. Through vows and ceremony, marrying couples assume a powerful mantel of cultural responsibility. As one such responsibility—their first—they ought through their ceremony to inspire the others in their community.

The Ring and Other Bling

> I give you this ring as a symbol of my vow, and with all that I am, and all that I have, I honor you. (*BCP*)

A last reason why a ceremony is appropriate as a way of marking and celebrating the couple's status change is the meaningfulness of its rituals. Its rituals illuminate the relational values that the marrying couple embraces. The individual customs of the *BCP* ceremony are awesome! The rings, the music, the flowers, and the Holy Communion are all instructive traditions: they are symbolic in particular of the emotional and sexual solidarity of marriages, down through the centuries. And their celebration on the day of the ceremony is a way for the marrying couple to learn more about their union.

Let's think more closely how two of these rituals help to distinguish the couple's new relationship from their old one. The ring exchange is one of the most moving parts of the *BCP* ceremony. The rings, being circular, and being intended to be worn until death, are signifiers of the eternity of the couple's love. Believe it or not, the rings are also symbolic as yokes: they represent the lasting promises of the husband and wife. Early Protestants like John Calvin were skeptical about the importance of the ring exchange because, in their day, rings were not yet symbols of commitment. But since that time the ring exchange has come to be more widely appreciated. Later theologians, like the seventeenth-century theologian Jeremy Taylor, did eventually acknowledge the ceremonial importance of ring exchanges and the capacity of rings to represent the holistic relationship of the couple. At our own wedding, my wife and I were enthusiastic ring-givers! Our aim was to offer each other tangible signs of our commitment. The ring blessing that our minister gave was particularly beautiful: "Bless, O Lord, these rings to be a sign of the vows by which this man and this woman have bound themselves to each other, through Jesus Christ our Lord. Amen."

Think for a moment about the values that the ring exchange celebrates. One such value is care: the husband and wife are formally pledging to care for each other in a way that they were not previously obligated to do when they were unmarried. They are swearing to offer each other comfort and support, in sickness and pain, no matter the cost. What an incredible, stupendous promise! So the ring exchange is also an acknowledgment of their vulnerability. Why is it customary for the rings to be worn on the fourth finger of the left hand? The medieval legend was that the vein from that finger went directly to the heart!

Another of the rituals of the *BCP* ceremony that conveys the couple's status change is the Holy Communion. The minister at our wedding—my wife's father—was the Communion celebrant. Both of us assisted, working alongside him at the altar and offering the bread and wine to our guests. The Communion is exciting because its focus is on the sacrifice of God the Son and because it highlights the mystery of marriage. Often in the Scriptures that sacrifice is illustrated through metaphor and story. The Communion's emphasis is on the reconciliation and forgiveness the sacrifice makes possible. At our own wedding the Communion ritual was also a tangible way of serving our guests. My wife and I made it our goal to show them our appreciation and affection for their involvement in our lives. We wanted likewise to set a precedent of service. Previously we were two individuals who served others on our own. Now we were a united couple, a one-flesh-union, devoted together to service. The point was to show our dedication, as husband and wife, to our families, friends, and neighbors. We loved every minute of it!

The classical rituals are also an expression of the couple's creativity. They illustrate the couple's artistry and, at the same time, convey the marriage values being celebrated. The deep transformation that the rituals mark furnishes an opportunity for the couple to be sober, joyous, and even boisterous—all at once! A classical ceremony simultaneously faces two directions: at the same time it honors both the past and the future, both wisdom and innovation. In one sense, it asks the marrying couple to conform to established patterns and values. Its liturgy is a coherent gloss on those patterns and values. In another sense, it is an innovative look to the years ahead: it offers the couple their own authentic spin on the classical rituals.

Its flowers, clothing, music, venue, and decorations all enable the couple to express their creativity, and their excitement about their union. The classical ceremony orients them toward the future, illustrating their differences from their past status. Its resources are hopeful and stirring, and they are worthy markers of the couple's emergence as a new and living entity.

At our own wedding my wife and I wanted our guests to experience a day of aesthetic beauty. Also, at the same time, we wanted our guests to feel the beauty of marital love. My wife took every opportunity to teach me about wedding artistry. She involved me in the planning and made the ceremony an authentic celebration of our personalities. The venue choice was an example of this. The building that we chose was her long-standing Methodist church home. Church buildings are special places: houses of worship that are dedicated to God. A wedding at our long-time church was a way for us to recognize the importance of God in our lives—or perhaps even more aptly, our lives in God's. Our aim also was for the building to be aesthetic and meditative. Through a strategic and intentional choice of location, a marrying couple can be simultaneously two things: creative and traditional, individual and communal. They can take pride in the past, but look expectantly toward the future. They can devote their happy day to God and at the same time throw an energetic party. God loves a good party!

Conclusion: The Adventure of Marriage

> Eternal God, give them wisdom and devotion in the ordering of their common life, that each may be to the other a strength in need, a counselor in perplexity, a comfort in sorrow, and a companion in joy. (*BCP*)

So why should couples marry, and how does ceremony illustrate their reasons for marrying? The reasons for marriage are numerous: showing each other mutual love, enjoying each other's care and support, starting a family, honoring God, and finding relational stability. Central also as a reason for marriage is a public pledge of sexual fidelity. The wedding tradition festively celebrates these values in abundant and joyful ways. Its liturgy, teaching, and music are all devoted to the emotional, spiritual, and sexual "yes" of marriage. At its best, a ceremony captures, artistically and mysteriously, reasons for marriage that are too complex for rational argumentation. What makes its illustration of marital change so beautiful is that its truths are deeper than anything that the most rigorously logical or rational defense of marriage can muster.

Finally, marrying couples do not need a *BCP* ceremony in order to distinguish themselves from unmarried couples or to make their day a special occasion. I have highlighted the *BCP* ceremony here just because it stands so robustly for the values of a successful marriage. It embodies the aspirations of the marrying couple, and it conveys the depth of their union. But there are many different kinds of ceremonies that affirm the values of marriage and that mark the profound changes in marrying couples! The common element in all such ceremonies is that they show that couples are a different and richer relational entity than they otherwise would be. By its reflectiveness, community, and hope for the future, the ceremony powerfully makes and marks those marvelous differences.

Part 2

Christian Sexuality for Singles

5

Why Young Christians Wince at Old-School Sexual Ethics

BRETT MCCRACKEN

I'm a millennial who has made a career of exploring and writing about the way young Christians engage culture and understand their Christian identity in a complicated world. I attended an evangelical Christian college (Wheaton) and have been on staff at another Christian college (Biola) for the last nine years. At Biola I have taught classes as an adjunct and have regular interactions with students. My wife, Kira, also works at Biola and we are both active in our local church, where we specialize in ministry to young adults and college students. We are surrounded by millennial Christians and love them, though our goal is to help them grow rather than just affirming them where they are at.

When it comes to their views on traditional Christian sexual ethics, younger Christians (roughly those between the ages of 18–35) are not a monolithic group. Opinions vary widely, and this chapter makes no claims to represent all the perspectives out there. But some trends are discernable.

Studies show that American millennials (born between 1981 and 1996) are much less likely than older Americans to see sex as something meant for marriage or primarily for procreation. On the other hand, millennials are far more likely than older adults to say the purpose of sex is self-expression and personal fulfillment.[1] Meanwhile, millennial Christians are dramatically more accepting of homosexuality than their older counterparts. Pew found in 2014 that 51 percent of evangelical Protestant millennials said homosexuality should be accepted by society, compared with a third

1. Barna Group, "What Americans Believe about Sex."

of evangelical baby boomers. Positive attitudes toward homosexuality have risen across the denominational spectrum in the last decade, even among traditionally conservative denominations like Southern Baptists, where the share saying homosexuality should be accepted increased from 23 percent to 30 percent between 2007 and 2014.[2]

We could drill down into all the statistics and cull insights from the many studies out there, but for the sake of space I'll simply list some of the common trends I have observed (from years of interacting with millennials and from a series of interviews conducted for this chapter) about how younger American Christians think about sexual ethics:

- They don't attach a shame-based stigma to premarital sex (particularly in committed relationships).
- Marriage is less compelling to them as it was to previous generations and singleness is acceptable and even desirable to many, except in churches where singleness is stigmatized.
- Many of them see overly legalistic approaches to sex (for example in the "do's and don'ts" community rules of Christian colleges) as unhelpful and out of touch. They want to be trusted to navigate their sexuality on their own, without referees standing by with whistles.
- "Purity culture" is viewed with suspicion as a potentially menacing ideology that supports patriarchal power and abuse.
- Many young Christian women see "modesty" as retrograde. They see their sexuality and embodiment as a beautiful gift to unashamedly celebrate.
- They view gender as more complex and fluid than the rigid male/female binary, even if most of them don't endorse every aspect of gender theory.
- While they see gender as fluid, they often view sexual orientation as fixed, largely siding with the "born this way" hypothesis and critiquing assertions that people choose to be gay or can be "healed" of their gayness.
- Many of them have friends or family members who identify as LGBT or at least experience same-sex attraction.
- Many struggle to reconcile their respect for biblical passages and traditional Christian teaching on homosexuality with their personal relationships with LGBT people.

---

2. Murphy, "Most U.S. Christian Groups Grow More Accepting."

- Having grown up within a sex-saturated media landscape, many younger Christians have been conditioned to see everything as sexual and everything sexual as political. For them, sex is a totalizing and sacred avenue for understanding identity.
- On the other hand, the digital environment and ubiquitous access to online pornography has amplified gnostic views of sex as a bodily function or release that need not be tied to relationships or anything particularly human. Many young Christians thus compartmentalize their sexuality and engage privately in pornography, perhaps amplified by the residual morality and shame associated with sexual entanglements in the real world.

Again, not *every* Christian young person in America lines up with all of the above. This is not a scientific study. But even if these views are only held by a segment of Christian millennials, what do we make of it? How did these views, which often directly or indirectly undermine traditional Christian sexual ethics, come to be?

In what follows I'm going to suggest that the thematic linchpin to all of this is the question and location of *authority*. We can only understand what's happening with young Christians and their beliefs about sexual ethics by understanding what is simultaneously happening with their beliefs about authority in its various forms. And it's a bit of an alarming picture.

The Loss of Moral Authority

One of the biggest authority questions that has shaped young Christians' beliefs about traditional sexual ethics is the loss of moral authority on the part of the church. The story goes like this: churches and Christian leaders who taught about the importance of sexual ethics were time and again discovered to be inconsistent or hypocritical on these matters. Catholic priests who taught sexual piety were found to be molesting young boys. Evangelical megachurch pastors preaching against homosexuality were found to be in adulterous affairs. The result has not been surprising: a severe mistrust of church authority on sexual dictates of any sort.

Meanwhile, the church's witness on sexual ethics has been sadly inconsistent and viewed by many young people as arbitrary. Why is so much made of the Bible's teaching on homosexuality while the majority of evangelical churches are silent on divorce? Why was the American church so loud in condemning the 2015 Supreme Court ruling to legalize same-sex marriage but silent in speaking out in 1969 when Ronald Reagan signed the first no-fault divorce law? Scripture is as clear in prohibiting no-fault divorce as it is in prohibiting gay sexual relations. What gives? Inconsistencies like this amplify existing suspicions among many young Christians that the church is driven more by homophobia than consistent hermeneutics.

Hypocrisy and theological inconsistency amplify existing suspicions about church leadership, but so does the perception that churches are not safe places for people to wrestle openly with sexuality. To the extent that churches push True Love Waits–style purity or simplistic messages about homosexuality without creating space for their people to be open about their real struggles, they can be perceived as harsh and oppressive. Many young people are afraid to bring their gay or sexually broken friends to church for this reason. There is a feeling in many churches that sex is a thing of shame, not to be spoken of openly. Over time this leads to the unfortunate belief that churches are *the last* places to go to get real talk, good advice, and healthy counsel on matters of sex. The church has simply lost its moral authority on the subject, and this is a huge reason why young Christians today draw from other sources in defining their sexual ethics.

But even if young Christians do not have much respect for what "moral authorities" have to say about sexual ethics, there is at least the authority of Scripture, right? And yet Scripture, too, has undergone its own weakening as an authority in the modern era.

The Loss of Scripture's Authority

"The Bible says it. I believe it. That settles it!" This is not a phrase you hear many young Christians uttering today.

Higher criticism, deconstructionism, critical theory, science, and a whole host of other academic threads of modernity have eroded the Bible's epistemological authority. Belief in the Bible as a completely trustworthy, infallible document is no longer something all Christians take for granted. There are churches with "low" views of Scripture and those with "high" views, but both call themselves Christian.

And this brings up the problem of interpretation. How trustworthy can Scripture be on something like homosexuality when there are such wildly divergent and even contradictory readings of Paul and Jesus on the topic? It seems problematic that, on one hand, there are progressive Episcopal bishops and mainline theologians who argue that the New Testament does not forbid homosexual unions, while, on the other hand, scores of respected theologians and church leaders claim the opposite. Duke University scholar Richard Hays, for instance, says the New Testament "offers no accounts of homosexual Christians, tells no stories of same-sex lovers, ventures no metaphors that place a positive construal on homosexual relations."[3] Whose interpretation of the Bible is correct? The contentious interpretive debates on this issue (among others) leave young Christians reluctant to cite a handful of Bible verses as the ironclad basis for their position.

But this is even assuming young Christians have enough biblical literacy to know what passages to turn to in the first place. Do they know what Romans 1, 1 Corinthians 6, or 1 Timothy 1 say about homosexuality? Do they know how to answer questions about continuity and discontinuity between the Old and New Testaments on sexual ethics? Sadly, widespread biblical ignorance is another aspect of Scripture's weakened authority in today's world. Even if Scripture is trusted or appealed to, is it really known? Are sound hermeneutics widespread among churchgoing millennials?

Most often when Scripture *is* invoked for sexual ethics it is less a source of holistic definition than a cherry-picked proof text to justify one's *existing opinion*. Indeed, the authority of Scripture is in many cases trumped by the authority of personal experience. It's not so much what Scripture *means* as much as *what it means to me*. The "me and Jesus" rituals of highly individualistic evangelical culture (some call it "Moralistic Therapeutic Deism") have accelerated Scripture's loss of transcendent authority. If the Bible is just a therapeutic guidebook to "meet me where I'm at" in my "spiritual but not religious" journey, who can tell me I'm wrong when I say the most important theme from the New Testament is that "God is love"?

Martyn Lloyd-Jones once said, "We should not interpret Scripture in the light of our experiences, but we should examine our experiences in the light of the teaching of Scripture."[4] Unfortunately, interpreting Scripture (or simply using it) in light of our experiences is common practice among many in the church today.

The Loss of Tradition's Authority

One of the more surprising aspects of these dramatic opinion changes is how at odds the "new orthodoxy" is with the thousands of years of traditional moral teachings from across the spectrum of religions. Since its inception two millennia ago, Christianity, for example, has been remarkably

---

3. Hays, *Moral Vision of the New Testament*, 395.
4. Lloyd-Jones, *Joy Unspeakable*, 17.

consistent on sexual ethics across its various denominations and cultural contexts. Until recently.

The two-thousand-year history of traditional Christian ethics on sexuality and marriage is now being abandoned with shocking ease. As LGBT sexuality is increasingly normalized within Western societies, many Christians are becoming convinced that the church had it wrong all those centuries. Or (more likely) they were ignorant of their faith's theological tradition on sexual ethics all along.

The anemic place of Christian tradition in much of contemporary evangelicalism is a huge factor in all of this. For many younger evangelicals, all they have known of church has been a sort of trend-chasing, always-re-inventing-itself novelty where making God relevant to the current zeitgeist is the primary aim. The music styles, sermon topics, and pastor's facial hair are all dialed in according to a constant *"what's happening now"* fine-tuning, so why would anyone assume that *"what has been"* continuity is a value?

The loss of a sense of rootedness within tradition, combined with a low ecclesiology that is widespread within evangelicalism, has led us to see church so contextually that the "old-school" ways of belief and practice are easily dismissed as themselves products of now-outdated cultural contexts. Our obsession with trendiness and reinvention has unfortunately left us as hyper-contextualized orphans with no necessary commitment or deference to tradition.

"Tradition" may hold some quaint appeal for young evangelicals (think of hipster churches that dabble in pews, candles, and ancient hymnody), but mostly it is an abstraction for them that has connotations of oppression and hegemony. Any respect for the past they may have quickly falls apart when it conflicts with their relationships in the present: having a friend or family member who is gay, for example, shapes their theological beliefs about sexuality more than their respect for traditional church teaching.

This is a common story among evangelicals today. Take Christian ethicist David Gushee, for example. He once wrote in a textbook that "Homosexual conduct is one form of sexual expression that falls outside the will of God." But later his moral position shifted, not because of a new exegetical epiphany, but because (in part) his sister came out as a lesbian and he came to view homosexuality as "not primarily an issue of Christian sexual ethics," but "primarily an issue of human suffering."[5]

For Gushee and many twenty-first-century evangelicals, the realities of incarnation and compassion in the *immanent present* take precedence over the notion of scriptural truths or moral norms that are *transcendent*.

---

5. Gushee, "I'm an Evangelical Minister."

Against the day-to-day realities of relationships and authentic experience, the force of tradition as a binding authority is diminished.

It's important to empathize with this tension rather than simply decry it. I personally have close friends who are gay, and most of my Christian peers do too. How do we balance the relational and the theological? Love and truth? It's not easy. The suffering we see in the eyes of our LGBT friends and family is much nearer to us than the often cold, distant doctrines of tradition and Scripture. It's not difficult to understand how someone's compassion could lead her to favor the person over the principle. Nor is it difficult to understand why individual convictions are now weighted above even the consensus of one's community.

The Loss of the Community's Authority

Community is one of the best guardrails against heresy and errant subjectivism. Friends and family help shape our moral vision and keep us in check when we say or do crazy things. Historically, this has been seen in a positive light. When individuals surround themselves with trusted others and submit to them for the sake of accountability, they release themselves from the burden of unchecked autonomy.

Yet twenty-first-century American culture does not see unchecked autonomy as a burden. On the contrary, the subjective freedom of the individual is celebrated: the freedom to be and do whatever feels "true" to oneself. This freedom is amplified by the existing individualism that permeates late capitalism. We've been conditioned to believe that what we desire is good and that wish fulfillment is an inherent right. If we can dream it, we should be free to pursue it and no one should judge us or stand in our way.

The logic of consumerism and individualism does not abide the authority of community. When one's personal "truth" is questioned by others (friends or family, for example), it is written off as persecution, misunderstanding, or bigotry. "You're not me" is the justification for dismissing community pushback against individual autonomy.

This posture has unfortunately been just as prevalent within evangelical Christianity as it has outside of it. The highly individualistic, "personal relationship with Jesus" flavor of American evangelicalism, combined with the aforementioned weak ecclesiology and disconnection from historical context, creates an environment where one only has to feel something sincerely and express it "bravely" in order to justify its moral viability.

Take Glennon Doyle Melton, the popular Christian mommy blogger who in 2016 divorced her husband and started a lesbian relationship with soccer star Abby Wambach. Melton's Facebook post announcing the new relationship captures this sort of strident individualism that refuses to subject itself to anything outside the self. Melton sees her life as a model of the free, authentic living she encourages in her readers: "I want you to grow so comfortable in your own being, your own skin, your own knowing—that you become more interested in your own joy and freedom and integrity than in what others think about you. . . . The most revolutionary thing a woman can do is not explain herself."[6]

This freedom to not explain oneself or one's choices is indicative of a no-constraints individualism that refuses to be bound by the authority of community. This is especially true of sexuality, a deeply personal and vulnerable realm that is bound up with questions of identity. How could the community's input hold more weight than the individual's own deeply felt longings and sense of who she is sexually?

Gay students at Christian colleges present an interesting case study of the tension between the authority of a disapproving community (in the sense of not affirming LGBT sexuality) and the authority of personal identity/expression. In her recent research on this topic, communications scholar Christine Gardner interviewed 103 students, administrators, faculty, and alumni at nine Christian colleges. In her article published in *Communication and Critical/Cultural Studies*, Gardner notes that LGBT students often appeal to essentialism and utilize "God created me this way" rhetoric to navigate the tensions of their sexual and spiritual identities.[7] By not only invoking the "born this way" rhetoric of the larger culture but putting a "*God made me* this way" Christian spin on it, these students are subtly attempting to reconcile their subjective, experiential authority with their faith commitment and deference to God. If God created me this way, how could it be wrong? Invoking divine creational intention is the ultimate authority trump card. Who cares what Scripture, tradition, or community say when one's felt experience of God's love is that "He created me this way and loves me just as I am"?

Pushing Back against Purity Culture

For millennial Christians growing up in the United States or other Western contexts, the reality of the dominant culture's open, celebratory view of sex feels at odds with the "purity" contours of conservative Christianity.

---

6. Glennon Doyle Melton, Facebook post on November 13, 2016, https://www.facebook.com/glennondoylemelton/posts/10154703803624710:0.

7. Gardner, "'Created This Way.'"

The former feels positive and liberated, while the latter feels negative and repressive. While this dichotomy is surely simplistic and obscures a more complicated spectrum, it is nevertheless a popular narrative shaping the moral vision of young Christians.

On one hand, there is the jubilant world of Hollywood celebrities like Beyonce and Justin Bieber, Kim Kardashian and Taylor Swift, Ellen Degeneres and Caitlyn Jenner, whose unabashed embrace of their own sexuality functions as a sort of anthemic empowerment for the masses to flaunt their bodies and express their sexuality without shame. This is the world of no-guilt sexuality, where pornographic novels like *Fifty Shades of Grey* are no longer stigmatized and nudity on film and in television is far less taboo than it once was. The prevailing message of sexualized bodies seems to be: "What's to be embarrassed about? The human body is beautiful in an almost transcendent way, and don't let the prudish Republican Christians tell you any different!"

On the other end of the spectrum is the ominous "purity culture," a sort of mythologized bogeyman that stands in for any strain of conservative religious tradition that favors modesty, boundaries, and sexual restraint. A student writer at a conservative evangelical university recently described purity culture as the "injection into the subconscious that sex should be avoided at all costs" and a system that reduces women's bodies to "mere objects to keep clean."[8] The church, this writer observes, tends to make the desire for sex "idolatrous," which means purity culture is not only physically but emotionally restrictive: "When Christians begin longing for the human desire for intimacy that the church has craftily rebutted, feelings of dirtiness and confusion arise, often leading to internalized shame."[9]

The alleged oppression of purity culture not only breeds shame but also perpetuates *patriarchy*, a villainous word increasingly heard in the classrooms and coffee shops of Christian colleges. "Sexual purity is a patriarchal notion that has been mistaken for a Christian one," wrote feminist book critic Jessa Crispin recently, suggesting that purity is a patriarchal tool to keep men empowered against the threat of female sexual freedom.[10]

Indeed, "the patriarchy" has become code for any conservative male (or male-dominated institution) who favors traditional ideas of binary gender, heterosexual marriage, and religious restrictions on sexual behavior. Most religious groups (but especially American evangelicals) are lumped

---

8. Lu, "Birds and the Bees"
9. Ibid., 39.
10. Crispin, "Maiden America."

into the Patriarchy Purity Complex and blamed for all manner of bigotry, homophobia, and epidemics of sexual assault.

Most popular youth culture (with the exception of some country and rap music) sets itself against the patriarchy, urging a subversive sexual freedom and gender fluidity. Whether on the HBO show *Girls* or in the pansexual escapades of (formerly Christian) Miley Cyrus or Kristen Stewart, the notion of unrestrained female sexuality is one example of it. The normalizing of queer sexuality on "domestic" family shows like *Glee*, *Modern Family*, and *Transparent* is another.

This is the cultural context in which today's young Christians are figuring out their stances on sexual ethics. It's a context in which sex is not so much about procreation as it is about power, pleasure, and personal expression. When the birth control pill became widely available in the 1960s, sex was detached from procreation and freed to morph into the expressive force that it is today. This paved the way for talk of "sexual identity." No longer primarily about a *biological purpose*, sex became more of a psychological state of mind. Sex became *sexuality*, a cultural construct and free-form aesthetic mode of being in the world. If no longer about *that thing* (man and woman conceiving a child), sex was released to become *everything*. It can now be anything one wants it to be. The last fifty years has seen the gradual sexualizing of everything, such that sex has now become a transcendent reality and divine right. To live without it or to have it constrained is unthinkable. In such a context, it's no wonder that traditional Christian sexual boundaries (abstinence outside of marriage, marriage only between a man and a woman) seem so strange, boring, and outdated.

Though it's unlikely that many millennial Christians are enthusiastic endorsers of the sexual politics of Lena Dunham or Caitlyn Jenner, the reality is that most are also unenthusiastic about anything resembling the Patriarchy Purity Complex. The negative "don't" disposition of religious postures toward sex does not appeal to them. If religious sexual ethics means avoidance, repression, guilt, shame, and the inability of non-heterosexual people to experience romantic love, many young Christians are uninterested in signing on.

Young Christians today are not embarrassed by sexuality. They want to talk openly about it. They want the church to acknowledge sex as a beautiful part of God's created order, not only for procreation but also for pleasure. Many of them have memories of awkward youth groups fumbling through topics like pornography and abstinence. They wish the church had been better equipped to address the complexities of sexuality. They wish the church today could be a safe place to express, discuss, and wrestle with sex. Could the church be that for them again?

Recommendations for the Church

How might the church reassert itself as a trustworthy, caring, and compelling authority on sexual ethics, a source not of shame but of clarity and hope for young believers seeking to live faithfully in a changing culture? I will end this chapter with eight recommendations—by no means exhaustive—for how churches can better position themselves to help their younger congregants thrive in this important area.

1. *Be compelling on sexual ethics.* Churches should lean in to biblical teaching on sex and not avoid it. Avoidance and embarrassment is not going to help anyone. On the contrary, churches must present biblical sexual ethics in a compelling way that positions it as part of God's good plan for human flourishing. Do a sermon series on the topic; hold seminars and classes; assemble the best readings and speakers on the subject. Be confident and yet compassionate in your teaching, acknowledging the reality of sexual brokenness and yet showing the witness of Scripture to be refreshingly clear in the midst of confusion.

2. *Be consistent on sexual ethics.* It is critical that if churches are to teach biblical sexual ethics at all, they must do so holistically. Picking and choosing, emphasizing some aspects over others, is part of what led to the church's loss of authority on the subject in the first place. Clarity on divorce should be emphasized alongside clarity on homosexuality. A church should not shrug at a heterosexual couple having premarital sex while condemning a homosexual couple for the same thing. A church should not refuse to perform same-sex weddings while simultaneously performing weddings for cohabiting heterosexual couples or weddings for unbiblically divorced couples.

3. *Don't stigmatize sexual confusion, but don't perpetuate it either.* Churches should have open doors for sexualities of every sort: gay, straight, transgender, and everything in between. Churches should acknowledge and provide room for people to seek wisdom, pastoral counsel, and discipleship in areas of sexual confusion, without fear of stigma or condemnation. But it is crucial that churches do not simply accept sexual confusion as a permanent, unchangeable reality in these people's lives. Rather, churches must walk with people in these areas toward repentance and renewal, from confusion and toward clarity, seeking to redeem sexual brokenness just like any other area of sin.

4. *Deconstruct the notion of "sexual identity."* Churches mustn't perpetuate the fallacy of "sexual identity," but must instead offer a fuller, richer,

more beautiful picture of identity in and union with Christ. The idea of a "sexual orientation" and the elevation of sex to an ontological level, as an identity, are very recent innovations in history (thanks Freud!). For most of human history, sex was a physical reality tied to procreation and one among many facets of existence, but not a fundamental, immutable definer of personhood. Churches should show how "sexual identity" talk is actually constricting, reductionist, and unhelpful. As Rosaria Butterfield has said, "the sexual identity orientation system is anti-gospel, because it replaces union with Christ."[11]

5. *Celebrate singleness and celibacy.* Churches should be mindful of not creating an implicit hierarchy in which married members have higher status than "second-class" single members. The fact that Jesus and Paul were single (the latter commended it as a worthy vocation: 1 Cor 7:8–9, 25–40) should mean churches celebrate singleness and celibacy for the sake of mission as a worthy, dignified calling. Churches should seek out and include singles in every aspect of church life, ensuring that they are seen and understood to be full-fledged members of the family.

6. *Create a culture where relational intimacy thrives beyond sexuality.* One way singles and celibate members of a church family can thrive is if their Christian community is characterized by deep relational intimacy. The family of God should be a place where profound spiritual friendship and intimacy between members of the same sex (and across sexes) can happen without the sexual charge that is ubiquitous in secular culture.[12] Love is deeper and wider than sexuality, and the church can be a countercultural exemplar of this in a sex-saturated world. Churches should find ways to foster deep, diverse, intergenerational community between married couples and singles, providing tangible ways for the body of Christ to experience the interdependence of its various members.

7. *Celebrate the dignity of embodiment, beyond sexualization.* Churches should find ways to be body-positive without sexualizing bodies. What does this look like? It looks like celebrating embodied activities like movement in worship, sport, physical exercise, dancing, the beauty of eating and drinking together, and so on. It looks like hugging and holding hands and not being so awkward around one another's physicality. It also looks like celebrating and protecting the image-of-God dignity of human bodies by decrying the various ways our culture

---

11. Butterfield and Bock, "Sexual Identity Issues and Union with Christ."
12. See Wesley Hill's excellent book *Spiritual Friendship*.

cheapens and assaults that dignity: pornography, prostitution, casual hookups, Tinder, sex trafficking, abortion, and so on. This was one of the ways the earliest Christians in the hyper-sexualized Roman Empire set themselves apart,[13] and it is one of the ways the church today can offer hope to a sex-weary world.

8. *Show (don't tell) the beauty of authority.* If the weakened authority of Scripture, tradition, and community is the root problem of our confusion on sexual ethics (as I've argued), it is critical that churches find ways to rebuild trust and live in deference to these authorities in ways that are compelling. This looks like servant leadership and humility. It looks like the church as a diverse family of interdependence and mutual discipleship where Spirit-empowered connection is profound. It looks like worship that is Scripture-centric and focused on encountering a big, holy, supernatural God. Churches should be places that push against the me-centric tendencies of consumerism ("what I got out of the service") and instead cultivate awe and reverence before a mighty God. They should engage hearts and bodies in addition to minds. Submitting to transcendent authority is hard to do rationally for modern people, but it becomes easier when the presence of God is tangible. If Christianity is only ever experienced as a human system or a social club, its authority is easily dismissed. Only when the faith is experienced as a divine encounter, and the church as sacred liminal space, is it possible for cracks to open in our modern defenses and our "buffered selves,"[14] allowing us to trust and submit to authorities, truths, and standards beyond the self.

Bibliography

Barna Group. "What Americans Believe About Sex." Research Releases in Culture & Media. January 14, 2016. https://www.barna.com/research/what-americans-believe-about-sex.

Butterfield, Rosaria, and Darrell Bock. "Sexual Identity Issues and Union with Christ." *The Table Podcast*, January 17, 2017. DTS (Dallas Theological Seminary) Voice. http://www.dts.edu/thetable/play/sexual-identity-issues-and-union-christ.

Crispin, Jessa. "Maiden America." *The Baffler*, December 5, 2016. https://thebaffler.com/salvos/maiden-america-crispin.

---

13. For an excellent study of how early Christian sexual ethics offered something radically novel in late antiquity, see Harper, *From Shame to Sin*.

14. A term used by philosopher Charles Taylor to describe the self in "disenchanted" modernity, lacking any sense of the transcendent. See Taylor, *Secular Age*.

Gardner, Christine J. "'Created This Way': Liminality, Rhetorical Agency, and the Transformative Power of Constraint among Gay Christian College Students." *Communication and Critical/Cultural Studies* 14.1 (January 2, 2017) 31–47.

Gushee, David. "I'm an Evangelical Minister. I Now Support the LGBT Community—and the Church Should, Too." *Washington Post*, November 11, 2014. https://www.washingtonpost.com/posteverything/wp/2014/11/04/im-an-evangelical-minister-i-now-support-the-lgbt-community-and-the-church-should-too.

Harper, Kyle. *From Shame to Sin: The Christian Transformation of Sexual Morality in Late Antiquity*. Cambridge, MA: Harvard University Press, 2016.

Hays, Richard. *The Moral Vision of the New Testament: Community, Cross, New Creation: A Contemporary Introduction to New Testament Ethic*. New York: HarperCollins, 2013.

Hill, Wesley. *Spiritual Friendship: Finding Love in the Church as a Celibate Gay Christian*. Grand Rapids: Brazos, 2015.

Lloyd-Jones, David Martyn. *Joy Unspeakable: The Baptism and Gifts of the Holy Spirit*. Edited by Christopher Catherwood. London: Kingsway, 2008.

Lu, Leah. "The Birds and the Bees: How Purity Culture Affects the Church." *The Point* 13.1 (Fall 2016) 38.

Murphy, Caryle. "Most U.S. Christian Groups Grow More Accepting of Homosexuality." Pew Research Center, December 18, 2015. http://www.pewresearch.org/fact-tank/2015/12/18/most-u-s-christian-groups-grow-more-accepting-of-homosexuality.

Taylor, Charles. *A Secular Age*. Cambridge, MA: Belknap Press of Harvard University Press, 2007.

6

How to Trust God with Your Body

Anna Broadway

Every few months—if not weeks—it happens: another Christian publishes an article on sex lamenting some trend, event, or book out of step with the biblical sexual ethic. Such pieces rarely lack sincerity or urgency, even wisdom, but underneath they carry a familiar futility. The typical recommendations either boil down to marrying early, trying harder to find someone (be less picky; ask your pastor to arrange singles events), trying harder at contentment (maybe you were meant for celibacy after all), or finding a way to accommodate the trend of delayed marriage.

Beneath all the hand-wringing, such pieces usually betray a fixation on the Christian ethic's *boundaries* for sex. No wonder, then, that Christians' views on sex tend to focus on the single, the gay, and the unfaithful more than the selfish or abusive.

By contrast, the authors usually seem far less concerned with the reputation and character of God. Did he just forget that he built his children with libidos that kick in early in life, even as marriages happen later and later? Doesn't he see how women continue to outstrip men in church attendance? Yet discussions about such practical challenges tend to focus more on what we followers should do than on how God's sovereignty fits into this painful and frustrating picture.

Doubts about God's goodness have tested every generation in history, but in this case I submit that the American church and Christian culture have contributed to the problem by overemphasizing the boundaries of the biblical sexual ethic, at the expense of the actual ethos for treating others. Thus, the God who invented sex becomes God the sex police.

Such emphasis makes typical "church" teachings an easy target for writers like Jennifer Wright Knust. In her book *Unprotected Texts*, Knust ruffled many feathers by claiming that the Bible has virtually nothing clear or consistent to say about sex. (In saying this, she relies partly on a determined conflation of reportage with endorsement.)

Though Knust writes from the perspective of a Baptist minister, in many ways she also speaks for those outside the church who recoil at how God's people use the Bible to talk about sex and justify certain positions. Little wonder Christians rarely get invited to join the broader discussion about sexual mores in our society. Should we be surprised when any involvement in helping to teach and bracket sexuality for our communities' most vulnerable—the young—so often prompts suspicion and hostility?

A large part of the problem stems from an all-too-often disembodied theology. As James K. A. Smith argues in his provocative book *Desiring the Kingdom*, "worldview"-focused responses to sin are usually doomed from the start because they misapprehend the nature of our humanity. They assume we are primarily thinking beings whose problems can be remedied either by correcting our thinking or by trying harder to think the right thoughts.

Ah, the old temptation to Gnosticism, and putting the mind above the material. But as Smith vividly conveys, the most powerful forces at work on us aren't ideas but multisensory experiences. They don't win because they have the best arguments; they win because they're more fun. Not coincidentally, this pleasures comes through highly embodied practices. As Smith puts it:

> While the mall, Victoria's Secret, and Jerry Bruckheimer are grabbing hold of our gut (*kardia*) by means of our body and its senses—in stories and images, sights and sound, and commercial versions of "smells and bells"—the church's response is oddly rationalist. It plunks us down in a "worship" service, the culmination of which is a forty-five-minute didactic sermon, a sort of holy lecture, trying to convince us of the dangers by implanting doctrines and beliefs in our minds . . . While secular liturgies are after our hearts through our bodies, the church thinks it only has to get into our heads. While Victoria's Secret is fanning a flame in our *kardia*, the church is trucking water to our minds.[1]

This, I would respectfully submit, is why so much of the church's teaching on sexuality has failed to accomplish its aim—greater submission to God

---

1. Smith, *Desiring the Kingdom*, 126–27.

in this part of our lives—and why each new hand-wringing piece, even if it runs to the length of a book, does little better. Words alone have little effectiveness in a general pedagogical sense. And we think they can separate two people who have the hots for each other?

Not having sex when you're *un*married—and lovingly sharing bodies with just your spouse *when* married—entails massive self-denial. In both cases, we must submit ourselves to an unseen God, trusting that he knows better than we do when and how to use our bodies. In both cases, we must fight the powerful selfishness wired into us from birth.

Trusting God with our bodies may be one of the hardest things we undertake as Christians. From the earliest days, mankind's rebellion against God has centered on issues of trust and doubt: Does God really know what's best for us? Should we listen to him and obey even when the present circumstances suggest he didn't anticipate this situation or wanted to spoil our fun? Over and over again in the first five books of the Bible, the same challenge plays out among the people of Israel: Will they trust God to fight for them? Will they trust God to provide? *Will they trust God?*

Not coincidentally, trust almost always involves our bodies. Trust for Adam and Eve would have limited what they could taste (Genesis 3). Trust for the Israelites would have meant marching into enemy-held territory based on the good reports of two optimistic scouts, Caleb and Joshua, and God's promise to give the land of Canaan to his people (Numbers 13). Trust often requires us to put our very bodies on the line—to show with physical action that we believe what we say we do.

In this we face both challenge and gift. Throughout the Old Testament, the Israelites struggled to serve a God who could not be touched or seen, only heard. More than once they tried to create a visible depiction of him, or turned to more palpable gods. The challenge remained even after God took on human form in the person of Jesus. We still can't touch or smell God; we mostly "see" him as imagined by people of European ancestry; and Western Christians rarely hear the audible voice or whisper that Moses did.

Sometimes our relationship with this being can seem just as disembodied. Many American churches have shunned the bodily practices used by our brothers and sisters around the world and throughout history. Rejecting icons, we often limit our church decorations to crosses, the walls showing only the faces of the congregation's missionaries. Rejecting incense, we bring only the perfume of our body wash and shampoo to church—and flinch from those without access to either. Reducing the Lord's Supper, we may take a nonalcoholic and barely caloric Communion once or twice a month.

To worship in many American churches takes little more than eyes and ears serving a brain and a soul. The God of these congregations seems little interested in noses or tongues, hands or feet. So when we learn that he might just want us to lock up our most pleasure-giving parts as well, not even using them ourselves . . . well, who could blame us for thinking, "How *dare* he!" or "Hands off my clitoris!"?

Why should we trust a God who seems only to care for our bodies when they might bring us a little enjoyment in this hard, often painful world?

If you find yourself asking that question, you're not alone, and you shouldn't be ashamed of wondering. But a question that serious deserves an equally serious reckoning. For starters, are all the assumptions in that question true? Does God only care about our bodies when it comes to sex? Is God good? Does God even *exist*?

For at least twenty years, my own reluctant chastity as a single woman has forced me to wrestle with each of those questions in turn. I would not be here, still struggling but committed to God and even writing for you about this topic, if I were not convinced of God's existence and his deep, abiding, delighted love for every person he's made. But it's been hardest and taken me longest to see that God also loves every part of my body and cares about *all* the ways I use it, all the ways it helps me connect to others and to him.

Trust Takes a Different Mindset

The lie that God cares only about your genitalia may be one of the greatest barriers to trusting God with your body. In 1 Corinthians 6:19 the apostle Paul writes, "Do you not know that your body is a temple of the Holy Spirit who is in you, whom you have from God, and that you are not your own? For you have been bought with a price: therefore glorify God in your body" (NASB). The surrounding context mainly applies this idea to sexual relationships, but Paul repeats it in Galatians 2:20, this time with much broader implications: "I have been crucified with Christ, and it is no longer I who live, but Christ lives in me; and the life which I now live in the flesh I live by faith in the Son of God, who loved me, and delivered Himself up for me."

Those of us who call ourselves Christians have died to ourselves and given up the right to call the shots for our lives. That includes our bodies. Because this can be so difficult to obey, the Bible lays out not one but several bodily practices that leave room for God and serve as a powerful reminder of whose we are.

Fasting. For various reasons, God's people in both the Old and New Testament regularly give up food. Sometimes this accompanies repentance or purification; other times it is part of seeking God's will. Prayer almost always accompanies fasting.

Sabbath. Following God's example in the story of creation, Jews and Christians have long observed a day of rest and enjoyment to set aside work, worship God, and enjoy the fellowship of our loved ones. During the Israelites' wandering in the desert (as recorded in Exodus 16), God even calls the people to stop collecting the miraculously provided manna on the Sabbath. That day, and that day only, God lets their food from the day before last without going bad.

Tithing. Whether work yields a tangible harvest or funds automatically deposited in a bank account, God calls his people to consistently give a portion back to him—both to crowd-source salaries for spiritual laborers and help care for the needy in our communities.

Service. The ethic of self-sacrifice runs all through the Bible—from the gleaning laws and call to show kindness to foreigners (Leviticus 19 and Deuteronomy 24) to the underlying command to "love your neighbor as yourself." The Bible consistently calls God's people to always reserve some—and sometimes a great deal—of our energy for others.

Chastity. Just as we can't hoard all of our time, money, or energy, the Bible consistently teaches that God's people must resist the temptation of a self-absorbed sexuality. In marriage, this means mutual self-giving in sex (as Paul discusses in 1 Corinthians 7:3–5); in singleness, this means sexual abstinence. In both situations, we depend on God to meet unfulfilled needs and desires as he sees fit.

To a lesser extent, sleep, silence, and other practices provide additional ways for us to yield our bodies to God.

Trust Changes Your Approach

Viewed by itself, the chastity of singleness can seem oppressive, retrograde, and deeply unfair. That starts to change once you realize the same principles extend into marriage. Whether due to illness, menstruation, or other disruptions, married couples don't get endless sex-on-demand either. They too must regularly deal with some sexual frustration.

Chastity changes most dramatically, however, when you recognize its continuity with the many other ways God asks us to trust him with our bodies. As a now late-thirties single woman, I've spent most of my life seeing chastity in terms of lack, absence, hunger, and missing out. But that thinking falls apart when I consider chastity as but one of many embodied spiritual practices.

At various times in the past decade, I've taken one day a week to fast and pray. Though I often long for the moment when I can eat, the fast entails much more than simply waiting to eat. Fasting remains a spiritual mystery to me, but I take the greatest consolation in its unseen work on the days I do the worst job of praying.

In my thirties, I've also come to a deeper appreciation of silence in the Christian life—both through occasional silent retreats[2] and the regular practice of listening prayer. It is unfathomable that I would define silence as "waiting to speak," considering how rich this practice sometimes proves.

More recently, I've been trying to allow more time for sleep. Though I know more rest will give me more daytime focus, increase emotional resilience, and make me feel better in general, I struggle immensely to do even less each day in order to make room for sleep. Yet even as I chafe against my supposedly reduced productivity, I would never think of sleep as merely waiting to wake. It may challenge me to block out eight or more hours of utter bodily stillness, but I know these long stretches offered to God and the night play an immensely important role in my well-being.

Tithing proved a crucible of my twenties, during a season of unemployment that left me with only $50 a week for food and transit.[3] Had I not tithed, I could have "freed up" more money to eat on each week, but I felt convicted that God's call to financial independence did not involve an income threshold . . . so I tithed. And during the week I had the least money for groceries, God provided nonperishable food in a give-away box I passed on someone's stoop.[4] Since then, tithing has become an important habit in my life. I do not always know how God uses it, but I would never reduce tithing to just mere waiting for more money, or a delay of my next purchase. In fact, I hardly think of tithing as waiting at all, even if it delays some consumption.

Sabbath, too, became important in my twenties, as unemployment gave way to a season of part-time freelance work. Because of poor time management and weak discipline, I regularly struggled to put in the hours needed each week. Many times I was tempted to cut into my Sunday to make up the time. But as I continued to honor God's command to rest, I found the day increasingly liberating. Sundays gave me space to pursue pastimes and leisurely conversations with friends without guilt about what

---

2. Broadway, "To Sleep, Perchance to Grow."
3. Broadway, "Eating on Fifty Dollars a Week."
4. Broadway, "Manna on the Stoop."

I wasn't doing. I'd reserved the time for such things. What's more, the break gave me a way to let go of the past week's failures and start fresh Monday morning. Sabbath-keeping never, ever feels like time spent merely waiting to resume work. Instead, I often wish Sundays lasted longer.

Of all these practices, service shows perhaps most clearly how God brings forth fruit from the ground that we leave "fallow" for him. During the four years I spent in New York, I had some of my most profound experiences of God's presence during moments when I stopped to talk with a homeless person and hear more of his or her story. And over more than three years of friendship, one homeless woman in San Francisco has become the person with whom I most regularly exchange the words "I love you."

In all its many forms, service to others provides perhaps *the* way we get to emulate Jesus and show his love to others. Though it can prove difficult, draining, and painful, service is much more than waiting to serve ourselves.

What then of single chastity? Is it only waiting for sex?

All these years I've mostly seen it that way, though in better moments I might at least deem it obedience to God. Even as I began to see beyond the sexual boundaries many Christians stress—to what the biblical sexual ethic calls us *to*—I ached. As God allowed me to stay single into my early thirties . . . then my middle thirties . . . and now my late thirties, when the hope of motherhood has begun to quiver with uncertainty, I've felt like I'm hearing more "no" than "yes" from my heavenly Father.

Seeing chastity's continuity with so many other spiritual practices has begun to change that. Though the loneliness and pain remain, for the first time I can see chastity not just as fallow ground, but as fruitful. Sure, I might wish God had chosen a different means, but everything I know from practicing these other bodily disciplines leads me to believe God has a present purpose and project underway in my abstinence.

When I serve others, I trust that God uses my bodily denial of power to accomplish unseen spiritual ends, too. When I practice Sabbath, I trust that God uses my sacrifice of time to accomplish spiritual ends. When I tithe, I trust he's using money for a spiritual end. When I sleep, he uses my rest from physical sight to sometimes heighten spiritual sight. When I listen instead of speaking, he trains my spiritual hearing. And when I fast, God must somehow use my bodily hunger toward spiritual ends, too, perhaps by reordering my desires.

If all these practices mysteriously connect my body to the spiritual, so, too, must chastity. Like fasting, what God does through the chastity of singleness remains largely a mystery to me, but I'm increasingly hopeful that what, from one stance, looks like two barren decades has actually been a more fruitful season than I can presently see. And for all that has *not* happened in human romantic relationships, God has brought incredible depth and intimacy in my relationship with him these past twenty years of singleness.

As a freshman in college, I turned back to God after reading his promise in Jeremiah 29:13–14: "'You will seek me and find me, when you search for me with all your heart. And I will be found by you,' declares the Lord." Based on the two decades since, I can tell you he *does* keep that promise. He *does* reveal himself to those who seek; he *does* reveal himself to those who wrestle through all their anger, doubt, and questions.

Strategies to Develop Trust

Maybe you've read this far and you're thinking, "I'd like to trust like that. I'd like to have a relationship like that . . . but I don't." How do you get there? You have to start practicing trust, even if you do not feel it.

The New Testament book of James famously says that faith without works is dead. In a similar sense, the *God* in whom we put faith without works can seem pretty dead, too. And no wonder: a faith without works involves no risk.

If I have "faith" that a certain Lyft driver can operate a car safely, but never ride along as her passenger, I take no risk on that person's skill and ability to focus on the road. My "faith" costs me nothing. So what if I have to hire that driver to cross a snowy mountain pass? Could I trust her to avoid the distraction of text messages? To navigate icy roads safely? To stay awake through long, monotonous night stretches that may be worsened by very poor visibility?

If I'm in a desperate situation, I may have to trust the driver whether I like it or not. But if I have some choice, a lot of my decision to take that risk or not will depend on information I can gather from others (how well other passengers rated him or her, how *many* ratings the driver has and whether any past passenger suffered injury, etc.). Ideally, I would hire a driver with whom I'd happily and safely ridden before. If I needed to make an unusually demanding trip, I'd ideally have taken not just an in-town trip with that driver, but at least a short ride on the highway, too—a way to forecast if I could really trust her to handle long-haul freeway driving safely.

Trusting God works much the same. The bigger the risk, the harder it is to trust him; the bigger the risk, the more we want to know that he'll prove trustworthy. The bigger the risk, the more it helps to have personal experience of his goodness. But here's the rub: you cannot get personal experience of God's trustworthiness without *taking* a risk.

Trusting God about chastity—especially in singleness—is somewhat like setting out on a long-distance road trip, through treacherous terrain, with different kinds of bad weather forecasted at each stretch along the way: dust storms, ice storms, hurricanes, tornadoes, and even blizzards. Worst of all, even if you trust that he'll get you to your destination safely, you cannot even be sure what that destination will be: lifelong singleness, a marriage that sours over time, a marriage that ends in divorce, a marriage cut short by death . . . or a happy and nourishing marriage that lasts decades. We have to trust God about an outcome or resolution far in the future, based largely on present circumstances that may often appear quite grim or even hopeless.

Fortunately, we have a lot of information about what's happened to other people who have taken similar risks with God. The Bible gives us dozens of stories about people who interacted with him. If you've never read it through cover to cover, consider doing so, so you can see the entire story (and it really is a story) in context. You'll probably need more than a year to get through it, unless you can consistently block off thirty to sixty minutes a day to read, but you'll get the best account we have of God's faithfulness to people, despite repeated distrust, disobedience, and rebellion. For a Cliff Notes version or helpful reading companion, pick up Craig Bartholomew and Michael Goheen's *The True Story of the Whole World*.

In addition to the Bible, we also have the stories of Christians throughout history and around the world. If you're not much of a reader, ask some of the Christians in your life—especially older ones—to tell you about their experience of trusting God and why they're still committed to him. You probably won't hear that trust resulted in them getting *everything* they wanted, but you'll likely hear what I've found: that God proved faithful and good, even as life threw its worst at them.

Years ago, I attended a church in New York that had a very charismatic, well-known pastor. One of the sermon illustrations I remember most, however, came from an assistant pastor whose sermons didn't stand out in the same way. And *that* illustration came from the life of someone Howard Thurman would probably call "disinherited."[5] One Sunday the pastor told us about his conversation with an older immigrant woman who did domestic work for his family. At almost no point had she enjoyed the privileges and boons others are born into—and on top of this, she experienced several other kinds of suffering. Life gave her almost none of even the ordinary

---

5. Thurman wrote the classic work *Jesus and the Disinherited*, which Martin Luther King Jr. was said to carry around with him. In the book, Thurman explains why he follows Jesus despite Christians' terrible involvement in the transatlantic slave trade, lynching, segregation, and other forms of race-based oppression.

sweetness, as I recall the account, yet when her experience of God came up, this woman told the pastor, "He's been like honey to me."

Sitting there then, I felt something like the psalmist also stirs in me, in passages where he says, "When I awake, I will be satisfied with seeing your likeness" (17:15, NIV) or, "You will fill me with joy in your presence, with eternal pleasures at your right hand" (16:11). *Who is this God?*, I wonder. *What have they found that I haven't—and how?*

To what extent I *have* tasted and seen God's goodness, it has come through an ongoing cycle of seeking and trust, wrestling and obedience. Chastity has played a large role in that, but it's certainly not the only way to develop trust in God. As I've tried to argue throughout this chapter, the Bible and Christian communities throughout history give us a large set of interconnected, embodied practices all meant to help us love God and others more deeply, while fostering greater trust and obedience with our doting heavenly Father. So, if you're considering or attempting chastity, don't just work on that by itself—take more risks in other practices, too. We're meant to give God our whole body—not just a hair here or toenail there.

Tithing. The less we take the Bible at its word—and put weight on those claims—the less we may actually experience firsthand the living, powerful God depicted on page after page. Tithing is one of the best and most practical ways we can strengthen spiritual muscles of trust in God.

During college, I watched with occasional envy as God repeatedly provided for the material needs of my younger sister and others in surprisingly dramatic fashion. *Why not me?*, I sometimes wondered. But as I looked at my own finances, I began to see that I rarely gave God room to come through for me: when I didn't have money in the bank to buy groceries, I went to the store anyway and paid with a credit card.

The more I resisted the temptation to spend what I didn't have, however, and sought to obey God in my finances, the more I began to see him provide in unexpected ways. He never provided the same way—and these days he provides more through the security of a stable job—but the more I trusted God in my finances, the more he proved that he could provide what I needed and often beyond that. What's more, in my leanest days, I often found that God gave me some surprise, above-and-beyond provision followed soon after by an encounter with someone whose need *I* could now help meet. As I heard a pastor say years ago, God blesses us so that we can be a blessing to others.

Fasting. For those wrestling with sexual self-control and restraint, fasting provides a powerful, physical reminder of the importance of sometimes denying even our most basic desires.

Why link the two? For me it began several years ago, when I joined a growing group of people, connected by an email list, who fasted and prayed every Monday about marriage and singleness. Each week, we asked God to provide marriage for those who desire it or should be married, and to change men and women where we needed it. Over the years I fasted with them, I got pretty good at being hungry, but prayer remained a persistent struggle on my hungry Mondays. Even so, fasting proved a powerful, palpable way to offer my body to God and remember that it belongs first to *him* and not to me.

More recently, I have begun a small email list for people to fast and pray weekly about the church's response to racism and race-based injustice.[6] This return to fasting has brought back my old struggles and yet a renewed sense that somehow God uses our physical hunger to serve a spiritual purpose we cannot see.

Living in community. Longing for connection often accompanies singleness. Typical adult living arrangements only serve to increase this. Living alone or with only one housemate does not provide much sense of family, much less the continued character formation afforded by close living arrangements. But singleness doesn't have to mean a life of isolation and loneliness; we can choose housing arrangements that foster connection.

For much of my adulthood, I've lived in community—first sharing a house with a rotating cast of other single adults, and now living in a former convent with a few families and single adults. The first arrangement gave me a sense of brothers and sisters while also continually challenging me to work through the frictions and tensions of close relationships. The present situation has deepened my community even further, providing an incredibly rich sense of family through this intergenerational living experience.

With all such community, you have to compromise on cleanliness and noise, and a host of others issues that arise. At the same time, you have to learn to love others not in ways that feel most comfortable to you but in ways that most make them *feel* loved. Yet I wouldn't trade this experience for anything. Since moving in, I've watched a tiny, barely mobile child move from sounds to simple "yes" and "no" answers to forming independent sentences and questions. I've gotten to introduce him to some of the most famous works of classical music and greatest hits of B. B. King. And I've learned firsthand that God truly does set the lonely in families, whether or not they proceed through our bodies.

Cooking for the church. One of the things I miss most about having a family is being able to cook for them the way my mother did for us when

---

6. For more information, email fastingforjustice@gmail.com.

we were growing up. Participating in my church's meals service for families with new babies or other needs, as well as the weekly house dinners at the convent, gives me a chance to cook on that larger scale. I may not have my own biological family to cook for, but in many ways I *do* cook for my family. The form of that family may change over time, but God's provision for our relational needs does not.

Participating in multigenerational (mixed life-stage) groups. Over the last several years, I've been part of multiple community groups, many of which combined singles and young families. In each case, this diversity has been a great blessing that both reminds me of the challenges of family life and childrearing (undermining any tendency to romanticize that life season!) and gives me a chance to experience family even though I don't have my own kids. At the same time, this contact has shown me ways that I can use my greater flexibility and free time to sometimes help share the load of my friends with kids.

Actively remembering God's faithfulness. I have not yet seen or participated in this to the degree I suspect the church should practice it, but the Bible—especially the Old Testament—strongly emphasizes storytelling and recollections of the faithfulness of God. This practice in particular reinforces our *trust* in God, especially when we're most discouraged and doubtful.

I'm not sure I would have made it this far in my often-reluctant chastity if not for a dramatic experience of God's kind intervention sixteen years ago, which gave me a taste of what's possible when I am out of control and he is *in* control. What he did that day, though it did not turn out how I thought it would, was a powerful repudiation of the ever-seductive, ever-destructive lie that God does not know best, that the path away from his will is somehow better. On that day, years ago, I had a taste of the truth that *God* knows better, and though I've never quite forgotten it, how I need to be reminded, again and again, to tell and retell that story.[7]

Regular church attendance. All the foregoing assumes this, but if you don't currently attend church regularly, start doing so. For years I attended church more from a sense I *should* do so than because I thought I needed those relationships. Even when I did go, I assumed God did most of his work through sermons. While you can certainly gain a lot through good teaching, the older I get, the more I realize how much God forms us through community. I would not have experienced the church as such a rich source of family—which it has been to me—if I were only going on Sundays and leaving immediately after the service ends.

---

7. Broadway, *Sexless in the City*.

I've been extremely fortunate in my churches, while others can be less welcoming, but don't let that discourage you. If no one says "hi" to you, try to make another newcomer feel welcome. Ask about community groups or Bible studies and start going to one. As you reach out, ask God to keep his promise to establish you in community.

This chapter was adapted from the essay "Practicing Trust," which first appeared in the January/February 2012 issue of Books and Culture.

Bibliography

Broadway, Anna. "Eating on Fifty Dollars a Week." *Comment*, November 7, 2008. https://www.cardus.ca/comment/article/728/eating-on-fifty-dollars-a-week.

———. "Manna on the Stoop." *Art House America*, September 29, 2011. http://www.arthouseamerica.com/blog/manna-on-the-stoop.html.

———. *Sexless in the City: A Memoir of Reluctant Chastity*. New York: Doubleday Galilee, 2008.

———. "To Sleep, Perchance to Grow." *Art House America*, July 17, 2014. http://www.arthouseamerica.com/blog/to-sleep-perchance-to-grow.html.

Smith, James K. A. *Desiring the Kingdom: Worship, Worldview, and Cultural Formation*. Cultural Liturgies 1. Grand Rapids: Baker Academic, 2009.

Thurman, Howard. *Jesus and the Disinherited*. Boston: Beacon, 2012.

7

From Lizards to Stallions
Exercising Moral Faith

David Baggett with Marybeth Baggett

Asking a philosopher to talk about sex is a dicey proposition. Exhibit A: a book called *Great Philosophers Who Failed at Love*.[1] Its jacket features this charming preview of coming attractions: "Few people have failed at love as spectacularly as the great philosophers. Although we admire their wisdom, history is littered with the romantic failures of the most sensible men and women of the age."

Novelist Neal Pollack describes the volume as a funny and oddly moving tale of philosophy as tortured erotic dysfunction. Take Friedrich Nietzsche, for example, who once wrote that women make the highs higher and the lows more frequent. His bitterness is understandable, given that he had been rejected by everyone he proposed to, even when he kept asking and asking. This makes Nietzsche one of dozens of great thinkers whose words we revere but whose romantic decisions we should avoid at all costs.

For this reason, I thought it best to ask my wife to help me.

Philosopher or not, writing on a topic like this feels a bit like walking a tightrope, with the opposing prospects of rabid fundamentalism and godless liberalism a scant hair's breadth away in either direction. Yet the challenge is a welcome one, not least because as Christians we have to be willing to discuss challenging topics. We cannot merely shy away from them. We should be confident about the truth claims of Christianity and unafraid to articulate those convictions and to apply them to various questions that arise. Part of the evidential force of the Christian worldview is its ability to

---

1. Shaffer, *Great Philosophers Who Failed at Love*.

provide analysis and insight—wisdom—to difficult questions, both old and new. Harry Blamires notes that the Christian mind is one trained, informed, and equipped to handle the data of secular controversy within a framework of reference that is constructed of Christian presuppositions.

Not that sex is a secular topic, of course. The Bible contains the erotically charged Song of Solomon, after all. Sex was God's idea, and intended to be practiced in a way consistent with his plan for us as human beings. Sex is a gift of God, and like all his gifts meant to point beyond itself to God himself. But there is little question that a secular mindset and worldview is driving the agenda of sexual discussion today, surely not a Christian understanding of sexuality.

As I write this, next week at a neighboring college Reid Mihalko, the self-styled "Sex Geek," is scheduled to do a talk called "How to Be a Gentleman and Still Get Laid: Navigating Consent, Sexual Freedom, Partying, Dating Relationships, and What It Means to Be a Man on Campus." That sort of title makes me think, among many other things, that this essay should have a snazzier heading. It's a little emasculating otherwise. So how about this for a subtitle? "Why a Christian Understanding of Sex Refuses to Venerate Autonomy, Deny Who We Are, Commodify and Deify Sex, Fragment the Psyche, Desacralize a Good Gift of God, and Construe Something Sacramental as Something Crassly Reductionist. So, There's That."

At any rate, that such a secular view of sex prevails outside the church and in the larger culture is hardly surprising. What *is* surprising, and disappointing, is the extent to which so many professing Christians' sexual lives are functionally atheistic. Let me explain.

Kantian Moral Faith

The great German philosopher Immanuel Kant, who was steeped in the Lutheran tradition, wrote about many things, one of which was "moral faith." Faith in today's world often gets a bad rap, construed as belief despite lack of evidence, or worse. Sam Harris, for example, calls faith "conviction without sufficient reason, hope mistaken for knowledge, bad ideas protected from good ones, good ideas obscured by bad ones, wishful thinking elevated to a principle of salvation."[2]

Needless to say, that construal, charming as it is, bears precious little resemblance to biblical faith: a God-infused sense of assurance in the trustworthiness of God rooted in evidence of all sorts, principled confidence

---

2. Harris, *Moral Landscape*, 175.

more than able to sustain and strengthen us through times of difficulty and doubt, trouble and tribulation.

So, setting aside today's misconceptions of faith, let us ponder a bit what *moral faith* is about when it comes to sexuality. For Kant, moral faith has two parts. First, that the moral life is possible. And second, that morality and happiness go together; they are deeply consistent and coherent with one another. Applied to sexuality, then, moral faith involves these two convictions: (1) sexual integrity is possible, and (2) it is profoundly consistent with happiness and joy.

These two aspects of moral faith correlate with two main ways in which today's society tends to communicate just the opposite message. It's easy to assume that these ubiquitous societal voices speak the truth, to absorb reigning ideas as axiomatic without even realizing the need to subject them to scrutiny. C. S. Lewis writes about this phenomenon in the fourth chapter of *The Problem of Pain*. He invites readers to remember a time when they lived in a pocket of society—a school, regiment, or profession—that featured a toxic atmosphere, a place where even minimal civility was seen as unrealistic or impractical. Exiting such a context opens our eyes to how dysfunctional the place had been. Then he adds, with his characteristic insight, "It is wise to face the possibility that the whole human race . . . is, in fact, just such a local pocket of evil—an isolated bad school or regiment inside which minimum decency passes for heroic virtue and utter corruption for pardonable imperfection."[3]

Even if most Christians do not buy into prevailing casual sexual attitudes at a conscious level, it remains tempting, unless we are vigilant, to let such ideas affect our behavior. What shapes how we live can arguably be said to reflect our truest beliefs, even more so than those beliefs we assent to at a cognitive and conscious level. Numerous studies indicate that this indeed is the case—that the sexual behavior of professing Christians, including evangelical Christians, is not substantially better, if at all, than that of folks who are not Christians or evangelicals. Various chapters in this volume document such studies with meticulous care.

These sorts of findings are significant, telling, and disturbing because they go to show an entrenched way in which professing Christians and evangelicals are saying one thing about sex and, in great numbers, doing another; or saying and doing the same thing, but something contrary to God's best. Perhaps this means we need to return to some basics. Rather than discussing, say, gay marriage, let us be clear: heterosexual evangelicals in great numbers are failing sexually.

---

3. Quoted from Lewis, *Complete C. S. Lewis Signature Classics*, 584.

So this chapter will focus on the 96.6 percent of the population that claims to be straight, according to recent NHIS data reported by the *Washington Post*. It will invite readers to think about Kantian moral faith, because its two parts are powerfully relevant to how we can think Christianly about this topic of sexuality.

Can we be sexually holy? And does sexual holiness conduce to joy? What does secular society say, and what does Christian theology say?

Can We Be Sexually Holy?

The secular message today, in answer to the first question, is "no": we can't be sexually holy. It insists that sexual purity is out of the question for most of us. Face it, we are told: People have sex, including high school kids, and most certainly college kids. Appeals to abstinence do not work. Chastity is a joke; its proponents are worthy of mockery. The subtext of all this condescension is that a life of sexual purity is beyond our reach. Besides which, such puritanical, repressive schemes are false to the human condition and recipes for dysfunction, we are soberly informed. This is part of a prevailing secular narrative with which we are bombarded on a daily basis.

We may be Christians, but this secular script is the cultural message filling our ears incessantly. And plenty of professing believers today are more steeped in, influenced by, and even comfortable with the prevailing views of secularism than they are by elements of classical Christian thought. Indeed, their very views about Christian teaching and doctrine are often shaped by worldly perspectives, leading them to think, if not say, that certain of such old-fashioned teachings, however quaint and cute, are altogether impracticable.

This is reminiscent of a character in C. S. Lewis's *Screwtape Letters* who, though a Christian, also fancied himself rather enlightened at the same time. So he looked down on his non-Christian friends for missing the spiritual part of reality, while also looking down on his Christian friends for missing out on aspects of the world with which he was familiar and reconciled. With an attitude featuring equal measures of pride and derogation, he thought himself better than and above them all. Unsurprisingly, this was exactly where the demon Screwtape wanted him to remain, realizing how precarious a condition such spiritual condescension was.

Christian writer Matt Walsh recently took on this logic that says parents should not bother to tell their kids to refrain from sex because, after all, they are going to partake anyway. He asked:

> What is your job as a parent? Is it to give your child low bars, easy goals, and mild challenges to meet? Or is it to point her towards what is right and good, and then give her the tools to attain it? Also, do you, in any other situation, elect to forgo teaching your kid to do what is right and instead prepare him to do the next best thing? Do you ever tell your child to shoot for a C in math class? Do you ever tell her to make sure she only engages in reasonable levels of bullying and gossip?[4]

Why is it important to ask whether we *can* meet a moral demand? The likely answer is that we deem it unjust to be expected to match a standard that we are intrinsically unable to meet. As ethicists like to say, *ought implies can*. We cannot be obligated to do something we simply cannot do. This is intuitive, for the most part, but interestingly enough the Bible suggests otherwise. We *are* obligated to meet the moral demand, yet the demand, ultimately, is for nothing less than perfection. Yet we cannot be perfect, as hard as we try. Invariably we fall short.

At this point, Yale ethicist John Hare writes that one has three choices: lower the demand, exaggerate one's capacities, or seek assistance to do what one cannot do on one's own.[5] Lowering the demand seems to be the most common tack nowadays, but this is not really a legitimate prerogative for believers who take biblical revelation seriously. Exaggerating our capacities, especially in light of our sinful predilections, also seems the wrong answer. So what is left?

The Christian answer is clear: Appeal to God for help. Ask God to do what we cannot do on our own. Acknowledge our weakness, our helplessness, our utter need for him, and trust that he will do in our lives what needs to be done. We cannot meet the moral demand in our own strength, through sheer dint of effort and grinding our teeth. We become holy only by relying on the strength God provides to be conformed to the image of Christ.

We are forgiven by grace through faith. Likewise, we are made holy by grace through faith. It's required of God's servants that they be found faithful, and holiness is not merely optional. We need to ask God to shape us, to change us, to transform us, by the power of his Spirit. God has more work to do in us. He wants to enable us truly to love him with all of our heart and soul and mind and strength, and our neighbor as ourself. He wants to be our

---

4. Walsh, "Why I Won't Teach My Kids about Safe Sex."
5. Hare, *Moral Gap*.

Lord, not just our Savior. He wants to sanctify us, and make us to be not just *better* men and women, but *new* men and women. Holiness is possible only as we submit to him. Some sins will be too much for us to resist unless we appropriate God's way of escape. That may sometimes require fleeing rather than standing and fighting. It calls for accountability, Internet filters, intense prayer, fasting, observing the Sabbath, confession, memorization of Scripture, practicing devotional disciplines, taking spiritual formation seriously.

Perhaps our hesitancy to embrace these resources stems from a misconstrual of God's character. All too many people labor under a misunderstanding, harboring deep-seated doubts about the love of God, as if God is veritably champing at the bit for us to mess up so he can dole out punishment. God upholds standards not for punitive reasons, but because he knows what's best for us. He doesn't want merely to *impute* righteousness, but to *impart* it, to transform us, to sanctify fully, to make us holy as he is holy, knowing that our deepest joy requires it. God is not looking for an excuse to cut us off or out. He loves us, with an eternal love. Often we hear nowadays that it's easy to believe in a God of love, by which is usually meant a degraded notion of watered-down, permissive love. But real love isn't like that; no good parent gives his child everything he wants and lets him grow spoiled rotten in the process. That isn't real love, but just the opposite.

God truly desires what is best for us, which is what real love entails. Love is not just what God *does*. It's who he *is*. We have all fallen short in various ways, and he extends his forgiveness and redemption, even of our sufferings produced by sin. God is that kind of redeemer. Hosea (13:10–13) tells us God's people experienced birth pangs because they had trusted in their corrupt kings, but the people repented and the Lord healed their apostasy in bringing in the new age of salvation. God's willing to take even the sufferings caused by sin and use them in redemptive ways—turning them into birth pangs for the messianic age. What a remarkable picture of who God is: perfect in love, yearning to see us flourish and experience the joy for which he created us.

Such joy is possible only in relationship with him. The resources for a holy life are the same resources we need for a pure sexual life. When it comes to our sexuality, before abundant life comes, something else has to happen first. And it is not marriage. Marriage is wonderful, but it is not the answer to our sexual short-falling. Wrong ceremony. It's a funeral that's needed instead. A single person who indulges lust to his heart's content and thinks marriage will solve it is on a trajectory to become a married person constantly committing adultery in his heart. The lust must die, and stay dead.

Single or married, sexual healing and health are possible by God's grace, but this raises an important point. Why did Jesus ask a man on a particular occasion, "Do you wish to be healed?" (John 5:6). Shouldn't the answer be obvious? Everyone wants to be healed, right? Not necessarily. For we may vaguely want a particular end result—say, deliverance from lust—without wanting to endure what it takes to get there. I (Marybeth) love the idea of playing the piano brilliantly, but have precious little desire to devote the time it would take to learn to do so. We may want health without being willing to endure the healing, to take the medicine, to let some things die. Or we may so closely identify the sickness with who we are that we're unwilling to let it go, sure that *its* death will result in *our* death. But God will only let those parts of us die that need to die as we trust him.

This is what Kant meant by a revolution of the will. This is what those in certain Christian traditions are getting at when they talk about complete devotion to the purposes of God, or being wholly sanctified.[6] Is holiness possible, including sexual holiness? Yes, but only by tapping into the resources at our disposal, by getting serious about our faith, by letting the Holy Spirit do his work in our lives. Augustine once said that God bids us to do what we cannot in order that we might learn our dependence on God.

And that requires death. Death to the idol of sexuality and to the tyranny of lust. Martin Luther once said, "You cannot keep birds from flying over your head but you can keep them from building a nest in your hair." A thoroughgoing secularist, Rosaria Champagne Butterfield was an English professor at Syracuse University, a practicing lesbian who taught gay studies. Her book *The Secret Thoughts of an Unlikely Convert* makes for an engaging read. It's about her conversion to historic Christianity and the way she left her lesbian lifestyle behind. She writes, "What good Christians don't realize is that sexual sin is not recreational sex gone overboard. Sexual sin is predatory. It won't be 'healed' by redeeming the context or the genders. Sexual sin must simply be killed."[7]

Killing the Demon

This is not a popular teaching. Nor is it easy—apart from God's, grace it's well-nigh impossible. Perhaps that's why it too often goes untried. The Bible's prescription for sexual purity is radical. The demon of lust has to die. One of the more vivid fictional portrayals of this Christian corrective is the

---

6. The holiness tradition is a salient example, according to which we are sanctified by grace through faith, typically involving a crisis moment subsequent to justification.

7. Butterfield, *Secret Thoughts of an Unlikely Convert*, 83.

latter half of the eleventh chapter of C. S. Lewis's *The Great Divorce*. Here is the context: a bus-full of people-turned-ghosts who reside in hell have arrived at the entrance to heaven on holiday, and are encouraged by various inhabitants there to let go of the sin that afflicts and assails them. Doing so is a prerequisite to entering into the joy of the presence of God.

In one of those stories, the narrator describes a Ghost on whose shoulder sat a little red lizard twitching its tail like a whip and whispering things in his ear. After a while, the Ghost starts to retreat back toward the bus (to return to hell). He explains to a flaming Spirit Angel that, since the lizard won't hush, he has no choice but to go home. What follows is a remarkable exchange between the Ghost and the Bright Spirit (or Spirit Angel), in which the latter repeatedly asks the Ghost if he would like the lizard to be killed.

The Ghost really does not want the lizard killed, though. Nothing as drastic as that. He would rather him simply be silenced, especially since the lizard's incessant chattering is proving so embarrassing while at the precipice of heaven. In fact, this is but the first of a litany of excuses not to permit the Spirit Angel to kill the lizard: *Let's put the operation off—the need for deliverance isn't so great after all . . . I'll be able to keep it in line . . . Let's deal with the problem gradually and incrementally instead . . . I'm not feeling well today or I would.*

Perhaps the most significant reason for the Ghost's ambivalence then becomes clear: fear that the Bright Spirit killing the lizard will kill the Ghost himself. To which the Angel admits it will be painful, but assures the Ghost it will not be fatal. The Ghost would have preferred the lizard to be killed already, wanting the end result without the process. But the Angel informs him that it can't happen without his permission, the very permission the Ghost has been trying so hard to rationalize withholding. Finally, once more, the Angel asks,

> "Have I your permission?"
> "I know it will kill me."
> "It won't. But supposing it did?"
> "You're right. It would be better to be dead than to live with this creature."
> "Then I may?"
> "Damn and blast you! Go on can't you? Get it over. Do what you like," bellowed the Ghost: but ended, whimpering, "God help me. God help me."
>
> *Next moment the Ghost gave a scream of agony such as I never heard on Earth. The Burning One closed his crimson grip on the reptile: twisted it, while it bit and writhed, and then flung it, broken backed, on the turf.*

"Ow! That's done for me," gasped the Ghost, reeling backwards.[8]

We'll return to the rest of this story momentarily, but here's the point: the demon of lust had to die. And there is something else to emphasize here of great importance for those who are serious about sexual holiness, namely, that there may be yet worse sins lurking in the vicinity of lust. Sodom was known for its sexual impurity, but in Ezekiel 16:48–50 we find God comparing Jerusalem to Sodom, saying Sodom's sin is less offensive to God than Jerusalem's. We find out that the root of sexual sin functions at the base of a myriad of sins—some worse than sexual sins. In reverse order, they are listed as lack of discretion and modesty, lack of mercy, ungodly trust in wealth, an entertainment-driven worldview, and, most of all, pride.

Why *pride*? Pride, says Butterfield, is the root of all sin. It puffs up with a false sense of independence. Proud people always feel that they can live independently from God and from other people. Proud people feel entitled to do what they want, when they want.

God can heal us even from our pride—from our self-consumption, from those sins that so easily beset us, from being turned inwardly on ourselves—and he will heal us if we let him. But only if we're willing to let some things die. It will not kill you. It may feel like it, but it won't. Ultimately, the pain required for transformation and conformity to the image of Christ is far less than the pain of being held in the grip of sin and death and hell. It is the way of the transgressor that's most difficult and riddled with pain. The yoke of Christ is easy, and his burden light, by comparison.

Do Our Deepest Joy and Sexual Holiness Cohere?

What about the other aspect of moral faith? The convergence of happiness and holiness? The world says you can't be sexually pure, and that if you actually try in prudish fashion to refrain from sex until the appropriate time, you're bound to be unhappy and repressed and miserable anyway. It will not make you happy; it will make you depressed. Rules against sex are just an overactive superego writ large, a shame-based way to keep us in line. Morality, and likely God, too, are nothing but cosmic killjoys, aimed to keep you away from fun and a good time. Indulging our sexual desires is the most natural thing in the world. Don't believe otherwise, we're told. Partake; you won't regret it.

---

8. Quoted from Lewis, *Complete C. S. Lewis Signature Classics*, 524.

Put like this, perhaps readers can recognize that this temptation has a long tradition. From *Paradise Lost* to *Faust*, literature, echoing hard reality itself, is replete with cautionary tales and colorful illustrations of the futility of choosing darkness over light. Even still, however transparently it is cast, the temptation proves insidiously effective time and again. Even we as Christians, when we fall short and fail, sexually or otherwise, buy into the lie that God doesn't really know best. We do. We believe we will be happier by choosing the sin, yielding to the temptation, indulging the self. And in our obstinacy we go down that path, yielding less and less fruit and fulfillment, and more and more heartache and regret.

Here it does us great good to ponder for a moment what morality from a Christian perspective is all about. This generation, probably not altogether unlike every previous one, has largely gotten snowed on this score. Morality tends to be too easily reduced to rules—do this, don't do that—and it's easy when ethics gets understood in such terms to lose sight of vitally important truths.

Rules strike us as arbitrary impositions, as if God delights in foisting on us capricious dictums in an effort to keep us from having a good time or, even worse, to catch us in every mistake, heaping on us guilt at every infraction. As always, bad theology leads to bad behavior—legalism on the one hand, license on the other.

What God wants for us is joyful obedience, abundant life, freedom in Christ from sin and shame, ultimately a life of wondrous love. For God actually does love us—with an eternal love, with perfect love. He loves each of us differently, and each of us infinitely. Although plenty of believers down deep really doubt that, it's true. Love is who God is. It always has been, always will be, in the (perichoretic) relationship between the members of the Trinity.

This means that we can rest assured that if God tells us not to do something, it's not because he doesn't like us. No, he likes us. He loves us, more than we can begin to imagine. We may not always fully understand the point of the prohibition, but there is one. Jesus came that we might have life, and life more abundantly. When we doubt God's love, we should remember the cross, and when we doubt we can live a holy life, we should remember the resurrection. The same power that raised Jesus from the dead can be at work within us, giving us the victory we seek in vain in our own strength.

God wants what is best for us. Too often we settle for too little—crumbs instead of a smorgasbord, disparate cacophonous notes rather than a mellifluous symphony, a few stolen physical pleasures when, if we could but see, God offers us a feast of infinite delights. We are meant for glory, nothing less. Our bodies will be resurrected, which is why Paul says not to perform sexual sins with it (1 Cor 6:18). We, and our very bodies, are meant for more.

Wrenching the sexual ethics of Christianity from its context and considering it in isolation, especially juxtaposed with the so-called enlightened ideals of the contemporary world, can make what we believe as Christians seem silly or superstitious. To understand Christian ethics we need to understand Christianity—and in more than a shallow, superficial way. It's time to cultivate some theological sophistication.

The Christian understanding of sex is built, of course, on an Old Testament understanding of sexuality, which stood in diametric opposition to various pagan mythic understandings among the religions of the ancient Near East. According to those religions, this is a world inhabited by debased, impulsive, and sexed gods, where sexuality rituals were conceived in magical fashion as able to manipulate the gods in order to achieve various ends.

The transcendent faith of the Jews offered a significantly altered picture, a radically different paradigm, one that assigned primacy to the faithful character of God superintending the world—a God, though known as Father, who is supra-sexual, manifesting both male and female features, but not essentially gendered. This true God cares about the whole of the created order, and especially human beings, made in his image. The world is fallen, but he's in the process of setting it right. God has imbued human beings with value, and intends their good, and sexual behavior among them is a good gift from him, but to be confined to marriage relationships between a man and a woman. The New Testament picks up this theme and stands firmly in this tradition.

We are to understand our sexuality, and everything else, in relation to the core identity God has given us. We need to remember who we are. As the church, it is our job to remind each other why God's ways make such sense, to the extent we can understand them though we still see through a glass darkly. We are the children of promise called to manifest God's character in the world, the people of God to showcase the values of the kingdom of God. We are the promissory note of a world restored to its original intention, the saints of God animated by the power that raised Jesus from the dead, modeling eternal life by our lives, meant to show what the Spirit of God can accomplish in sanctified people: individuals and a community that demonstrate God's intention for a redeemed humanity and a world set right.

The resurrection by Old Testament lights was to come at the end of the age, but Christianity came as a surprise in this sense. Resurrection happened not at the end, but in the middle. Jesus was raised from the dead, which means the end has already made its appearance, in a real sense, and yet in another sense it hasn't. The kingdom of God has arrived, and from now until the general resurrection all the resources are available for us to live as kingdom people, redeemed and able to live victoriously in a perilous world rife with temptations that buffet us from every direction.

When Jesus reaffirms the traditional Jewish standards of sexual behavior, and when the apostle Paul, speaking in a largely Gentile context, spells out a bit more clearly what is and what isn't part of the new creation lifestyle for those "in Christ," it was as counterintuitive then as it is today. But the constraints aren't mainly a matter of what behaviors are allowed or prohibited. To ask the question that way is already to admit defeat, to think in terms of behavior as a set of quasi-arbitrary and hence negotiable rules. We should instead ask what this new creation God launched in Jesus looks like, and how we can live well as genuine humans, as both a sign and a means of that renewal. The entire biblical sexual ethic is deeply counterintuitive.

In an interview with Jonathan Merritt, N. T. Wright adds that "all human beings some of the time, and some human beings most of the time, have deep, heartfelt longings for kinds of sexual intimacy or gratification that don't reflect the Creator's best intentions for his human creatures—intentions through which new wisdom and flourishing will come to birth. Sexual restraint is mandatory for all, difficult for most, and extremely challenging for some."[9]

When we do it God's way, relinquishing everything, he can and will redeem what we give back to him. He will take what we have sacrificed in obedience to him, cleanse it, and use it for his purposes. The earlier excerpt from *The Great Divorce* features a beautiful illustration of God's power to forgive, deliver, and transform. Recall we left the story right after the lizard was killed. After that, the lizard transforms into a mighty stallion, silvery white but with a mane and tail of gold.

> It was smooth and shining, rippled with swells of flesh and muscle, whinnying and stamping with its hoofs. At each stamp the land shook and the trees dindled. In joyous haste the young man leaped upon the horse's back. Turning in his seat he waved a farewell, then nudged the stallion with his heels. They were off, already they only like a shooting star far off on the green plain, and soon among the foothills of the mountains, till near the dim brow of the landscape, so high they finally vanished into the rose-brightness of that everlasting morning.[10]

---

9. Merritt, "NT Wright on Homosexuality, Science, Gender."
10. Lewis, *Great Divorce*, 524–25.

A Few Loose Ends

We Christians need to know what we believe, and why we believe it. We need to catch a vision of the love of God that animates the Christian ethic, so we know it's not an arbitrary set of rules, but rather the truth about the kingdom of God and the human condition, meant for his glory and our deepest joy. We need to remember who we are. We need good theology, sound doctrine, the courage of our convictions, and to take our call to holiness seriously. We must see the relevance of our faith and worldview in any and every area of our lives, and most surely our sexuality—and refuse to be in lockstep with the world. We simply have to stop trivializing sin for which Jesus died.

Exactly because sex is so good, its twisted variants and unintended expressions are corrupt, predatory, and idolatrous. "There you go," some might say. "We knew you were just scared of sex after all. We're *not* scared of sex. It is harmless fun."

No, it is not. For lots of reasons. Here are a few million. Since 1973 over fifty million unborn babies have been slaughtered in their mothers' wombs. For what? Just having harmless fun? God knows what he's talking about when he tells us how to conduct ourselves. He really does. There are nightmare scenarios we can avoid, and goods beyond words we can safeguard and relish by obeying him.

It is not about "safe sex," as if a thin piece of latex could make sex safe. It's not supposed to be safe. It's about vulnerability and intimacy and two eternal creatures physically manifesting their love and God's love. The world treats it as copulation and satisfaction and stolen inebriated gropings in the dark. It was never meant to be tawdry, never meant to be dirty or cheap. It was meant to be beautiful. It was meant to be heavenly, in the true sense of the term. We shouldn't settle for less, and by God's grace we don't have to. We can be forgiven for having fallen short, and we can be empowered to walk uprightly.

What defines this moment in history isn't the latest secular transvaluation of values, sexual revolution, or widespread acceptance of gay marriage as normative—a debate that's been around since Plato, by the way, nothing new there. No, what marks the moment, despite all appearances to the contrary, is that God is at work in this world, setting things right, accomplishing his purposes. The question is a simple one: Will we submit to his lordship in every area of our lives, or not? That is what will determine whether we're on the right side of history, not the dictates of a tyrannous culture of political correctness and normative promiscuity.

We need moral faith when it comes to sex. We need to embrace the radical truth that, with God's help, sexual holiness is possible, and, in his will, obedience to God's plan for our sexuality conduces to our deepest joy.

Bibliography

Butterfield, Rosaria Champagne. *The Secret Thoughts of an Unlikely Convert: An English Professor's Journey into Christian Faith*. Pittsburgh: Crown & Covenant, 2012.

Hare, John E. *The Moral Gap: Kantian Ethics, Human Limits, and God's Assistance*. Oxford: Clarendon, 1996.

Harris, Sam. *The Moral Landscape: How Science Can Determine Human Values*. New York: Free Press, 2011.

Merritt, Jonathan. "NT Wright on Homosexuality, Science, Gender." *Religious News Service*, June 3, 2014. http://religionnews.com/2014/06/03/nt-wright-homosexuality-science-gender/.

Lewis, C. S. *The Complete C. S. Lewis Signature Classics*. San Francisco: Harper SanFrancisco, 2007.

Shaffer, Andrew. *Great Philosophers Who Failed at Love*. New York: Harper, 2011.

Walsh, Matt. "Why I Won't Teach My Kids about Safe Sex." *The Matt Walsh Blog*, August 5, 2014. http://themattwalshblog.com/2014/08/05/i-will-not-teach-my-kids-about-safe-sex.

8

What Would Saint Paul Say about "Making Out"?[1]

GERALD HIESTAND

One of the more vexing issues facing evangelical pastors today is the question of premarital sexual ethics. Simply put, we pastors are not quite certain how to counsel singles and teens regarding appropriate sexual boundaries. Of course, we still (for the most part) teach that sexual intercourse should be reserved for marriage. But beyond this, there is no consensus among evangelical clergy about where the boundaries should be drawn. Instead we tend to push the burden of this question back onto singles. One pastor typifies the counsel regularly given by evangelical clergy:

> You may want me to tell you, in much more detail, exactly what's right for you when it comes to secular boundaries [in dating relationships]. But in the end, you have to stand before God. That's why you must set your own boundaries according to His direction for your life. . . . I want you to build your own list of sexual standards.[2]

But do we really mean to say that Christian singles should "build their own list of sexual standards"? Certainly this can't be right. Is oral sex permissible? Fondling? Mutual masturbation? Passionate kissing? No one seems to really know. Certainly many Christian singles don't know.[3] And

---

1. An extended version of this chapter first appeared as "A Biblical-Theological Approach to Premarital Sexual Ethics: or, What Saint Paul Would Say about 'Making Out.'" *Bulletin of Ecclesial Theology* 1.1 (2014) 13–34.

2. Clark, *I Gave Dating a Chance*, 108–9.

3. According to one study, the percentage of evangelical teens who believe it is

the confusion here is no small matter. There is every reason to suspect that our lack of clear direction regarding premarital boundaries is putting singles in a precarious position. The September/October 2011 edition of *Relevant* magazine included a remarkable look into evangelical sexual ethics.[4] In the article "(Almost) Everyone's Doing It," author Tyler Charles, drawing on data gathered by the National Campaign to Prevent Teen and Unwanted Pregnancy, informs us that among evangelical singles between the ages of eighteen and twenty-nine, 42 percent are currently in a sexual relationship, 22 percent have had sex in the past year, and an additional 10 percent have had sex at least once. Assuming the accuracy of such data, this means only 20 percent of young evangelicals have remained abstinent.

Even if the survey's data were wrong by half,[5] the numbers would still be concerning. And, as a pastor, I am indeed concerned. In my experience, I see a significant amount of confusion and compromise among Christian teens and singles, particularly as it relates to premarital sexual ethics. Sometimes Christians flounder because the church fails to address crucial issues; sometimes Christians flounder because the leaders of the church address crucial issues wrongly. Both the former and the latter are at work here. On the one hand, evangelical scholars and theologians have devoted little attention (if any) to the issue of premarital sexual ethics; and when pastors do speak explicitly to this issue, we send a confusing and mixed message. We've told Christian singles that it's fine (or at least might be fine, or at least we can't say it's not fine) to prepare the meal—just as long as they don't consume it. We've left the door open to sexual foreplay, while insisting that singles refrain from consummating that foreplay. In essence, we're telling Christians singles that it is (or might be) permissible to start having sex, just as long as they don't finish. It is little wonder, then, that many Christian singles, while largely agreeing that intercourse should be reserved for marriage,[6] find themselves unable to live out their own ideal.

"always or sometimes appropriate for two people who are in love, but not married" to engage in the following activities is as follows: embracing and some kissing (97 percent); heavy French kissing (81 percent); fondling of breasts (35 percent); fondling of genitals (29 percent); sexual intercourse (20 percent). See McDowell and Hostetler, *Right from Wrong*, 278.

4. Charles, "(Almost) Everyone's Doing It." The article gets its data from the National Survey of Reproductive and Contraceptive Knowledge, conducted by the National Campaign to Prevent Teen and Unwanted Pregnancy, December, 2009.

5. There may be reasons to suspect the survey does not represent a completely accurate picture of evangelical sexual conduct. For a helpful analysis regarding the methodology of the survey, see DeYoung, "Premarital Sex and Our Love Affair with Bad Stats."

6. Charles goes on to note that "76 percent of evangelicals believe sex outside of

If the pastoral community is unclear on this issue, it is unsurprising that singles are likewise unclear. Given the present lack of consensus within the pastoral community, this chapter will explore the New Testament's sexual ethic with a view to constructing an objective sexual ethic for all premarital relationships. Supported by a christocentric hermeneutic, it will conclude that fidelity to the ethic of Scripture necessitates *reserving any and all sexual activity for the marriage relationship*. Or, to state it again, the New Testament conveys—both theologically and exegetically—that all premarital relationships are to be completely nonsexual. Or one more time: premarital "making out" is a sin.[7] We begin with a close reading of the New Testament's premarital sexual ethic.

The New Testament's Premarital Sexual Ethic

The sexual mores of the first-century Greco-Roman world were in most every respect more liberal than our contemporary culture. Prostitution was viewed as a legitimate way for a man to satisfy his sexual urges; keeping a personal mistress or a slave for sexual gratification was normal for those who could afford such things; homosexual acts between men and boys, while not without its critics, was largely viewed as normal and permissible (more so in the Greek tradition than the Roman). But the one place where the Greco-Roman culture was more conservative than our contemporary culture was the way in which it viewed premarital sexual relations between a man and another man's virgin daughter.

The ability of a respectable young woman to find a suitable marriage partner was, in no small part, contingent upon her father's ability to prove her chastity. Since a daughter's contribution to the family was often found in her ability to secure a socially or economically advantageous marriage, a father in the ancient world typically took pains to protect the sexual integrity of his daughter's reputation until the day of her marriage. Respectable young women did not leave the home unescorted, and the practice of cloistering (i.e., where a young woman was kept in the home and secluded away from any male nonrelatives) was often employed. Suffice it to say, respectable young virgin women in the ancient world were, in many respects, not easily afforded the opportunity to engage in sexual misconduct.[8]

---

marriage is morally wrong." See Charles, "(Almost) Everyone's Doing It," 65.

7. In many respects, this chapter represents a more detailed defense of the opening two chapters of my book written with Jay Thomas, *Sex, Dating, and Relationships*.

8. This is not to say that female promiscuity never occurred, only that it was generally condemned in ways that male promiscuity was not. *The Art of Love*, written by

Given the cultural dynamics of the ancient world, New Testament proof texts on premarital sexual ethics are in short supply. In a culture that prized virginity in unwed women, utilized arranged marriages, and often practiced cloistering, the authors of the New Testament had no need to be overly specific regarding chastity rules for premarital relationships. Simply put, the reigning ethic—even in the pagan culture—was, "Keep your hands off my daughter." Thus we cannot expect the Bible to offer us a detailed list about which activities (e.g., fondling, kissing, oral sex, etc.) are permissible in premarital relationships.

Yet, despite the lack of an explicit statement about "how far is too far" in premarital relationships, the New Testament does offer us a clear sexual ethic: *sexual relations are to be reserved for the marriage relationship*. Adultery (Rom 2:22), homosexuality (1 Cor 6:9), prostitution (1 Cor 6:12–20), fornication (1 Thess 4:3–8), and polygamy (1 Tim 3:2) are all explicitly condemned in the New Testament. Additionally, the New Testament uses the term πορνεία (*porneia*—sexual immorality) as a catch-all term to forbid all extramarital sexual activity. The New Testament's use of πορνεία is properly understood against the backdrop of the Levitical purity codes of the Old Testament, and thus adultery, fornication, bestiality, incest, homosexuality, and prostitution—all condemned by Old Testament law—fall within its range of meaning.[9]

We find a working example of this basic ethical framework, specifically as it relates to premarital sexual activity, in 1 Corinthians 7:1–9. Discussing celibacy and marriage, Paul writes,

> I wish that all were as I myself am. But each has his own gift from God, one of one kind and one of another. To the unmarried and the widows I say that it is good for them to remain single as I am. But if they cannot exercise self-control, they should marry. For it is better to marry than to burn with passion. (7:7–9, ESV)

---

the first-century Roman poet Ovid, is a bawdy and comical window into the sorts of shenanigans a male lover had to go through to seduce a maiden or another man's wife. Ovid's poems show that such seductions were especially guarded against, but nonetheless took place.

9. Etymologically, πορνεία (transliterated *porneia*) referred to prostitution or fornication, but was frequently used more broadly to denote any and all forms of sexual misconduct. For an analysis of the use of πορνεία in the New Testament, see Collins, *Sexual Ethics and the New Testament*, 80–83; Loader, *Sexuality in the New Testament*, 71–76; Countryman, *Dirt, Greed, and Sex*, 73. For the full range of terms denoting sexual misconduct, see the entry on sexual misbehavior in Louw and Nida, *Greek-English Lexicon of the New Testament*, 271–82.

Here Paul is responding to a series of questions posed to him by the Corinthians. Many at Corinth viewed celibacy as the ideal Christian state. Even married individuals, it seems, were attempting to live a celibate life.[10] Paul notes his own commitment to celibacy and agrees that celibacy is indeed ideal for increasing one's capacity to serve in Christ's kingdom. Yet Paul recognizes that the ability to live a chaste and celibate life is a unique gift from God—one that God has not given to everyone. Given the ever-present temptation toward sexual immorality, Paul instructs those who have a strong desire for sexual intimacy (i.e., "burn with passion") to fulfill that desire within the context of a marriage relationship.

The ESV rightly glosses "to burn" (from πυροῦσθαι) as "to burn with passion" (v. 9). Viewing unfulfilled sexual desire as a "burning" was a common-enough metaphor in Paul's world. The picture of lovers "aflame with love" and lying in each other's arms "on fire" is found throughout Greco-Roman literature.[11] In this respect, Paul's analysis of sexual desire is common to his times; his solution, however, is unique. In the ancient world, the solution to "burning" with sexual desire was release through intercourse. In other words, sex—not marriage—was the solution to passionate burning.[12] But for Paul the marriage relationship is the only legitimate context for satisfying one's sexual passions. To choose celibacy without the χάρισμα ("gift") would be a mistake. Indeed, Paul not only recommends marriage as a bulwark against sexual temptation, but in fact commands it; Paul uses the imperative form of γαμέω ("to marry") in verse 9. Failure to seek legitimate means of sexual release places oneself in harm's way, and creates temptation toward illegitimate sexual activity. Those who have a strong desire for sexual intimacy should not continue to "burn" indefinitely, nor seek to quench that burning in illegitimate ways outside the marriage bounds. The sexual ethic here is clear: sexual activity is to be reserved for the marriage relationship. The working assumptions that drive Paul's logic in 1 Corinthians 7 are operative throughout the New Testament. The church, in keeping with this New Testament ethic, has historically viewed sexual relations as appropriate only within the context of a monogamous, permanent, heterosexual marriage.

---

10. My brief reconstruction here follows the standard interpretation of 1 Corinthians 7, i.e., that Paul is addressing a form of asceticism. For interpretations along these lines, see Wright, *Paul for Everyone*, 77; Collins and Harrington, *First Corinthians*, 253.

11. Xenophon of Ephesus, *An Ephesian Tale* 1.3.3 and 1.9.1. For additional examples, see Alexander, "Better to Marry than Burn." Note also Sirach 23:17: "Desire, blazing like a furnace, will not die down until it has been satisfied; the man who is shameless in his body will not stop until the fire devours him."

12. See the helpful comments of Garland, *First Corinthians*, 274–75.

So far we have broken no new ground. Nearly all evangelical pastors and ministry leaders agree that sexual activity should be reserved for the marriage relationship.[13] But it is here that evangelical sexual ethics begin to flounder. Our problem is not that we have failed to recognize the New Testament prohibition against premarital sexual activity. Rather, we have failed fully to reckon with the reality that there is more to sexual activity than intercourse. Oral sex, fondling, and mutual masturbation, for example, are all sexual activities. It is inconceivable that the New Testament's ethic—insofar as it is an extension of the Torah—intends to leave room for such activities outside of marriage. Once we embrace the biblical ideal that sexual activity must be reserved for the marriage relationship, the question "How far is too far?"—a perennially vexing question for contemporary singles—is easily answered. If an activity is sexual, it is to be reserved for the marriage relationship.

Yet for the sake of clarity we must press this further. Beyond the seemingly obvious activities noted above, there is real confusion among evangelicals about what constitutes sexual activity. There is a wide array of physical activities that are inherently nonsexual: holding hands, a kiss on the cheek, a peck on the lips, hugging, walking arm in arm, etc., are all nonsexual activities. While sexual arousal may indeed accompany such activities, the activities themselves are not inherently sexual. But there are other physical activities that are exclusively sexual. It is these activities (at least) that must be reserved for the marriage relationship. But how are we to tell which is which?

Perhaps the most objective way to determine the sexual nature of a physical activity is to consider it against the backdrop of the family relationship. Within the context of family relations, there are certain physical forms of affection that are inappropriate (fondling, oral sex, etc.). And the reason such actions are inappropriate is precisely because such activities are sexual. Thus we can quickly intuit which activities are sexual by considering an activity within the context of the family relationship. If an activity would be *sexually* inappropriate between a mother and a son, then that action is clearly of a sexual nature. Or again, the activities that we intuitively exclude from family relationships *because those activities are sexual* are, in fact, sexual activities. To clarify, note here that this way of identifying sexual activity is not primarily concerned about what *I* would (or would not) do with *my* mother, but rather about what is deemed to be generally

---

13. The "Colorado Statement on Biblical Sexual Morality" offers us a standard evangelical articulation: "Sex outside of marriage is never moral. This includes all forms of intimate sexual stimulation that stir up sexual passion between unmarried partners." Quoted in Heimbach, *True Sexual Morality*, 370.

appropriate between biological relatives. While a particular man might never hold hands with his mother (given the interpersonal dynamics of their relationship), that same man would not view it as sexually inappropriate for a mother and son to hold hands. If Genesis 26:8–10 is any indication, even ancient pagan cultures distinguished between sexual and nonsexual activity via the context of the family relationship.[14]

This criterion becomes enormously helpful when considering appropriate premarital boundaries, particularly as it relates to one of the most common physical activities in contemporary dating relationships: passionate kissing. Many (perhaps most) Christian dating couples regularly engage in passionate kissing. And, for the most part, evangelical pastors and leaders have not provided definitive biblical counsel here. Clearly some forms of kissing are nonsexual. Fathers kiss their children, and sons their mothers. But there are other forms of kissing that men and women reserve exclusively for their lovers. And the reason they do so is because such forms of kissing are sexual. When we consider passionate kissing against the backdrop of the family relationship, it quickly becomes clear that passionate kissing is not merely affectionate, but sexual. Under no circumstances would it ever be appropriate for a brother and sister to engage in passionate kissing. Thus we conclude the following:

1. All sexual activity must be reserved for the marriage relationship.
2. Some forms of kissing are sexual. Therefore,
3. Sexual forms of kissing must be reserved for the marriage relationship.

In order to legitimize sexual forms of kissing in a premarital relationship, one would need to (1) provide a cogent rationale for why passionate kissing is not sexual or, alternately, (2) legitimize sexual activity outside of the marriage relationship. The first is counterintuitive to the way human sexuality actually functions. The second runs counter to the ethic of the New Testament.

The objective definition provided by the family test is not the last word on sexual purity. There is, of course, more to purity than how one behaves with the body (Matt 5:27). And every "objective" boundary can be worked around with enough creativity. But, in spite of its limitations, it does provide a solid framework for clearly identifying which bodily activities are inherently sexual. Humans are embodied beings; as such, we need

---

14. Even in ancient pagan Greek culture (not known for espousing a moderate sexual ethic), familial relations were assumed to be nonsexual. Note Alcibiades' comment, regarding his attempted seduction of Socrates, "My night with Socrates went no further than if I had spent it with my own father or older brother!" Plato, *Symposium* 219d.

an embodied ethic. While it *may* be a sexual act for a particular man to look at (talk to, etc.) a particular woman, it is *always* a sexual act when he does something with her that would be sexually inappropriate between immediate blood relatives.

Pastors and ministry leaders have been sending a mixed message about premarital sexual activity. On the one hand, in keeping with the sexual ethic of the New Testament, we've clearly articulated that sexual activity should be reserved for the marriage relationship. But on the other hand, we've largely ignored—or actually legitimized—sexual forms of kissing. We are in effect saying that while sexual activity *is not* permissible in premarital relationships, sexual activity *is* permissible in premarital relationships. If the preceding sentence doesn't make sense to the readers of this chapter, that's because it doesn't make sense.

At its heart, the New Testament sexual ethic calls for premarital relationships to be completely nonsexual. Sexual forms of kissing fall afoul of this ethic, likewise any activity that is sexually inappropriate between immediate blood relatives. Simply put, if an activity is inherently sexual, it is to be reserved for the marriage relationship.[15]

For many, the above argument will suffice as a clear explication and contemporary application of the New Testament's teaching on premarital sexual ethics. But some will want more. The remainder of the chapter offers a christological reading of Scripture that supports the premarital ethic argued for above.

---

15. With the rise of postmodernity, the need to take seriously the cultural distance between the world of the Bible and our own has been increasingly felt. Is it legitimate to import Scripture's vision of sexual ethics directly into today's culture, given that the first-century context didn't have "dating relationships"? A true enough, but largely irrelevant, observation. To point out that there were no "dating relationships" in the first century is a non sequitur. Of course there weren't. What the Bible offers us is a clear sexual ethic for unmarried men and women: *sexual activity is to be reserved for the marriage relationship*. And it is this explicit sexual ethic that must inform contemporary premarital relationships. Evangelicals err when they allow transient cultural structures (i.e., dating relationships) to negate Scripture's clear transcultural sexual ethic. The logic of, "Since we are 'dating,' we don't have to follow the New Testament's sexual ethic for unmarried couples," is not the sort of logic that squares with a proper reading and application of Scripture. As the New Testament scholar N. T. Wright correctly observes, "We cannot relativize the epistles by . . . suggesting any intervening seismic cultural shifts which would render them irrelevant or even misleading." Wright, *Last Word*, 125–26.

A Christocentric Reading of Sex:

Sexual Union as a Type of Christ's Spiritual Union with the Church

In his provocative book on hermeneutics, *The Bible Made Impossible*, Christian Smith argues that the only right way to read and apply the Bible is to examine its ethical teaching through the lens of Christ and the gospel. The Bible, Smith argues, does not offer us a discernibly coherent and unified stance on any one topic. Thus, for Smith, all attempts to arrive at a "biblical" position on any topic (e.g., sexual ethics, finances, relationships, politics, etc.) are doomed from the start. Instead, we are to use the Bible solely as a means of understanding Christ and the gospel. Smith writes:

> The Bible is not about offering things like a biblical view of dating—but rather about how God the Father offered his Son, Jesus Christ, to death to redeem a rebellious world from the slavery and damnation of sin. . . . This is not to say that evangelical Christians will never have theologically informed, moral and practical views of dating and romance . . . they may and will. But the significance and content of all such views will be defined completely in terms of thinking about them in view of the larger facts of Jesus Christ and the gospel.[16]

Smith goes on to muse, "Perhaps God has no interest in providing to us [through the Bible] all of the specific information people so often desire . . . perhaps God wants *us* to figure out how Christians should think well about things like war, wealth, and sanctification."[17] According to Smith, Christians are to use the Bible as a means of gaining a picture of Christ and the gospel, and then use this picture as a means of developing one's own appropriate ethic. In some instances, a christocentric reading of the Bible may lead us in a different direction from the actual stated imperatives of the New Testament.

I do not here highlight Smith's work because I believe it to be the best representation of a christocentric hermeneutic. Indeed, I find Smith's approach significantly problematic.[18] But insofar as critics of my position on

---

16. Smith, *Bible Made Impossible*, 111.

17. Ibid., 112.

18. Smith's proposal represents a departure from the way the Bible has been historically read by the church catholic (not just evangelicals). The fact that we do not share total agreement on a given issue does not mean that we have no agreement. Evangelicals may have four views on the Lord's return, but we all believe he is coming again. The church, broadly and universally construed, has not shared Smith's severe pessimism

premarital sexual ethics tend to resonate with Smith's work, I intend to show that Smith's christocentric hermeneutic—like the more traditional christocentric readings of other evangelical scholars—actually supports the central argument of this chapter.

Fortunately, when it comes to sexual ethics, searching for a christocentric starting point need not take us long. As it happens, Paul provides us with an obviously christocentric reading of sex in Ephesians 5:30–32. In what is certainly the New Testament's most developed treatment of sex and marriage, Paul pointedly describes the sexual relationship within marriage as an image of the spiritual relationship between Christ and the church. For Paul, sex and marriage typologically point beyond themselves to an ultimate fulfillment in Christ's marriage to the church. Which is to say, sex is fundamentally about Christ and the gospel. Note carefully the significance of the last sentence of verse 32 within its context:

> For no one ever hated his own flesh, but nourishes and cherishes it, just as Christ does the church, because we are members of his body. "Therefore a man shall leave his father and mother and hold fast to his wife, and the two shall become one flesh." This mystery is profound, *and I am saying that it refers to Christ and the church*. (5:30–32, ESV, emphasis added)

Paul is here discussing the relational dynamics of Christian marriage. And as he gives instruction to husbands and wives about how they are to treat one another, he draws a tight parallel between human marriage and Christ's relationship with the church. The way Christ treats the church, Paul tells us, serves as the pattern for the way a husband is to treat his wife. And the way the church relates to Christ is the way a wife is to relate to her husband. But by what logic does Paul ask husbands and wives to relate to one another as Christ and the church? The answer is found in verse 32. The sexual oneness of human marriage, Paul tells us, "*refers* to Christ and the church." Drawing on the ancient marriage formula of Genesis 2:24, Paul reveals that sexual oneness within marriage was created by God to serve as a typological foreshadowing of the spiritual oneness that has now begun to exist between Christ and his church. The New Testament's many references to the church as the "bride" of Christ, and to Christ as the "bridegroom," further highlights this parallel. Additionally, many of Christ's parables use the wedding motif as an illustration of his return and consummate union

---

about the legitimacy of attempting to discern and apply the imperatives of Scripture—however difficult this may be to do well. For a more balanced hermeneutic that takes seriously the challenges of applying the biblical imperatives across cultures, see Vanhoozer, *Drama of Doctrine*; and Wright, *New Testament and the People of God*, 121–44.

with the church. And the book of Revelation explicitly refers to the wedding supper of the Lamb as inaugurating the dawn of the eternal age.[19]

What Paul says here about marriage is equally true about sex itself. True Christian marriage cannot be constituted apart from sexual union. The phrase οἱ δύο εἰς σάρκα μίαν ("the two shall be one flesh"), used in 5:31, speaks specifically about sexual union, not simply marital union in a general, legal sense (see 1 Cor 6:16, where Paul deploys the identical "one flesh" phrase to denote sexual union with a prostitute). Within the context of the Ephesians passage, the metaphor of bodily union (i.e., head to body) is tied intimately to the sexual relationship. For Paul, sex establishes and creates the bodily union upon which true marriage is based.[20] Thus Paul's statement that marriage is a type of Christ's relationship to the church is at the same time a statement that sexual union is a type of Christ's spiritual union with the church (again see 1 Cor 6:16–17 for this close parallel).

And of course this makes sense when we consider the relational dynamics of sex. Sex, when understood from a christocentric framework, is the mutual self-giving and joyful receiving of the husband and wife. John Paul II, in his *Man and Woman He Created Them: A Theology of the Body*, pushes back against the Cartesian depersonalization of the body and rightly presses home the point that man does not simply *have* a body, but in a certain sense *is* a body. Thus sex, as the union of male and female bodies, is properly (and theologically) understood as a form of personal communion—a "gift of self." Thus, when a man pursues a woman sexually,

---

19. The church has traditionally understood the marriage relationship through a typological framework. See *2 Clement* 14:2; Augustine, *On Forgiveness of Sins, and Baptism*, I.60; Thomas Aquinas, *Summa* III.42.1. Calvin, commenting on Ephesians 5:23, states, "Christ has appointed the same relation to exist between a husband and a wife, as between himself and his church." Calvin, *Commentaries on . . . Galatians and Ephesians*, 317–18. So too, Luther, while denying that types are inherently sacramental, still affirms, "Christ and the church are . . . a great and secret thing which can and ought to be represented in terms of marriage as a kind of outward allegory." Luther, *On the Babylonian Captivity of the Church*, 223. Jonathan Edwards states explicitly, "[Christ is] united to you by a spiritual union, so close as to be fitly represented by the union of the wife to the husband." "The Excellency of Christ, 1758," in Edwards, *Sermons of Jonathan Edwards*, 186. Karl Barth also follows this pattern in his extended comments on the relationship between men and women. See Barth, *Church Dogmatics* III/2.285–324. Many modern evangelical commentators embrace this typological interpretation as well.

20. In the ancient world—far more than today—sex was viewed as the means by which a marriage was constituted. However, even in the ancient world there was more to marriage than sex (e.g., see John 4:18 and the woman at the well). Marriage in the ancient world began at betrothal—generally a formal agreement between the families of the bride and groom—and was consummated through sex on the wedding day. For more on marriage in the ancient world, see Campbell, *Marriage and Family in the Biblical World*.

what he desires (even if he does not realize it) is not simply the surrendering of her body to him as a material object, but rather her *personal* openness to receive him as a gift. In sex the man offers himself to the woman as a gift, and he finds his joy in her opening herself to receive him as the gift he offers of himself. And she, for her part, finds her joy in yielding herself to another before whom she is vulnerable, who seeks her joy in the giving of himself, who uses his strength to bless rather than totalize. And in this way she too is gift to him, for she gives herself as gift to him in that she opens within herself a place for him to dwell, trusting and receiving the man's gift of self, and returning it in like kind. Most significantly, this mutual giving and receiving of the self may result in new life—a child. The man places his very life in the woman, and she receives and nurtures it (and thus him) in an expression of personal communion so profound that it actually has the power to instantiate the *imago Dei*.

All of this finds its deepest meaning in Christ's relationship with the church. We give ourselves as gift to Christ in the free surrender of ourselves, that we might joyfully receive him as gift. He *himself* is the gift of grace that we receive, and we *ourselves* are the gift that we give to Christ. We find our joy in opening to him and making room for him to dwell within us, and he finds his joy in placing himself—and thus his life, via his Holy Spirit—inside of us and being joyfully received by us. Thus Paul frames for us a view of sex and marriage whereby they are not ends in themselves, but rather are *types* of something higher, pointing to the deeper reality of the believer's union with Christ. Just as the sacrifice of the Passover lamb in the Old Testament foreshadowed Christ's atoning sacrifice in the New, so too the mutual self-giving and joyful receiving of spousal love "refers to Christ and the church" (Eph 5:29).[21]

Even without considering the explicit imperatives in the New Testament, Paul's christocentric reading of sex provides us with a theological framework for thinking about the whole of sexual ethics. Because sexual union functions as a living witness of the spiritual oneness between Christ and the church, our sexual conduct should be patterned after the way in which Christ and the church relate spiritually. The prohibitions against homosexuality, polygamy, incest, prostitution, fornication,

---

21. This typological reading of sex can be found throughout church history. Among the fathers, Origen is noteworthy; see his *Commentary and Homilies on the Song of Songs*. Medieval exegetes likewise read spousal love in this way. See especially John of the Cross, *Spiritual Canticle of the Soul*; and Bernard of Clairvaux, *Sermons on the Song of Songs*. For recent interpretations, see John Paul II, *Man and Woman He Created Them*, 500–503; and Leithart, "Poetry of Sex."

bestiality—indeed all forms of πορνεία—find their ultimate explanation against the backdrop of this reality.[22]

And most significantly, it is within this christocentric framework that we can begin to think constructively about premarital sexual activity. Were we to look beyond the direct imperatives of Scripture (as Smith would have us do) and construct our own premarital sexual ethic based exclusively on a christocentric reading of sex and marriage, we would be pointed toward a conclusion consistent with what I've argued for above. God has ordained sex and marriage as a means of foreshadowing the one-spirit relationship between Christ and the church; therefore, we misuse our sexuality when we express it outside the context of the marriage relationship.

Most fundamentally, our sexuality has not been given to us simply for our own use and pleasure. We are not self-referential. As *eikons* made in the image of God, all of our humanity—not least our sexuality—exists as a means of representing the One in whose image we have been made. Premarital sexual activity, therefore, must be assessed in light of this fundamental context of meaning. Given the theological and typological import of sexual relations, it is difficult (if not impossible) to justify *any* amount of sexual activity outside the context of the marriage relationship, even if that sexual activity stops short of intercourse. Men or women who use their sexuality in a premarital relationship fail to express their sexuality in a way consistent with the ordained intent of sex. God calls us to reserve our sexuality for the marriage relationship, because it is only in the marriage relationship that the image of Christ's relationship to the church can be lived out.

Conclusion

St. Ambrose once said, "The condition of the mind is often seen in the attitude of the body. . . . Thus the movement of the body is a sort of voice of the soul."[23] Indeed it is. And nowhere does the voice of the soul speak louder than in our sexuality. Sex carries such significance in our lives because it was ordained by God to point toward that which is most significant: Christ's relationship with the church. So the misuse of sex damages us in ways that other bodily sins do not. As the apostle Paul states, "Every other sin a person

---

22. In brief, homosexuality fails to denote the union of the masculine and the feminine; prostitution, divorce, and adultery fail to denote Christ's single-minded fidelity to his bride; incest fails to portray the union of dissimilar natures (i.e., the divine and human).

23. Ambrose, *On the Duties of the Clergy* 1.18.

commits is outside the body, but the sexually immoral person sins against his own body" (1 Cor 6:18).

While "thou shalt not make out" is not as explicit as "thou shalt not commit adultery," the Bible does indeed offer us a clear sexual ethic: sexual activity is to be reserved for the marriage relationship. When we combine this sexual ethic with an intuitive understanding that sexual activity includes more than sexual intercourse, we can confidently conclude that all forms of sexual activity—even sexual forms of kissing—must be reserved for the marriage relationship.

For too long pastors and Christian leaders have neglected to provide definitive instruction about the appropriate boundaries of premarital relationships. Telling singles that the Bible has nothing explicit to say about premarital sexual activity beyond its prohibition against intercourse is an unacceptable fulfillment of our pastoral responsibility. The stakes are simply too high, and human sexuality simply too important.

The reigning premarital sexual ethic of evangelicalism is muddled and unclear. The pressing need of the moment is for evangelical pastors and leaders to articulate a clearer, more pastorally responsible premarital ethic—one that is biblically authoritative, theologically robust, and sufficiently objective.[24] May this chapter be a step in that direction.

Bibliography

Alexander, L. A. "Better to Marry than Burn: St. Paul and the Greek Novel." In *Ancient Fiction and Early Christian Narrative*, edited by Ronald F. Hock, J. Bradley Chance, and Judith Perkins, 235–56. SBL Symposium Series 6. Atlanta: Scholars, 1998.
Ambrose, St. *On the Duties of the Clergy*. Benediction Classics, 2010.
Barth, Karl. *Church Dogmatics III/2. The Doctrine of Creation*. Translated by G. W. Bromiley et al. Edited by G. W. Bromily and T. F. Torrance. London: A & C Black, 2004.
Calvin, John. *Commentaries on the Epistles of Paul to the Galatians and Ephesians*. Translated by William Pringle. Electronic ed. Bellingham, WA: Logos, 2010. https://www.logos.com/product/9495/commentaries-on-the-epistles-of-paul-to-the-galatians-and-ephesians.
Campbell, Ken M. *Marriage and Family in the Biblical World*. Downers Grove, IL: InterVarsity, 2003.
Charles, Tyler. "(Almost) Everyone's Doing It." *Relevant*, September 3, 2011. http://archives.relevantmagazine.com/life/relationships/almost-everyones-doing-it.
Clark, Jeramy. *I Gave Dating a Chance: A Biblical Perspective to Balance the Extremes*. Colorado Springs, CO: Waterbrook, 2009.

---

24. Embracing this ethic will inevitably necessitate a rethinking of contemporary dating relationships. For my views on this, see Hiestand and Thomas, *Sex, Dating, and Relationships*.

Collins, Raymond F. *Sexual Ethics and the New Testament: Behavior and Belief.* New York: Crossroad, 2000.

Collins, Raymond F., and Daniel J. Harrington. *First Corinthians.* Sacra Pagina 7. Collegeville, MN: Liturgical, 1999.

Countryman, Louis William. *Dirt, Greed, and Sex: Sexual Ethics in the New Testament and Their Implications for Today.* Minneapolis: Fortress, 1989.

DeYoung, Kevin. "Premarital Sex and Our Love Affair with Bad Stats." *The Gospel Coalition*, December 13, 2011. https://blogs.thegospelcoalition.org/kevindeyoung/2011/12/13/premarital-sex-and-our-love-affair-with-bad-stats.

Edwards, Jonathan. *The Sermons of Jonathan Edwards: A Reader.* Edited by Wilson H. Kimnach, Kenneth P. Minkema, and Douglas A. Sweeney. New Haven, CT: Yale University Press, 2008.

Garland, David E. *1 Corinthians.* Baker Exegetical Commentary on the New Testament. Grand Rapids: Baker Academic, 2003.

Heimbach, Daniel R. *True Sexual Morality: Recovering Biblical Standards for a Culture in Crisis.* Wheaton, IL: Crossway, 2004.

Hiestand, Gerald. "A Biblical-Theological Approach to Premarital Sexual Ethics: Or, What Saint Paul Would Say about 'Making Out.'" *Bulletin of Ecclesial Theology* 1.1 (2014) 13–34.

Hiestand, Gerald, and Jay S. Thomas. *Sex, Dating, and Relationships: A Fresh Approach.* Wheaton, IL: Crossway, 2012.

John of the Cross, Saint. *A Spiritual Canticle of the Soul and the Bridegroom Christ.* Lulu. com, 2016.

John Paul II, Pope. *Man and Woman He Created Them: A Theology of the Body.* Translated by Michael Waldstein. Boston: Pauline, 2006.

Leithart, Peter. "The Poetry of Sex." *First Things*, January 13, 2012. https://www.firstthings.com/web-exclusives/2012/01/the-poetry-of-sex.

Loader, William. *Sexuality in the New Testament: Understanding the Key Texts.* Louisville: Westminster John Knox, 2010.

Louw, J. P., and Eugene Albert Nida. *Greek-English Lexicon of the New Testament: Based on Semantic Domains.* 2nd ed. United Bible Societies, 1989.

Luther, Martin. *On the Babylonian Captivity of the Church.* Translated by Albert T. W. Steinhaeuser. Edited and modernized by Robert E. Smith. Online ed. Project Wittenberg, 2002. http://www.projectwittenberg.org/etext/luther/babylonian/babylonian.htm.

McDowell, Josh, and Bob Hostetler. *Right from Wrong.* Dallas: Word, 1994.

Smith, Christian. *The Bible Made Impossible: Why Biblicism Is Not a Truly Evangelical Reading of Scripture.* Grand Rapids: Baker, 2012.

Vanhoozer, Kevin J. *The Drama of Doctrine: A Canonical-Linguistic Approach to Christian Theology.* Louisville: Westminster John Knox, 2005.

Wright, N. T. *The Last Word: Beyond the Bible Wars to a New Understanding of the Authority of Scripture.* New York: HarperCollins, 2009.

———. *The New Testament and the People of God.* Christian Origins and the Question of God. London: Fortress, 1992.

———. *Paul for Everyone: 1 Corinthians.* Louisville: Westminster John Knox, 2004.

9

What About Sex?

Habits of Heart for a Fulfilling Sexual Relationship and a Happy Marriage

Mary Rice Hasson

Sex. We talk about it openly. The culture is saturated with it. Images of sexual activity not only fill the big screen but also arrive (perhaps unbidden) on our personal media devices—explicit sexual imagery, personalized and delivered, in a matter of seconds. Popular dating apps, like Tinder, Grindr, and others, put casual sex at our fingertips, literally, with a "swipe right" and then a rendezvous. Although the "hookup culture" has been somewhat exaggerated,[1] and singles routinely overestimate how often *other* singles are having sex, 45 percent of millennials (those born between 1982 and 2004) say that they have engaged in casual sex.[2]

Research consistently has shown that men and women both report feelings of regret from casual sexual encounters, although women are more likely than men to report regret or develop depressive symptoms and guilt feelings.[3] Still, a strong majority of millennials (58 percent) believes there's nothing at all wrong with premarital sex.[4] "Millennials," as one researcher

---

1. Lapp, "Transforming Hookup Culture."
2. Shire, "Millennials Are Very Mixed Up about Sex."
3. Garcia et al., "Sexual Hookup Culture."
4. Twenge, Sherman, and Wells, "Changes in American Adults' Sexual Behavior and Attitudes," 2273. The study found: "Adults in 2000–2012 (vs. the 1970s and 1980s) had more sexual partners, were more likely to have had sex with a casual date or pickup or an acquaintance, and were more accepting of most nonmarital sex (premarital sex, teen sex, and same-sex sexual activity, but not extramarital sex). The percentage who

noted, "hold the most permissive sexual attitudes of any generation," although they "have sex with fewer partners" than adults of previous generations at the same age.[5] Traditional norms about sex have been thrown to the curb, leaving just one "rule of the road" to be followed: get consent.

That's the general cultural script anyway. But surely Christians approach sex differently? Well, not exactly.

As Christians, we understand sexual intercourse as a deeply intimate expression of love within marriage. It's a one-flesh, pleasurable union of man and woman that bonds us more deeply to one another. It carries with it the awe-inspiring power to be co-creators with God of new human beings who will live forever. Sex is celebrated in the Song of Solomon and enriched by the poetics of St. Paul's description of love in 1 Corinthians 13:4–8. It's an integral part of God's plan for marriage, a way to generate love and new generations here on earth. In short, sex is a wonderful gift from God, our Creator!

It's also powerful. When misused, our sexual desires can become a source of misery, pain, exploitation, and jealousy. When severed from love and its procreative potential, sex is at risk of becoming a tool for personal gratification, a selfish, solitary act in which one person is used for another's fleeting pleasure. When it's not "handled with care," sex can detonate a series of sins, from selfishness to lust to jealousy to rage. So it's not surprising that the God who loves us also provides us with clear instructions about how to use—or not use—such a powerful gift.

When it comes to premarital sex, the biblical commands seem clear enough: premarital sex is morally wrong. In Mark 7:20–23 (RSV), Jesus identifies "fornication" as one of the particular sins that "defile a man."[6] St. Paul warns against sexual immorality in numerous passages, including Galatians 5:19–21 ("The acts of the sinful nature are obvious: sexual immorality, impurity, and debauchery"), 1 Corinthians 6:18–20 ("those who sin sexually sin against their own bodies"), and 1 Thessalonians 4:3–5

---

believed premarital sex among adults was 'not wrong at all' was 29 percent in the early 1970s, 42 percent in the 1980s and 1990s, 49 percent in the 2000s, and 58 percent between 2010 and 2012.... [T]he trend toward greater sexual permissiveness was primarily due to generation."

5. Twenge, Sherman, and Wells, "Changes in American Adults' Sexual Behavior and Attitudes." Comparing sexual attitudes and behaviors from the 1970s through 2010s, the researchers found that while only 29 percent of adults in the 70s approved of premarital sex, 55 percent approved of it four decades later.

6. Mark 7:20–23: "And he said, 'What comes out of a man is what defiles a man. For from within, out of the heart of man, come evil thoughts, fornication, theft, murder, adultery, coveting, wickedness, deceit, licentiousness, envy, slander, pride, foolishness. All these evil things come from within, and they defile a man.'"

("you should avoid sexual immorality . . . learn to control your own body in a way that is holy and honorable not in passionate lust like the pagans, who do not know God"). Overall, more than twenty biblical passages teach against sexual immorality (or *porneia*, which is commonly interpreted to mean fornication).[7]

Nevertheless, while religious and nonreligious young adults diverge when it comes to their lifetime number of sexual partners[8] (churchgoers tend to have fewer), Christians don't seem convinced that avoiding premarital sex is all that important. According to a recent survey of subscribers on a Christian dating site (Christian Mingle), 61 percent of Christians say they are willing to have premarital sex.[9] A 2009 study of young Christian adults (18–29) found that 80 percent of them had engaged in premarital sex.[10] A more recent survey by Gallup (2016) shows that 50 percent of Protestant adults and 68 percent of Catholics say that premarital sex is morally acceptable.[11] In recent years, moreover, a growing number of Christian denominations, theologians, and writers have backed a "contextualized" interpretation of the Bible that approves of various nonmarital sexual activities as long as they occur in the context of a loving relationship.[12]

---

7. See, for example, Gal 5:19–21: "The acts of the sinful nature are obvious: sexual immorality, impurity, and debauchery; idolatry and witchcraft; hatred, discord, jealousy, fits of rage, selfish ambition, dissensions, factions, and envy; drunkenness, orgies, and the like. I warn you, as I did before, that those who live like this will not inherit the kingdom of God." Also: 1 Corinthians 6:18–20: "Flee from sexual immorality. All other sins people commit are outside their bodies, but those who sin sexually sin against their own bodies. Do you not know that your bodies are temples of the Holy Spirit, who is in you, whom you have received from God? You are not your own; you were bought at a price. Therefore, honor God with your bodies."

8. Twenge, Sherman, and Wells, "Changes in American Adults' Sexual Behavior and Attitudes." On the other hand, older adults, including religious adults, may be making up for lost time. So-called gray divorce, divorce among married couples over fifty, has spiked in recent years, nearly doubling over the past several decades. See Stepler, "Led by Baby Boomers, Divorce Rates Climb."

9. O'Neil, "Christians Are Following Secular Trends."

10. Blake, "Why Young Christians Aren't Waiting Anymore."

11. Jones, "U.S. Religious Groups Disagree." Of all denominations, Mormons expressed the strongest commitment to traditional sexual morality, with just 29 percent agreeing that premarital sex is morally acceptable.

12. For example, the blog of the organization The Christian Left argues that injunctions against premarital sex reflect the ancient context in which women were property and virgins brought a higher bride price. See Toy, "Premarital Sex." Christian author Bromleigh McClenghan takes a permissive stance towards premarital sex in McClenghan, *Good Christian Sex*. The Evangelical Lutheran Church in America (ELCA) approved in 2009 a social statement on "Human Sexuality" that does not disapprove of premarital sex per se, but of "non-monogamous, promiscuous, or casual

These are troubling trends for two reasons: first, the statistics suggest that many Christians regard biblically based moral norms about sex as purely optional, a personal preference. Indeed, many young Christians seem to relate to God as "Moralistic Therapeutic Deists," a term coined by Notre Dame sociologist Christian Smith.[13] God's role, it seems, is to be a problem solver and to make people happy. A person whose approach to the Christian moral life is more therapeutic deism than discipleship "will tend not to have strong opinions about sex, beyond affirming the importance of consent. Intercourse outside of marriage, masturbation, the use of contraception, homosexuality (including same-sex marriage), transgenderism—none of it will register as raising significant moral or theological issues and problems," according to Smith.[14]

Unfortunately, therapeutic deism numbs the conscience and renders the heart lukewarm—not the signs of a committed Christian![15] Moral and sexual integrity *do* matter in our relationships with God and others. The virtuous Christian life requires them. When we acknowledge God as our Creator, loving him because "he first loved us" (1 John 4:19), we are called to humbly submit our entire being to him, including our sexuality. These are essential truths about the Christian life.

There's much to unfold about these foundational truths (and some of the other chapters in this book do so quite well). But my purpose here is really to focus on the second reason why current sexual trends are quite troubling.

The easy slide among Christians towards permissive sexual attitudes is worrisome. But equally worrisome is the *unrecognized* impact of our sexualized culture on the assumptions and habits of believing Christians. Although Christians still tend to hold more conservative views on sexual morality—at

---

sexual relationships" because they fail to "create the context for trust in sexual intimacy." Catholic teachings on sexuality clearly prohibit premarital sex. Catechism of the Catholic Church, "The Sixth Commandment" (par. 2353). Some Catholic theologians reject this teaching, arguing for contextual approaches that permit "loving" nonmarital sexual relationships. E.g., see Farley, *Just Love.*

13. Smith and Denton, *Soul Searching.* They describe Moralistic Therapeutic Deism as "the de facto dominant religion among contemporary teenagers in the United States." Teenagers they interviewed believed that "[a] God exists who created and orders the world and watches over human life. . . . God wants people to be good, nice, and fair to each other. . . . The central goal of life is to be happy and to feel good about oneself. . . . God does not need to be particularly involved in one's life except . . . to resolve a problem. . . . Good people go to heaven when they die."

14. Linker, "Why So Many Conservative Christians Feel like a Persecuted Minority."

15. See Rev 3:15–16: "I know your works: you are neither cold nor hot. Would that you were cold or hot! So, because you are lukewarm, and neither cold nor hot, I will spew you out of my mouth."

least compared to their nonreligious peers—those differences should not be interpreted to mean that Christians, generally speaking, "get it right" on sexual integrity. In fact, much has been written about the high divorce rates among self-professed Christians (the Bible Belt has a high rate of marriage dissolution). How seriously we adhere to Christianity matters a great deal. Thus, it is not surprising that those who attend church most frequently (one sign of intentionality about faith) also have the lowest divorce rates.[16] We carry the common human burden of sin and weakness in the face of temptation. That's to be expected. Throwing aside traditional Christian norms on sexuality, without even putting up a fight (so to speak), is not.

Much of the problem lies in the culture. Christians breathe the same cultural air, walk the same broken paths, and struggle to see over the horizon of same confusing cultural landscape, just like their non-Christian peers. Christians need to be wary of absorbing the culture's firmly embedded, but faulty, narratives about sex. Unless those false narratives are recognized for what they are and resisted, they inevitably will influence personal attitudes, expectations, and actions. Individuals who unwittingly build up harmful habits of heart—by engaging in premarital sex, for example—eventually discover that they may have undermined their prospects for long-lasting happiness. Toxic habits of the heart can render a sexual relationship meaningless, lackluster, or exploitative. They can destroy relationships by shattering trust, eroding commitment, and causing unhappiness—even among good people who intended "forever marriages."

Anyone who hopes to live with sexual integrity, enjoy human flourishing, and embrace God's plan for marriage must appraise critically the cultural assumptions now in play—and then examine his or her own habits of heart. By intentionally turning towards greater virtue, young adults can become loving, generous spouses well on the road to happy, mutually fulfilling, lifelong marriages.

In the pages that follow, I identify two toxic assumptions that underlie permissive sexual ethics. They are hidden land mines that become embedded early in a sexual relationship, and risk detonating and destroying not only the sexual relationship but also an eventual marriage. Writ large, these assumptions are changing who we are as a society, with troubling consequences for the most vulnerable among us.

---

16. French, "Little Religion Is Terrible for Marriage." For a good summary of the studies in this area, see also Stokes et al., "Bit of Religion Can Be Bad for Marriage."

The Consent Mentality: Permission to Use You for My Pleasure

Sexual ethics in today's culture can be reduced to two words: "get consent."[17] Among adults, anything goes as long as all parties agree.[18] The underlying mindset is selfish, solo, and egoistic: sex is really about me, and about getting permission to use someone else for my personal pleasure. Christianity, in contrast, understands human sexuality in the context of relationship: we are made one for another, and the one-flesh union of marital sexuality reflects a mutual, permanent, personal commitment of our entire lives to each other. "They are no longer two, but one flesh," called to mutual love in an indissoluble relationship (Matt 19:6). As St. Paul wrote, "Husbands, love your wives, as Christ loved the church and gave himself up for her, that he might sanctify her. . . . For this reason a man shall leave his father and mother and be joined to his wife, and the two shall become one. This is a great mystery, and I mean in reference to Christ and the Church" (Eph 5:26–27, 31–32). The Christian view of marriage and relationships stands in stark contrast to the transactional framework of modern relationships.

Changes in law, as well as culture, have stripped sexuality of its relational context and reinforced the "consenting adults" paradigm. Aside from laws prohibiting prostitution, polygamy, and sexual crimes (which by definition lack consent), few legal constraints on adult sexual behavior remain on the books.[19] These changes reflect deep ideological and moral divides. In the bigger picture, public discourse around sexuality no longer centers on

17. Because reports of sexual assaults on college campuses have increased, the Obama Justice Department sought to "change the conversation" around sexuality, ostensibly in response to campus rape fears, and normalized a transactional view of sex in the process. The Affirmative Consent Project promotes the "Yes Means Yes" campaign and "Affirmative Consent Kits" (sex agreements) to colleges and advocacy groups, creating an expectation that sexual consent, an expression of personal sexual autonomy, must be explicit, never assumed. Feminist groups admirably raised the issue that intoxicated young women are unable to consent to sexual intercourse, but their solution emphasizes a mechanized process of affirmative consent rather than mutual respect and sexual self-restraint.

18. In today's culture, a small but growing number of sexual relationship include other parties, such as temporary threesomes, "open" marriages, or polyamorous relationships.

19. Laws restricting the sale of contraceptives, outlawing abortion, and prohibiting sodomy have all been struck down. Laws against prostitution ("sex work"), polygamy, and even incest are current targets of legal reformers, fueled by the rising visibility of polyamory, the continued deconstruction of kinship relationships, and the shifting definitions of "family." Adultery is one exception to this liberalizing trend: by large majorities, Americans still believe adultery is wrong; and it remains illegal in twenty-one states, but is rarely prosecuted. Rhode, "Why Is Adultery Still a Crime?"

religion, morality, or personal responsibility, but on "sexual rights" as a new subset of human rights.[20] By and large, sexual rights are rooted in atheistic individualism and sexual autonomy. According to the International Planned Parenthood Federation (IPPF), sexual autonomy means that each person has the right to make personal decisions "on matters related to sexuality, to choose their sexual partners, to seek to experience their full sexual potential and pleasure, within a framework of nondiscrimination and with due regard to the rights of others and to the evolving capacity of children."[21] IPPF's *Declaration on Sexual Rights* (2008), written to "explicitly identify sexual rights and support an inclusive vision of sexuality," frames "sexual rights" as "an evolving set of entitlements related to sexuality."[22]

Don't miss the important word: entitlements. It's indicative of the mindset at work: individuals are *entitled* to sexual pleasures and experiences, limited only by the need to obtain consent from other participants.[23] From the start, then, the individual approaches sex as a consumer rather than as a lover or a giver.

Individual sexual entitlement helps drive the current emphasis on consent as the only relevant boundary in sexual relationships. The consent boundary is the downstream result of an ideology that takes God out of the conversation, rejects moral absolutes, and equates the good with my choice. As Timothy Hsiao observed in a piece for *Public Discourse*, "The most obvious problem with basing sexual morality on consent is that we can consent to things that are bad for us. . . . Consent only has value insofar as it is used to make decisions based on knowledge of what is good for us. The issue then becomes one of determining what is in fact good for us as human beings."[24]

---

20. Progressive groups work transnationally to codify the concept of sexual rights or "sexual and reproductive health and rights" in international law and human rights conventions. To date, they have been unsuccessful. Sexual rights and sexual autonomy appear only in nonbinding United Nations documents and resolutions. See the Sexual Rights Initiative, http://www.sexualrightsinitiative.com/sexual-rights/intro-to-sexual-rights. The International Planned Parenthood Federation has advocated for sexual rights, including the sexual rights of adolescents, for years. In 2008 it published *Sexual Rights: An IPPF Declaration* in more than a dozen languages, and in 2011 published a version dedicated to youth sexual rights.

21. International Planned Parenthood Federation, *Sexual Rights*.

22. "Sexual rights are constituted by a set of entitlements related to sexuality that emanate from the rights to freedom, equality, privacy, autonomy, integrity, and dignity of all people." Ibid.

23. The idea of sexual entitlements is complex in today's casual sexual environment. Campus sexual assaults are interpreted in some universities as a problem of male sexual entitlement, but women claim their own sexual entitlements—the right to have casual sex and be promiscuous without being "slut-shamed."

24. Hsiao, "Limits of Consent."

Put differently, the problem with the consent standard is that it asks too little. It fails to take into account either the inalienable dignity of the human person (which cannot be disregarded, even with consent) or the objective reality of good and evil (i.e., what God desires for us and what God forbids). Authentic sexual decision-making asks not, "Have all parties consented?" but rather, "In light of the dignity of the person in front of me, and my own dignity, and the good that God desires for us both, how must I act?"

So what happens when a Christian absorbs the cultural mindset that consent is the only requirement that matters? He or she will likely set sexual boundaries accordingly. Little by little, everything is on the table, from whether or not to engage in premarital sex, to the use of pornography, to kinky practices. He or she may begin to see his or her partner differently—less as a person to be loved and cherished and more as a means for one's own sexual release or excitement. Selfishness and insensitivity may creep into their intimate moments, sowing seeds of resentment or sadness.

In real life, because we are persons, it's hard to contain selfish habits to one area of life. A person who is selfish in the bedroom will become selfish with her time outside the bedroom. A person habituated to using another sexually is at risk of bringing a transactional approach into other areas of his life. Interestingly, a survey of "morning after" feelings found that both women and men experienced negative feelings connected with sexually "using" (or being used by) another person—even where there was consent all around. Although women felt more negatively about allowing themselves to be used during casual sexual encounters, a fair number of men also expressed regret over having used young women sexually.[25] Down deep, we know there's something wrong about treating ourselves or others like things, of little value, to be tossed aside when they are no longer useful or are all used up.

When we lose sight of others as persons to be loved, no matter what, it's easy to begin measuring the "costs" and "benefits" of the relationship. No relationship can stand up to such metrics in the long haul, because the truth is that we are all dependent, needy, and difficult at times. As Scott Stanley observed, "To really avoid the possibility of heartache and family instability, one would need to avoid love, sex, and children altogether."[26] The personal "benefits" of the sacrifices needed in married life are not always easy to see. A sacrificial heart and the rock-solid commitment that enable a marriage to

---

25. Campbell, "Morning after the Night Before." And it has been suggested that women have evolved adaptations for this strategy. One piece of evidence supporting such a female adaptation would be that women find the experience of a one-night stand as affectively positive as men.

26. Stanley, "How to Lower Your Risk of Divorce."

go the distance are fashioned by the habitual practice of love and generosity, precisely when it's tough.

So what's an unmarried Christian to do, amidst the cultural pressures to be sexually intimate? First, be at peace. The Lord God who gave you this great gift of sexuality will help you live in a way that honors him. As you turn to him, it will be easier to keep sight of others' God-given dignity and eternal destiny. In humility, partners in a relationship must acknowledge the preeminent place of each person's relationship with the Lord. (The couple's personal relationship, when it's working right, should draw both people closer to the Lord, rather than away. If not, consider it a sign that something's seriously amiss.) Second, integrate your sexuality more fully into your Christian identity. Act with respect and love in all circumstances. Respect for the other's dignity before God means keeping the whole person in view, developing a respect and appreciation for the *person*, rather than lusting after sexual body parts. A sexual ethic based on dignity and love never treats the other person as a thing to be used or a means to an end. It means never asking the person to engage in degrading sexual activities or to do something contrary to the Lord's commands. It means having the clarity of mind and conviction of heart to refuse to engage in demeaning, degrading, or sinful activities even if the other person invites or "consents." (Because our dignity is inalienable, we have no right, before God, to consent to degradation or disobedience.)

Perhaps a simple (though absurd) example will illustrate the inadequacy of consent (as opposed to human dignity) as the boundary of sexual decision-making. Let's say you knock on my door and offer to pay me $10,000 if I will let you amputate my right arm and practice a new surgical technique to reattach it. You are a fledgling surgeon, you need practice, and you hope your new technique will help other patients in the future. And you're excited about trying something new with a willing participant (we're longtime friends). Because I am short of cash, and I want to help you out, I say yes. You numb me up, cut off my arm (after checking with me at various junctures to be sure I was still willing), and are about to try reattaching it when the police arrive and arrest us both (sending me to the hospital first).

My consent to be experimented upon won't keep you out of jail, because it cannot justify your actions, or mine. Why? Because, as a human being, I have an inherent dignity and value. It's wrong to treat me as a means (a surgical practice dummy or a source of biological spare parts) to a good end (making you a better surgeon or putting my bank account in the black), no matter how many times I consent. It is wrong for *anyone* to treat me in a degrading or dehumanizing way, even if I have apparently given permission.

It's a ludicrous example, but it makes the point: human beings have a God-given dignity and purpose and our actions are good only to the extent they respect that dignity and align with that purpose—consenting to be treated in a lesser way doesn't change this truth.

So it is in the sexual realm. As a person with an inalienable dignity, I have no authority to give you permission to treat me in a degrading fashion. Even if I do not recognize my own dignity, your duty towards me, as a fellow human being, is to treat me with dignity anyway. Consider the woman who prostitutes herself or appears in pornographic videos quite willingly—a Christian man who "hires" her or lusts after her from afar is using her for selfish ends. He exploits her—and her permission does not change that fact. Similarly, Christian singles who are lonely, sexually frustrated, or just looking for a fun or exciting evening have no right to use another person to fulfill their sexual or emotional desires, consent notwithstanding. Even engaged couples need to be cautious here; although they love one another and *intend* to enter into that lifelong commitment, they are not there yet. Commitment-to-be-committed isn't the same as commitment-in-fact. They have no right to each other's bodies until they freely give themselves to each other in marriage, in a lifelong exchange of their persons, fully committed to love each other until death.[27] The *meaning* of sex is to express a lifelong commitment—it is literally a personal gift of oneself. The giving and receiving of a gift so incredible—literally the gift of another person—should happen only in the context of a loving, permanent relationship, such as marriage. Making that commitment publicly, in the company of family and friends who will support the couple and hold them accountable to their commitment, emphasizes the nature of the commitment.

The consent framework for relationships, with its accompanying consequentialist mindset, causes problems for married couples as well. When consent is the only gatekeeper, married couples may begin justifying sexual activities that degrade each other or dishonor their commitments to fidelity. ("We're married, after all, so there's nothing we can't do.") For example, a husband who pressures his wife to watch pornography with him breaks his commitment to be faithful (even a virtual other woman is still another woman) and degrades his wife by his request. A wife who suggests to her

---

27. The married couple exchanges vows and then, in consummating the marriage, exchanges the gift of persons, becoming one flesh, giving and receiving the other in a lifelong bond. This language of the body echoes the language of the vows exchanged. When a couple has sex without being married, the language of the body is a hollow sound—deprived of its true meaning, because there is no genuine giving and receiving of the other, no mutual promise to love the other, unconditionally, no permanent commitment.

husband that they engage in sexual bondage or sadomasochism similarly degrades him and their relationship. (The bestseller status among women of the *Fifty Shades of Grey* series is an indication of the degree to which the consent mentality has dislodged mutual respect and authentic sexual ethics.) Mutual consent does not legitimize those practices, which rely on domineering and demeaning the other, inflicting pain, and treating the other as a thing to increase one's own sexual pleasure.

In sum, relying on consent in premarital relationships has the potential to create difficulties later in marriage. It's hard to unlearn attitudes. In addition to selfishness and disregard for the dignity of the other person, the consent mindset tends to be legalistic, and thus more easily loses sight of the other person's humanity and need for unconditional love. It feeds the habit of using the other person for one's own self-gratification (albeit with the other person's permission), and it fails in respect and genuine charity. As Christians, surely we can do better.

Sex Makes Babies: Let's Take that Seriously

The second toxic assumption relates to children. It's no secret that contraception was a game-changer for the sexual revolution. The pill made it possible for women to be more like men—to have sex without worrying about making babies. And that's been the promise for the past fifty years—that sex is now different. Babies are optional. With the connection between sex and procreation severed (by hormones, barriers, surgery, and whatnot), singles over the past few decades have celebrated their "freedom." Casual sex, hookup sex, multipartner sex, "monogamish" marriages—it's all possible, and indeed incentivized, because medicine has off-loaded the "burden" of children from the natural biological process. Once children were no longer considered to be a predictable consequence of sexual intercourse, children's interests took a back seat to adult interests, both in government policy and in family, religious, and neighborly conversations about sex, intimacy, marriage, and cohabitation.

But reality has a way of intruding. Sex still makes babies. And contraception fails. So children show up, needing mothers and fathers, together when possible. Data supports the view that children generally do better when born and raised in a married, two-parent home.[28] And sex continues

---

28. Goodnow, "Why Do the Kids of Married Parents Do Better?"; Regnerus, "Married Mom and Dad Really Do Matter." Sawhill, in *Generation Unbound*, agrees that children do better in married, two-parent families, but she argues that the decline in marriage is irreversible and can be offset by discouraging unwed pregnancy (through

to makes babies, even with contraceptives widely used. A 2006 study, for example, reported that 84 percent of abortion-seeking women had used contraception during the month they conceived, and only 16 percent said they were not using contraceptives when they became pregnant.[29] Women must face the reality that having sex within an uncommitted (unmarried) relationship, or one not well-suited to raising children, is a risky proposition. Unmarried couples that have children together are likely to split up.[30] One recent study found that 93 percent of parents who are still together by the time their child is sixteen are *married* parents; far fewer cohabiting parents go the distance together.[31]

Children's needs are forcing the conversation anew, but the answers sound like "more of the same." The proposed fix for the current reality (that sex still makes babies) is contraception: more effective contraception, free contraception, wider access to contraception, and (of course) abortion as the fail-safe.[32] Scholar Isabel Sawhill, the author of *Generation Unbound: Drifting into Sex and Parenthood without Marriage*, recognizes the problems created when children are raised in fractured or never-formed families, typically headed by single women. Her solution is to urge the creation of a new cultural default—an expectation that "adults only have children when they are ready to be a parent."[33]

That sounds like a great idea. Except that she is not suggesting that parents, pastors, teachers, or policy-makers start communicating to teens and young adults that sex is something to take seriously. Nor is she suggesting that adults think very carefully, before engaging in sex, about whether their potential sexual partner is ready to be a parent. Although she acknowledges that marriage is the best place to raise children, and that sex begets children, she is unwilling to draw the logical conclusion: that

---

long-acting reversible contraception) and supporting single or cohabiting parents.

29. Schünmann and Glasier, "Measuring Pregnancy Intention and Its Relationship with Contraceptive Use"; Tsui, McDonald-Mosley, and Burke, "Family Planning and the Burden of Unintended Pregnancies."

30. "According to the 2013 National Marriage Project's *Knot Yet Report*, children of cohabiting parents in their twenties are three times more likely to experience the dissolution of their family than children born to married parents. See also the Fragile Families & Child Wellbeing Study, which found that "nearly half of parents who are cohabiting at the time of their child's birth break up within five years, compared to only 20 percent of married parents." Elhage, "For Kids, Parental Cohabitation and Marriage Are Not Interchangeable."

31. Bingham, "Almost No Couples with Children Who Stay Unmarried Stay Together."

32. Richards, "Protecting and Expanding Access to Birth Control."

33. Sawhill, *Generation Unbound*.

sex belongs in marriage. Instead, Sawhill favors interventions that provide long-acting reversible contraception, such as IUDs, to teenagers and low-income single women—the women least ready to be parents. This policy raises numerous red flags, including the possibility that pressuring poor women to use long-acting forms of contraception, which temporarily sterilize them and which cannot be undone without medical intervention, is perilously reminiscent of the coercive, eugenics-based practices of the past. It also is unrealistic. There is no perfect contraception. A culture invested in perpetuating the sex-without-babies myth will always clamor for abortion as a backup. Sawhill's position spotlights our cultural bargain: we'd rather pay a bloody price for sex without commitment than to treat sex seriously, reserving it for marriage.

And so, our grown-up conversations about sex and relationships ignore the built-in connections between sex and babies, except when we problematize babies. To be a responsible adult is to prevent the "problem" (a child) from occurring, until the perfect time arrives. In the life of a sexually active single, there is no room for babies. The relationship is inherently unstable, defined by its lack of commitment. Sexual intimacy that lacks the stable context of the marital relationship develops a built-in reluctance towards new life (with good reason, practically speaking). If sex occurs soon after a couple meets, it's often a "test run" for whether a relationship is worth pursuing. Preventing pregnancy seems prudent for a woman who is not even sure she wants to be getting texts from her sex partner a week later.

The larger point here is this: for sexually active singles, the prospect of conceiving a child is framed almost universally in negative terms. Premarital sexual relationships, then, become a training ground for a mentality eager for sex but with a strong antipathy towards getting pregnant. During years of premarital sexual activity, young adults habituate themselves into thinking about children as a burden, an obstacle standing in the way of the rest of their life. The culture sends a firm message to sexually active teens and young adults: getting pregnant unexpectedly is a disaster.[34] And

---

34. The public health literature aimed at discouraging unwed childbearing rarely reports on an additional consequence of pregnancy—happiness. Multiple studies show that "many women who experience unintended pregnancies nonetheless report high levels of happiness." The majority of "unintended pregnancies," in fact, are not "unwanted" pregnancies but "mistimed" pregnancies—the mom hoped for a baby, but perhaps six months down the road. The oft-reported data that outcomes for children are worse if the pregnancy is unintended prove to be not quite true: the correlation is weak, and the measure ("unintended pregnancy") is the target of "numerous thoughtful critiques," suggesting it is no longer an appropriate measure of childbearing intentions or policy development. More complex data analysis shows that women's receptivity to pregnancy is related to *who* her partner is. One subset of women who say that their pregnancies

in times of economic strain the message intensifies: there's "never a good time to have a child."³⁵ Of course, this negative rhetoric is targeted towards the child who results from premarital sex, rather than toward the behavior (premarital sex) that results in premarital pregnancy.³⁶

As with the problematic consent mentality, selfishness and fear are hard to cordon off to a single corner of life. Hearts adamantly foreclosed to new life can become less elastic towards others outside their circle of two and less generous to the needs of each other, especially if those needs become unpredictable and demanding. The physical, emotional, or financial needs of one partner will challenge and often break even long-term sexual relationships, because those relationships lack the scaffolding of commitment and the habits of generosity to support them.

In addition, it's hard to unlearn patterns of self-centeredness, anxiety, and worry that center around the possibility of getting pregnant. Couples who spend their first years together making love behind a metaphorical wall designed to keep children out will not find it easy to tear down that wall with the passage of time. It's not easy to open one's heart in generosity towards a new, unique human being after spending years fearing or dreading their very existence. When I speak to newly pregnant *married* young women, their fear is heartbreaking. They worry about how the baby will change their relationship with their husband. They worry about whether they will enjoy being a mother, or if they will even like the baby. They are fearful of the demands of motherhood. They worry they will be less attractive and unsexy to their man. They worry they won't be a good enough mother. They are angry and fearful about the daunting prospect of balancing work and family. And worst of all, they fear the reality that there's no do-over—having a baby is a decision they can't take back. After ordering their lives for so many years around avoiding the disaster of pregnancy, it's hard to shake that foreboding

---

are "unintended" actually mean that they did not want to become pregnant "with this partner." Kost and Lindberg, "Pregnancy Intentions, Maternal Behaviors, and Infant Health." This points again to the problem of separating sex from procreation in the public mindset—we are habituating people, women especially, to forget that sex makes babies. In so doing, we encourage singles to skip over an incredibly important question (a question that should be asked before sex, not after a pregnancy): is my potential sexual partner someone I believe would be a good father or mother to my children?

35. Gribaldo, Judd, and Kertzer, "Imperfect Contraceptive Society."

36. Public discussions about the negative consequences of premarital sex focus disproportionately on pregnancy. Even aside from the possibility of pregnancy, unmarried sex is never consequence free. Possible negative consequences (apart from pregnancy) include sexually transmitted diseases, broken hearts, unstable relationships, intimate partner violence, emotional stress, regret, depression, disappointment, infertility from delayed childbearing, higher risk of divorce, and more.

feeling. They have taken the culture's message to heart: babies are a fearsome and burdensome thing.

These habits of thought contribute also to a consumer mentality towards children. Once a couple marries, it may be difficult to flip a switch and reframe the possibility of pregnancy as a good or even desirable thing. Yes, some cohabiting couples move towards marriage precisely because they want to have a child. But spending years with a heart in lockdown towards new life also risks creating a consumer attitude towards children—"Ok, I'm ready to buy. But I want the perfect one, not the Down syndrome one, by the way." It will take personal growth and spiritual maturity for a couple to retrain their hearts to accept *all* life as a good, even when not perfectly timed. And if the child God sends looks different from the child of their dreams, they will need to learn that loving the child unconditionally ("as is") means letting go of *their* dreams of the perfect family. It means realizing that a child deserves love simply because she exists, not because of the fulfillment or joy we hope to experience because of her. But these are not lessons easily learned in half-committed relationships that stubbornly, or indifferently, refuse to make room for another.

Taking sex seriously again means acknowledging the goodness of God's design for sex. Our sexual activity is meant to be relational, a gift of self to the other, inherently fruitful and life-giving. The culture has reduced sexuality to a self-gratifying search for pleasure, a drive to consume rather than create. But we can recover the truth and beauty of sexuality. This means rediscovering the intrinsic link between sexual intercourse and *another person*, the connection of sexual love *to relationship* and *to fruitful love*, and appreciating children and family as a beautiful blessing.

Finally, a Word about Trust

> We used to think of sex as you crossed the line now you are in an intimate zone, but now sex is almost a given and it's not the intimate part. . . . The intimate part is getting to know someone and going on a date.[37]

Why do men and women have sex? It's pleasurable, of course. But sex is deeper than that. It's meant to bond men and women together, to create and sustain an intimate relationship built on love, fidelity, and trust. Every

---

37. Kimberly Resnick Anderson, sex therapist, quoted in Bowerman, "Sleeping Together before a First Date." The article refers to *Singles in America*, a Match.com survey and report of five thousand single millennials, available at http://www.singlesinamerica.com/2017.

heart yearns for love and intimacy. And no doubt many men and women think a premarital sexual relationship will become the love relationship they desire. As one marriage expert, Scott Stanley, writes, "Chemistry is great. You want to have that. But chemistry is best developed in a sequence, not as a blinding, binding glue in a relationship you'd otherwise never have chosen."[38] When sex occurs outside the supportive context of a marital commitment, however, it creates a pseudo-intimacy. The sheer fact of being naked with one another creates the illusion of a deeper intimacy. But it's a skin-deep baring of self that simultaneously requires a person to raise the emotional drawbridge ("mustn't get too attached or appear needy"). As one Christian writer observes, casual sex "fails to meet the deeper need for intimacy that sex was designed to give. . . . Multiple partners create mistrust, performance anxiety, and comparison evaluations that are barriers to the deepest levels of intimacy."[39]

At this point, a wise person might raise the obvious question: why become sexually intimate with someone you barely know or is not a suitable relationship partner? A recent survey by Match.com surfaced some contradictions in the way young people approach sex. On the one hand, 48 percent of millennials say they are likely to have sex with a person in order to "see if they have a connection"—to test the prospects for intimacy on other levels. At the same time, 19 percent of men and 19 percent of women say that one-night stands are the "worst sex" ever (while 29 percent of men, but just 15 percent of women, say one-night stands are the "best sex" ever).[40]

In talks to single women, I often raise the question of trust. I ask them how long they would have to know someone before they'd feel comfortable sharing with him their bank account passwords. Almost every time, they come back with lengthy time periods—a year or more, if they'd share their passwords at all. They know, at least when it comes to money, that not all people are trustworthy. They realize they need to know someone for a while and to understand their values, motives, and priorities in order to decide if the person is trustworthy. But when it comes to relationships, the very same women will *trust strangers without reason*. They will open their bodies in the most vulnerable way to someone they barely know, or to an acquaintance they wouldn't trust with their debit card, or to a boyfriend whom they could never envision as the father to their child. At the same time, *they distrust the Lord*, who knows them intimately and whose love

---

38. Stanley, "How to Lower Your Risk of Divorce."
39. McBurney, "Christian Sex Rules."
40. *Singles in America.*

is unshakable, the God whose law will help them find the happiness they seek, if only they will trust him.

If we're going to take sex seriously, then it's time to challenge today's sexually active men and women to ask themselves some hard questions, based on the ideas in this chapter and other chapters as well. First, is your sexual partner willing to make a commitment to you? (The only commitment that really counts is marriage. Unmarried couples who move in together do not have a commitment; they have a hedged bet, with one eye kept peeled for other options in case things don't work out.) Second, is your partner likely to be a good mother or father? And third, are you willing to trust God? He is your Father who loves you and wants the best for you. Trust in that love, obey his commandments, and cultivate habits of heart that honor him. Be confident that he is "the way, the truth, and the life." Honor him by living with sexual integrity, and know that he will delight in blessing you abundantly!

Bibliography

Bingham, John. "Almost No Couples with Children Who Stay Unmarried Stay Together, Study Claims." *Telegraph*, May 22, 2013, sec. Women. http://www.telegraph.co.uk/women/mother-tongue/10074614/Almost-no-couples-with-children-who-stay-unmarried-stay-together-study-claims.html.

Blake, John. "Why Young Christians Aren't Waiting Anymore." *CNN Belief Blog*, September 27, 2011. http://religion.blogs.cnn.com/2011/09/27/why-young-christians-arent-waiting-anymore.

Bowerman, Mary. "Sleeping Together before a First Date Is a-OK, but Cracked Phones Are a Put Off." *USA Today*, February 6, 2017. https://www.usatoday.com/story/news/nation-now/2017/02/06/sex-before-first-date-intimacy-online-app-dating-sites-match-singles-america-dating-taboos/97341904.

Campbell, Anne. "The Morning after the Night Before." *Human Nature* 19.2 (June 1, 2008) 157–73.

Catholic Church. *Catechism of the Catholic Church*. 3.2.2.6, "The Sixth Commandment." http://www.vatican.va/archive/ccc_css/archive/catechism/p3s2c2a6.htm.

ElHage, Alysse. "For Kids, Parental Cohabitation and Marriage Are Not Interchangeable." Institute for Family Studies blog, May 7, 2015. https://ifstudies.org/blog/for-kids-parental-cohabitation-and-marriage-are-not-interchangeable.

Evangelical Lutheran Church in America. "Human Sexuality: Gift and Trust." ELCA Social Statement, adopted August 19, 2009. http://www.elca.org/Faith/Faith and Society/Social Statements/Human Sexuality.

Farley, Margaret. *Just Love: A Framework for Christian Sexual Ethics*. London: Bloomsbury Academic, 2008.

Fragile Families & Child Wellbeing Study. Princeton University and Columbia University. http://www.fragilefamilies.princeton.edu.

French, David. "A Little Religion Is Terrible for Marriage: Here's Why." *National Review*, "The Corner," July 16, 2014. http://www.nationalreview.com/corner/382901/little-religion-terrible-marriage-heres-why-david-french.

Garcia, Justin R., Chris Reiber, Sean G. Massey, and Ann M. Merriwether. "Sexual Hookup Culture: A Review." *Review of General Psychology* 16.2 (2012) 161–76.

Goodnow, Natalie. "Why Do the Kids of Married Parents Do Better?" *AEIdeas*, September 5, 2014. http://www.aei.org/publication/why-do-the-kids-of-married-parents-do-better.

Gribaldo, Alessandra, Maya D. Judd, and David I. Kertzer. "An Imperfect Contraceptive Society: Fertility and Contraception in Italy." *Population and Development Review* 35.3 (September 1, 2009) 551–84.

Hsiao, Timothy. "The Limits of Consent." *Public Discourse*, September 23, 2015. http://www.thepublicdiscourse.com/2015/09/15171.

International Planned Parenthood Federation. *Sexual Rights: An IPPF Declaration*. May 25, 2011. http://www.ippf.org/resource/sexual-rights-ippf-declaration.

Jones, Jeffrey. "U.S. Religious Groups Disagree on Five Key Moral Issues." Gallup, May 26, 2016. http://www.gallup.com/poll/191903/religious-groups-disagree-five-key-moral-issues.aspx.

Knot Yet Report: The Benefits and Costs of Delayed Marriage in America. National Marriage Project (University of Virginia), National Campaign to Prevent Teen and Unplanned Pregnancy, and RELATE Institute, 2013. http://twentysomethingmarriage.org.

Kost, Kathryn, and Laura Lindberg. "Pregnancy Intentions, Maternal Behaviors, and Infant Health: Investigating Relationships with New Measures and Propensity Score Analysis." *Demography* 52.1 (February 1, 2015) 83–111.

Lapp, Amber. "Transforming Hookup Culture: A Review of American Hookup." Institute for Family Studies blog, February 15, 2017. https://ifstudies.org/blog/transforming-hookup-culture-a-review-of-american-hookup.

Linker, Damon. "Why So Many Conservative Christians Feel Like a Persecuted Minority." *The Week*, March 13, 2017. http://theweek.com/articles/684365/why-many-conservative-christians-feel-like-persecuted-minority.

McBurney, Louis, and Melissa McBurney. "Christian Sex Rules." *Today's Christian Woman*, September 2008. http://www.todayschristianwoman.com/articles/2008/september/christian-sex-rules.html.

McCleneghan, Bromleigh. *Good Christian Sex: Why Chastity Isn't the Only Option—and Other Things the Bible Says about Sex*. San Francisco: HarperCollins, 2016.

O'Neil, Tyler. "Christians Are Following Secular Trends in Premarital Sex, Cohabitation Outside of Marriage, Says Dating Site Survey." *Christian Post*, January 27, 2014. http://www.christianpost.com/news/christians-are-following-secular-trends-in-premarital-sex-cohabitation-outside-of-marriage-says-dating-site-survey-113373.

Regnerus, Mark. "A Married Mom and Dad Really Do Matter: New Evidence from Canada." *Public Discourse*, October 8, 2013. http://www.thepublicdiscourse.com/2013/10/10996.

Rhode, Deborah L. "Why Is Adultery Still a Crime?" *Los Angeles Times*, June 2, 2017. http://www.latimes.com/opinion/op-ed/la-oe-rhode-decriminalize-adultery-20160429-story.html.

Richards, Cecile. "Protecting and Expanding Access to Birth Control." *New England Journal of Medicine* 374.9 (March 3, 2016) 801–3.

Sawhill, Isabel V. *Generation Unbound: Drifting into Sex and Parenthood without Marriage.* Washington, DC: Brookings Institution Press, 2014.

Schünmann, Catherine, and Anna Glasier. "Measuring Pregnancy Intention and Its Relationship with Contraceptive Use among Women Undergoing Therapeutic Abortion." *Contraception* 73.5 (May 2006) 520–24.

Shire, Emily. "Millennials Are Very Mixed Up about Sex." *Daily Beast*, May 6, 2015. http://www.thedailybeast.com/millennials-are-very-mixed-up-about-sex.

Singles in America. Match.com, 2017. http://www.singlesinamerica.com/2017.

Smith, Christian, and Melina Lundquist Denton. *Soul Searching: The Religious and Spiritual Lives of American Teenagers.* Oxford: Oxford University Press, 2009.

Stanley, Scott. "How to Lower Your Risk of Divorce: Advice to Singles." Institute for Family Studies blog, February 11, 2015. https://ifstudies.org/blog/how-to-lower-your-risk-of-divorce-advice-to-singles.

Stepler, Renee. "Led by Baby Boomers, Divorce Rates Climb for America's 50+ Population." Pew Research Center, March 9, 2017. http://www.pewresearch.org/fact-tank/2017/03/09/led-by-baby-boomers-divorce-rates-climb-for-americas-50-population.

Stokes, Charles, et al. "A Bit of Religion Can Be Bad for Marriage." *The Federalist*, July 8, 2014. http://thefederalist.com/2014/07/08/a-bit-of-religion-can-be-bad-for-marriage.

Toy, Charles. "Premarital Sex: Is It a Sin or Not?" The Christian Left blog, November 19, 2013. http://www.thechristianleftblog.org/1/post/2013/11/premarital-sex-is-it-a-sin-or-not.html.

Tsui, Amy O., Raegan McDonald-Mosley, and Anne E. Burke. "Family Planning and the Burden of Unintended Pregnancies." *Epidemiologic Reviews* 32.1 (April 1, 2010) 152–74.

Twenge, Jean M., Ryne A. Sherman, and Brooke E. Wells. "Changes in American Adults' Sexual Behavior and Attitudes, 1972–2012." *Archives of Sexual Behavior* 44.8 (November 1, 2015) 2273–85.

10

Continence, Character, and the Morality of Masturbation

Matthew Dugandzic

Setting the Stage

The aim of this chapter is to argue that masturbation is morally wrong. In order to do that, it will first analyze the Sermon on the Mount in Matthew's Gospel to derive an understanding of how Christians ought to act in order to follow Christ's command to "be perfect." After that, it will use this understanding of proper Christian action to argue that the act of masturbation, by disordering the passions of the one who engages in it, is incongruous with a life of pursuing Christian perfection. Finally, it offers some more practical advice on how to deal with the vehement passions that can lead one to masturbate.

Be Perfect (Because Jesus Wasn't Kidding)

Perhaps the most shocking injunction in our Lord's most well-known discourse, the Sermon on the Mount (Matthew 5–7), is this: "You, therefore, must be perfect as your heavenly Father is perfect" (5:48).[1] This phrase summarizes the essence of the Christian moral life as inspired, expounded, and *commanded* by Christ.[2] The command is not optional; we must strive

---

1. All English quotations from the Bible in this chapter are from the NIV.
2. For example, Evans says, "'Be perfect' means to demonstrate a complete love, a love that expresses itself toward enemies as well as toward family and friends. This is the kind of love that our heavenly Father has." Evans, *Matthew*, 136. Furthermore, Osborne

for perfection in all that we do. But to do that, we must know *what* perfection is and *how* to attain it.

Fortunately for us, our Lord provides answers to these questions in the rest of the sermon. Jesus tells us that he will save not those who merely preach and act in his name, but rather those who do the will of the Father (7:21). This shows that it is not enough for us to say that we are Christians. We must also act like Christians. Actions speak louder than words.

But our Lord's prohibition against feeling anxious (6:25) shows that a life in pursuit of perfection involves more than acting rightly; it also involves *feeling* rightly. Meditating briefly on 5:21–22 clarifies why this is the case. In these verses Jesus condemns not only murder but also anger. The reason is that murder doesn't happen spontaneously; it requires a cause. People murder one another out of unjust anger. In order to prevent murder, therefore, it isn't enough merely to ban murder. People must be rid of the feelings that lead them to become murderers. Doing away with unjust anger does away with murder.

But again, our Lord tells us that doing away with evil feelings and that acting according to the law are not enough. We must also act according to good intentions. For example, Jesus condemns those who give alms in order to be seen (6:1–4). These people do the right thing, but for the wrong reason. Giving alms should be done for the sake of charity. A person who gives alms in order to be seen is more a show-off than an alms-giver. A true alms-giver gives alms for the reason why alms are given: to help the poor.

In sum, then, the perfect life commanded by Christ involves doing God's will. But to do God's will, one must act for the sake of doing God's will (and not to be seen or for some other ulterior motive), and one's feelings must be so ordered that one can do so readily and easily.

Sexuality is no exception. Jesus himself applies these standards to sexuality when he says that "anyone who looks at a woman lustfully has already committed adultery with her in his heart" (5:28).[3] Although not a complete

---

and Arnold write, "'[To be perfect]' means 'have the same perfect love as your Father does.' At the same time it provides the conclusion for all of [Matthew] 5:21–48, where it means ethical/moral perfection." Osborne and Arnold, *Matthew*, 214.

3. It is worth pointing out that some biblical scholars see in this verse and in the following verses an injunction against masturbation. Osborne, for example, points out on that the term "right hand" in Matt 5:30 may be a euphemism for the act of masturbation or for the sexual organ. Osborne and Arold, *Matthew*, 196. Although this example shows that there are some biblical scholars who believe that the issue of masturbation is directly addressed in the Bible, I have chosen to avoid the controversies that exist within biblical scholarship on this issue so as to focus instead on uncontroversial biblical principles from which I derive an argument not only *that* masturbation is wrong, but also *why* it is wrong.

picture of sexual ethics, this statement provides a helpful jumping-off point. So far we have learned that proper action is not enough, for one cannot act well unless one is properly motivated by good feelings. Here, it is specified that lustful feelings lead to lustful actions.

In Romans 1, St. Paul sheds light on this phenomenon. In speaking about Gentiles who knew God through created things (1:20), he tells how, in refusing to love God above all, they were given up to "sinful desires of their hearts to sexual impurity for the degrading of their bodies with one another" (1:24). This improper ordering of desires leads to a cascade of moral degradation. Once declining to worship the Creator so as to worship creatures instead (1:25), the rest of their nature was thrown out of order. Men and women experienced illicit desires, and they became wicked, envious, and murderous.

The point of this is to show that the human person is a unity. Disorder in one area leads to disorder in other areas. A child who, for example, does not respect her parents enough to tell them the truth may, if she continues to lie to them for a long period of time, lose so much respect for them that she no longer considers it a problem to steal from them. A liar, by lying, can predispose herself to become a thief.

The perfect life, the Christian life, then, is to be striven for by acting so as to train your feelings to work harmoniously with one another to motivate you to pursue the will of God with ease, readiness, and joy. It is my contention that masturbation, by disordering the passions, can impede you in your pursuit of the life of Christian perfection.

Shifting Gears (but Not Manually)

From the above biblical analysis, I have derived three components of the sort of action that will put a person on the path toward perfection. We must do the right thing, for the right reason, motivated by the right feelings.

In order to apply this schema to sex, the first question to ask is this: what does sex do? The most obvious answer to this question is that sex is procreative: it makes babies. Secondly, sex is unitive. It not only makes a husband and a wife feel closer to one another, but it also binds them through their children, all of whom need (and deserve!) the love and support of both of their parents. Finally, sex is pleasurable, and in two ways. On the one hand, sex is physically pleasurable in a way that can be similar to other physical pleasures. On the other hand, sex involves the pleasure of desiring another person and being desired by that person in a specifically sexual way.

A little reflection reveals that these three ends which people can seek through sex are connected to one another. Pleasure serves as a motivation for action. The action in particular is unitive and procreative at the same time. The question then is this: is it right to separate these ends from one another? Presumably not, but this is precisely what masturbation does.

Masturbation, most broadly defined, is self-stimulation of one's genitals outside of the sexual act. Why would somebody want to do that?

The first answer that comes to mind is that masturbation is done for the sake of physical pleasure. Although there are some actions that may be sought purely for the pleasure they bring, such as when a man strokes his beard while listening to a lecture, it is clear that there are many other actions that should not be motivated solely by the pleasure that they bring. Consider eating. If a person ate only for pleasure, then he would quickly become extremely unhealthy. Such a person should instead eat for the sake of nourishment and enjoy the resulting pleasure as a reward for having acted well. This is not to say that a person cannot eat for the sake of pleasure, but only that a person cannot eat for the sake of pleasure *to the detriment of nourishment*. That is, on many occasions, it is fine for him to eat simply because he wants to eat, but he cannot forget that how he eats will affect his health.

When sex enters the picture, the rule that pleasure should not serve as the sole motivation for action becomes even more crucial because sex is oriented toward another person—another person whom Christ commands us to love as he loves us. When a person masturbates, he does what is most pleasurable to himself. There is no concern for what the other person might want; indeed, there cannot be, since there is nobody else present with him. It follows that the more a person masturbates, the more he habituates himself to care only about his own gratification. Later on, if he gets married, for example, he will have trained himself to focus on his own pleasure. He will not be attuned to his wife's needs and desires, which are unlikely to be wholly compatible with his own.

Things become even worse when you consider the second sort of pleasure associated with sex, that of desiring and being desired. First of all, as was the case above, this sort of pleasure is not a sufficient motivation for action if sought alone. For example, our Lord said, "You have heard that it was said, 'You shall not commit adultery.' But I tell you that anyone who looks at a woman lustfully has already committed adultery with her in his heart" (Matthew 5:27–28). This, of course, means that mere desire for sexual union does not legitimate such union. At the very least, such union needs to occur within marriage.

Even in marriage, is desire for sexual union always appropriate? No. To make this case, I need to appeal to Aquinas' distinction between two different kinds of love: *amor amicitiae* and *amor concupiscentiae*. In English, these are "love of desire" and "love of friendship," respectively.[4] Love of desire exists because humans have needs that they have to fulfill in order to complete themselves. I desire food in order to nourish myself and shelter in order to protect myself. This type of life is necessarily self-regarding. I desire things insofar as they are good for me.

Love of friendship, on the other hand, is focused on another person. In this mode of loving, I desire things for the sake of my friends. That is, I see things that are good for my friends and desire these things for them. If my friend is thirsty, I desire to give her water. If my friend is upset, I desire to console him. I do not desire these things because they are good for me, but because I care about my friends and I see that these things are good *for them*. Many times these self-interested and other-regarding desires may correspond, but genuine friendship requires that one's motivations go beyond the former alone.

It is clear that, as far as masturbation is concerned, it is not possible to act on the basis of love of friendship. There is no one else whose good I am concerned for except my own. There is simply nobody else there.

Now, love of desire is not in itself a bad thing, but imagine, for example, what it would be like for a friendship to be motivated entirely by love of desire. I have a certain friend. I like his sense of humor, his enthusiastic attitude, and his quirky obsession with crossword puzzles. These things please me. I often invite him over so that I can enjoy these characteristics of his. But I don't have any concern for him *as a person*; I only care about him for my own enjoyment, not his. So when his anxiety gets the best of him and he feels upset, I don't see it as worth my while to console him. When his enthusiasm becomes just a bit too much and gets on my nerves, he's no longer pleasing me, so I tell him to leave.

Clearly, this person will not stay friends with me for very long. In fact, he was never really my friend, but my toy. And now that he's gone, I can enjoy his attributes even more. I can sit by myself and imagine the sort of jokes he would tell. I can fixate on a picture—mental or physical—of him indulging in this love of crossword puzzles. Thus, I have now isolated all of the features of him that I like and have separated them from everything that I dislike.

But it gets even better (or worse). Now that I've focused in on what I like, I can augment these features in my mind to bring me even more pleasure. Now, instead of being a mere real-life crossword enthusiast, he's

---

4. Aquinas' discussion of these two forms of love can be found in his *Summa Theologiae*, I-II, q. 26, a. 4.

instead a mere invention of my mind who is a crossword super-genius and does crosswords all day, never stopping to take care of human needs such as eating or drinking.

At this point it should be clear that I've perverted myself, my understanding of friendship, and my expectations of other human beings. I now enjoy the company of people who can exist in my mind only. No living person can come close to matching my expectations. I have destroyed my ability to form friendships. I have destroyed my ability to love. Life goes well beyond active fantasies sanitized of life's messiness and challenges that are the fixtures of actual reality.

On the other hand, if our relationship is a love of friendship, the attributes of him that I like fill me with appreciation for him. This appreciation motivates me to desire what is good for him. I try to fulfill his needs and satisfy his wants simply because I care about him.

Clearly, in marriage this latter type of relationship is preferable, and masturbation will not help one get there since it is concerned with no other person but oneself. All of the actions are self-directed. In the words of C. S. Lewis:

> For me the real evil of masturbation would be that it takes an appetite which, in lawful use, leads the individual out of himself to complete (and correct) his own personality in that of another (and finally in children and even grandchildren) and turns it back: send the man back into the prison of himself, there to keep a harem of imaginary brides. And this harem, once admitted, works against his *ever* getting out and really uniting with a real woman. For the harem is always accessible, always subservient, calls for no sacrifices or adjustments, and can be endowed with erotic and psychological attractions which no real woman can rival. Among those shadowy brides he is always adored, always the perfect lover: no demand is made on his unselfishness, no mortification ever imposed on his vanity.[5]

All of this is particularly apropos today in a day and age of social media in which so many "friendships" are superficial and self-consumed, requiring precious little or absolutely no sacrifice or forbearance. By a click of the button the friendship can be severed if it becomes challenging or onerous. People are discardable, easily written off; relationships are disposable; others are there for one's own gratification. It's easy to profess love for humanity

---

5. Lewis, "Letter to Keith Masson," June 3, 1956. Quoted from Lewis, *Yours, Jack*, 292–93; emphasis in original.

when few actual human persons, with all their faults and foibles, actually need to be loved.

The person that Lewis is describing has perverted himself in the same way that the "friend" described before had perverted himself. Both have become so concerned with their own wants that they have rendered themselves incapable of caring about the good of another person. What we do puts us on a trajectory of who we are becoming.

Indeed, you may think, "Is every situation this extreme?" Well, no, but we're talking about marriage here. Marriage requires a great deal of self-sacrificial love over a long period of time. Anything that can make it any harder than it already is ought to be avoided. A marriage in which a spouse is disproportionately concerned with his own desires, and with how the other may please him, is only going to crash and burn. Rather, spouses must have friendships toward one another and, as spouses, this love of friendship takes on the particular character of married life, which includes sex.

Both St. Thomas Aquinas and C. S. Lewis discuss how our desires can be transformed in a relational context. For Aquinas, the love of friendship is so strong that it can even compel us to love things that we would otherwise hate. This is how we are able to follow the command of Jesus to love our enemies; we love God so much that we grow to love everything that he loves.[6] For Lewis, Eros transforms Venus from an appetite into an appreciative pleasure that rejoices in the beloved in her totality. Astoundingly, since Eros is concerned entirely with the other person, it can even, "without diminishing pleasure, [make] abstinence easier."[7] In these contexts, love of friendship and a relationship dominated by Eros—everything that the spouses do for one another, including making love—is done to a large degree *for the sake of the other.*

Masturbation, existing for the sake of the pleasure of the person engaging in it, can do nothing but favor love of desire or Venus over love of friendship or Eros. Although it is not a bad thing to want to experience the pleasure connected with sex, this must always be done in a context that keeps the good of one's spouse in mind.

Now I can return to the three aforementioned components of a perfecting action. It should now be clear that masturbation affects your feelings for the worse. By choosing one's own pleasure repeatedly, one becomes habituated to acting for the sake of one's own pleasure. Even if someone might want to have fulfilling, unitive sex with their spouse, their feelings, fortified by habits, will fight against their good intentions.

---

6. Aquinas, *Summa Theologiae*, II-II, q. 23, a. 1, ad 3.
7. Lewis, *Four Loves*, 97.

Many people may be asking, "But what if I'm not married?" or, "What if I never get married?" This may be a hard word, but I would submit that it nevertheless remains the case that masturbation disorders the passions. As in the example above of the child who started out as a liar and became a thief, so a person who masturbates will train himself to see people as objects to be used, not as persons to be loved. This is not hard to see. A person who masturbates imagines himself with another person and focuses in on those aspects of the person that please him most. He does not—indeed, cannot—take into account the totality of the other person. He will meet no competing needs or concerns and will not encounter any undesirable characteristics. Such action, especially considering that it is likely repeated many times, can do nothing but inhibit a person from being able to relate to others in a wholesome way.

That's not all. A person in the habit of masturbation has trained himself to deal with sexual urges by relieving them immediately though physical stimulation. This means, first, that when he has lustful thoughts his manner of dealing with them will be to relieve himself over, and over, and over. But this doesn't solve the problem. In fact, it perpetuates and exacerbates it. Instead, such a person should try to diagnose what is causing her to have such thoughts in the first place and should try to devise a more constructive way of dealing with them (to be discussed below).

Such a person is also likely to be highly incontinent, that is, unable to restrain himself from indulging his impulses. How will this affect his relationships with people of the opposite sex? Such a person is more likely to feel overwhelmed by the impulses he may feel around members of the opposite sex, making him more likely to engage in, and even coerce others into, illicit behavior. Furthermore, even in marriage it is not always appropriate to make love. An incontinent person is more likely to compel his spouse to have sex when the time is not opportune, or when his spouse simply does not want to.

What to Do about It

A final point that remains to discuss is how to handle the impulses that lead one to masturbate. For this section I will first turn to advice from St. Augustine himself, who was all too familiar with struggles against sins of the flesh.[8]

8. The following discussion is derived from Augustine's remarks in his sermons 21, 63, 72, 177, 250, 265, 279, 306, and 315. A detailed discussion of their interpretation can be found in Byers, *Perception, Sensibility, and Moral Motivation in Augustine*.

Augustine divided the passions into a number of categories, one of which was *propassiones,* or "preliminary passions." These passions arise without any rational thought. Think, for example, of when you hear a loud noise and instantly feel scared, or of when you smell some food and begin to feel hungry. These passions are spontaneous and independent of any judgment of reason. Often, when a person feels tempted to masturbate, preliminary passions are to blame. A person does not think, "It would be good for me to masturbate now," but instead feels an overwhelming urge that clouds his judgment and makes masturbation seem like an attractive option. A large part of the battle against masturbation will therefore involve learning how to handle preliminary passions.

St. Augustine first recommends *premeditatio,* or "prerehearsal" of possible future events. Here's how this works: you anticipate the events that give rise to unwanted passions and concentrate on how you want to respond emotionally. That is, think about whatever sights or sounds or thoughts make you feel lustful and think about how you should feel in reaction to such stimuli. For Augustine, this was not a means of merely avoiding sin, but it could also be used to help one participate more actively in the liturgy, for example, by prerehearsing the experience of joy upon hearing the proclamation of the gospel. Thus we can train ourselves to respond positively to those stimuli that usually trigger unwanted passions in our hearts.

Augustine also advocated *recordare,* or "remembering" the greatness of God and the virtues of Christ. That is, when you feel yourself being tempted, try to focus your mind on the greatness of God. To do this, focus on mental images—Augustine's favorite was the resurrection—that call to mind God's greatness. Remember that he can do anything and you will feel comforted in his infinite ability to save you from any evil. Holiness can be achieved only by availing ourselves of God's offer of sanctifying grace, so that we can do what we otherwise would be unable to do in our own strength.

Additionally, Augustine recommended *meditatio,* or "meditation" on the law. Though it doesn't sound like much fun, this approach does have strong scriptural backing. Consider Psalm 1:2, "[his] delight is in the law of the LORD, and [he] meditates on his law day and night." Or from Psalm 119, "Oh, that my ways were steadfast in obeying your decrees! Then I would not be put to shame when I consider all your commands. I will praise you with an upright heart as I learn your righteous laws. I will obey your decrees; do not utterly forsake me." Or, finally, Joshua 1:8, "Keep this Book of the Law always on your lips; meditate on it day and night, so that you may be careful to do everything written in it. Then you will be prosperous and successful." Augustine believed that meditating on the law would prepare one to obey it readily and easily, even in the face of difficulty.

Finally, there is *referre*, or "referring" to the metaphysical hierarchy. God, being the greatest good from which all else derives its goodness, is ultimate. Everything else is placed below according to its own goodness. What is important to remember is that God deserves primacy and that everything else is loved for God's sake. As with Aquinas' love of friendship, the idea here is to fall so deeply in love with God that you want to do whatever he wants you to do. What seems a heavy burden can become light.

In addition to these prayerful approaches to pursuing the virtue of chastity, there are also many practical approaches. First and foremost, you should avoid whatever stimuli provoke sexual temptation in you. If you find yourself tempted by certain websites, avoid them, or try installing filtering software on your computer. Covenant Eyes is a good option. Next, it would also be a good idea to find a friend or groups of friends with whom you can hold yourself accountable. I've done this myself. The fear of letting your friends down combined with their emotional support both serve as strong deterrents in the battle against sexual sin.

Finally, be healthy. It's simple. Eat well, exercise, get enough sleep, and structure your day. Unhealthy bodies lead to grouchy attitudes and a decrease in willpower. As St. Peter says, "Be of sober spirit, be on the alert. Your adversary, the devil, prowls around like a roaring lion, seeking someone to devour. But resist him, firm in your faith, knowing that the same experiences of suffering are being accomplished by your brethren who are in the world" (1 Pet 5:8–9).

Lastly, I encourage you not to be dismayed if your struggles with masturbation persist. Sinful as masturbation may be, our Lord is one who loves us more than we can comprehend and forgives us our sins time and again. Trust that if you are persistent in your efforts and prayers, you, like the neighbor who asked for bread (Luke 11:5–8), will eventually be given what you need in order to prevail.

A Response to Erin Dufault-Hunter

In her chapter, Dufault-Hunter acknowledges that if masturbation cannot be separated from lust, then it is always wrong to masturbate. Unlike me, she does think that masturbation can be done in a nonlustful way. She does not argue for this claim, but rather provides two examples of situations in which masturbation would be nonlustful and would promote virtue. For the sake of brevity, I will reply to the first of her examples here.

Dufault-Hunter says that people sometimes experience strong, unwanted sexual desires. She says that it would be better to masturbate in order to rid oneself of these desires, rather than ignore or repress them. This way, one is not hindered by unwanted desires, but is rather freed from them and made able to engage on other, virtuous activities. On the surface, this sounds like a reasonable solution, but I have three reservations.

First, this solution assumes that indulging, ignoring, or repressing sexual desires are the only ways of dealing with them. However, great Christian thinkers throughout history have extolled the act of resisting temptation as a way of growing in virtue. When Jesus was fasting in the desert, the devil used his hunger to tempt him to disobey his Father. But Jesus did not give into his hunger, nor did he ignore it, nor did he repress it. Rather, he acknowledged that he was hungry and, nevertheless, for the sake of obeying his Father, refused to turn the stones into bread. We can follow his example and accept our temptations humbly, refusing to give into them out of love for God, and thereby grow in the virtue of piety.

Second, Dufault-Hunter seems to overlook the fact that desire always has an object. That is, I never simply desire sex; I always desire sex *with someone*. Similarly, one does not masturbate with a blank mind, but rather with a mind full of images. Of whom are these images? If they are of a person to whom I am not married, then I am guilty of lust, as Jesus forbade in the Sermon on the Mount. If they are of someone who does not exist, then, as C. S. Lewis said above, I am preferring my imagination to reality, constructing a "harem of imaginary brides" with which no woman can compete.

Thirdly, humans are creatures of habit. If you resort to masturbation as a way of releasing sexual tension, you are going to predispose yourself to do so again in the future. Furthermore, you may even make yourself more likely to experience unwanted sexual tension, for which your solution will be masturbation, which will result in an addictive feedback loop. A better way to deal with sexual tension would be to refuse to indulge in it for the sake of obeying God, which, I promise, gets easier with time.

Bibliography

Byers, Sarah Catherine. *Perception, Sensibility, and Moral Motivation in Augustine: A Stoic-Platonic Synthesis*. New York: Cambridge University Press, 2013.

Evans, Craig A. *Matthew*. New Cambridge Bible Commentary. New York: Cambridge University Press, 2012.

Lewis, C. S. *Yours, Jack: Spiritual Direction from C. S. Lewis*. Grand Rapids: Zondervan, 2008.

———. *The Four Loves*. New York: Houghton Mifflin Harcourt, 1991.

Osborne, Grant R., and Clinton E. Arnold. *Matthew*. Zondervan Exegetical Commentary on the New Testament 1. Grand Rapids: Zondervan, 2010.

11

Chastity's Helping Hand?
How Masturbation Can Serve Virtue

ERIN DUFAULT-HUNTER

Regardless of whether one dubs the rhetoric liberal or conservative, progressive or traditional, much discourse on sexual ethics is a mere reaction to the culture. It is not a response from a distinctively Christian understanding of the significance of the erotic. One of the unintended consequences of such discursive habits is that one side's rhetoric stokes our shame while the other, in a rejection of our supposedly oppressive past, goes to great lengths to be "sex positive." Because virtue always connects moral concerns to an overarching, ordering narrative rather than to abstract rules ("don't do that") or principles ("sexual pleasure is good"), discussions of matters like masturbation provide opportunities for recollecting "how our lives mean"—that is, they force us to go back to the basics about how Christianity makes a difference in ordinary life.

From the perspective of virtue theory, the moral status of masturbation is only determinable in light of the Christian vision of the good life.[1] Virtue subordinates all human activities to this understanding of the good life, suggesting that even commonplace actions are significant insofar as they shape us—or misshape us—for that life. Thus virtue makes sense of why the God of Israel addresses not only broad moral questions like wealth distribution, but also ritual prescriptions vis-à-vis involuntary activities such as menstruation and involuntary ejaculation (Lev 15:15–17).[2] YHWH

---

1. Throughout this paper, "masturbation" refers to self-stimulation of genitals and not to mutual arousal.

2. While contemporaries read into this that "sex is dirty"—i.e., it is somehow

desires that Israel live into the ordinary with intentionality, consciously recalling the overarching narrative by which she patterns her life. The significance of the mundane is that it reminds Israel to lean into this drama in every part of her existence.[3]

There are many ways of articulating the Christian vision of the good life. But there is one articulation into which we are especially invited: God created humans in God's own image and then called a particular people into a covenantal relationship analogous to a marriage. When loyal in love of God, this community's way of life is a reflection of the character of the God in whom we trust. Like loyal lovers, we come to know and love this God, to gladly offer ourselves in adoration and joyful obedience. We see this sort of obedience most clearly in Christ, who lived as the fully Human One and offered himself to others in self-giving love.[4] Jesus shows us that we can lay ourselves aside for others. But it is not because we are self-sufficient or morally superior. We do not lay ourselves aside in order to meet some abstract ethical standard of behavior that God demands. Rather, we extend ourselves for others' good only because of the sort of God that God is: ever steadfast, God's fidelity means he has our back; God's triune nature overflows with gifts and provides for us; and God's power redeems not only the small daily "dyings" that love requires, but will also raise our bodies from the dead.[5] To put this into our contemporary romantic imagination, YHWH is the only lover

---

immoral or shameful—the Jewish tradition does not interpret them in this way. We cannot here investigate the ways moderns map current sexual anxieties onto biblical concerns for purity whose sociohistorical context differs considerably. As a general rule, states of *tohorah* (sacred, clean, or pure) are in contrast with *tum'ah* (everyday, unclean, impure). Rituals of purification then become occasions for recalling how even the mundane in Israel's life suggest her covenant with YHWH, and how this covenant reorders her everyday existence. See Goldingay below on this. On Leviticus and purity, see Milgrom, *Leviticus*.

3. Commands for being "all in" are summarized in God's characterization as a jealous God. Only a God like YHWH can be zealous for his own glory without diminishing his worshippers or instrumentally using them for his ends. Additionally, as Chuck Primus put it, "Any religion that doesn't tell you what to do with your pots and pans and genitals can't be interesting." Quoted in Hauerwas, *Hauerwas Reader*, 531.

4. The Common English Bible uses "Human One" rather than the more usual "Son of Man." Addressing Jesus's internal motivation, the writer of Hebrews states, "who for the joy set before him endured the cross, disregarding the shame, and has taken his seat at the right hand of the throne of God" (Heb 12:2, NASB).

5. Jesus expresses this dynamic in his comments to the competitive disciples: "But it is not to be so among you; but whoever wishes to become great among you must be your servant, and whoever wishes to be first among you must be slave of all. For the Human One came not to be served but to serve, and to give his life as a ransom for many" (Mark 10:43–45).

worthy of "all of me," deserving the bodily worship expressed in much of our culture's music and exemplified in Jon Legend's gorgeous ballad.[6]

Unlike other gods who require human subservience for their own schemes, the triune God does not need us. The Three-in-One is love, and this love overflows to create and sustain the world.[7] As humans, our main task is to posture ourselves so that we become able conduits of God's abundant gifts (including that of the Spirit, who transforms us for such a life). In this way we, too, become givers and images of the deep goodness of the God of Israel. Because we are made to rely on God by offering ourselves for others, we do not merely seek some external, final reward such as "salvation" or an entrance pass to a far-off heaven. Rather, we enjoy growing in Christlikeness, and over time we become the sort of people who find satisfaction and delight by enacting generosity toward others. In virtue language, we pursue rewards or goods "internal" to such a way of life. Finally, humans can also reject this posture, instead becoming fearful takers whose hearts and minds gradually shrivel as we cave in on ourselves, never developing the virtues necessary to love others generously and freely.[8]

In my telling of the story, notice that what matters is how we respond in the present; virtue accommodates the blessings and burdens of incarnate temporality by acknowledging that we flourish (or wither) over time. No one is born completed or whole. We may start from a state of incontinence (as *akratic*, or having a weak will), in which we initially want to do the right thing but give in to our wrong desires. Or we may find ourselves in a state of vice, in which we actually delight in wrong, mistaking it as good or true. But even the vicious can move toward continence. It is possible for us to turn, slowly practicing our resistance to wrongdoing and intentionally enacting the good in our minds and bodies—although we may find it difficult or painful to do so. Once virtuous, we can actually enjoy doing the good and resisting the bad. Particularly when it comes to sex, virtue provides a gracious context for learning chastity and recognizing that humans are not merely thinking or willing animals; it encourages us to celebrate our move away from vice, recognizing that even a state of incontinence is a small step toward God and his lovingkindness. As a model of the moral life, virtue

---

6. As of March 7, 2017, the official video for Legend's "All of Me" topped one billion hits. Clearly, we crave such all-encompassing, beautiful communion. Consider this song's immense appeal in the context of the meaning of the erotic explored below.

7. This is a way that YHWH interacts with humankind that is substantially different from other gods; consider also the Greco-Roman stories of human-divine relations, as well as the way the god of mammon devours us.

8. For an articulation of the Christian faith along these lines, see Volf, *Free of Charge*.

assumes a theological anthropology (widely supported by neuroscience) that we are psycho-social-biological-spiritual entities, all rolled into one; daily habits and routines of our bodies and minds are important for our formation. Our flesh matters precisely because our souls are inextricably linked to it.[9] Our sexual life matters, because only in and as bodies—bodies that are sexed and sexual—do we become generous lovers of others. We do so by posturing ourselves as receivers of God's good gifts. In the erotic, as in all areas of our life, we establish patterns or habits that bear on whether we are becoming such a person. The virtue traditionally associated with tending to our erotic life in this way is called "chastity," a disposition that even among Christians today sounds stuffy and unappealing but when understood richly becomes an attractive and—even erotically—desirable trait.

This background framework is essential to our understanding of the moral importance of masturbation. Does masturbation form or fail to form us as generous lovers and gracious receivers? In order to be virtuous, masturbation must be practiced in such a way that it moves us toward chastity, allowing us to focus our sexual energies so that we love others and are loved in return.[10] The assertion that masturbation can form us for virtue might lead some to be casual about their indulgences. But recasting self-stimulation as a possible moral resource also forces Christians to recall the overarching meaning embedded in our erotic life and to reconnect our sexuality to God's story.

The Dynamics and Danger of Lust

If the above account is right, then God's reason for proscribing certain behaviors while commanding others cannot be simply, "I said it. You believe it. That settles it."[11] Instead, YHWH's Instruction (or Torah) habituates Israel for a faithful relationship within particular sociohistorical contexts.

---

9. Joel Green argues against a dualist understanding of persons as immaterial souls and material bodies, and engages in neuroscience and its implications for theology and Scripture. Green, *Body, Soul, and Human Life*. Regardless of how one conceives of the human person, orthodox faith affirms the importance of the bodily life, as opposed to gnostic heresies that arise in various forms throughout history.

10. There are a variety of definitions of chastity. As Caroline Simon defines it, chastity is "the virtue that helps us focus our sexual energies on committed relationships." It also enables "the successful integration of sexuality within a person that results in inner unity between bodily and spiritual being." When we are chaste we are able to use our "sexual powers intelligently in the pursuit of human flourishing and happiness." Simon, *Bringing Sex into Focus*, 75–76.

11. A popular bumper sticker among conservative Christians reads, "God said it. I believe it. That settles it."

Obedience to it enacted Israel's trust in this God, and she reordered her relationships so as to embody *shalom* (and thus to enjoy the blessings of this covenant). Here we cannot explore why Christians insisted that certain Torah rules were still required regardless of culture (until recently, such as keeping Sabbath), while other habits about diet were largely abandoned.[12] While it is common to parse Torah into ceremonial, moral, or judicial law, John Goldingay notes that such cleaving is not possible, especially given how interwoven these elements were in ancient societies.[13]

An understanding of Torah's logic is crucial for discussions of sex, because we need to examine Jesus's reiteration of the law regarding lust, adultery, and commands to cut off body parts. Once we understand what lust means in the context of the Sermon on the Mount, we can comprehend the role of these proscriptions in the development of virtue. Then we will consider analogous situations in our own day and ask how we can embody Christ's command so that we, too, are formed for partnership with God. If masturbation *necessarily* entails lust as some insist, then as such it is prohibited. But if it does not, then we will need to consider other ways of comprehending this activity so that it sustains our growth as generous lovers and gracious receivers.

As we address Jesus's words in Matthew, we do so aware that even conservative Christians have disagreed about masturbation's link to lust. What is now widely accepted is that Scripture itself does not directly address it. While Genesis 38 was once widely cited as referring to masturbation, Onan most likely practices *coitus interruptus* in regard to Tamar (i.e., he withdraws from her before ejaculating and thus prevents pregnancy); this is the likely interpretation of what he did when he "spilled his seed" (Gen 38:9).[14] Many leading evangelical voices, such as James Dobson of Focus on the Family and ethicist Norman Geisler, acknowledge that masturbation can

---

12. The severing of eating from daily faithfulness proved an error, I would argue, as we see in our current ecological crisis. That, too, must be recast through how we witness in the ordinary to trust in God's faithfulness to us, rather than bow to convenience and consumerism at the cost of our own health and that of God's creatures and creation. For a helpful recasting of creation care and eating in this way, see the work of Ellen Davis, such as Davis, "Learning Our Place." Sabbath is also undergoing a revival among Christians, who recognize how ignoring rest has wrought havoc on our relationships. See Muthiah, *Sabbath Experiment*.

13. Goldingay, *Old Testament Theology*, vol. 1. Likewise, we often sever our contemporary rituals such as checking our phones or shopping on the Internet from our morality. See Smith, *Desiring the Kingdom*, for a meditation on humans as worshipping, liturgical animals shaped by our ordinary habits.

14. Relevant to our plum line for measuring sexual practices, Onan's sin lay in his unwillingness to extend generosity to his sister-in-law and to honor his dead brother via the sexual norms of his context.

be a done in a way that does not necessarily promote lustfulness.[15] They particularly warn against shaming those who practice it (especially younger, unwed men). However, many highly influential conservative writers are more fearful of masturbation's effects while less conservative ones seem rather cavalier about it.[16] What is often missing from these perspectives is that masturbation offers us an opportunity to reflect deeply on our sexuality and how it matters for our life with God and others. That is why we need to slow down as we read Jesus's warnings against lust in Matthew.

Toward the beginning of the Sermon on the Mount, Jesus insists that he has not come to abolish Torah but rather to fulfill it.[17] He then goes on into a series of antitheses ("You have heard it said . . .but I say to you") in which he reasserts Torah and reminds hearers of its intention as formation.[18] He states the second of these antitheses thus:

> You have heard that it was said, "You shall not commit adultery." But I say to you that everyone who looks at a woman with lust has already committed adultery with her in his heart. If your right eye causes you to sin, tear it out and throw it away; it is

---

15. See for example Geisler, *Christian Ethics*, 184 and 187. Dobson notes, "I'm not telling you to masturbate, and I hope you won't feel the need for it. But if you do . . . you should not struggle with guilt over it. I suggest you talk with God personally about this matter and decide what He wants you to do about it." Quoted in Dobson, *Preparing for Adolescence Group Guide*, 46. For a short articulation against masturbation, see Tushnet, "What Could Possibly Be Wrong with Christian Masturbation?"

16. I have in mind here especially the wildly popular Every Man series. See Arterburn and Stoeker, *Every Man's Battle*. They consistently offer "meeting God's standard for purity" as the motivation for restraint, promoting a rather warped vision of God. Importantly, this series, as well as "liberal" ethicists such as Patricia Jung, link masturbation and pornography and thus share unexpected concerns or even prohibitions of both—something we will consider below. See Jung, *Sex on Earth as It Is in Heaven*.

17. Matt 5:17–20: "Do not think that I have come to abolish the law or the prophets; I have come not to abolish but to fulfill. For truly I tell you, until heaven and earth pass away, not one letter, not one stroke of a letter, will pass from the law until all is accomplished. Therefore, whoever breaks one of the least of these commandments, and teaches others to do the same, will be called least in the kingdom of heaven; but whoever does them and teaches them will be called great in the kingdom of heaven. For I tell you, unless your righteousness exceeds that of the scribes and Pharisees, you will never enter the kingdom of heaven." This word for fulfill can also be translated "fill out" or "fill up," thus emphasizing the ways Jesus explains (and embodies) the content of Torah and its aims.

18. Matthew's Gospel harkens back to the formation of Israel, including through the giving of the law on Sinai (and its reiteration in Deuteronomy) as a way to reform people who had been enslaved under the fearful politics of Pharaoh. As Jewish folklore puts it, "It took four days to take Israel out of Egypt. It took forty years to take Egypt out of Israel." Torah provides practical ways that Israel expels the influence of Egypt by coaching her in new habits of life.

better for you to lose one of your members than for your whole body to be thrown into hell. And if your right hand causes you to sin, cut it off and throw it away; it is better for you to lose one of your members than for your whole body to go into hell. (Matt 5:27–30)

This first line literally translates as "everyone looking at a wife/woman with desire."[19] The word translated "lust" (*epithumēsai*) can also be translated "covet," and the LXX (the Greek version of the OT available in Jesus's day) uses this same word when it translates the Decalogue's prohibitions (i.e., "Thou shalt not *covet* . . .").[20] The word conveys strong emotion as well as intention, but it can also be used positively, as in 1 Timothy 3:1 and other places in the New Testament, when one desires something good and then acts according to that longing.[21] Thus we cannot assume that we know what Jesus means by the word that is translated into English as "lust" unless we consider the larger context of the prohibition.

As William Loader points out, the word commonly translated in this sentence as "woman" (*gunaika*) could also mean "wife," and he argues that "wife" (including one's betrothed) in fact is what is meant here. Otherwise, the sin would be the more general one of *porneia* or sexual immorality, rather than the more specific one of adultery. While we use "heart" to mean the center of emotion, in this period heart denoted the center that directs our actions or intentions as well as our passions.[22] Thus, putting these concepts together, Jesus specifically addresses those who look at another's wife with the intention to take and who nurture a longing for her, connecting the willingness to nourish these thoughts to the sin of adultery. In this context, lust names this consumptive gaze that forms us as takers. It makes us into persons who shatter covenantal relationships in order to get what we want, our own or others' commitments be damned (literally).

Given this close consideration of the context, translating the word as "lust" connotes much about the posture that leads to vice. Lust denotes wrongful desiring, the nourishing in mind and body of appetites that fracture or distort our connection with God and others. In this sense, greed and lust closely correspond to one another, as both set our hearts (in the NT

19. Loader, *Sexuality in the New Testament*, 114. Loader is widely recognized as an expert on sexuality in the intertestamental and New Testament period.

20. Paul uses this same word when citing these commandments in Rom 13:9.

21. 1 Tim 3: "The saying is sure: whoever aspires to the office of bishop desires [*epithumeō*] a noble task." See also, among others, Gal 5:16–17; Heb 6:11; and 1 Pet 1:12.

22. Sensible, given physical realities, the bowels rather than heart were considered the center of emotion, as when the Samaritan responds with compassion or "is moved in the gut" by the need of the man left on the roadside.

sense) on not receiving from God but rather on getting from others—including their adulation, envy, or attention.[23] The sermon plays out implications of these two basic stances: one that enacts openness and trust in God's provision, and another that embodies greediness and anxious taking.[24] In a culture like ours that consistently encourages fulfillment of our appetites yet struggles chronically with anxiety, the gospel comes again as good news—news that also requires intentional responses to it from us.

Given the high stakes for our well-being, Jesus then goes on to talk about gouging out eyes and cutting off hands—those members that enable scandalous *looking* and *taking*, the vehicles for the acquisitive stare and the consumptive grasp.[25] The overarching sensibility of the sermon contrasts anxious acquisitiveness with gracious giving, and matters of sexuality fall into this same framework. Remember that women were often vulnerable and had little power in that culture, including over their sexual life. In the teaching on divorce that immediately follows our text (Matt 5: 31–32), Jesus underscores men's culpability (i.e., "he makes her an adulterer") rather than blaming women for somehow deserving such treatment.[26] Jesus warns us that indulging our longing for another's wife (or, in our more egalitarian context, another's lover) puts us at tremendous risk; reject such covetousness and do whatever you must to focus on fidelity! Following this same logic of loyal love of God and neighbor, Jesus then teaches about speaking truthfully and keeping vows we have made.

---

23. Throughout the sermon, those who do not keep Torah are those who do perform obedience before others and thus train their bodies and minds to crave the reward of others' admiration. This is in contrast to those who obey in secret (with head, heart, and hands), and who position themselves to receive from a God who readily blesses his children.

24. Consider how Jesus chides those who worry or fearfully store up treasures rather than those who give alms faithfully, realizing that God sees their lives and cares for them. Or think about Jesus's teaching on prayer, in which he corrects our tendency to project onto God an attitude of grudgingly giving, rather than a heavenly Father who already knows what we need and provides accordingly.

25. Some propose that this comment about hands could include masturbation, but the difficulty is that the hand we are to slice off is the right one. The right side was generally reserved for "clean" activities, and the touching of the genitals during the toilet was done with the left hand. This continues to be the case in many countries and cultures. For more on this, see Loader, *Sexuality in the New Testament*, 128, including his comments about widespread disapproval of masturbation among rabbis.

26. Jesus is likely responding to two schools of thought about divorce: one that approved of men divorcing women "for any cause" (such as burning dinner), and another that took this same approach of sexual immorality of some sort as the only way to break this covenant. For more on divorce and these teachings, see David Instone-Brewer http://www.tyndale.cam.ac.uk/david-instone-brewer or Instone-Brewer, *Divorce and Remarriage in the Bible*.

Overall, Jesus warns about performing the letter of Torah without the spirit (e.g., his discussion of giving alms) or ignoring the letter by claiming to keep the spirit (e.g., his teaching about lingering on another's spouse or about divorce). He consistently challenges interpretations of Torah that foster a disposition to take what we want and to do so even when it ruptures the fabric of relationships (e.g., consumptive gazes destroy marriages; broken promises fracture relationships; being religious for others' commendation shuts out God's reward). But true righteousness enacts God's "perfection" or wholeness in a willingness to give good gifts, a charity that extends even to enemies (Matt 5:43–48). In all these ways, obedience to Torah tutors us in God's openhanded, noncoercive generosity. That's a far cry from ways Christians often disparage Torah (and Judaism) as stifling legalism.

While not addressing masturbation per se, Jesus's teaching on lust is important for our own approach to sexual desire today. In contemporary culture, some mock the earnestness with which we are to respond to lust's lure, often carelessly eliding covetousness with spontaneous arousal or pleasure. Having considered the teaching in context, we recognize that an unintended response (be it a spark of emotional delight or bodily desire) is not Jesus's worry. Rather, what concerns Jesus is what we *do* with that initial response, how we attend to it as those called to witness to his Father in heaven. Jesus's hyperbole seems warranted: if we have ever been sexually pressured or taken against our will, been haunted by a jealous lover, or had our beloved lured away from us, Jesus's rhetoric appears fitting. "Take charge of your eyes and hands to keep yourself from vicious grabbing! Repent! Better to maim your body than for you to destroy a brother or sister's marriage!" This charge becomes even more shocking in a tradition that forbade mutilation of any sort (e.g., Deuteronomy 14). Even if it costs you dearly, step away from vice and toward charity in mind and body, toward different treasures that await you in God's good reign. Notice that Jesus knows we desire; the question facing us is how we train and satisfy our appetite for "treasure" of all sorts.

Although this text about "looking lustfully at another's woman or wife" does not directly address masturbation, it does describe the temperament that forms us as sexual consumers and wreaks havoc in our relationships. For those bound to one another in the body of Christ, love limits our actions because we must choose how to honor one another, and love obligates us to respect and protect one another as diverse members of that body. To ignore Jesus's fierce warnings about sexual consumerism risks our salvation, because coveting cracks and shatters the bonds by which we are joined to one another.

Does masturbation *necessarily* entail this consumptive gaze and *always* habituate us into being takers rather than grateful receivers? We must consider how we masturbate, what dangers we face in doing so, and whether we can engage in this activity so as to serve chastity rather than vice.

What's in an Orgasm?: Training Our Bodies for Ecstasy

Our culture frames sexual desires as private and as deserving (or even requiring) satiation. We tend to laugh about our lusts. But Jesus states that internal sexual dispositions are not just personal (i.e., not just about satisfying my needs) and that sexual indulgence cannot be directed by our whims. Instead, we must intentionally order our sexual life according to God's intentions for a particular sort of community. We thus set our hearts to discipline our sexual life, so that in whatever form it takes (married, unmarried, divorced) or in whatever bodily state (young or old; able-bodied or disabled; gay, bisexual, or whatever) we slowly become more like Christ. As one important aspect of our collective and individual life, the erotic both reveals and shapes our character. Thus one of the most damning accusations against masturbation is that because it is an autoerotic activity, it trains us for personal pleasure outside such ecstasy's proper boundaries of mutuality and committed partnership. Additionally, we probably do so by objectifying others, something that is itself a sin, especially if we fantasize about others not as they exist in their own right but rather as instruments for our erotic satisfaction. These accusations must be addressed in part by considering masturbation's link to bodily pleasure, and then whether it necessarily reinforces a grasping, acquisitive disposition toward others rather than openhandedness.

In masturbation, an immediate reward is orgasm or, at the very least, bodily ecstasy. Anti-masturbation advocates rightly note that, far from being an activity bracketed from our sexual interactions with another human being, orgasm is a significant event precisely because we are embodied spirits. Self-stimulation triggers links between our neurons, thoughts, and genitalia; in doing so, it trains our mind-body for how we respond to *real* people. Against the casualness with which masturbation is taken by those seeking to be "sex positive," all sexual stimulation is a serious matter, given its capacity to habituate us in our relational patterns (including our habit of interacting with real people who play a part for others' fantasies, as in pornography), because we *are* our bodies. Further, orgasm itself must be theologically considered vis-à-vis our *telos*, considered for "how it means" from within the Christian vision of the good life. Thus if masturbation can serve virtue, we must first consider how sexual ecstasy (even if autoerotically achieved) might sustain us for our end in God. Then we can ask how masturbation can be practiced in alignment with these ends.

Dying to Live: A Short Theology of Bodily Ecstasy

The French expression *la petite mort*—"the little death"—offers one euphemism for orgasm. Although there are many ways to understand this phrase (and other experiences that bring similar sensations), here a Christian perspective on orgasm might utilize this secular allusion. The term "ecstasy" literally means "outside ourselves"; sexual ecstasy takes us "outside ourselves" only as we let go—as we die—to our inhibitions, as we nakedly and unashamedly give ourselves over to another (or to an experience). In our sexual life this is evidenced by involuntary, embarrassing convulsions of pleasure. While subject to distortion when sought as its own goal or fixation (even in sexual relationships), orgasmic pleasure is but one reminder that our ultimate joy lies in surrender—even unto death—and encourages us to be open to God's Spirit. The Spirit works best amid vulnerability, and enters us to remake us as gracious receivers who are united in the Trinity's work and communion. Like many signposts in the ordinary messiness of life that intimate God's nature and our personal end, orgasm (its embodied experience or its mere possibility) can remind us of the wonder possible when we generously stimulate another to ecstasy. It also recalls our own intense desire to find a space in which we can collapse into our yearning without shame or regret, and do so with joyful abandon.

Orgasmic ecstasy becomes its most twisted when we sever it from its role as an attachment behavior, as a space of seeking another's good, on one hand, or of willingly exposing our own privation. But to think of orgasm as *la petite mort* is to rethink blanket prohibitions on masturbation and to discern that it can be a means of putting the pleasure or good of another (our love of God or of neighbor) first. Because it can point us to cruciform love and to the Spirit's filling, we cannot summarily affirm it; all love entails loss or denials, and for some persons masturbation does not foster death for another's good. Autoeroticism by definition fails to make us generous, as it does not *directly* train us to put another's pleasure first. But in light of its link to orgasm, theologically considered, masturbation might support generosity in other ways. Perhaps it might demand of thoughtful practitioners a more careful consideration of God's interest in their erotic lives than is commonly true of happy and hapless lovers.

As the French hints, even the best orgasm seldom affords us utter gratification. Ironically, while we often justify such behaviors as sexual "satisfaction," erotic stimulation often leaves behind an emotional as well as physical residue, a melancholy or sense of loss involved in this peculiar form of dying. Orgasm recalls for us the force of our desire to offer ourselves fully to another, the potential cost of doing so, and the ultimate reality of a "not yet" world in which mere humans cannot sustain us in this kind of ecstasy; but demands for endless orgasm make us a weary lover or a driven, distracted masturbator. We can taste in orgasm a genuine good, as when our ecstasy deepens our attachment to another, or as it binds us in future fidelity when regular climaxes become but a dim memory. Like all appetites momentarily appeased, pleasures this side of heaven perpetually arise to niggle at us. Orgasmic excitement remains a teaser and it must not be mistaken as the end in itself (many a magazine or self-help book notwithstanding). Rather, it points us toward the surrender that is possible in another communion, the surrender that does not require the awkward mechanisms of sex to bring us such ecstasy.[27]

In short, rather than being an ultimate good or fixation, orgasm serves as a sign of our longing for the joy of self-forgetfulness—a self-forgetfulness that will finally arise in Christ. Its rightful place in human sexual relationships binds us in trust and mutual fulfillment. Given this, how can self-stimulation move us toward charity or chastity? How can masturbation be ordered as a means of readying us for union with God, as creatures made to receive and channel God's generosity?

Masturbation that Disciplines Us for Generosity and Opens Us to God's Grace

Because virtue takes our mind-body seriously as the only way in which we can become suited to our end, Christians cannot glibly affirm masturbation on the grounds that it satiates an animal appetite. We are animals, but we are not merely animals; we are honored and obligated by our capacity for intentionality, for directing our lives. If we choose to channel our desires so that we equip our bodies for openness to God, we must consider how our

---

27. Matt 22:29–32. Some church fathers such as Gregory of Nyssa ponder whether, when we are in full communion as Christ's body, we shall not only regularly enjoy a messianic feast (another appetite fulfilled), but will also experience ecstasy of communion as a natural marker of loving relationship in the resurrection. For reflections on the Song of Solomon and its insights into the close connection between our capacity for union with God and ecstatic transcendence, see Davis, "The One Whom My Soul Loves," in *Getting Involved with God*.

sexual responses can be disciplined to this end—including possibly through masturbation. Assuming that we comprehend chastity as the disposition of mind and body that frees us to focus our energies (sexual and otherwise) on our relationships, we then can ask if choosing self-stimulation in some situations may actually be a *controlling* of this energy rather than a *being controlled* by it. Let us thus for a minute take into account the way that the erotic reveals and shapes our character, and let us consider some of the ways in which masturbation may actually serve chastity by forming us for generosity toward others and openness toward God.

Masturbation can enable us to release our tensions about our erotic desire and, thus, to be liberated from a fixation upon it. It frees us from such diversions to attend to those around us—as befits our obligations to them as boyfriends, coworkers, neighbors, or acquaintances. We are an unusually sexually anxious culture; liberals tend to harp on our need for sexual fulfillment, while conservatives hammer away at purportedly biblical values of marriage, family, and purity.[28] In such a context, we might do well to simply release our sexual tensions, thus cutting off the energy supply to a restless libido that can distract us—through guilt or indulgence—from our participation in God's work.[29] We need not fuel our sexual tension or bodily cravings; rather than fixating on our need or "horniness," we can simply provide our body with an outlet and move on. It may be that over time we can develop other ways of dealing with our longings. But in certain seasons on our journey toward chastity, we might require a practical means of diverting our body's nagging: ovulating or pregnant women often have heightened libidos; the efforts of adolescents to wrestle with the physical, emotional, and psychological pressures of sex can lead them to engage in risky experimentation; one's anticipation of a date amplifies one's awareness of erotic desire and might detract from one's ability to be present for the date on his or her own terms.

28. The narrowing of purity to sexual concerns is an odd and unbiblical move, as even a cursory consideration of this language and its context conveys. For instance, John Goldingay says that in the Old Testament, "Purity means being wary of things that are inconsistent with God's nature, such as death and sex and idolatry and oppression." Goldingay, *Job for Everyone*, 32, commenting on Job 4:1–21. Of course, this means purity also concerns the erotic, which makes some more liberal-leaning folks squirm. Notice that not all on the list of what requires purification is morally wrong in itself (such as death or sex). Rather, each of these is contrary to YHWH's nature (i.e., God does not die, nor does God engage in sex, as many gods do).

29. I take this to be part of Paul's seemingly glib comment about marrying rather than burning with passion. An unmarried state is best for all the reasons he lists, but if one finds oneself hopelessly distracted from the good, then one should get married, deal with its complexity, and do it all within the meaning and direction of one's life in God. See 1 Cor 7:8–9 in its larger context.

Chastity in its deepest sense requires engaging in activities that focus our energies on the people around us—those to whom we are extending God's gracious gifts. Taking the possibility of vice seriously means that our sexual energies require direction (e.g., "cut it off"). When we allow sexual energy to disrupt our capacity to see and attend to those we are supposed to love, we look at them as outlets for our own sexual needs—and thus forgo the obligatory constraints that generous, self-offering love places on us. Far from being a virtue that makes us prudish boors, chastity requires focused consideration of our erotic feelings and longings. While thoughtless indulgence is one error, ignoring our desires or repressing them can also result in the manipulation of others, including efforts to be a "good Christian" by getting someone into a marriage bed in order to get my "need" for sex satisfied—even if marrying that person makes it more difficult for me to participate in God's work in the world. Rather than allowing sexual appetites to disrupt our relationships, masturbation can operate as a check on our consumption—recalling all the while that the final fulfillment of our desires is our union with others in Christ.[30]

The finality of this union emphasizes the "not yet" of life in this body, and Christian conceptions of virtue can train us to recall this reality. It is also possible in such a context for masturbation to be practiced as lament. What of those who have been divorced, who seek to live as unmarried abstainers, who are separated from a spouse, or who have lovers who, due to injury or illness, are no longer capable of sexual connection? For all of these, masturbation is not merely letting off sexual steam and getting on with one's life of generosity. In these and many other contexts, unleashing our sexual energy exposes us and connects us to our sorrow. Masturbation may not just end in ejaculation or multiple orgasms; the body's release may unleash tears of sadness at what was, what could have been, or what will not

---

30. Assumed in this section is the possibility that masturbation does not necessitate *porneia*. In doing so, we might well explore the difference between masturbation's relationship to porn discussed below and "erotica" in its best sense. Some define the difference between the two as the muddy but real line between material that expresses committed and affectionate sex (erotica) and that which portrays degrading, violent, or dehumanizing sexual acts (pornography). How such material shapes the viewer depends not only on its objective content but also on the character of the participant(s). From this perspective, the Song of Solomon qualifies as erotic but not pornographic. Although sexually explicit, films may highlight the vacuous or destructive nature of uncommitted sex. Whether individuals find such material inappropriate or sexually stimulating depends upon their maturity as well as their worldview. For Christians, then, determining if something qualifies as pornographic requires an honest analysis of the material's effect on those involved, including on those who are producing it. See Balswick and Balswick, *Authentic Human Sexuality*, 275–93. This also reminds us of the importance of learning to perceive rightly, itself an aspect of the virtuous life.

be. Masturbation as lament suggests the longing we bear as those who are faithful to Christ, as those who are seeking to love in ways that are faithful to God and others. Masturbation is a way of checking our envy or covetousness toward those whose erotic lives seem more fulfilling than our own, while also keeping us truthful about the losses love entails—including our love of Christ. Thus, rightly exercised, masturbation may not primarily be an escape but rather an unveiling of our soul, exposing us as we are undone in orgasm before the God who will finally take us all into a place of sheer repose, utter vulnerability, and unashamed need.

We could extrapolate from this a variety of other scenarios to foster chastity and orient us toward the good of others. But two things are worth underscoring. First, such a practice assumes a capacity to be honest about ourselves, and truthfulness about what the activity is doing for us. Our reticence to talk candidly about masturbation reveals that we would rather hide like Adam and Eve than confess that we are earthy animals also called to be partners with the One who made us capable of feeling such ecstasy. Virtue means maturing before God, acknowledging that many areas of our lives (economic, political, business, etc.) are consumptive. We should enter into masturbation with prayer—weird as this may seem—and with wise confidants, so that we nurture sexual generosity and alert ourselves to the self-deception to which we are all prone. Masturbation *may* serve chastity for some persons in some circumstances, but it also may not. For example, some may not be able to stimulate themselves without fantasies that objectify those neighbors they are called to serve. Virtue assumes that ensouled bodies are like plants: while we share general sensibilities, we are all different from one another, and thus we must figure out what nourishes good growth, feeding and pruning as befits the individual plant and the season. Masturbation may nurture growth—or it may not.

Such an approach to masturbation, by acknowledging our shared need for cultivating generosity and for starving our sexual greediness, guts the power of shame. When we push ourselves to consider masturbation within a larger context of erotic desire's end in God, we open up conversations about longings and unearth any embarrassments we may have. Because of strong links between sexuality and shame, Christians seldom openly ponder how our sexual appetite intersects with God's invitation to witness to lovingkindness and to come alongside the Spirit's love for the world.[31] We may well feel

---

31. Readings of Gen 2:25 and 3:7 express this connection, and psychoanalysis famously has investigated the sex-shame connection. See Thompson, *Soul of Shame*, for a discussion of shame broadly as well as its connection to sexuality, from a Christian psychiatrist's perspective. Note that the feminine pronoun here simply reminds us that God is not a man or woman, i.e., not sexed, as are most of the creatures she creates.

shame when we desire wrongdoing, and shame does good work when, step by step, it turns us back toward God. But too often shame makes a more negative home in us as Christians. We too often resist Christ's promise to address our shame, either through confession and forgiveness or through the recognition that this humiliation is not from God at all.[32] When shame settles in us and does not nudge us toward repentance or redemption, it undermines our pursuit of Christlikeness and ceases to promote chastity.[33] In such a circumstance shame eats away at us, causing us to shrink or withdraw from others and from God.

Pornography: Training in Taking

Pornography is one of the main ways in which "bad" shame arises. Anyone who hopes to enlist masturbation in the service of chastity faces a daunting challenge in our pornified culture.[34] When it comes to sexual expression, too many Christians believe our erotic life can be compartmentalized or nurtured apart from other life arenas—such as, for instance, social justice.[35] Because of this, some glibly affirm pornography as liberating or morally neutral. Even if this were once true of porn, it has since been exploded in the age of the Internet, fueled by the Web's famed "triple-A engine" (accessibility, affordability, and anonymity).[36] One can hardly understate the influence of pornography on the sexual landscape of the West and the rest of the world; even those of us who never view it find our relationships altered by it.[37]

This remains a distinctive feature of the God of Israel as opposed to other gods, who often beget worlds or demigods, or who are driven by their own sexual appetites to use humans as pawns in their escapades.

32. For a fascinating reflection on how shame functions in our common life, see Tarnopolsky, "Prudes, Perverts, and Tyrants."

33. For perspectives of male Christian therapists and the impact of masturbation on emotional, spiritual, and psychological health, see Kwee and Hoover, "Theologically Informed Education about Masturbation."

34. Among others, Pamela Paul popularized this term in her book *Pornified*.

35. Oddly, even many of my evangelical colleagues and friends splice justice from sexual appetite. Scripture knows better, and thus prophets are just as likely to cite economic gluttony and oppression alongside sexual immorality; God's *shalom* rightly orders all our relationships and knows nothing of "social" justice rather than simply justice that reclaims every aspect of our social and personal life to express God's true peace.

36. See Cooper, Delmonico, and Burg, "Cybersex Users, Abusers, and Compulsives." Cooper's original research and use of the term go back to an article he published in 1998.

37. See Regnerus and Uecker, *Premarital Sex in America*. They discuss this

Porn is regularly used for masturbation.[38] In his book on pornography and the male brain, neuroscientist William Struthers explains how using pornography to masturbate to orgasm rewires the brain. This is why treating compulsive porn viewing merely as a matter of rationality or moral choice usually fails. Many accountability groups that perceive compulsive porn viewing to be a "spiritual" problem also fail. Struthers explains how men's "peculiar proficiency" for relaying visual cues for sexual arousal makes quitting pornography difficult. He goes on to explain how porn affects male brains and thus how it becomes a reinforced neurological habit.[39]

For some among the generation of men who have grown up with easily available Internet porn, masturbating to porn has produced a distressing fruit: they cannot "perform" with actual women and suffer from porn-induced erectile dysfunction.[40] Also disturbing is the development of what Mitja Suncic calls "Single Techno-Sex, a novel form of sexual intercourse involving a lone human being and a computer showing por-

---

throughout the book, but see especially pp. 94–100 under the subheading "How Porn Affects the Sexual Economy."

38. Pornography may seem to be straightforwardly only about sex, but this is a naïve conception of porn's role in many lives. For reasons why men view porn, and for its link to anxiety and depression among other factors, see Struthers, *Wired for Intimacy*. While some continue to proclaim its good affects for couples, one survey of marriage and family therapists found that 76 percent of the respondents had seen individual clients and 74 percent had seen couples dealing with pornography issues. See, e.g., Ayres and Haddock, "Therapists' Approaches in Working with Heterosexual Couples," especially 63.

39. "Rewiring and Sanctification," in Struthers, *Wired for Intimacy*, 99. He explains, "As men fall deeper into the mental habit of fixating on these images, the exposure to them creates neural pathways. . . . Over time these neural paths become wider as they are repeatedly traveled with each exposure to pornography. They become the automatic pathway through which interactions with women are routed. The neural circuitry anchors this process solidly in the brain. With each lingering stare, pornography deepens a Grand-Canyon like gorge in the brain through which images of women are destined to flow. This extends to women that they have not seen naked or engaging in sexual acts as well. All women become potential porn stars in the minds of these men. They have unknowingly created a neurological circuit that imprisons their ability to see women rightly as created in God's image. . . . This neurological superhighway has been reconstructed and built for speed, able to rapidly get to the climax of sexual stimulation" (85). He contrasts this swiftness with the patience necessary for intimacy with another human being.

40. Luscombe, "Porn and the Threat to Virility." The article notes that while porn has many critics, these charges come from its most loyal customers. "Most of the men interviewed were quick to say it was not a matter of morals but rather of 'having functioning penises'" (43). Of course, virtue comprehends why such attempts to sever ethics and personal attachments prove false and literally impossible given the nature of the human creature.

nographic images," in which one masturbates with one hand while the other touches the screen.[41] While porn induced ED may seem extreme, the images and videos to which men (and some women) masturbate almost inevitably involves consumptive behavior. It means being sexually demanding and greedily taking from another in a way that causes his or her personality to disappear from us.[42]

Virtue theorists, now supported by this evidence from neurobiology, are unsurprised by the evidence that masturbating to pornography shapes us into erotic consumers: others become objects viewed for the sake of our sexual needs; we withdraw from the complexity of embodied erotic love into solo sexual performances; we focus our sexual energy on an endless pursuit of neurological and neurochemically induced highs.[43] In human creatures, mind, body, and spirit are interconnected. Unfortunately, we sometimes address our desires via mechanics as if our body were merely a machine. We find ourselves surprised when pornography overtakes our embodied spirit, driving us to do things we do not want to do and preventing us from becoming who we want to be. On the other hand, of course, virtue theorists agree with Struthers that it is possible for us to retrain our mind-body, to identify triggers for our porn appetite, and to note that often these triggers—the things that set our brains firing down particular pathways—are not themselves sexual.[44]

---

41. Sunčič, "Porn Drift," 65. I cannot here explore how porn has altered the sexual landscape, nor the ways many of the people affirming pornography remain unaware of how porn has shifted its content over the last decade or so, becoming increasingly violent and degrading toward women as well as demanding of male performers. Porn's sexual practices have "gone mainstream," especially among younger persons (thirty and younger), from shaving genital hair to anal sex to acts I will not explain here. For an example of concerns raised by sociologists about pornography's effect on gender relations, see Garlick, "Taking Control of Sex?"

42. Women's relationship to mainstream porn is, as noted in other places, complicated. However, women are just as likely as men to engage in the sin of *porneia*, in which we refuse to see another in his or her difference. This sin offers us a particular form of power, provides us momentary escape from daily stressors, and overall stokes the lie that we can be known without risk, naked without vulnerability. Women do this, too, even if we do so through other sorts of fantasies.

43. For an explanation of the chemical and neurological effects of porn (such as how hormonal responses reinforce pathways), see Struthers, *Wired for Intimacy*, 99–107. For an overview of the effects of pornography on our culture (now becoming outdated, given developments in the industry), see Layden and Eberstadt, *Social Costs of Pornography*.

44. Struthers, *Wired for Intimacy*, 177–89. This is another reason why "just stop it" can be cruel: We mistake masturbation and/or porn viewing as the problem, while the other needs or longings that are suggested by such activities remain unexamined (and thus unhealed).

In a short essay like this it is not possible to explore the theological implications of pornography and the ways that it illuminates sin's dull patterns and our erotic life's true end.[45] However, what *can* be stated is that the specific practices and pathways formed in us as we engage in cyberporn mean that the practice of masturbating to porn seldom (if ever) provides us with an avenue for training our sexual energies for generosity and the gracious reception of others.

Conclusion: Masturbation That Forms Us for Chastity's Generosity

In the 1980s, psychotherapist Peter Marin commented on what he saw as the failure of the sexual revolution to deliver on its promises to men and women. He noted that the pursuit of freedom in sexual matters does not itself foster the good. We "have not learned how to be kind to one another, how, in the midst of the confusions we have created, among the categories and styles and pretenses of sex that surround us—how we can sustain those we find at our sides or in our arms." He went on to diagnose our problem in a way that nicely coincides with the Christian vision of the good life.

> The problem is not that sex has been separated from love, as many people have suggested (though there is some truth to this). The more general problem is that sex—along with countless other activities—has been emptied of generosity. There is nothing specifically sexual about such generosity, nor is there anything unique in the place it ought to play in sex. Yet the hardest thing of all in sexual life, more difficult by far than having the world's finest orgasm, is to leave images and dreams behind, and to learn that the person in one's arms is a poor forked creature, subject to the same confusions and alarms as oneself. Beyond all will, beyond all imagining, beyond all sensation . . . there remains a human reality that yields itself to a kindness of touch but which remains closed to us, despite all our yearnings, until we can somehow learn to bring to sex, through generosity, precisely what it is that we seek there from others, and without which the sexual world remains a kind of limbo.[46]

---

45. See Dufault-Hunter, "'Porn Again.'" For an understanding of what porn is from a theological perspective and ways women's versions of porn may be wrongly perceived as harmless fantasy, see Dufault-Hunter, "Pornography," in Green, *Dictionary of Scripture and Ethics*.

46. Marin, "A Revolution of Broken Promises," reprinted in Scott and Warren, *Perspectives on Marriage*, 166–75; quote on 174.

This quote captures what I have argued here about the character sought by the people of God, and how the process of training for this disposition necessitates an alternative kind of community. Both liberals and conservatives tend to begin with sex or sexual acts as good or bad things, as liberating or dangerous. Marin reminds us that we need to know what sort of person we want to be—and indeed need to be—as sexual, erotically aroused creatures. He observes that we will put up with a great deal in our partnerships and relationships, including really bad sex or no sex at all. But what shatters our capacity to love and be loved is consumptiveness, a failure of generosity. Although written in a very different cultural climate, Marin's comments recall that the much-maligned virtue of chastity fixes us on just such openness. By orienting our lives toward chastity, we willingly embrace our vulnerability to our longings as well as to the finitude of others in ways that focus our energies to become genuinely kind.

In thinking about sexual desire, we must remind ourselves what we are *for*, what sort of creatures we are and for what ends we are created. Only in this way is it possible for us wisely to order our sexual appetites. By beginning with God's goodness, we can work backward to our own need to be trained—as willing, joyful participants. Our culture provides us with ample opportunities for training our mind-body for greedy taking, for fearful grasping at erotic pleasures that then drive our relationships. By contrast, virtue enables Christians to discern the right use of masturbation. We must not take such a subject lightly, because we are creatures made a little lower than the (celibate) angels. Nor must we take it too seriously, as we are (sexual) creatures of the earth.[47] The good life means becoming generous receivers of God's good gifts. Generous receivers are persons who invite others into their journey of charity and chastity, a venture requiring much patience and grace, as we sojourn together through time and into eternity. In a culture saturated by sex, marred by shame, and marked by aimless dissatisfaction, taking mundane things like masturbation into God's story creates an entré into this adventure for many who do not yet know the triune God who created them for explosive joy.

---

47. Scripture notes this in-between state of the human creature: we participate in the ruling and care of the world like the angels (who are forbidden sexual relations), and yet we are remarkably finite and fragile (including in our sexed and sexual embodiment). For instance, Ps 8:3–8: "When I look at your heavens, the work of your fingers, the moon and the stars that you have established; what are human beings that you are mindful of them, mortals that you care for them? Yet you have made them a little lower than God, and crowned them with glory and honor. You have given them dominion over the works of your hands; you have put all things under their feet, all sheep and oxen, and also the beasts of the field, the birds of the air, and the fish of the sea, whatever passes along the paths of the seas."

Bibliography

Arterburn, Stephen, and Fred Stoeker. *Every Man's Battle: Winning the War on Sexual Temptation One Victory at a Time*. Colorado Springs, CO: Waterbrook, 2009.

Ayres, Michelle M., and Shelley A. Haddock. "Therapists' Approaches in Working with Heterosexual Couples Struggling with Male Partners' Online Sexual Behavior." *Sexual Addiction & Compulsivity* 16.1 (March 4, 2009) 55–78.

Balswick, Judith K., and Jack O. Balswick. "Pornography and Erotica." In *Authentic Human Sexuality: An Integrated Christian Approach*, 275–93. Downers Grove, IL: InterVarsity, 2013.

Cooper, Al, David L. Delmonico, and Ron Burg. "Cybersex Users, Abusers, and Compulsives: New Findings and Implications." *Sexual Addiction & Compulsivity* 7.1–2 (January 1, 2000) 5–29.

Davis, Ellen F. "Learning Our Place: The Agrarian Perspective of the Bible." *Word and World* 29.2 (2009) 109–20.

———. *Getting Involved with God: Rediscovering the Old Testament*. Lanham, MD: Rowman & Littlefield, 2001.

Dobson, James. *Preparing for Adolescence Group Guide: How to Survive the Coming Years of Change*. Ventura, CA: Gospel Light, 2005.

Dufault-Hunter, Erin. "'Porn Again': What Pornography Can Teach Christians about Good Sex." Paper presented at the annual meeting of the American Academy of Religion, 2011.

Garlick, Steve. "Taking Control of Sex?: Hegemonic Masculinity, Technology, and Internet Pornography." *Men and Masculinities* 12.5 (August 1, 2010) 597–614.

Geisler, Norman L. *Christian Ethics: Contemporary Issues and Options*. Grand Rapids: Baker Academic, 2010.

Goldingay, John. *Job for Everyone*. Louisville: Westminster John Knox, 2013.

———. *Old Testament Theology*. Vol. 1: *Israel's Gospel*. Downers Grove, IL: InterVarsity, 2003.

Green, Joel B. *Body, Soul, and Human Life: The Nature of Humanity in the Bible*. Studies in Theological Interpretation. Grand Rapids: Baker, 2008.

———. *Dictionary of Scripture and Ethics*. Grand Rapids: Baker Academic, 2011.

Hauerwas, Stanley. *The Hauerwas Reader*. Edited by John Berkman and Michael Cartwright. Durham, NC: Duke University Press, 2001.

Instone-Brewer, David. *Divorce and Remarriage in the Bible: The Social and Literary Context*. Grand Rapids: Eerdmans, 2002.

Jung, Patricia Beattie. *Sex on Earth as It Is in Heaven: A Christian Eschatology of Desire*. Albany, NY: SUNY Press, 2016.

Kwee, Alex W., and David C. Hoover. "Theologically Informed Education about Masturbation: A Male Sexual Health Perspective." *Journal of Psychology and Theology* 36.4 (December 22, 2008) 258.

Layden, Mary Anne, and Mary Eberstadt. *The Social Costs of Pornography: A Statement of Findings and Recommendations*. Princeton, NJ: Witherspoon Institute, 2010. Available at http://www.socialcostsofpornography.com/booklet_download.pdf.

Luscombe, Belinda. "Porn and the Threat to Virility." *Time*, March 30, 2016. http://time.com/4277510/porn-and-the-threat-to-virility/?iid=toc_033116.

Milgrom, Jacob. *Leviticus: A Book of Ritual and Ethics*. Continental Commentaries. Minneapolis: Fortress, 2004.

Muthiah, Rob. *The Sabbath Experiment: Spiritual Formation for Living in a Non-Stop World*. Eugene, OR: Cascade, 2015.

Paul, Pamela. *Pornified: How Pornography Is Transforming Our Lives, Our Relationships, and Our Families*. New York: Macmillan, 2007.

Regnerus, Mark, and Jeremy Uecker. *Premarital Sex in America: How Young Americans Meet, Mate, and Think about Marrying*. Oxford: Oxford University Press, 2011.

Scott, Kieran, and Michael Warren, editors. *Perspectives on Marriage: A Reader*. Oxford: Oxford University Press, 2007.

Simon, Caroline J. *Bringing Sex into Focus: The Quest for Sexual Integrity*. Downers Grove, IL: InterVarsity, 2012.

Smith, James K. A. *Desiring the Kingdom: Worship, Worldview, and Cultural Formation*. Cultural Liturgies 1. Grand Rapids: Baker Academic, 2009.

Struthers, William M. *Wired for Intimacy: How Pornography Hijacks the Male Brain*. Downers Grove, IL: InterVarsity, 2009.

Sunčič, Mitja. "The Porn Drift: Pornography, Technology and Masturbation." *International Journal of Technoethics* 4.2 (July 1, 2013) 58–71.

Tarnopolsky, Christina. "Prudes, Perverts, and Tyrants: Plato and the Contemporary Politics of Shame." *Political Theory* 32.4 (August 1, 2004) 468–94.

Thompson, Curt. *The Soul of Shame: Retelling the Stories We Believe about Ourselves*. Downers Grove, IL: InterVarsity, 2015.

Tushnet, Eve. "What Could Possibly Be Wrong with Christian Masturbation?" *Christianity Today*, February 2016. http://www.christianitytoday.com/women/2016/february/what-could-possibly-be-wrong-with-christian-masturbation.html.

Volf, Miroslav. *Free of Charge: Giving and Forgiving in a Culture Stripped of Grace*. Grand Rapids: Zondervan, 2009.

Part 3

Christian Sexuality for Persons with Same-Sex Attraction

12

A Christian Response to the "Born This Way" Theology of Homosexuality

RAYMOND PHINNEY

Lady Gaga retweeted a modern pseudo-theology when she penned "Born This Way."[1] The mother in the song says, ". . . he made you perfect, babe." She uses it to endorse sexualities and orientations that do not fit traditional biblical sexual ethics: "*No matter gay, straight, or bi, / lesbian, transgendered life, / I'm on the right track baby, / I was born to survive.*" The refrain is a repetition of, ". . . 'cause I was born this way." With lyrics like, "It doesn't matter if you love him, or capital H-I-M"; "he made you perfect, babe"; and "God makes no mistakes, I'm on the right track baby, I was born this way" peppered through the song, she appeals to God as the author of these different sexualities.

While this can easily be dismissed as merely a pop song, to fill four minutes and twenty seconds of time, much of our culture's more serious moral reasoning follows the same pattern. When it does appeal to God as Creator, it does not go on to appeal to fallen human nature as also influencing the way things are. As such it is theistic, but not actually Christian, theology.

Chandler Burr, in an article for *The Atlantic* and in his book *A Separate Creation*, uses this theistic, unbiblical reasoning to argue that a homosexual orientation is likely an inborn, unchangeable trait. He says, "God made people this way . . ."[2] This presupposition that only God's creative power, and no other factor, is responsible for all aspects of my being, is also pres-

1. Germanotta and Laursen, *Born This Way*.
2. Burr, *Separate Creation*; Burr, "Homosexuality and Biology."

ent in numerous presentations of a biblical or Christian case for same-sex relationships, though it is not always stated explicitly.

Many different commentators, from pop icons to theologians and apologists, use "Born This Way" arguments that have certain theological entailments and implications. However, "Born This Way" theology is not typically presented as a theology per se. It is often a sort of cultural mantra that purports both to acknowledge God and be inclusive. But its acknowledgement of God is deficient and misleading. Its attempt at inclusion, though laudable, is also misdirected because of the theological errors in how it acknowledges God.

Unfortunately, the most common Christian responses actually accept and endorse "Born This Way" theology's bad logic, then attempt to refute it on its own invalid terms. This ends up being both uninclusive and unbiblical. Analyzing the presuppositions underlying "Born This Way" theology and evaluating how they differ from biblical theology can help us to rebut its underlying errors and respond on proper theological and logical grounds. This better response should also help the church combat anti-gay bias and to love, accept, and support those who feel same-sex attraction.

"Born This Way" Theology

"Born This Way" theology reasons that God, as Creator, is responsible for all my nature and my predispositions. It asserts that any natural predisposition (to same-sex attraction, for instance), or "natural human variation," is due to God's direct action.[3] Since God is all-powerful, it is then reasoned that he meant for the predisposition to exist. God's intention should then be honored by fully expressing and elaborating these God-authored predispositions. Failing to do so, finally, is reckoned to be morally wrong.

Well-Intentioned

This theology is often motivated by a desire to pronounce all people valuable, regardless of their differences. God truly loves all humans and we humans should do the same. In that sense, the Christian should agree with the motivation of "Born This Way" theology, even though we may disagree with its premises and conclusions. All persons are worthwhile and lovable—to God and through God. Many ways that Christians oppose "Born This Way"

---

3. White, *What the Bible Says—and Doesn't Say—About Homosexuality*. The Rev. White asserts that homosexuality has been judged as a natural human variation by scientists and is therefore not an automatically sinful lifestyle.

sound as if they are devaluing the people who think differently from themselves. A Christian response should perhaps start by stating where agreement is held. The value of persons is a good point to emphasize.

Conflating Love and Approval

While "Born This Way" theology is often well intentioned, it does not account for all the facts of life. Yes, we are all valuable to God and each other. He loves each of us more than we could ever know. But this does not mean that he approves of all our actions or predispositions. People often conflate the love of God (or others) with the approval of God (or others). God's love is unconditional and does not depend on one's actions. There is nothing one can do to lose or gain it. On the other hand, not all our actions are approved by God.

We have all sinned and fallen short of the glory of God (Rom 3:23). None of us is good enough to receive God's approval on our own. I am separated from God by sin and only receive his approval through Christ's sacrifice. Even after repenting and being justified by faith, the Christian then embarks upon a life of sanctification, of setting herself apart for God. This should include continued change as a response to God's righteousness and mercy. Justification and sanctification, along with glorification, are all part of the salvation process God brings us through. God loves us before we ever come to faith. He loves us while we are walking in repentance and growing in sanctification but have not yet been perfected. He loves us when we betray that salvation and sin again. He loves those who will never acknowledge him or his Scriptures. Clearly, God's love for me does not mean that any particular facet of me is holy, right, or acceptable to God.

Conflating God's love and his approval leads to two errors. Firstly, people who see the truth that God loves all of us sometimes misinterpret this as divine approval of all our actions. Secondly, people who understand God disapproves of homosexual acts sometimes misinterpret this as rejection of homosexual persons. Both these views conflate the love of God with the approval of God. Decoupling God's love and his approval can correct both errors. While it is my purpose in this chapter to state that God does not want his people to engage in homosexual behavior, it is also important to remember that God loves all people and his church should love and care for all people.

Just as we should not conflate God's love and his approval, we should not conflate our own. When I love someone, I should not blindly approve of all they do. When I disapprove of something, I should not withhold true love from a person who embraces it. Christians should remember this when opposing "Born This Way" theology. Ephesians 6:12 reminds us, "For our struggle is not against flesh and blood, but against the rulers, against the authorities, against the powers of this dark world and against the spiritual forces of evil in the heavenly realms" (NIV).

Refuting "Born This Way" Theology with Truth and Love

Arguing against "Born This Way" theology is one aspect of a loving response to the world. Christians should not shirk this task. But, sadly, those who do not avoid it often refute it in an unloving manner. The most common Christian response is, "You Weren't Born That Way." It ends up seeming uninclusive, and can allow or encourage anti-gay bias.

"Born This Way" theology should be opposed because it overturns any proper Christian concepts of sin, temptation, the fall, and redemption. But the commonly used "You Weren't Born That Way" does not refute it. Rather, it actually supports the improper "Born This Way" arguments and suffers from the same non-Christian presuppositions! It is itself incompatible with a biblical understanding of sin, temptation, the fall, and the need for redemption. Furthermore, it marginalizes and excludes anyone who experiences same-sex attraction.

A better response first addresses improper "Born This Way" presuppositions. Only then does it counter with a response. It stresses more careful parsing of the biblical statements, and leads to compassion, love, and acceptance for those who experience same-sex attraction.

The Problem: Creation with No Fall, No Redemption

Because it references God as Creator, "Born This Way" theology can sound Christian. Sayings like "God doesn't make mistakes" (and "He made you perfect, babe") are invoked to assert that we are fine just the way we are.[4]

---

4. Schachter, *Door to Door*. In this Emmy award-winning movie, William H. Macy plays Bill Porter, a man determined to become a salesman despite cerebral palsy. Porter's character says, "God created us all, Shelley. He doesn't make mistakes." While persons with disabilities (and persons who are gay, and other marginalized people) are as valuable as anyone else, failure to recognize and account for the fall, and the fact that the world and our natures are broken, is not the best way to argue for basic human dignity. It leads to other poor moral reasoning.

"Born This Way" is correct in naming God as Creator. The Bible tells us that God created all that there is (e.g., Gen 1:1; Ps 102:25; Isa 42:5; 44:24; 45:12; John 1:3; Heb 1:10, 11:3; Col 1:16) and our very selves (e.g., Ps 139:13; Isa 44:2; Zech 12:1). Directly after this creation he pronounced the universe "very good" (Gen 1:31).

But "Born This Way" is no Christian narrative. The Bible tells us we are not actually born as we were meant to be. What we now see around us is not as it was intended. We are fallen (Gen 3:1–8; Jer 17:9; Ps 51:5; Rom 5:12–19; 1 Cor 15:21–22; 1 Tim 2:12–13) and thereby the world is marred (Rom 8:18–22). Psalm 51:5 tells us we are born in sin. When humanity broke communion with God (sin, or "the fall") and broke the world, marring even ourselves, God allowed that state of affairs to stand. In making a universe of individuals with free will, he chose to work through the brokenness rather than destroying us and starting over. The redemptive work of Christ through the cross is our only way out of that depraved condition.

"Born This Way" theology completely ignores the fall and its consequences. It assumes that whatever I am like "naturally" is how God meant me to be and should be fully expressed. It is non-Christian because without a fall we don't need a redeemer and Jesus didn't have to die. If Jesus is not the "Lamb slain from the creation of the world" (Rev 13:8, KJV), then whatever god "Born This Way" theology refers to is not the God of the Bible.

Another Problem: No Sin

"Born This Way" theology has another premise, believed by many (even many Christians). The premise states that anything innate cannot be sinful. Even those who don't explicitly share this presupposition often implicitly accept it, and do not realize they are doing so.

For example, once when Joel Osteen was interviewed on *Chicago Tonight*, moderator Phil Ponce asked Osteen if homosexuality is a sin.[5] Osteen said it is. Ponce then eventually countered with, "If it [homosexuality] were innate then it would be hard to call it a sin." He pressed Joel with this false dichotomy, asking if homosexuality is innate or is a choice. While Joel tried to avoid conflict and said he didn't know all the details of how homosexual orientations form and so on, Ponce persisted with the innate-versus-choice dichotomy. Reverand Osteen eventually capitulated and said he thought homosexuality is a choice.

By the terms Ponce had laid out, it was the only answer that supported the proscriptions of Scripture. However, Ponce's terms were unsound.

5. Ponce, *Chicago Tonight*, August 2, 2011.

Answering such misconstrued questions on their own terms results in unfortunate responses. Answers such as "It's a choice" can trivialize sexuality and put it on the same level as choosing between coffee or tea this morning.[6] Proper answers cannot be given to such malformed arguments on their own terms. One must confront the invalid logic. It is based on assumptions that are inconsistent with biblical truth and common sense.

The question, as asked, cannot be answered biblically. If one's innate drives cannot be sin, as Ponce asserted, then no one has ever sinned in the history of the universe. According to this nativist logic, as long as one does what one feels naturally inclined to do, one cannot sin.

Assuming innate issues cannot be sin is the same thing as saying we are innately good. The Bible tells us just the opposite. We are fallen creatures and we are thus inclined to sin. Psalm 51:5 says we were born in sin. Ephesians 2:3 says we "were by nature children of wrath" (NRSV). Common sense also says that if innate issues can *never* be sin, then no one who follows their innate desires ever sins, period. From this perspective, there is no logical point to even having such a concept as sin. And if there is no such thing as sin, we do not need a savior. The central point of all Scripture, Christ's sacrifice for us, is undermined by such arguments.

This is one reason why "You Weren't Born That Way" arguments are not useful. They actually degrade the Christian story with the same problems inherent in "Born That Way" theology. They remove the problem of sin, which leaves no need for a savior, which makes nonsense of the gospel. No Christian should use such arguments.

Biological Fatalism

"Born This Way" also applies another concept, biological determinism. Chandler Burr's assertion that "God made gay people this way . . ."[7] follows the "Born This Way" template in ignoring the fall and additionally employs biological determinism. Gaga's arguments also do so. Biological determinism is not in and of itself at odds with a biblical worldview. It can be used

---

6. Even a simple choice like this might not be a momentary concern. Years of choosing and enjoying coffee can constrain one's response for coffee even though one is "free" to choose tea at any time. Since a person's choice at any one time is a combination of her predispositions, reinforcement history, and understanding of the choices, there is hope for a homosexual person to alleviate at least the personal history portion of the choice through normal behavioral science approaches. But it is important for third parties not to rush to judgment about how much behavioral and cognitive change is achievable, nor what the degree of change means for one's salvation or righteousness.

7. Burr, *Separate Creation*, 133.

simply to acknowledge that we are limited by our biology. For instance, when I leave a room, I simply cannot fly out of it. I do not have the biology to do so. But I do have a range of possible ways to leave. I could walk out, run out, crawl out, or perhaps try to duck behind others to leave the room unobserved by someone. My biology does not fully direct which method I will choose, but it sets the range of options available to me.

The way Burr and many others use determinism is better termed biological *fatalism*. It asserts not only that biology determines one's repertoire of behaviors, but that it forces us into a specific behavior. Mary Midgley draws a distinction between biological determinism, the idea that our biology constrains us, and biological fatalism, the idea that it directs us to a specific behavior or outcome within those options, not changeable by any environmental concerns. "The central issue here, then, is not about determinism. It is about *fatalism*, about the impression that we can make no difference to what happens. If we believe that we can make no difference to what happens. If we believe that we are powerless we become so. *This sense of powerlessness does not follow from scientific determinism*. It is merely a common, seductive dramatization of it, which proceeds by telling us that we are in the grip of ineluctable forces."[8]

Evolutionary Psychologists Marc Paratarelli and Krystal Mize note, "The consensus of opinion among knowledgeable geneticists and evolutionary biologists is that genes determine what any organism *can* become . . . . Given that there are both biological and cultural forces at work in the process of shaping human nature, the question has to be rephrased to ask, 'what do we become from the possible options/outcomes that exist in the human genome?'"[9]

These comments illustrate that biologists and geneticists actually view all behaviors and most other human variables as phenotypes, or properties that rely on both genetics (genotypes) and environment. From this perspective, one's biological inheritance is not the sole cause of behavior, nor even of one's physical attributes such as height. While one's height is strongly constrained by one's genetics, environmental factors can also exert strong control. Diet, exercise, and diseases can all affect height, sometimes powerfully. One's culture can of course affect one's diet and exercise regimens, or even what type of medicine one might pursue, indirectly affecting height.

For instance, in the above example of leaving a room, I could perhaps lie down and roll out of the room. But I will likely never do that. Nor am I likely to crawl. It is culturally inappropriate. My biology does not limit me

---

8. Midgley, *Ethical Primate*, 86; emphasis added.
9. Pratarelli and Mize, "Biological Determinism/Fatalism."

in this. My psychology does. I am concerned about how others will perceive me. Many versions of biological determinism amount to saying that my biology determines the exact way I will exit the room on any given occasion. But all it can really specify is the range of ways in which I might leave the room, and how much physical effort is required by those various ways. How I assess the relative costs and benefits of different ways I might exit the room is mediated by learning and environment. This cost/benefit analysis is what typically gets automated into my usual way of exiting a room. The possibilities come from biology, but the specifics are determined by my environment, learning history, and desired outcome.

In the context of homosexuality and the church, biological fatalism is employed to stipulate that a person with same-sex attractions will never enjoy a heterosexual marriage and cannot be content as celibate. Such arguments say that a biological predisposition to feel same-sex attraction requires same-sex relations be enacted. Construed this way, biological fatalism says that there is really no way a person with same sex attraction can be content with life other than when in a same-sex, intimate, sexual relationship. Fatalism says their biology not only allows same-sex relations, but actually requires them. The person's environment, choices, and values are assumed to have little or no influence over this situation.

This argument does not simply misinform homosexuality issues, but also upends heterosexual issues in Christian living, and pretty much any issues addressing responsible behavior. This same argument is often used to say heterosexual single persons must satisfy their sex drive with sexual relations even if they cannot find a spouse. So, "Born This Way" theology says we should not expect biblical sexual ethics from anyone, unless their biology magically does not drive them to sexual expression until the moment they are married, and then never pushes for sexual expression with anyone other than their spouse. When biological drives are seen as wholly determinative of one's specific actions, there really is no concept of choice left. People are assumed to be driven in specific and fatalistic ways by their biology.

Thus, the overall "Born This Way" argument is that we are currently exactly how God wanted us to be and should do all we can to fulfill our innate predispositions. Further, "Born This Way" stipulates that if things are innate they cannot be sin. This is in contrast to the biblical picture of sin as inborn. Finally, "Born This Way" says that if same-sex attraction is present in someone, not only is it innate, but it should be brought to fullest expression, lest God's creative will be thwarted. This reasoning is not compelling when applied to other issues besides sexuality. The problem is that most Christians try to answer "Born This Way" theology in ways that accept

"Born This Way" presuppositions and undercut the Christian story. Thus, the responses to it are as flawed as the original thesis.

Clearly, "Born This Way" is an apologetic for being free to do whatever one wishes, call it biologically driven, and then excuse it or even celebrate it. That must be opposed. But many Christians have chosen to oppose it in ways that also undercut Christ and his plan. Let us explore the pitfalls of this most common response to "Born This Way" arguments.

"You Weren't Born That Way" Also Leaves Out Sin, the Fall, and Redemption

The typical Christian response to "Born This Way" theology is "You Weren't Born That Way." It erroneously accepts the presupposition that our current attributes are there only because of God's creation. It also accepts the "Born This Way" assertion that something innate cannot be sin. So to preserve scriptural teaching that homosexual behavior is sin, it is asserted that no one could be "Born This Way."

Biblical Imprecision

"You Weren't Born That Way" then combines the erroneous presuppositions of "Born This Way" with one of its own errors. It argues that "Homosexuality is sin," which is an oversimplification of Scripture. It then asserts that if homosexuality is sin, and if nothing innate can be sin, then one cannot have been born homosexual.

But the Bible does not condemn the multidimensional concept our culture refers to as homosexuality. It does not condemn homosexual desire or orientation, which is part of what we mean when we use the term "homosexuality." The Bible does, however, specifically and consistently condemn homosexual behavior or relations. For instance, Leviticus 18:22 and 20:13 condemn lying with a man the way one lies with a woman. First Timothy 1:10 (NIV) speaks of those "practicing homosexuality." Romans 1:27 speaks of men who "abandoned natural relations with women and were inflamed with lust for one another," and then goes on to say, "Men committed shameful acts with other men, and received in themselves the due penalty for their error." This indicates that judgment was predicated on the act, not the desire or predisposition alone.[10]

---

10. Some people say this amounts to prohibition of male homosexuality but not female homosexuality. But they ignore certain verses to do this, such as Rom 1:26, which

"You Weren't Born That Way" condemns homosexuality (as our culture understands it) in its entirety, whereas Scripture only condemns homosexual relations (and lust) as sin. It does not condemn the orientation itself. This condemnation shares all the shortcomings of "Born This Way" theology, leaving out the fall and its consequences. But in addition to being unbiblical and illogical, it is also uninclusive. It ends up telling anyone with same-sex attraction that they cannot be reconciled to God if they still feel that attraction, as if their desires and temptations are somehow more sinful than the next person's.

Desire and Sin

In fact, no one's desires are sin. Desire can, however, become temptation. This temptation can result in sin—for instance, adultery, or even looking on a woman "to lust after her" (as in Matt 5:28, KJV). It is very common for both the "Born This Way" camp and the "You Weren't Born That Way" camp to conflate desire and sin.

Matthew Vines, in his defense of homosexual lifestyle for the Christian, contends that if homosexual relations are always sin then all homosexual desire is a sin.[11] He then notes that this would require the person with same-sex attractions to repudiate an unchangeable and innate part of herself or himself. He reasons God would never do this to a person and therefore same-sex relationships can be God-honoring if consensual and monogamous.

His reasoning has at least two weak points. First, he commits the main "Born This Way" error of not accounting for the fall. He is wrong to suppose that repudiating an innate part of himself is not part of God's salvation plan. We all, every one of us, must repudiate innate parts of ourselves. We were all born into sin, into a fallen world, with a sinful nature. Repenting of our sinful acts and our sinful nature can displace our judgment onto Christ. We can then enjoy fellowship with God.

Second, Vines is perhaps not properly parsing the difference between desire and sin. The mere fact of feeling homosexual desire is not necessarily sin any more than is heterosexual desire. It does not necessarily require self-repudiation. In other words, whereas homosexual sex is always a sin, homosexual desire is not always sin.

Let us look at heterosexual desire, for comparison. Heterosexual desire is not always sin, even for the unmarried. It is only sin when it causes one to

---

says, "Even their women exchanged natural sexual relations for unnatural ones."

11. Vines, *God and the Gay Christian*.

pursue or enact sexual relations outside of biblical marriage. Matthew 5:28 illustrates this point, even though it is often misinterpreted to say exactly the opposite. Many Christian laypersons and clergy use the verse to assert that any felt sexual desire is lust, which is a sin. However, proper exegesis actually supports the argument that not every sexual desire is sin.

In Matthew 5:28 (NIV) Jesus says, "You have heard that it was said, 'You shall not commit adultery.' But I tell you that anyone who looks at a woman lustfully has already committed adultery with her in his heart." The NIV's use of the adverb "lustfully" implies a look that has the property of being sinful or lustful. But the original Greek grammar is better reflected in the King James translation, "But I say to you that whoever looks at a woman to lust for her has already committed adultery with her in his heart." The Greek grammar clearly indicates the look is motivated by lust (here a verb); it does not merely happen to be lusty.

In fact, the Greek word translated as "lust" here is neither inherently sexual nor inherently sinful. It is *epithumeô*, a strong desire of the soul. The same word is used in Luke 22:15 when Jesus says, "I have *longed* to eat this Passover with you before I suffer." *Epithumeô* is also used in the Tenth Commandment in the Greek Septuagint version and is translated "covet" in English translations. In commenting on this passage, R. T. France says, "Jesus's intention is therefore to prohibit not a natural sexual attraction, but the deliberate harboring of desire for an illicit relationship."[12] Merely looking and then recognizing her beauty, and maybe feeling a pang of desire, is not the sin. It is the action in service of the motivation that makes this a sin.[13]

Some may be concerned that any desire for a thing that is necessarily sin must itself be a sin. Vines himself seems to think so. I suggest that while homosexual relationship is not part of God's plan for us, the desire for sexual fulfillment is not sin. The fact that one's sexual desires are homosexual rather than heterosexual, to the degree that it may be predicated on factors outside of a person's simple, direct control, is more of a cosmic sin than a personal sin. That desire is not what God originally intended. It is part of the fall, a brokenness, under which the creation groans. But it is not necessarily something one can choose, in the moment, not to feel.

Sexual actions, however, are always something one can choose to engage in or not to engage in. A homosexual person's struggle with same-sex attraction is comparable to a heterosexual person's struggle with sexual desire.

---

12. France, *Matthew*, 121.

13. He is likely also addressing a common cultural understanding of that time that it is the woman's fault if a man feels covetous toward her. Jesus here says it is the man that is to blame. For an argument supporting the idea that there is a sexual desire that is neither precisely marital nor sinful, see also Bower, "Jesus and the Lustful Eye."

While they cannot engage in sexual behavior, they do have innate desires for sex. These can lead to temptation and sin, but can also simply be desires. The immediate fulfillment of those desires would be sin, since one must be married first. But the desires are not sins in and of themselves.

In this line of thought, neither homosexual nor heterosexual desire is intrinsically sinful. It is simply a natural desire, need, or drive. There comes a point at which desire can blossom into sin. Since "the look" in Matthew 28 might not appear to an onlooker to be a sinful sexual behavior, third parties may not be able to specify for each person when they have moved from desire to sin. Each person must search his or her own heart.

In summary, Christians should not use "You Weren't Born That Way" responses because they reinforce the erroneous premises of "Born This Way," omitting the fall and its consequences. It usually involves imprecise use of Scripture relative to homosexuality, and it often conflates desire and sin. This is uninclusive, devalues homosexual persons, and condemns them in a biased manner. It is not simply an ineffective argument, upsetting the people it is levied against. It literally destroys the Christian story, making nonsense out of the doctrine of sin. So how should Christians respond?

A Better Way

A Christian response should put love front and center. God does not want his people involved in homosexual relationships, but neither does he want his people condemning others. So how should Christians proceed? Some Christians actually accept "Born This Way" theology because they believe the lie that any adherence to biblical proscriptions on homosexual relations is biased. So, in their mind, they must choose between "traditional" or "loving." They choose the latter. But this is a false dichotomy. We must stand for God's ways while affirming the value of persons. This keeps us from making oversimplified statements like "Homosexuality is sin," or "God made you that way, so it must be OK." In our age of 140-character Twitter communication, moving beyond unhelpful sound bites is difficult. However, we must push past this to construct more nuanced arguments.

Love

First, Christians must start with love. We should behave towards the homosexual, and the "Born This Way" apologist, in a way that says they really do matter. More than mere words are required. A good, minimal start is simply to not be biased. The sin of homosexual relations is no more of a sin than a heterosexual couple having sex outside of marriage. So let us not shun them as if they were any worse sinners than ourselves. Neither should we speak against them just because we know they are gay or a gay ally. There may come a time to speak a word about biblical sexuality, but just as if you were meeting a heterosexual person, that time would not be early in the relationship. Sometimes people go years without ever speaking about sexuality between friends. It is personal. There is a certain strength of relationship that is needed before it is productive to broach such things. Like anyone else, "They don't care what you know until they know that you care." We must care for those in the LGBT community who cross our path—not dismiss them, and not politely ignore them. In fact, Christians need to find a way to be gay allies. We need to provide a safe, caring space.

Those who speak about biblical sexuality from the pulpit should always word their message as if they were speaking to a dear friend who is gay—with understanding and compassion. I have heard preachers use the fully flawed "You Weren't Born That Way" argument from the pulpit. Or they attack the orientation or feelings of same-sex attraction as less than normal humanity. These are not biblical arguments (see below). If the message is too strident, a gay person will simply leave the church, and perhaps step away from God. Or they will stay in a closet and not seek out their good friends in the church to process that message. They will feel rejected by everyone, and sink deeper into fear, depression, and desperation.

The Bible

The next step is proper biblical understanding. Scripture should be our rule of faith and practice. It should not merely be a starting point from which we make generalizations. When confronted with "Born This Way" arguments, the proper response is to first assert a biblical frame for the questions and issues. Do not start with the proscriptions. Start with the affirmations. The proscriptions only make sense in that larger context. God created sex. He placed the man and woman in the garden and said it was "very good" (Gen 1:28, 31). The union of man and wife is a divine analogy to Christ and the church (Eph 5:21–33). The limits come later. For instance, one should not marry a close relative such as a parent, step-parent, grandchild, grandparent, sibling, aunt or uncle, or half-sibling (Leviticus 18).

Homosexual relations, not orientation, are condemned

As to direct proscriptions on homosexuality, Scripture clearly condemns homosexual relations, as discussed above (see "Biblical Imprecision"). However, be aware that many LGBT Christians call those passages "texts of terror" and feel abused when people quote those to them. Those passages are nonetheless inspired by God, but we need to use wisdom in how we speak to others. It is easy to be insensitive when one does not feel that the verse reprimands themselves, but only others.

The church also needs to remember that there are many ways people are sexually broken, not just in orientation. One person may want sex more often than his spouse, another less. One may wish to have sex with many people she sees, another may marry yet never really want sex. Many of these are not sin in themselves, but people often use the pain felt through such brokenness to justify their sinful behavior, and hurt one another in the process.

The man who wants sex more often than his wife may coerce her or manipulate her into it. Or he may blame her for his unhappiness. A woman who wants sex less often than her husband may ignore his needs and desires and make him feel as if he is "dirty." These are sexual sins even if they do not lead to adultery. They are relational sins even if they do not lead to divorce.

This is only a partial list of the most "acceptable" forms of sexual brokenness and sin. Often we forget that such sexual sins and brokenness are rampant in our own life or in the lives of others to whom we do not presume to pontificate. A biblical approach is to humbly remember how broken we are and speak with care into the lives of others.

While the Bible does condemn homosexual behavior, it does not condemn issues of orientation or desire. One person may be more or less biologically wired for anger and aggression, but he must still "Be angry and and do not sin" (Eph 4:26, NIV). Likewise, there may be a more or less biological predisposition to homosexual orientation. One must still not "lie with a male as with a woman" (Lev 18:22, NRSV) and so on. Therefore, we should help a Christian with same-sex attraction to see that God does not hold her responsible for the orientation itself, but for the way she responds to it. She need not repudiate herself (as Vines thinks) for feeling same-sex attraction, any more than any other person would for any other desire or temptation. But it is best not to dwell on the desire in a way that leads to temptation, or to sin.

Sin Is Innate

The Bible can also be used to show that "Born This Way" theology is mistaken in the way it construes innate attributes. Our attributes are not present only because God made them and wants them there. They are a result of both creation and the fall. Our innate drives are not necessarily good. The biblical view is that we all are born in sin (Jer 7:19; Ps 51:5) and must repent of that and walk according to the Spirit (see Gal 5:16–24) through faith in Christ. Though we innately sin, we do not all feel the same strength of inclination toward each sin. However, Scripture clearly states we are naturally sinners. This scriptural framing of innate attributes and sin is the best strategy for refuting "Born This Way" thinking. It is also an important point to raise with those who engage in "You Weren't Born That Way" arguments, since they, too, are endorsing wrong views.

Do Not Use "You Weren't Born That Way"

Since the amount of innateness does not actually bear on the sinfulness of a behavior, there is then no more need to argue over whether homosexuality is innate or a choice. We ought to be able to move past this red herring. The issue of whether homosexual relations are sin does not hang on arguments about how innate and how immutable homosexual orientation might be.

This understanding can help the Christian acknowledge an important truth. There is surely some biological influence over one's sexual orientation. The pro-LGBT movement has advanced an overly fatalistic view of biological determinism in sexual orientation to bolster the "Born This Way" view that if it is inborn, it should be acceptable. This misuse of biology does not excuse those Christians who dismiss the biological aspects of sexual orientation. Rather than argue about whether sexual orientation is innate, we should redress how "Born This Way" invokes biological fatalism. I am not required by my biology to always engage my predispositions in a particular way. This is a fundamental fact of all sin.

Compassion

Seeing that a person may have a stronger or differently directed biological drive than another may help us to be more compassionate to those of our fellow Christians who feel same-sex attraction—and not to look down on them as being "less than." This can help with the bias issue raised before. My thoughts and feeling towards the homosexual should be the same as for the heterosexual. The person who feels same-sex attraction is not someone who should be rejected on that basis. If she does not pursue such a relationship out of love for and obedience to God, she should be respected as a chaste overcomer, just as I would respect any other person who kept herself pure. My compassion for the difficulties of being single and living a chaste life should not suddenly dissipate just because a person is staying celibate from homosexual sex. The same point applies to those who do not fully embrace God's standards. A man in my church who has a male sexual partner is no worse a sinner than a man who is having sex with his girlfriend. Both are having sex outside the marriage covenant.[14] The heterosexual version is not better than the homosexual version. We must also remember that "there but for the grace of God go I."[15] Since many heterosexuals actually feel repulsed by homosexual thoughts, they may not easily sympathize and see

---

14. Some feel this comparison is unfair to the homosexual. They argue that a heterosexual can simply marry their sexual partner to find godly sexual fulfillment in marriage, whereas the homosexual cannot. But this is not necessarily as unfair as "Born This Way" supporters suppose. First of all, marriage may still not be the godly answer for the heterosexual couple. Even if he wants them to marry, he likely wants them to spend some time in proper celibacy before the wedding. After the wedding, they still could be in sin. Their heterosexuality is not righteous in and of itself. The couple might have selfish reasons for marrying and may never have the self-giving love God expects between spouses in the marriage bed (and the rest of life). In that sense, they may marry and yet not embody the holy sexuality God intended for them. While all godly sex occurs within a marriage, not all marital sex is godly.

Second, the fact that the homosexual cannot marry their same-sex partner is not the inequitable deprivation some say it is. Matthew Vines (in chapter 3 of *God and the Gay Christian*) argues that "mandatory celibacy" for gay Christians is different than the celibacy engaged by heterosexuals and that the Bible does not actually require celibacy of gay persons. He says the forced celibacy of one who is told she cannot marry a same-sex partner is nothing like the positive choice made by a heterosexual person to live celibate. He says the latter cases all involve a spiritual gift of celibacy. This line of reasoning is another bad fruit of "Born This Way" thinking. Vines views heterosexual celibacy as unproblematic because he does not really account for the fall and he presumes biological fatalism. He thinks it is self-evident that if one lived a celibate life, one must have been given a special constitution to bear that. But many people I know who live celibate lives do not have the "gift of celibacy." They simply lack the circumstances (and willing partner) to enter into a godly marriage. I personally know several who would like to marry but cannot find the person and the situation to enter into a God-honoring marriage. God does not waive the celibacy requirement for them simply because it is discomfiting. Most Christians who are celibate are not choosing celibacy as a ministry to God. It just happens to them. They live it out with a measure of contentment as worship to God. They do this not because they prefer it, or were "meant for it," but because that is how circumstances unfolded in their lives.

15. For instance, Gal 6:1: "Brothers and sisters, if someone is caught in a sin, you who live by the Spirit should restore that person gently. But watch yourselves, or you also may be tempted."

themselves as also vulnerable. But if they realize how quickly it is possible for them to fall into their own version of sexual sin, such as manipulating a spouse or looking at pornography, they might then be more merciful to gay Christians whose sinful forms are different from their own.

On a side note, Christian heterosexuals could also be more compassionate in how we treat Christian homosexuals even if we dogmatically believed it's "just a choice," and disregarded any biological predisposition. Imagine you love eating a candy bar each day at 3 p.m. You do so for ten years. One day you become convinced it's immoral. You resolve to stop. You repent of it. It is difficult to cope with 3 p.m. each day, but somehow you do. Then one day, as you throw away an empty candy bar wrapper, you are overwhelmed with guilt as you realize that you've just broken your promise. How could you have done such an immoral thing? It felt so natural. You did not even have to think about it. The habitual behavior perhaps even felt *innate*.

We live in a nation where two thirds of adults are overweight and most cannot seem to change. For most, this is not a genetic problem. It is an over-eating, under-exercising problem. This is a learned problem, and not an innate one. Yet many Christians find weight management problematic. So even if homosexual behaviors are learned and not innate, we should still recognize that change is hard—and be compassionate. A homosexual person who embraces God's view of sex might still stray in ways that seem deliberate, but are in fact just habitual.

Psychologists call such behaviors "automatic." They are so well learned that they do not require much conscious control. In fact, efforts at conscious control are often unsuccessful or awkward. Changing these automatic behaviors takes a lot of time and numerous attempts. These behaviors occur on autopilot, as it were. The autopilot experience can lead one to feel as if the behaviors are fundamental to one's person, in ways that cannot change. If even simple habits like the 3 p.m. candy bar are difficult to change, how much harder is it to change a habit that included most of a person's self-concept for years or decades? And, if in fact there is a biological component to one's feeling of sexual orientation (just as there is to one's hunger drive), there will be even more to overcome. Clearly, Christians who do not experience homosexual attraction should be more compassionate and less judgmental toward those who do.[16]

---

16. Also, Christians need to note that there is no reason for a non-Christian to see a homosexual lifestyle as immoral at all. So we should be more compassionate and understanding of non-Christians who seem to push a pro-gay agenda in the world even though we know God does not want them to do so.

None of these biological arguments is meant to minimize God's power to supernaturally change a person. I know people who were alcoholics and got saved. They never touched another alcoholic drink in their life. Their operant conditioning, classical conditioning, and biological predispositions were all at once, supernaturally, dealt with by the Holy Spirit. But I also know those who had to work very hard to beat their addiction when they came to Christ. While we should all hope, believe, and pray for God's instant, supernatural deliverance, he seems to have his own reasons for when and why he provides instantaneous healing to one person and a long process to another.

Some in the church have taught that if the gay person were just properly repentant, he would never again feel same-sex attraction. This has set up many gay Christians to feel pain, self-loathing, and failure that they did not have to feel. We must be careful not to expect a gay Christian who prays for God's deliverance to suddenly have no more trials or struggles with same-sex attraction. Feeling same-sex attraction is a result of biological, social, and psychological factors, any of which can be resistant to change. The church should not expect an end of all same-sex attraction in a convert any more than it should expect an end to any other temptation.

On the other hand, a Christian should be sober and avoid situations that might inflame her temptation to sin. Well-meaning Christian friends, hoping to help their gay friend, will often tell them not to identify or think about themselves as gay. In seeing how many members of the gay community oppose biblical morality, they worry such identification can lead the person to ruin. But telling them what labels they should or should not use for themselves can just pile more guilt or anxiety on them. Identifying as gay and a Christian is not in and of itself sinful. Nor is it indicative of a weak faith. Wesley Hill's book *Washed and Waiting* is an excellent resource, written by a powerful, committed Christian who is comfortable identifying as gay or homosexual.[17] He writes from a biblical perspective on Christian living. It is an encouraging book for gay Christians who are trying to understand how to feel about themselves and what labels they wish to accept or avoid.

However, if identifying with gay culture and being active in the LGBT community exposes one to more temptation than might otherwise occur, it may be at least advisable to limit one's participation in that culture. For instance, hanging out in gay hookup spots can make inappropriate sexual encounters more likely. If identifying oneself as gay leads to this, it is wise not to do so. Referring to oneself as "gay" might signal others that one is open to advances from other gay persons. This might also increase

17. Hill, *Washed and Waiting*.

temptation and lead to more sinful behavior than would result if one did not identify as gay. Some choose to say they are "same-sex attracted," but wish to deny the label "gay" since they see the gay culture as opposing biblical standards. While some Christians who identify as gay, as well as some gay allies, may feel this stance is hurtful to the gay community, it should be noted that the person who refuses such labels should also have the right to do so. Each person should prayerfully consider for himself or herself how (or whether) to publicly identify. Individuals should be given the leeway to find their own way to refer to themselves and feel comfortable and safe doing so within the church.

Conclusion

In the face of our culture's mores, it is difficult to keep to God's word and endorse what it says. The Bible clearly says that God's plan is for sex to be within marriage, between one man and one woman for life. Agreeing with "Born This Way" thinking and retreating from this biblical position is not the proper way to be inclusive. However, the church must also remove any anti-gay bias from the way it confronts attempts at redefining faithful and proper sexuality. This includes rejecting "Born This Way" theology. But it also includes rejecting "You Weren't Born That Way" responses.

Discounting biological influences in sexual orientation by saying "You Weren't Born That Way" is not useful in discipleship, apologetics, or evangelism. The church should quit trying to prove that sexual orientation is completely or primarily environmentally determined. Degree of innateness does not settle whether something is sin. Some people are more predisposed than others to same-sex attraction, for a variety of reasons—some biological, some environmental. None of these factors is easily overcome or diminished. Ignoring and minimizing the biological contributions to sexual orientation only decreases our compassion for the struggles of gay Christians.

Biblically imprecise overgeneralizations like "Homosexuality is sin" are also damaging and cause harm. The Bible does not comment on homosexual orientation or desire. It only condemns homosexual relations. Furthermore, let us not engage in gay bias by acting as if homosexual sins were greater than other sins. Homosexual desire is no more a sin than heterosexual desire. Either can become temptation and sin. While homosexual relations are always sin, heterosexual relations are not always holy. The mere prefix homo- does not make it better or worse than if it were hetero-.

Being in the world and not of it is difficult. There are no good, quick sound bites to carry the conversation. We must engage the nuanced issues and be kind, patient, and long-suffering in speaking God's word to our congregations and our culture.

Bibliography

Bower, Kent. "Jesus and the Lustful Eye: Glancing at Matthew 5:28." *Evangelical Quarterly* 76.4 (2004): 291–309.

Burr, Chandler. *A Separate Creation: The Search for the Biological Origins of Sexual Orientation*. New York : Hyperion, 1996.

———. "Homosexuality and Biology." *The Atlantic*, June 1997. https://www.theatlantic.com/magazine/archive/1997/06/homosexuality-and-biology/304683.

France, R. T. *Matthew: Evangelist and Teacher*. Eugene, OR: Wipf & Stock, 2004.

Germanotta, Stefani, and Jeppe Laursen. *Born This Way*. Musical album. Interscope, 2011.

Hill, Wesley. *Washed and Waiting: Reflections on Christian Faithfulness and Homosexuality*. Grand Rapids: Zondervan, 2016.

Midgley, Mary. *The Ethical Primate: Humans, Freedom and Morality*. London: Routledge, 2002.

Ponce, Phil, host. *Chicago Tonight*, WTTW, August 2, 2011. http://chicagotonight.wttw.com/2011/08/02/joel-osteen.

Pratarelli, Marc, and Krystal Mize. "Biological Determinism Fatalism: Are They Extreme Cases of Influence in Evolutionary Psychology." *Theory and Science* 3 (2002). https://www.researchgate.net/publication/259739261_Biological_determinism_fatalism_Are_they_extreme_cases_of_influence_in_Evolutionary_Psychology.

Schachter, Steven, director. *Door to Door*. Movie. Warner Bros., 2012.

Vines, Matthew. *God and the Gay Christian: The Biblical Case in Support of Same-Sex Relationships*. New York: Crown, 2015.

White, Mel. *What the Bible Says—and Doesn't Say—about Homosexuality*. Lynchburg, VA: Soulforce, 2006.

13

Same-Sex Attraction and the Calling of God

Ron Belgau

Over the last few decades, gay rights have become one of the most divisive issues in Western culture.[1] Conservative Christians have led the opposition to gay rights, and for a long time their position enjoyed the support of a cultural majority. In the past decade, however, both the law courts and public opinion have increasingly favored the gay rights movement. Today, Christian political advocates are spending less and less of their time actually opposing gay rights, and more and more of their time just fighting for their freedom to hold and live out traditional Christian beliefs about homosexuality.[2]

The divisions about homosexuality have arisen not only in the culture wars that have divided conservative Christians from the larger society,

---

1. I am grateful to All Saints Presbyterian in Austin, Texas, for inviting me to present an earlier version of this chapter. Feedback from that presentation helped me to revise and strengthen this chapter. Thanks go to Ashleen Bagnulo, Jonathan Balmer, Beverley Belgau, Thomas Bell, Kyle Blanchette, Chris Damian, Jeramy Gee, Michael Hauser, Chad Huelsman, and Aaron Taylor for discussing the content and providing feedback on the manuscript as I revised it. Thanks also go to Matt Canlis, the friend who first introduced me to *A Severe Mercy* and thus to C. S. Lewis's thinking about homosexuality and vocation. Again, I am grateful to John Cavadini and Sr. Ann Astell of the Center for Church Life at the University of Notre Dame; Christopher Roberts; and Wesley Hill, Eve Tushnet, and all of the writers at the *Spiritual Friendship* blog. All have provided an inestimable amount of inspiration and feedback as I have developed my ideas on vocation, friendship, and chastity. And finally, to Jerry Walls, Dave Baggett, and Jeremy Neill, for their patience and support in working with me on this chapter.

2. Anderson, *Truth Overruled*.

but also, increasingly, within the Christian community itself. For almost twenty centuries—despite divisions over many other aspects of Christian teaching—Christians have agreed that God created human beings male and female, and intended for marriage to be a faithful, lifelong union between a man and a woman.[3] They also agreed that both the Old and New Testaments prohibit homosexual acts under any circumstance.[4]

Until recent decades, Christian writers simply assumed the sinfulness of homosexuality, usually with nothing but a quick proof text. Beginning in the 1970s, however, lesbian, gay, and bisexual[5] advocates began to formulate a variety of arguments to reconcile same-sex marriage with Christian teaching.[6] The debate has since then been growing steadily and, as a result, virtually every major Christian denomination has now faced significant conflicts over marriage, ordination, and other issues related to homosexuality. These issues have divided individual churches, caused local churches to leave or be kicked out of their larger denominations, and even broken up the denominations themselves. In response, numerous authors have written exegetical and theological arguments defending the traditional interpretation that the Bible prohibits any and all same-sex sexual relationships.[7] Their negative argument makes clear the boundaries of Christian behavior. Although it may be necessary, it is not sufficient.

---

3. See Gen 1:27–28; 2:24; Matt 19:4–6; Mark 10:6–9; 1 Cor 7:1ff.; Eph 5:22–33.

4. Lev 18:22; 20:13; Rom 1:26–27; 1 Cor 6:9–11; and 1 Tim 1:10. Many exegetes also based the prohibition on homosexual acts on the story of Sodom and Gomorrah, found in Gen 18:16–19:29. However, the men of Sodom proposed to gang rape the angels who came to Lot, which makes the passage less directly applicable to those who argue for marriage-like same-sex relationships. Moreover, Ezek 16:49–50 blames the destruction of Sodom on a variety of sins without explicitly naming homosexual acts. Given these factors, the case for prohibition is clearer in Leviticus and the Pauline passages.

5. In contemporary discussion, it's common to lump lesbian, gay, bisexual, and transgender into a single acronym, LGBT. However, lesbian, gay, and bisexual deal with sexual orientation, and transgender deals with gender identity. Since the discussion in this chapter focuses on how Christians should respond to those with same-sex attractions, not on questions of gender identity, I only reference gay, lesbian, and bisexual persons. For an evangelical Christian perspective on transgender issues, see Yarhouse, *Understanding Gender Dysphoria*.

6. For a more academic revisionist argument, see Brownson, *Bible, Gender, Sexuality*. For personal narratives aimed at a more popular audience, see Lee, *Torn*; Vines, *God and the Gay Christian*.

7. For an accessible presentation of this traditional interpretation of the Bible's teaching, see DeYoung, *What Does the Bible Really Teach about Homosexuality?* For a more in-depth academic argument, see Gagnon, *Bible and Homosexual Practice*. See also "Homosexuality" in Hays, *Moral Vision of the New Testament*, 379–406. For a presentation of both sides of the debate, see Sprinkle, *Two Views on Homosexuality, the Bible, and the Church*.

In this chapter, I want to explore a different question. Suppose a gay, lesbian, or bisexual person accepts the traditional interpretation of the Bible. How should he or she live? As Eve Tushnet has observed, ". . . you can't have a vocation of not-gay-marrying and not-having-sex. You can't have a vocation of No."[8]

While a lot of attention has been focused on politics and biblical exegesis—on making clear what Christians oppose—there has been a lot less focus on the question of the positive vocation that a same-sex-attracted Christian might have. Surprisingly perhaps, this question was addressed as early as 1953, in a letter from C. S. Lewis to Sheldon Vanauken. Vanauken was an American who studied at Oxford shortly after World War II and converted to Christianity under Lewis's influence. After returning to the United States, he taught at Lynchburg College, where he and his wife led an informal ministry to students. In the fall of 1953, after two students approached the couple to talk about their own struggles with homosexuality, Vanauken wrote to Lewis for advice.

Lewis began by asserting something that was much less controversial in 1953: that any homosexual activity is sinful.[9] But he didn't stop with that prohibition. He insisted that even those with a serious struggle, like being attracted to the same sex, still have gifts and a calling to serve the body of Christ: "in homosexuality, as in every other tribulation," the works of God can be made manifest. That is, "every disability conceals a vocation, if only we can find it, which will 'turn the necessity to glorious gain.'"[10]

This should not surprise us as much as it perhaps does. Every human struggles with temptation and sin, and yet the mysterious and glorious message of the gospel is that God still gives us gifts and calls us to serve him. In his first letter to Timothy, just after calling homosexual acts sin, the apostle Paul gives thanks that Christ "judged me faithful, appointing me to His service, though formerly I was a blasphemer, persecutor, and insolent opponent," and insists that "Christ Jesus came into the world to save sinners, of whom I am the foremost" (1 Tim 1:12–13, 15).[11] This does not mean that blasphemy or persecution is good in God's eyes, any more than homosexual acts are. But God calls all sinners to repentance and gives them gifts to serve his church. In a profound meditation on spiritual gifts and God's calling, Paul wrote:

---

8. Tushnet, "Botany Club." Also, Tushnet, *Gay and Catholic*.
9. Vanauken, *Severe Mercy*, 147.
10. Ibid.
11. All biblical quotations in this chapter are from the ESV.

> The eye cannot say to the hand, "I have no need of you," nor again the head to the feet, "I have no need of you." On the contrary, the parts of the body that seem to be weaker are indispensable, and on those parts of the body that we think less honorable we bestow the greater honor, and our unpresentable parts are treated with greater modesty, which our more presentable parts do not require. But God has so composed the body, giving greater honor to the part that lacked it, that there may be no division in the body, but that the members may have the same care for one another. If one member suffers, all suffer together; if one member is honored, all rejoice together. (1 Cor 12:21–26)

Thus, my argument in this chapter is shaped by two convictions—one negative and one positive. On the negative side, I stand with the long-held Christian belief that gay or lesbian sexual relationships are always contrary to God's plan for human love and human sexuality as revealed in the Bible. I believe that sexual attraction to a person of the same sex is a temptation, and a result of the fall. On the positive side, however, I affirm that God gives *every* Christian gifts for the purpose of building up the body of Christ, and that our struggles with temptation and sin do not change this—"the gifts and the calling of God are irrevocable" (Rom 11:29).

In the balance of this chapter I will affirm that God calls us to obey his commandments (see John 14:15). But I will also argue that God's call is the distinctively positive context for understanding the pastoral care of same-sex-attracted Christians. In order to develop this positive theology of vocation for same-sex-attracted Christians, I will explore three major vocation-related themes: marriage, celibacy, and friendship.

The Calling to Marriage or Celibacy

In the pre-Reformation Catholic Church, the idea of vocation, or a call from God, was primarily associated with celibate vocations to the priesthood or religious life. Marriage was not regarded as sinful, but a person who was married was seen as a kind of second-class Christian. In reaction against this, many of the Protestant Reformers stressed that Christians in any form of life could glorify God.[12] The Protestants believed that Christians were called to sanctify every aspect of human life, and not to withdraw into a monastic life apart from the world. With regard to the sanctification of work, the differences between the two approaches at times

---

12. For an introduction to these ideas, see McGrath, "Calvin and the Christian Calling."

were not so great. The Benedictines, for example, stressed that both work and prayer were essential to their monastic calling. Still, at the same time, the general vocational teaching of Roman Catholics tended to focus on the priestly and religious callings, while the focus of the Protestant Reformers was on the call to sanctify every aspect of human life. For Protestants, this included marriage, and not just secular work. More recently, the emphasis of Catholics since the Second Vatican Council has been on the universality of God's call.[13] Pope John Paul II, in particular, emphasized the importance of marriage as a path to holiness.[14]

The emphasis of the Protestant Reformers on marriage as a calling from God was a helpful correction. But the Reformers, in reaction to the Catholic emphasis on celibate vocations, often treated celibacy as a questionable, if not downright dangerous, lifestyle—in spite of Christ's words about choosing to give up marriage for the sake of the kingdom, and Paul's wish that everyone could remain single, as he was (Matt 19:12; 1 Cor 7:7, 38).[15]

The overemphasis of Protestants (and some Catholics) on marriage has shaped the debate over homosexuality in two important ways. The first is that it is one of the factors that contributed to the failure of the ex-gay movement. After the Stonewall Riots in 1969,[16] the gay rights movement became increasingly visible in American culture. Even before the rise of the Christian Right's opposition to gay rights (which began around 1977), some Christians had begun ministries to those struggling with homosexuality. One of the earliest of these, Love in Action, was formed in 1973. Other ministries formed, and in 1976 Exodus International was founded as an umbrella organization for such ministries. Because of the strong emphasis on marriage in evangelical culture, the ex-gay ministries focused on the

13. See, for example, Paul VI, *Dogmatic Constitution on the Church*.

14. John Paul II, *Love and Responsibility*; John Paul II, *Man and Woman He Created Them*.

15. For a contemporary example of Protestant skepticism about single pastors, Al Mohler, an influential Southern Baptist leader, was quoted as telling his students that "if they remain single, they need to understand that there's going to be a significant limitation on their ability to serve as a pastor." Eckholm, "Single and Evangelical?"

16. The Stonewall Riots are widely viewed as the catalyst for the modern gay rights movement. In the early morning hours of June 28, 1969, the New York Police Department raided the Stonewall Inn, a gay bar in Greenwich Village. Homosexual conduct was illegal, and such raids were routine in the 1950s and 1960s. At the Stonewall Inn, however, the patrons resisted police, and the clash led to riots that continued for two nights. The riots led to the formation of an organized gay liberation movement. The first gay pride parades were organized in June, 1970 to commemorate the riots. Within the modern gay rights movement, they have a symbolic value similar to the Battles of Lexington and Concord in American self-consciousness, marking the first battle in a long fight for freedom.

testimonies of gays and lesbians who had not only stopped engaging in homosexual activity, but had married someone of the opposite sex.[17] The theology behind this promise of "healing"—which often drew on ideas from the charismatic movement or the prosperity gospel—was at odds with many evangelicals' beliefs about how God answers prayer in other areas of life. Nevertheless, the widespread belief that marriage is almost the only way to have meaningful Christian life made this seem like the only way to offer a positive message to gay and lesbian Christians, who were being told that they could not pursue same-sex relationships.

In time, however, the idea of orientation change proved for many to be a false hope, which led, among other things, to shattered families. John Paulk, the former chairman of the board of Exodus International, was caught in a gay bar; later he divorced his wife, renounced his ex-gay beliefs, and is now pursuing relationships with other men. Alan Chambers, the former president of Exodus International, has rejected his past statements about orientation change and is now more open to supporting those in gay relationships, although he personally remains committed to his wife, Leslie.[18]

Ironically, the belief of many Christians that marriage is almost the only viable form of love has also strengthened the argument for same-sex marriage in many people's minds, especially as the ex-gay narrative began to come apart. If marriage is necessary for flourishing, and opposite-sex marriage isn't possible for most gays and lesbians, then the alternative must be same-sex marriage. Forced celibacy seems like an unbearable burden.

For example, Matthew Vines has argued that Christians have always regarded celibacy as a spiritual gift and calling, and not something that can be forced on people. It is only for those who have a special gift and freely choose to embrace it.[19] Vines claims that both Jesus and Paul taught this view, but, like many of Vines's claims, this is not supported by the biblical text. One of the key biblical passages for understanding celibacy is Matthew 19:12: "There are eunuchs who have been so from birth, and there are eunuchs who have been made eunuchs by men, and there are eunuchs who have made themselves eunuchs for the sake of the kingdom of heaven.

---

17. The most prominent of these testimonies was John Paulk's, which he described in Paulk, *Not Afraid to Change*. For a more general overview of ex-gay beliefs, see Davies and Rentzel, *Coming Out of Homosexuality*; Chambers, *God's Grace and the Homosexual Next Door*.

18. Alan Chambers has told the story of his evolving beliefs on homosexuality in Chambers, *My Exodus*.

19. Vines, *God and the Gay Christian*, 44. Vines is the founder of the Reformation Project, an organization that advocates for same-sex marriage and other gay rights issues within the church.

He who is able to receive this, let him receive it." Vines's mistake stems, at least in part, from his focus on only a third of what Jesus says in this verse. If those in the last category of eunuch voluntarily chose celibacy for the sake of the kingdom,[20] those in the first two categories had no choice. For them, marriage was excluded either by an accident of birth or by something imposed on them by force at a young age. We should also remember that many people who would like to marry are unable to do so due to various circumstances. For example, the prophet Isaiah speaks of a day when the men of Israel will fall by the sword, when, with so few available husbands, seven women will ask one man to marry them (Isa 3:16—4:1).

Christians are born unmarried. Getting married is a momentous decision, and not merely a stage of life that everyone automatically traverses unless they are given a special gift. When Jesus talks about the depth of commitment required for marriage, some of the disciples say, "If such is the case of a man with his wife, it is better not to marry" (Matt 19:10). When the apostle Paul writes to the Corinthians about marriage, he advises them, "I want you to be free from anxieties. The unmarried man is anxious about the things of the Lord, how to please the Lord. But the married man is anxious about worldly things, how to please his wife, and his interests are divided" (1 Cor 7:32–34). He makes a similar point about unmarried women, and then concludes, "I say this for your own benefit, not to lay any restraint upon you, but to promote good order and to secure your undivided devotion to the Lord. . . . So then he who marries his betrothed does well, and he who refrains from marriage will do even better" (1 Cor 7:35, 38).

While the ex-gay movement often provided a false hope of orientation change, this does not mean that Christians should just out-and-out dismiss marriage as a vocation for same-sex attracted Christians. For example, although Alan Chambers has admitted that he didn't experience the orientation change that he had hoped for, he nevertheless loves his wife and remains committed to fulfilling the promises he made to her at the altar a couple of decades ago.

Human sexuality is a complex thing. While some people are either exclusively attracted to the same sex or exclusively attracted to the opposite

---

20. In his comments on an earlier draft of this chapter, Kyle Blanchette suggested that if a Christian has a clear sense that he or she is being called by God to become "a eunuch for the sake of the kingdom," obedience to this is not "voluntary" in the sense that a person could either "take it or leave it." Elisabeth Elliot discussed her own struggle to discern whether the call she felt to be a missionary was also a call to give up marriage in Elliot, *Passion and Purity*. Elisabeth wanted to marry Jim Elliot, but they were both sure that they were called to be missionaries. They waited to marry until they were sure this would not get in the way of God's call to the mission field. So even the third category of "eunuch" may not always choose as freely as Matthew Vines suggests.

sex, others experience some attraction to both sexes. Attraction itself is a complex concept. Some people start out with a strong sexual attraction to their future spouse, and, having almost no knowledge of their character, only later determine that this is a person who is not only physically attractive, but also someone with whom they could spend the rest of their lives. Others are drawn first to the person's character, or intelligence, or humor, or artistic abilities. For such persons, the physical attraction might only come later. Still others function differently. There are many different roads to the altar.

Often, happily married couples who age and lose the kind of physical attractiveness that drives Hollywood and Madison Avenue nevertheless learn how perpetually to rekindle their attraction, even as their attraction may become more difficult to understand from the outside. Over many years of getting to know gay, lesbian, and bisexual Christians who ended up in opposite-sex marriages, I've heard some interesting stories about how their attractions developed. Such stories are very difficult to reduce to a simple label like "gay," "ex-gay," or "bisexual."[21] Generally speaking, however, I've heard persons speak first of developing a deep friendship with someone of the opposite sex, and then gradually realizing that they did not just feel a deep spiritual connection to this person; they also could see themselves spending the rest of their lives together as husband and wife. They often went through a period of doubt—what if they married and then, like John Paulk or numerous other ex-gay leaders, left to pursue a gay relationship? This is a serious worry that every couple in this situation should face head-on. However, it's not unique to same-sex-attracted men or women who are contemplating an opposite-sex marriage. Heterosexual desire is no guarantee of long-term marital stability.

If a person with strong same-sex attractions has fallen in love with someone of the opposite sex, a lot of the questions he or she needs to ask are questions that any couple considering marriage should ask. However, there are also some questions that should arise that are situationally unique. For example: Am I really attracted to this person? Can I imagine living as husband and wife? And do I understand my own sexual struggles sufficiently under control that, with God's grace, I can remain faithful to my husband or wife as long as we both shall live? No engaged couple can easily answer these questions, but if there is a genuine mutual attraction to a person of the

---

21. The *Spiritual Friendship* blog, which I cofounded, has tended to focus more on Christian theology related to celibacy and homosexuality than it has on opposite-sex marriage. However, we have published a number of reflections by same-sex-attracted men and women in opposite-sex marriages describing their own experiences and sharing what they have learned about marriage. To read some of these stories, see the articles at https://spiritualfriendship.org/2014/06/04/marriage-roundup.

opposite sex, the fact that there are also attractions to people of the same sex should not necessarily be an obstacle to marriage. It should just be part of the mix of issues that the couple would discuss with each other, their pastor, premarital counselor, and trusted friends and family members—in the same way any couple would try to sort through potential challenges.

On the other hand, lesbian or gay Christians who accept the traditional interpretation of the Bible and try to live by it should not be pressured into marriage by well-meaning friends or family members who see this as the only possible solution. Remember that the apostle Paul worried that marriage would bring unnecessary anxiety (1 Cor 7:32–35); he certainly would not have pressured persons into marriages they did not want. Nor should lesbian or gay Christians themselves assume that if they are not married they are cut off from God's promises. In addition to the passages from Matthew and 1 Corinthians cited above, the prophet Isaiah said, "let not the eunuch say, 'Behold, I am a dry tree.' For thus says the Lord: 'To the eunuchs who keep my Sabbaths, who choose the things that please me and hold fast my covenant, I will give in my house and within my walls a monument and a name better than sons and daughters; I will give them an everlasting name that shall not be cut off'" (Isa 56:3–5). Likewise, in the Gospel of Mark, Jesus tells His disciples,

> Truly, I say to you, there is no one who has left house or brothers or sisters or mother or father or children or lands, for my sake and for the gospel, who will not receive a hundredfold now in this time, houses and brothers and sisters and mothers and children and lands, with persecutions, and in the age to come eternal life. But many who are first will be last, and the last first. (Mark 10:29–31)

For those Christians who are unable to marry, these verses set out a calling that may at times seem difficult to heed. For the rest of the church, they offer a different kind of calling: how can we make our church a place where this calling can be fulfilled?

Friendship and Vocation

An important part of the answer to this question, I believe, is recovering a Christian understanding of friendship. The *Spiritual Friendship* blog, which Wesley Hill and I cofounded several years ago, has tried to explore this problem from a variety of angles.[22] Friendship is more important in the

---

22. https://spiritualfriendship.org. See also Hill, *Spiritual Friendship*.

Bible than many Christians realize. The books of James and 2 Chronicles call Abraham a friend of God (2 Chr 20:7; Jas 2:23). God "spoke to Moses face to face, as a man speaks to his friend" (Exod 33:11). At the Last Supper, on the night when Christ instituted the new and eternal covenant, he said to the Twelve, "No longer do I call you servants, for a servant does not know what his master is doing; but I have called you friends, for all that I have heard from my Father I have made known to you" (John 15:15). He also frames his own sacrifice on the cross—the definitive act in salvation history—as an act of friendship: "Greater love has no man than this, that he lay down his life for his friends" (John 15:13).

Since we sought to explore the Christian meaning of friendship, we named our blog after a series of dialogues on spiritual friendship by a twelfth-century Cistercian monk named Aelred of Rievaulx. He wrote the dialogues to provide "rules for a pure and holy love," and to show that some ideas of friendship found in the ancient philosophers—particularly Cicero—could be "supported by the authority of the Scriptures."[23] In order to explain this teaching on friendship, I will turn to ancient philosophy, Scripture, and the ancient and medieval Christian writings that fused the two together.

In the first chapters of the Letter to the Romans, the apostle Paul argued that it is possible for humans to know certain things about God and about how they ought to live, and that we actively suppress these truths. In exchanging the truth about our ultimate good for false goods, our love for both God and neighbor was corrupted. However, even without the revelation of God's will that was given to the Jews, some pagans recognized the true good and tried to pursue it (Rom 1:18–32; 2:14–16; see also Acts 17:16–34). A medieval Christian like Thomas Aquinas could agree with a pagan philosopher like Aristotle that human beings always act to gain what they perceive to be good. However, when philosophers examined the kind of goods that most human beings pursue, they recognized that most pursue false goods—e.g., pleasure, wealth, honor, power, glory.[24] Even the pagan Aristotle, however, could see that these were false goods, and that the highest good was virtue and a kind of contemplation of ultimate reality.[25] Aristotle's was a view not too distant from that of Aquinas, who recognized that the highest good for human beings is the beatific vision of God.[26]

---

23. Dutton, *Aelred Of Rievaulx*, 53 (prologue, paras. 6–7).

24. Aquinas, *Summa Theologiae*, Ia-IIae 2, 3; Aristotle, *Nicomachean Ethics*, 1.4–5. See also Rom 1:18–32.

25. *Nicomachean Ethics*, 1.6–7; 10. See also Rom 2:13–16; Acts 17:27–28.

26. Aquinas, *Summa Theologiae* Ia-IIae 3.8.

Friendship is based on the shared interests or pursuits that draw friends together, and the nature of the friendship is determined by the nature of those shared interests.[27] Aristotle recognized that those who focused on different kinds of goods would develop different kinds of friendship. Those who understood the highest good to be pleasure would form their closest friendships with those who also sought pleasure, and their friendships would be shaped by that shared pursuit. (Much of the pre-AIDS gay liberation movement was a particularly extreme version of this kind of "friendship.") Those who valued worldly success—wealth, honor, power, glory—would be drawn to those with the same goals, and their friendship would take shape from their shared goals.

But the only true friendship was to be found among those who pursued the genuine goods of virtue and contemplation.[28] This division of friendship was picked up and adapted by later Christian writers, including Aelred of Rievaulx and Thomas Aquinas. Aelred distinguishes spiritual friendship from carnal friendship, based on the mutual pursuit of pleasure, and worldly friendship, based on the pursuit of wealth, honor, power, and glory.[29] Pleasure and wealth are fleeting, he argues, and only when friendship is based on shared Christian discipleship and mutual encouragement in Christ can it fulfill the promise that "A friend loves at all times" (Prov 17:17).[30] Indeed, David and Jonathan swore a covenant with each other, making a formal commitment to seal their friendship (see 1 Sam 18:1; 20:17).[31]

Those who value pleasure or worldly success, like the prodigal son, take the gifts that have been bestowed on them, go to a far country, and spend them on fulfilling their own goals and desires. On the other hand, those who see that God is their highest good will seek to use the gifts he has given them to respond to his call. Thus true friends in Christ will help each other to discern God's gifts and his call, and encourage each other in using their gifts to fulfill that call.

Friendship isn't just a nice saying from the Last Supper, or a concept in a medieval treatise. As American culture becomes more hostile to Christianity, it will become more important for Christians to foster communities where they can support and encourage each other. Hosting a small group dinner, hiking trip, or movie night can be ways for people with common

27. Dutton, *Aelred of Rievaulx*, 62; also, John Cassian, *Institutes*, 16.2.
28. *Nicomachean Ethics*, 8.2–6.
29. Dutton, *Aelred of Rievaulx*, 61–64 (bk. 1, paras. 33–49).
30. Ibid., 102 (bk. 3, para. 63). See also Belgau, "Love, Covenant, and Friendship."
31. At that time, a covenant was a binding legal agreement. For a discussion of Byzantine covenant friendships, see Rapp, *Brother-Making in Late Antiquity and Byzantium*.

interests to get to know each other better. Churches that encourage their members in these kinds of community-building activities can go a long way toward nurturing the kind of Christ-centered friendships Aelred described. Even more radically, Rod Dreher suggested that Christians might build single-sex group houses for single members to live in prayerful fellowship.[32] Even where these kinds of community initiatives are not in place, Christians who recognize the value of Christ-centered friendship can be more proactive about trying to cultivate good friendships.

Responding to God's Call

I've already said a bit about discerning whether or not one is called to marriage, and a bit about how friendship in Christ can provide encouragement and support—both for unmarried and married Christians. But for a gay, lesbian, or bisexual Christian—as with any Christian—God's calling cannot be reduced to marital status, even if marital status does do a lot to give shape to that calling.

Sometimes, God's call is fairly clear. We find ourselves facing a choice where the Bible speaks clearly against one of the choices. We need only consult its teaching to know that we cannot choose that. I believe that the Bible's teaching on sexuality rules out marriage to another man as a legitimate calling for me.

Or, when choosing between two potentially good pathways, we pray and have a clear sense that God is calling us to follow one path rather than another. Although I see both marriage and celibacy as possible good ways of serving God, I have long had a clear sense that I was called to celibacy.

Again, we may look back at past decisions and realize that we've ignored God's word, or we've failed to seek his guidance in prayer, and then, like the prodigal son, we hear him calling us to repent and return to him. I have found that it is often when I feel most sure that God is calling me *here* rather than *there* that I drift away from prayer and allow myself to rely on my own guidance and abilities, rather than remembering my dependence on God. When this happens, I may have a moment of clarity where I see how I have drifted off track, and realize that I need to turn back.

Often, however, our walk with God isn't quite like this. We may agonize over decisions, and pray for clarity, without receiving a clear sense of which path God calls us to take. A recent conversation with a friend of mine facing a time of transition gave me some perspective on this kind of trust. He has been in the military for several years. In a few months, he will be

---

32. Dreher, *Benedict Option*, 213.

transitioning back to civilian life. As he sorts through his post-military options, finding and fulfilling God's calling for him is one of his most important considerations.

In his conversation with me he contrasted his experience in the military with his experience of faith. In the military, he said, he always knows where he's supposed to be. If he's ordered to Iraq or Afghanistan, he goes. If he's sent to training at Fort Benning, he goes. And there are very serious consequences if he disobeys an order. In short, he knows clearly what the military wants him to do, and he would know very quickly if he failed to do it. So far, however, he doesn't have that kind of clarity about where God is calling him next. The decisions he makes in the next few months will do a lot to shape what the rest of his life looks like, where he will live, and what career path he will take. One of the insights that has helped him, however, is the realization that no matter where he goes or what he does, there will be men and women who need to hear the gospel and know the love of God. God can use the gifts he has given my friend in many different ways. He must to be attentive to God and trust that God will show him what he needs to do just when he needs to do it. So he has realized that responding to God's call is not just about getting big, life-altering decisions "right." It's also, once those decisions are made, about trusting God and becoming sensitive to his guidance day to day.

Responding to this call also requires trust. Fr. John Kavanaugh was one of my mentors in graduate school. Over lunch one day, I was talking with him about my own vocational uncertainty, and he told me a story. In the 1970s, near the beginning of his life as priest, he spent a year in India to focus on prayer, service, and ministry to the poor. During his time in India, he spent a month working at Mother Teresa's House of the Dying in Calcutta. While he was there, he sought Mother Teresa's counsel for his own future. Should he go back to the United States and become a philosophy professor, or should he continue to work with the poor in India or Africa? He asked that she pray that he would have clarity regarding which choice was God's will for him. Much to his surprise, she refused to pray that he would have clarity. What he needed, she said, was trust. "She said that she never had clarity," he recalled; "all she had was trust." Ultimately, he came back to the US and taught at St. Louis University until his death in 2011.[33] The lesson here, however, is that fulfilling God's call is not just about making the *right* decision about where or how to serve, but about trusting God each

---

33. Fr. Kavanaugh also told this story to Clayton Berry. See Berry, "SLU Jesuit Philosopher Recounts Transforming Time Spent with Mother Teresa."

day, wherever he places us: "let each person lead the life that the Lord has assigned to him, and to which God has called him" (1 Cor 7:17).

Conclusion

A single chapter like this cannot hope to address all of the issues raised by the gay rights movement or by the increased visibility of lesbian, gay, and bisexual people in our families and churches. What I hope I have done, however, is provided a place to start.

Every Christian struggles with temptation and sin. However, God's grace restores us when we fail, and gives us strength to resist temptation. We have also all received gifts and a call to serve him and his people. We can examine our own gifts or help others to discover how God may have equipped them to build up his church. As we encourage each other to grow in grace and use our gifts, we will become more grateful for just how much God has given to all of us.

Whether we marry or not is an important question that will give shape to the way we respond to this call. Opposite-sex marriage may be an option for some same-sex attracted Christians, but it should not be rushed into or pushed as a solution by well-meaning families, pastors, or friends. In contemporary Christian culture, it's easy to see marriage and family life as a way of loving and being loved. But it's harder for many to imagine how a single life can be a way of loving and being loved. This is especially true when the surrounding culture treats sexual fulfillment and romance as essential for a healthy human life.

In order to combat this, I have tried to provide at least a small glimpse of the importance of friendship in the Christian tradition, and pointed to biblical examples, like David and Jonathan, of friends who cared deeply for each other. Because friendship is generally based on common interests, there is no one-size-fits-all plan for how to cultivate friendships. However, I have tried to suggest both simple and radical ways for Christians to cultivate deeper friendships.

It would be nice if I could provide a complete roadmap for this process. Often, however, we do not understand in advance the role God has for us. We must strive to follow what he has made clear, while trusting that he will give us opportunities to love and serve, and also put others in our lives who will provide us with the support that we need to fulfill his call. This trust can be difficult, especially when we don't see how obedience can lead to a life that will be good for us. Renewed attention to what the Bible has to say about friendship and celibacy, and how that teaching has been understood and lived out by Christians in the past, will give us greater hope and insight to face the challenges of today.

And so, as the Christian community confronts the challenges of the sexual revolution in general, and the gay rights movement in particular, gift and vocation, marriage and celibacy, and Christ-centered friendship can provide us with waymarks that will help us to recover and live a more gospel-centered vision.

Bibliography

Anderson, Ryan T. *Truth Overruled: The Future of Marriage and Religious Freedom.* Washington, DC: Regnery, 2015.

Brownson, James V. *Bible, Gender, Sexuality: Reframing the Church's Debate on Same-Sex Relationships.* Grand Rapids: Eerdmans, 2013.

Belgau, Ron. "Love, Covenant, and Friendship." *Spiritual Friendship*, September 15, 2015. https://spiritualfriendship.org/2015/09/15/love-covenant-and-friendship.

Berry, Clayton. "SLU Jesuit Philosopher Recounts Transforming Time Spent with Mother Teresa." Saint Louis University, September 4, 2007. Reproduced with permission at http://www.catholiceducation.org/en/faith-and-character/faith-and-character/jesuit-philosopher-recounts-time-with-mother-teresa.html.

Chambers, Alan. *God's Grace and the Homosexual Next Door.* Eugene, OR: Harvest House, 2006.

———. *My Exodus: From Fear to Grace.* Grand Rapids: Zondervan, 2015.

Davies, Bob, and Lori Rentzel. *Coming Out of Homosexuality: New Freedom for Men and Women.* Downers Grove, IL: InterVarsity, 2009.

DeYoung, Kevin. *What Does the Bible Really Teach about Homosexuality?* Wheaton, IL: Crossway, 2015.

Dreher, Rod. *The Benedict Option: A Strategy for Christians in a Post-Christian Nation.* New York: Penguin, 2017.

Dutton, Marsha L. *Aelred of Rievaulx: Spiritual Friendship.* Trappist, KY: Liturgical, 2010.

Eckholm, Erik. "Single and Evangelical? Good Luck Finding Work as a Pastor." *New York Times*, March 21, 2011. https://www.nytimes.com/2011/03/22/us/22pastor.html.

Elliot, Elisabeth. *Passion and Purity: Learning to Bring Your Love Life under Christ's Control.* Grand Rapids: Revell, 2013.

Gagnon, Robert A. J. *The Bible and Homosexual Practice: Texts and Hermeneutics.* Nashville: Abingdon, 2010.

Hays, Richard. *The Moral Vision of the New Testament: Community, Cross, New Creation: A Contemporary Introduction to New Testament Ethic.* New York: HarperCollins, 2013.

Hill, Wesley. *Spiritual Friendship: Finding Love in the Church as a Celibate Gay Christian.* Grand Rapids: Brazos, 2015.

John Cassian. *John Cassian: The Conferences.* Translated by Boniface Ramsey. Ancient Christian Writers 57. New York: Paulist, 1997.

John Paul II, Pope. *Love and Responsibility*. Translated by H. T. Willetts. San Francisco: Ignatius, 1993.

———. *Man and Woman He Created Them: A Theology of the Body*. Translated by Michael Waldstein. Boston, MA: Pauline, 2006.

Lee, Justin. *Torn: Rescuing the Gospel from the Gays-vs.-Christians Debate*. New York, NY: Jericho Books, 2012.

McGrath, Alister. "Calvin and the Christian Calling." *First Things*, June 1999. https://www.firstthings.com/article/1999/06/calvin-and-the-christian-calling.

Paul VI, Pope. *Dogmatic Constitution on the Church: Lumen Gentium*. 2nd ed. Boston: Pauline, 1965.

Paulk, John, with Tony Marco. *Not Afraid to Change: The Remarkable Story of How One Man Overcame Homosexuality*. Mukilteo, WA: WinePress, 1998.

Rapp, Claudia. *Brother-Making in Late Antiquity and Byzantium: Monks, Laymen, and Christian Ritual*. Oxford: Oxford University Press, 2016.

Sprinkle, Preston, editor. *Two Views on Homosexuality, the Bible, and the Church*. Grand Rapids: Zondervan, 2016.

Tushnet, Eve. "The Botany Club: Gay Kids in Catholic Schools." *American Conservative*. May 5, 2012. http://www.theamericanconservative.com/2012/05/30/the-botany-club-gay-kids-in-catholic-schools.

———. *Gay and Catholic: Accepting My Sexuality, Finding Community, Living My Faith*. Notre Dame, IN: Ave Maria, 2014.

Vanauken, Sheldon. *A Severe Mercy*. New York: HarperCollins, 2011.

Vines, Matthew. *God and the Gay Christian: The Biblical Case in Support of Same-Sex Relationships*. New York: Crown, 2015.

Yarhouse, Mark A. *Understanding Gender Dysphoria: Navigating Transgender Issues in a Changing Culture*. Downers Grove, IL: InterVarsity, 2015.

14

The Sexual Pluralist Revolution

Reasons to Be Skeptical

JAMES S. SPIEGEL

This generation has seen a decisive move away from the Judeo-Christian sexual norms that have prevailed in the West for centuries. The shift has involved a move toward *sexual pluralism*, the view that any sexual behavior is morally permissible so long as it takes place between mutually consenting adults. In fact, this is nothing short of revolutionary, as it constitutes a radical and abrupt change of practice and moral perspective. And it should be troubling to anyone who prizes the values of the Judeo-Christian tradition, because it flouts both natural law and biblical teaching on sexuality. But it is also troubling for non-theological reasons. Here I will note some reasons why we should be especially skeptical of the rise of sexual pluralism. I will give special attention to homosexual conduct both because it is so heavily emphasized by sexual pluralists and because it is now a point of controversy even within some Christian communities.

I believe that, even aside from biblical considerations, we should be skeptical of sexual pluralism because this movement *has not been driven by rational argument*. The driving forces behind this cultural revolution have nothing to do with theological argument, scientific discoveries, or any other actual evidence. Rather, they have to do with popular culture and lifestyle choices.

The Problematic Scientific Argument for Sexual Pluralism

Many sexual pluralists insist that there is a good argument for their view, specifically the argument from nature—that science has proven our sexual orientation to be innate, not under one's control. And what is not under one's control is not properly subject to moral assessment. After all, as Kant famously maintained, "ought implies can."[1] However, this so-called argument from science is spurious. No credible studies have proven a biological basis for homosexual orientation.

The most interesting studies related to this issue regard identical (monozygotic) twins. Such studies inquire into the degree of similarity, or "concordance," between twins regarding the occurrence of various traits. If homosexuality has a completely genetic cause, then there should be 100 percent concordance (hetero- or homosexual) between identical twins. And this should be true for all identical twins, whether raised together or adopted away from one another. One of the earliest studies was conducted by Franz Kallmann, who found a 100 percent concordance rate among male homosexual twins.[2] But the study was seriously flawed. Among the problems is the fact that the subjects studied were all institutionalized or mentally ill. But, most importantly, no adopted-away twins were included, which of course constitutes a failure to eliminate home environmental factors as a common determining factor. Also, subsequent research on identical twins undermined the findings of the Kallmann study, even as early as the Rainer, et al. study of 1960.[3] Later studies have also undermined Kallmann's study, as I explain below. Remarkably, the Kallmann study is still sometimes cited as definitive evidence for the biological basis thesis.

Among more recent studies, Bailey and Pillard found a 52 percent concordance for identical (monozygotic) twins raised together as compared to a 22 percent concordance for nonidentical (dizygotic) twins.[4] This would seem to suggest genetics as one contributing cause. But critics have noted that the sample source of this study was obtained through homophilic publications, and concordant twins tend to respond more frequently to research

---

1. Precisely, Kant says: "The action to which the 'ought' applies must indeed be possible under natural conditions." Kant, *Critique of Pure Reason*, 473. Elsewhere, he puts it like this: "if the moral law commands that we ought to be better human beings now, it inescapably follows that we must be capable of being better human beings." Kant, *Religion and Rational Theology*, 94.
2. Kallmann, "Twin and Sibship Study of Overt Male Homosexuality."
3. Rainer et al., "Homosexuality and Heterosexuality in Identical Twins."
4. Bailey and Pillard, "Genetic Study of Male Sexual Orientation."

advertisements. Also, in the Bailey and Pillard study the sexual orientations of both twins were not reported directly in most cases. Finally, later studies have suggested other problems with their research. For instance, the King and McDonald study found lower concordance rates than Bailey and Pillard and inadvertently discovered a high frequency of sexual relations between identical twins.[5] Such behavior could account for a significant percentage of the concordance rate among identicals (confirming what some earlier researchers had theorized about the role of incest). King and McDonald concluded that "discordance for sexual orientation in the monozygotic pairs confirm[s] that genetic factors are an [sic] insufficient explanation of the development of sexual orientation."[6]

In addition to the many twin studies, some researchers have looked at neuroanatomic factors as potential biological bases for homosexuality. For example, Simon LeVay's much-discussed 1991 study found that some hypothalamus cells were more numerous in heterosexual men than in homosexual men.[7] Even if this research is completely reliable, it is difficult to know what to conclude from this. Critics have complained about the small samples (thirty-four and forty-one subjects) used in the study and the fact that all of those studied had AIDS, the complications of which could have had a causal impact on the number of certain hypothalamus cells.[8] A later study conducted by Allen and Gorski found that the anterior commissure (a nerve bundle connecting the two cerebral hemispheres) is smaller in homosexual men than in women and heterosexual men.[9] Again, it is difficult to say what the implications of these findings might be. But the study itself is problematic because, again, the samples used were obtained mainly from men who died of AIDS (a significant uncontrolled variable). Moreover, neither of these studies rule out the possibility that the discovered neuroanatomic differences were caused by environmental factors. Behavior and

---

5. King and McDonald, "Homosexuals Who Are Twins."

6. Ibid., 407.

7. LeVay, "Difference in Hypothalamic Structure between Heterosexual and Homosexual Men."

8. Even LeVay himself rightly disclaims certain implications of his study, noting, "It's important to stress what I didn't find. I did not prove that homosexuality is genetic or find a genetic cause for being gay. I didn't show that gay men are born that way, the most common mistake people make in interpreting my work. Nor did I locate a gay center in the brain." Quotation from Nimmons, "Sex and the Brain."

9. Allen and Gorski, "Sexual Orientation and the Size of the Anterior Commissure in the Human Brain."

trauma can significantly alter brain structure and function, as new research is increasingly confirming.[10]

Now for all of the problems with these studies, it must be emphasized that even if they were all successful in proving the biological basis thesis, the point is moot vis-à-vis sexual pluralism, which is a *moral* thesis. Supposing there were a demonstrable genetic or neuroanatomical disposition toward homosexual attraction, this proves nothing regarding whether homosexual practice is ever *morally* appropriate. For even if homosexual orientation is biologically determined, this does not imply that such people *must choose to behave accordingly* or that they are not morally culpable for their sexual choices. To insist so is to embrace hard determinism, the view that since human choices are caused we are neither free nor morally responsible for our behavior. The fact that sexual pluralists often appeal to such deterministic thinking suggests a lack of evidential grounds for their view.

The Historical and Global Consensus among Christian Scholars

This leads us to another reason we should be skeptical of sexual pluralism, namely, the fact that *significant disagreement about the issue within the church is historically unprecedented*. Never before the last generation was there ever serious debate among Christian theologians or ethicists regarding the moral legitimacy of homosexual behavior. From the founding of the church until the late twentieth century, every major (and minor) Christian theologian who addressed the issue of sexual ethics affirmed the traditional, orthodox view of sexuality and condemned same-sex sexual activity.[11] In fact, there has been considerably more debate in the church about such fundamental doctrines as the Trinity and the divinity of Christ than there has been about sexual morality. Some sexual issues (e.g., polygamy) have been debated, of course. But not until recently have Christians seriously debated the moral permissibility of homosexual practice.

No major theologians challenged the traditional Christian view of sexuality until the late twentieth century, likely beginning with Jürgen Moltmann and Hans Küng. Today there is division among Christian theologians

---

10. Kolb, Gibb, and Robinson, "Brain Plasticity and Behavior"; Hanson et al., "Early Stress Is Associated with Alterations in the Orbitofrontal Cortex"; McCrory, De Brito, and Viding, "Research Review"; Wilson, Hansen, and Li, "Traumatic Stress Response in Child Maltreatment and Resultant Neuropsychological Effects"; Shonkoff et al., "Lifelong Effects of Early Childhood Adversity and Toxic Stress."

11. Fortson and Grams, *Unchanging Witness*.

in the West regarding the morality of homosexual conduct. But the fact that this difference of opinion among theologians (in this part of the world) is such a new and unprecedented phenomenon in church history should not be taken lightly. When an overwhelming majority of experts agree regarding any issue, their position deserves deep respect. In fact, where there is near consensus this warrants a presumption in favor of that view such that the burden of proof lies on the shoulders of those who disagree. As we've already seen, the most popular argument for disregarding this consensus is deeply problematic, so there are no grounds to maintain that the burden of proof has been met by those who challenge the orthodox view.

In light of this, it appears that for a Christian to casually discard the traditional orthodox view of sexuality is a sign of either ignorance or arrogance. That is, it shows either that (1) one is *unaware* of the uniform voice with which the greatest theological minds in church history have spoken to the matter of sexual ethics or (2) one doesn't really *care* enough about this historical consensus of Christian theologians and ethicists such that it could have significant bearing on one's own opinion about the matter. The former demonstrates a lack of *understanding* and the latter a lack of *respect* for the authoritative witness of uniform Christian scholarship throughout history.

Here some object that, for all we know, there might have been astute Christian theologians and ethicists down through history who would have affirmed sexual pluralism but did not do so for fear of reprisal. The potential repercussions of affirming the sexual pluralist thesis in, say, the Middle Ages or the early modern period in the West would simply have been too severe to take the risk. Hence, these scholars kept their convictions to themselves. This line of response is problematic for several reasons. For one thing, it is an entirely speculative supposition. There is no historical evidence to support this hypothesis. But the suggestion is also problematic because it doesn't gel with historical fact. The danger of dissent on other theological issues hasn't deterred scholars or lay people from publicly renouncing orthodoxy. Throughout church history, from the ante-Nicene days to the modern period, numerous people have boldly declared all sorts of controversial beliefs, often resulting in their severe persecution and even execution. If theological heretics were often willing to be burned at the stake for their views on the Eucharist, baptism, ecclesiology, and atonement theories, then why wouldn't at least some sexual pluralists (who would be *moral* heretics) be willing to do the same?

Despite the lack of Christian theologians defending sexual pluralism throughout church history, some scholars have nonetheless looked for precedents of *tacit* approval of same-sex relations in the form of church *practice*. The most serious, and notorious, such attempt was made by medieval studies scholar John Boswell, who focused on the church rite of *adelphopoiesis*. In some Roman Catholic and Eastern Orthodox traditions, *adelphopoiesis* is the practice of "brother-making," sometimes also translated as "fraternization," where two men or two women are bound by rite as spiritual brothers or sisters.[12] The most renowned example of spiritual brothers who provide inspiration for *adelphopoiesis* rites are Sergius and Bacchus, the fourth-century Roman soldiers who together suffered martyrdom and were subsequently venerated as saints in the Roman Catholic and Eastern Orthodox churches.[13]

In his book *Same-Sex Unions in Premodern Europe*, Boswell claimed to have discovered that various medieval versions of these brother-making rites were essentially the homosexual equivalent to heterosexual marriage ceremonies.[14] In fact, as many reviewers subsequently showed, they were nothing of the kind.[15] In both Roman Catholic and Eastern Orthodox traditions, *adelphopoiesis* rites were, during the medieval period and beyond, entirely about a *phileo* and *agape* spiritual bond rather than being erotic or romantic. The historical record is entirely bereft of any evidence for such unions having a sexual dimension, let alone being tantamount to traditional Christian marriage. On the contrary, most history scholars have concluded that these ceremonies merely represented a form of ritualized kinship.[16]

Boswell's embarrassing failure to discover a historical precedent in church history for same-sex marriage is instructive. That a scholar would need to so radically distort church history in order to create the impression of such a precedent only confirms its absence. It is likewise noteworthy that no scholar has yet even attempted to find historical precedents of Christian

---

12. For an in-depth study of the ritual of *adelphopoiesis*, see Rapp, *Brother-Making in Late Antiquity and Byzantium*.

13. For a historical study of the suffering and martyrdom of these two men, see Woods, "Emperor Julian and the Passion of Sergius and Bacchus."

14. Boswell, *Same-Sex Unions in Premodern Europe*.

15. Boswell's book prompted many critical, even scathing, scholarly reviews. Brent Shaw accused Boswell of "tear[ing] words, sentences and larger statements out of the social and literary contexts in which they were imbedded." Shaw, "Groom of One's Own." Regarding Boswell's book, Archimandrite Ephrem Lash laments that "had this volume been submitted as a doctoral dissertation I should unhesitatingly have rejected it on the grounds that the author clearly did not possess even the minimum technical equipment to deal with the subject." Lash, "Review of Same-Sex Unions in Premodern Europe," 50. And Robin Darling Young writes, "Despite its façade of scholarship, the book is studded with unwarranted a priori assumptions, with arguments from silence, and with dubious, or in some cases outrageously false, translations of critical terms." She concludes, "Boswell's insouciance about historical accuracy would be unacceptable in an undergraduate paper." Young, "Gay Marriage," 44.

16. Herman, *Ritualised Friendship and the Greek City*.

scholarly (whether philosophical or theological) defenses of same-sex marriage. Again, this is because they are nonexistent. Apparently, not a single Christian scholar seriously defended the sexual pluralist thesis until the late twentieth century. Prior to this time—nearly two thousand years of church history—Christian scholars seem to be completely united in affirming that sex is only appropriate between married heterosexuals.

The implications here for today's Christian sexual pluralists are enormous. It means they must maintain that *all* of the greatest Christian minds in history were wrong about this issue. For the entire reach of Christian history, *every* theologian and moral philosopher who wrote on the subject came to the wrong conclusion about sexual morality. Not just some or most, but *all* of them. Let that sink in. The sexual pluralist might reply by noting that each of the greatest Christian minds down through history has been wrong about some issue or other. They are not infallible, after all. But that is to miss the point. It is the *unanimity* of opinion on sexual morality that is crucial here. It is one thing to claim that all Christian scholars are fallible and inevitably get it wrong somewhere, or even that a large percentage of Christian thinkers got a particular issue wrong, as, for example, might be the case regarding certain doctrinal positions regarding hell, eschatology, or baptism. It is quite another to reject the unwavering view of Christian scholars, East and West, for two millennia on an extremely important moral issue. As for those Christians who nonetheless reject this uniform conviction in favor of sexual pluralism, as I suggested above, it is difficult not to see this as profoundly arrogant, historically myopic, or both.

What this amounts to is powerful historical grounds to be skeptical about sexual pluralism.[17] But the church consensus about sexual ethics is not just historical. It is also, at least relatively, *global*. Contemporary debate in the church about sexual issues has occurred almost exclusively in North America and parts of Europe. Christians in Africa, Asia, and South America almost uniformly affirm the traditional view.[18] Because of this,

---

17. One might wonder whether a similar sort of historical argument could be made against the use of contraceptives. For, after all, Christian scholars generally opposed the practice until the twentieth century. This analogy is problematic for a couple of reasons. First, the general consensus regarding this issue was never absolute or uniform among Christian scholars as it was regarding sexual morality. Second, condemnations of contraceptives for most of Christian history are complicated by the fact that so many ancient methods (e.g., from pennyroyal, opium, and opopanax, to sitting over a pot of boiling onions) were either a health hazard to the women who used them or they also worked as abortifacients. It wasn't until the mid-twentieth century that artificial contraceptives were developed that were safe, reliable, and clearly distinguishable from abortifacients.

18. Jenkins, *Next Christendom*.

it is extremely misleading, even ethnocentric, to glibly declare, as some are wont to do, that "Christians today are divided on the homosexuality issue." Consult a typical Christian in Kenya, China, or Brazil about their thoughts on the growing presence of sexual pluralism in the American church, and they will shake their heads in disbelief, perhaps even asking, "What is wrong with American Christians that they could actually disagree about this issue?" Good question.

So the casual dismissal of the traditional view by a North American Christian, despite the strong global consensus in its favor, could reasonably regarded as ethnocentric. It is not as if those of us in the West are privy to a body of evidence that is inaccessible to Christians in Asia, Africa, and South America. Nor, obviously, are Western Christians any more rational or intelligent than our global brothers and sisters on these other continents. A wise and humble approach, then, would be to take seriously the strong global church majority and to be skeptical of the rising sexual pluralism that is a peculiarly Western, mostly North American, aberration as well as a historical anomaly.

The Cultural Roots of Sexual Pluralism

Despite the fact that in the church sexual pluralism is a historical and global aberration, it is nonetheless noteworthy that today many Christians in the US are sexual pluralists and these percentages are on the rise. In fact, as I have suggested, we are witnessing a revolution of thought when it comes to the theology of sexuality. Does this trend suggest that there is something to the claim that the traditional Christian sexual ethic should be reconsidered? That all depends on whether this revolution of thought is *rational*.

I believe that the sexual pluralist revolution is not fundamentally rational. Unlike other revolutionary developments throughout history, such as the scientific revolution, the Protestant Reformation, and the abolitionist movement, the sexual pluralist revolution has been prompted by a variety of cultural factors rather than evidence-based arguments. We have already seen that the alleged scientific grounds for sexual pluralism are spurious both because of (1) the inconclusiveness of genetic and neuroanatomic studies when it comes to establishing innate determination of homosexual attraction and (2) the ultimate irrelevance of these studies when it comes to the moral question at issue. And as for the now-popular permissivist reinterpretations of the relevant biblical texts (e.g., Gen 19; Lev 18:22; Lev 20:13; Rom 1:26–27; 1 Cor 6:9; 1 Tim 1:9–10), these did not become popular until fairly recently, long *after* the cultural tide had already turned on the issue.[19] Besides that, it is not as if biblical scholars have discovered anything strikingly new in the last few decades to warrant a radical hermeneutical reassessment of these passages. And, anyway, it would be absurd to suggest that our secular culture would be significantly impacted by biblical exegetical studies.

So, ruling out scientific and theological arguments as causal impetuses for the sexual pluralist revolution, what are more plausible candidates? One obvious factor is pop culture. While it is self-evident that pro attitudes towards sexual promiscuity and same-sex relations are ubiquitous in Hollywood film, television programs, popular music, and the fashion industry, the cultural effects of this can be overlooked. Consider television programming in particular. The positive portrayal of LGBT characters is now a regular feature of television dramas, comedies, variety shows, and even animated programs. Meanwhile, surveys routinely find that kids aged eight to eighteen typically spend more than thirty hours per week watching television.[20] The cumulative psychological impact of the pro-LGBT slant in these media is no doubt significant. Such programs rarely present a rational argument for their implicit alternative sexual ethic. They don't need to.

Another factor driving the sexual pluralist revolution is more subtle but no less powerful, and that is ethical relativism—the notion that moral values derive entirely from cultural preferences. This entails a rejection of the idea that there is a fixed *telos* for human relationships and conduct. And when applied to sexual practice, sexual pluralism is the result, again embraced sans argument. Now some may claim that ethical relativism is itself a rational position, particularly when construed as an aspect of postmodern skepticism. However, given that the postmodernist perspective essentially undermines confidence in reason and eschews the notion of absolute truth commitment, it's difficult to see how such a perspective could be *rationally* defensible.

A third factor instrumental in the rise of sexual pluralism is a confused view of tolerance. Properly understood, tolerance is the public virtue of permitting the expression of views that one believes to be false. As the term is commonly used in contemporary American society, however, to be "tolerant" of certain views is not just to permit their public expression but actually to *affirm* them. Thus, to be tolerant of homosexuals, it is not enough to accept their presence and allow them to express their views. Rather, one must

---

19. Not long ago, permissivist interpretations of Scripture were almost unheard of in the evangelical world, much less seriously defended in print by Christian authors. Today such books are appearing with regularity. These include Lee, *Torn*; Wilson, *Letter to My Congregation*; Vines, *God and the Gay Christian*.

20. Rothman, "Kids TV Survey."

embrace their sexual conduct as morally legitimate. To suggest that their lifestyle is immoral is itself immoral, according to the popular redefinition of tolerance. The irony, of course, is that such a view forecloses *in favor* of sexual pluralism. That is, the new view of tolerance entails that dissent from sexual pluralism is unacceptable. And the routine censure of public figures who express skepticism about sexual pluralism shows just how intolerant the sexual pluralist movement is.[21] The new tolerance of sexual pluralism is really a (not so well) disguised dogmatism.

These factors help to account for this recent and relatively local drift from moral-theological orthodoxy. And there is a further reason to be skeptical about the notion that this trend should be morally compelling, namely, the fact that the rise of sexual pluralism in the West has been co-incident with the pornography epidemic. Pro attitudes toward sexual pluralism, and homosexual conduct in particular, began to increase steadily with the advent of popular pornographic publications in the 1950s and 60s. As porn was slowly mainstreamed into the film industry, sexual pluralism gained yet more steam. And with the exponential surge of porn on the Internet since the 1990s, sexual pluralism has similarly surged. In short, the rise of sexual pluralism is strongly correlated with the general pornification of American culture.[22]

Admittedly, such correlation doesn't prove a causal connection. But it is consistent with and suggestive of such a connection. And the inference is reasonable considering the pervasiveness of porn and the impact it has on viewers. As for its pervasiveness, pornography is now a $13 billion yearly industry in the US and approximately $100 billion worldwide. Twelve percent of websites (twenty-seven million) are porn sites, and one of every eight Internet searches is for porn. As for the church, a Barna survey found that 21 percent of Christian men admit to being *addicted* to pornography. And surveys consistently find that about half of all Christian men regularly look at porn. As for its deleterious effects, studies show that regular exposure to pornographic materials increases a viewer's tendency to approve of inappropriate forms of sexual conduct.[23] And this hardening effect appears proportional to the degree of graphic content.

---

21. The list is long, from NFL star Reggie White to Phil Robertson of *Duck Dynasty* fame.

22. For some bracing studies of the latter phenomenon, see Paul, *Pornified*; Dines, *Pornland*.

23. Zillmann and Bryant, "Pornography and Sexual Callousness"; Peter and Valkenburg, "Adolescents' Exposure to a Sexualized Media Environment"; Sun et al., "Pornography and the Male Sexual Script."

These cultural factors—pop culture influences, postmodern skepticism, the redefinition of tolerance, and the rise of the pornography industry—have had an enormous cultural impact, particularly as regards the shaping of public views of sexual practice. I believe they have been the principal driving forces behind the sexual pluralist revolution. Yet none of them are genuinely rational in nature. Together their reinforcement of sexual pluralism has made the appeal to reason and argumentation unnecessary.

Conclusion

I have argued that there are significant reasons why we should hold fast to the historic Judeo-Christian sexual ethic and maintain a strong skepticism toward sexual pluralism. Throughout church history, until the past generation, there has been uniform endorsement of the traditional Christian sexual ethic among Christian theologians and ethicists, and even today sexual pluralism is a very small, relatively localized minority position in the global Christian church. Moreover, the sexual pluralist revolution is not a consequence of rational argument but rather of nonrational cultural dynamics, such as pop culture influences, postmodern assumptions, a warped view of tolerance, and the rise of pornography.

All people should hold in high regard the greatest thinkers in their tradition. For the Christian, this matter of historical precedent is especially germane to moral and theological questions. As Christians, we should take seriously the wealth of moral and theological wisdom that has preceded us historically, and where there is strong consensus about an issue, as there is on the sexual conduct question, this creates a strong presumption in favor of the prevailing view. Since sexual pluralism constitutes a rejection of the Christian consensus about sexual ethics, then, to say the least, we ought to be rather skeptical of this view.

Standing firm on this issue in the coming years will be increasingly difficult, since this will demand a firm resolve to resist powerful cultural currents. Those on the side of orthopraxy will be dismissed or, worse, persecuted. And although sexual pluralism has no rational grounds—theologically, historically, or scientifically—it might be useless to resist with rational argument. For a view that rises to prominence by abandoning reason can hardly be defeated through the use of reason.

Bibliography

Allen, L. S., and R. A. Gorski. "Sexual Orientation and the Size of the Anterior Commissure in the Human Brain." *Proceedings of the National Academy of Sciences* 89.15 (August 1, 1992) 7199–202.

Bailey, J. Michael, and Richard C. Pillard. "A Genetic Study of Male Sexual Orientation." *Archives of General Psychiatry* 48.12 (December 1, 1991) 1089–96.

Boswell, John. *Same-Sex Unions in Premodern Europe.* New York: Knopf, Doubleday, 2013.

Dines, Gail. *Pornland: How Porn Has Hijacked Our Sexuality.* Boston: Beacon, 2010.

Fortson, S. Donald, and Rollin G. Grams. *Unchanging Witness: The Consistent Christian Teaching on Homosexuality in Scripture and Tradition.* Nashville: B & H, 2016.

Hanson, Jamie L., Moo K. Chung, Brian B. Avants, Elizabeth A. Shirtcliff, James C. Gee, Richard J. Davidson, and Seth D. Pollak. "Early Stress Is Associated with Alterations in the Orbitofrontal Cortex: A Tensor-Based Morphometry Investigation of Brain Structure and Behavioral Risk." *Journal of Neuroscience* 30.22 (June 2, 2010) 7466–72.

Herman, Gabriel. *Ritualised Friendship and the Greek City.* Cambridge: Cambridge University Press, 2002.

Jenkins, Philip. *The Next Christendom: The Coming of Global Christianity.* New York: Oxford University Press, 2011.

Kallmann, Franz J. "Twin and Sibship Study of Overt Male Homosexuality." *American Journal of Human Genetics* 4.2 (June 1952) 136–46.

Kant, Immanuel. *Critique of Pure Reason.* Translated by Norman Kemp Smith. New York: St. Martin's, 1964.

———. *Religion and Rational Theology.* Translated and edited by Allen Wood and George Di Giovanni. Cambridge: Cambridge University Press, 2001.

King, M., and E. McDonald. "Homosexuals Who Are Twins: A Study of 46 Probands." *British Journal of Psychiatry* 160.3 (March 1, 1992) 407–9.

Kolb, Bryan, Robbin Gibb, and Terry E. Robinson. "Brain Plasticity and Behavior." *Current Directions in Psychological Science* 12.1 (February 1, 2003) 1–5.

Lash, Ephrem. "Review of Same-Sex Unions in Premodern Europe." *Sourozh* 59 (February 1995) 50–55.

Lee, Justin. *Torn: Rescuing the Gospel from the Gays-vs.-Christians Debate.* New York: Jericho, 2012.

LeVay, Simon. "A Difference in Hypothalamic Structure between Heterosexual and Homosexual Men." *Science* 253.5023 (August 30, 1991) 1034–37.

McCrory, Eamon, Stephane A. De Brito, and Essi Viding. "Research Review: The Neurobiology and Genetics of Maltreatment and Adversity." *Journal of Child Psychology and Psychiatry* 51.10 (October 1, 2010) 1079–95.

Nimmons, David. "Sex and the Brain." *Discover*, March 1994. http://discovermagazine.com/1994/mar/sexandthebrain346.

Paul, Pamela. *Pornified: How Pornography Is Transforming Our Lives, Our Relationships, and Our Families.* New York: Macmillan, 2007.

Peter, Jochen, and Patti M. Valkenburg. "Adolescents' Exposure to a Sexualized Media Environment and Their Notions of Women as Sex Objects." *Sex Roles* 56.5-6 (March 1, 2007) 381–95.

Rainer, J. D., et al. "Homosexuality and Heterosexuality in Identical Twins." *Psychosomatic Medicine*, July 1960. http://journals.lww.com/psychosomaticmedicine/Fulltext/1960/07000/Homosexuality_and_Heterosexuality_in_Identical.3.aspx.

Rapp, Claudia. *Brother-Making in Late Antiquity and Byzantium: Monks, Laymen, and Christian Ritual*. Oxford: Oxford University Press, 2016.

Rothman, Lily. "Kids TV Survey: How Much TV Kids Watch." *Time*, November 20, 2013. http://entertainment.time.com/2013/11/20/fyi-parents-your-kids-watch-a-full-time-jobs-worth-of-tv-each-week.

Shaw, Brent. "A Groom of One's Own." *New Republic*, July 24, 1994. https://newrepublic.com/article/79049/groom-ones-own.

Shonkoff, Jack P., Andrew S. Garner, et al. "The Lifelong Effects of Early Childhood Adversity and Toxic Stress." *Pediatrics* 129.1 (January 1, 2012) e232–46.

Sun, Chyng, Ana Bridges, Jennifer A. Johnson, and Matthew B. Ezzell. "Pornography and the Male Sexual Script: An Analysis of Consumption and Sexual Relations." *Archives of Sexual Behavior* 45.4 (May 1, 2016) 983–94.

Vines, Matthew. *God and the Gay Christian: The Biblical Case in Support of Same-Sex Relationships*. New York: Crown, 2015.

Wilson, Kathryn R., David J. Hansen, and Ming Li. "The Traumatic Stress Response in Child Maltreatment and Resultant Neuropsychological Effects." *Aggression and Violent Behavior* 16.2 (March 1, 2011) 87–97.

Wilson, Ken. *A Letter to My Congregation: An Evangelical Pastor's Path to Embracing People Who Are Gay, Lesbian, and Transgender in the Company of Jesus*. Canton, MI: Read the Spirit Books, an imprint of David Drumm Media, 2014.

Woods, David. "The Emperor Julian and the Passion of Sergius and Bacchus." *Journal of Early Christian Studies* 5.3 (September 1, 1997) 335–67.

Young, Robin Darling. "Gay Marriage: Reimaging Church History." *First Things*, November 1994. https://www.firstthings.com/article/1994/11/gay-marriage-reimagining-church-history.

Zillmann, Dolf, and Jennings Bryant. "Pornography, Sexual Callousness, and the Trivialization of Rape." *Journal of Communication* 32.4 (December 1, 1982) 10–21.

Part 4

Pastoral Wisdom for Christian Sexuality

15

The Place of Forgiveness in the Marriage Bed

Stephanie Ellis

Few people have a "perfect" sexual history. Common concerns regarding sexual behavior and the covenant of marriage are sexual experience (with your spouse or someone else) before marriage, sexual intimacy with someone else during marriage, and sexual fulfillment found outside of marriage in other ways (e.g., pornography, romance novels). Questions about how spouses (or engaged couples) should handle these situations are less than clearly answered in the Scriptures. For example, is divorce required, recommended, or only allowed when infidelity is the issue (e.g., Mark 10:11–12)? To what degree is full disclosure required or recommended (e.g., Jas 5:16)? What qualifies as a "hint" of sexual immorality (Eph 5:3) and how does Jesus's reference to adultery in the heart apply (e.g., Matt 5:27–28)? Even the term *porneia,* in the verse that commands Christians to flee from such acts (Matt 5:31–32), is variously translated as sexual immorality, sexual sin, fornication, adultery, unfaithfulness, whoredom, and the like.

While the concept of sexual immorality may be less than clear, in light of God's grace and the injunction to *forgive each other so that we might be forgiven* (Matt 6:14–15; Col 3:13), the imperative to forgive is less equivocal. The many references to forgiveness—such as the call to love our neighbors as we love ourselves (Matt 22:39), for husbands to love wives as Christ loved the church (Eph 5:25), and the example of the relationship of forgiveness of Hosea and Gomer (Hosea 1–3)—suggest that forgiveness, even of sexual sin, is an important part of thriving, healthy, holy relationships. At the bottom of almost every concern about sex and marriage is the need to forgive: forgiveness for oneself or one's partner, usually both.

Forgiveness

The call to forgiveness is not an easy one. Why is forgiveness so difficult? Why is it sometimes harder to forgive your spouse than anyone else? Why is it so especially hard to forgive when it comes to sex?

Forgiveness is difficult in large part because of a constellation of universally experienced negative emotions, including anger, sadness, disgust, and fear.[1] In marriage relationships, the depth of intimacy experienced in marriage brings many blessings, but also dangers. The degree of intimacy increases our negative feelings when expectations are violated. We are obviously more hurt by the betrayal of a loved one than by a careless barb from a stranger. In addition, expectations for significant others are higher than those we place even on friends and relatives; often these expectations are unrealistically high. The closeness of the relationship also gives us access to knowledge about our partner's thoughts and behaviors that we would have no opportunity to scrutinize in other relationships. Further, the act of sex is intimate by its nature and this increases the difficulty, especially because most people feel particularly vulnerable in this area.

Although intimacy in some ways hinders the process of forgiveness, the closer a relationship is before the need for forgiveness arises, the more likely partners are to be able to give and receive forgiveness effectively.[2] People in committed romantic relationships and marriages, as opposed to casual relationships or friendships, are usually willing to fight hard for themselves and their significant others. The scarceness of this person as a resource (you only have one spouse), the relational foundation (the original bonds of affection and love that have sustained the relationship thus far), and the investment made in the partner (in terms of time, effort, shared memories and property, etc.) dispose both partners to put forth effort in the continuance of the relationship. This means that you (and your partner) are more likely to apologize sincerely, and you are both more likely to be able to develop *empathy* for each other's experience, which is critical to forgiveness.

Empathy is often confused with sharing the other person's feelings, agreeing with them, or feeling sorry for them. In contrast, empathy is about "thinking with"—it is getting into the other person's world and mind enough that you can understand their perspective.[3] What follows is a guide through

---

1. Ekman, "Argument for Basic Emotions," 169.
2. McCullough et al., "Interpersonal Forgiving in Close Relationships," 1586.
3. Rogers, *On Becoming a Person*.

some of the common emotional responses to sexual sin in marriages. Examining your own thoughts and understanding the emotions you are both experiencing can help us develop more empathy for our partners and help ourselves in the forgiveness process.

Forgiveness Is Hard Because of *Anger*

I wanted the perfect wedding night. She should have waited for me. She's ruined it! What kind of a woman just gives herself away like that? She should have told me sooner!

He promised me fidelity and broke that promise! How dare he!

I can't believe I was so stupid. I never should have let it go that far. I hate myself.

Anger is about injustice. It's the feeling we get when we recognize that one of God's own creations is being treated unfairly. It's what we feel when we want to pound our fists on those who abuse children or rage against political injustice. Most often, we feel it on behalf of ourselves—when we have been gossiped about, or denied an earned promotion, or been the victim of any number of perceived wrongs. When it comes to being wronged by our partners, we are especially likely to feel the kind of anger we call "righteous indignation."[4] What naturally follows that feeling is a desire for revenge,[5] which, of course, is not healthy for relationships. However, anger can be very useful—when it is rightly earned—because it motivates us to take action to correct the injustice, on behalf of our own dignity or on behalf of the powerless. So, we need to figure out if our anger with our significant other is *rightly earned,* and this is how we can do that.

These are the three thoughts that tend to accompany the feeling of anger:

1. I was treated unfairly.
2. I deserve better.
3. They did it on purpose, to hurt me.

If all three are true (that is, congruent with the reality of the situation), then the anger is rightly earned, and movement to correct the injustice may be warranted. If any of the three is *not* true, and we can bring ourselves to

---

4. Gottman, "Theory of Marital Dissolution and Stability," 57.
5. McCullough et al., "Interpersonal Forgiving in Close Relationships," 1586.

realize it fully, often at least some of the anger dissipates on its own. Let's look at some examples:

> You've found out your fiancée has prior sexual experience. Have you been treated unfairly? Well, if that experience was before you were together (possibly even before she was a Christian), you really haven't been treated unfairly. You aren't getting what you wanted; you are disappointed. It's certainly reasonable to have an emotional response. But if what you're feeling is anger, look deeper. That's likely "secondary anger," the kind that covers up sadness or another emotion.
>
> Your spouse cheated. Were you treated unfairly? Yes, there was a promise of fidelity made and broken. Do you deserve better? You may be tempted to say yes, if you haven't cheated. On the other hand, you married a fallen human person. You are also a fallen human person. If we, the fallen, are called to marriage, we are called to marry sinners. Maybe you haven't committed the same sin, but have you never sinned? Be careful about casting those stones (John 8:7). As to whether they did it on purpose, to hurt you, chances are they didn't. Though it did hurt you, and they did treat you unfairly, it's unusual for punishment to be the reason. Although it is relatively common to use the pain of the first sting to justify your own revenge, then you are satisfying condition three and doing it to hurt *them*. Be very wary of this kind of quid-pro-quo thinking. It never works out as cleanly as you plan. Stay open; you may find as you pursue this more deeply that there is more to the story than you realize.
>
> You've pushed your own boundaries. You said you wouldn't look at that kind of thing, or do those kinds of things. Were you treated unfairly? Well, maybe. Maybe you treated yourself unfairly, in the way that Paul says we do the things we hate to do (Rom 7:15). And you perhaps deserve better, in the sense that we are called to perfection and when we keep our sin in check, we find blessings there. But I doubt you did it to yourself (or your spouse) on purpose. Did you think to yourself, "I'm certainly looking forward to inflicting pain and regret on myself"? Of course you didn't. It is not that you need to give yourself an *excuse*, but it might be worth it to realize you probably didn't intend it—at least not all the consequences—when the behavior happened.

Realizing that your spouse's intention was not to hurt you gives you some mental space to listen more attentively, to consider their perspective, to begin building empathy. What motivated your partner's actions, if not simply an evil purpose to make you miserable? Was it impulsive? Was it unintended? Did it start small and get out of hand? Did they possibly experience some of the other feelings you are experiencing? Again, this is not an expedition in making excuses, just in getting more information.

Perhaps you find that your anger dissipates as you examine the sexual sin in your or your partner's past. If you don't, and you find that your anger is "justified," make sure your partner knows that they have wronged you (Luke 17:35). Even spouses can't read minds, so it is prudent to tell them overtly; this can help to avoid more unfairness or wrongdoing in the future. We are told that if our brother sins, we ought to rebuke him (Luke 17:3). If your partner, fiancé, or spouse has sinned against you, you do have the right and the expectation to tell them it hurt you. That fosters good, free communication between you. Just know that the scripture continues in the next breath (indeed, in the same sentence, 17:3) that, if he repents, we ought to forgive him. And remember that justice belongs to the Lord. Though it is "natural" to want to exact revenge (Rom 12:19), it never satisfies. This is someone you are committed to; pride, resentment, bitterness, punishment, and the like only cause more grief in relationships.

If you realize that perhaps your anger was not quite as rightly earned as you had thought, but you still feel angry, consider that many people experience anger as a secondary emotion.[6] This means that anger is experienced in a way that covers up another emotion, like sadness or fear (for example, because it is more culturally acceptable to express anger than fear, or because it's less painful to express anger than sadness). So, next, we will look at some of the other emotions that make forgiveness difficult, which may underlie the anger that is often the most salient.

Forgiveness Is Hard Because of *Sadness*

I thought he loved me more than anything.

She must not have cared or she would never have done this.

Things will never be the same.

Sadness is usually about loss. When we talk about sexual issues in marriage, we're often talking about the loss of comfort, trust, security, joy, closeness, pleasure, and more. Sadness can take the form of disappointment when we

---

6. Greenberg and Paivio, *Working with Emotions in Psychotherapy*.

experience the loss of something hoped for, not yet realized, like the hope for a virgin bride.

When we find out that our partner is not all that we imagined—they have sexual experience with someone else or they let us down by becoming intimate with someone else—we are hurt. We have feelings of hurt because we (and the relationship) have been damaged; whether they meant to hurt us or not, the pain is still there. It's completely natural that once we have been hurt we want to avoid the person and situation that caused the pain,[7] but it isn't helpful in this case.

These hurts need to be expressed in order to heal. Certainly, your partner needs to hear them, but it might also be helpful to share them with someone else or write about them in a journal beforehand. You also want to work through the anger first (even though the anger is in part fueled by the pain). You may find that you begin to cultivate empathy for your partner as you work through the anger, and this conversation will go much better if you can express your pain without the blame (and volume) that are typically associated with angry conversations. That will only send your partner into a defensive, non-listening stance. This is the opportunity that you have to help your partner cultivate empathy *for your experience*. This will help you feel heard, and it will help your partner know how much they have hurt you and how. They need to know that—if they are going to be able to begin to heal the damage done and to move into the future with you and not hurt you further.

Consider *all* of your hurts and losses. There is almost certainly a sense of separation that wasn't there before, so there is the loss of relational closeness. There is probably a loss of trust, and with it the security of having a confidant. The sense of safety, of the relationship being the place you can always run to, is often shattered. That means that even when there are difficulties outside the relationship (e.g., work stress or in-laws) there isn't a shelter from the storm. Hopefully, you can rely on God to be the primary source of refuge during this time of rebuilding.

There are probably physical losses, too, if you and your partner are not being sexually intimate while you are working through this, and the loss of other affectionate touch, like hugs. These kinds of touch are very important to our mental and physical well-being. They release chemicals in the nervous system that act to support our immune functioning, buffer us in stressful times, and promote feelings of happiness and closeness. So you also lose one of the coping strategies that helps you through tough times. That may well be a good enough reason to express your hurt to your partner and

---

7. McCullough et al., "Interpersonal Forgiving in Close Relationships," 1586.

see if you can begin to feel safe enough to incorporate some of those kinds of touch back into your relationship.

It's important to make sure that the losses you are sharing with your partner are losses that belong to *this* relationship. Often what happens is that a partner hurts us in a way we have been hurt before, and the hurt is compounded. It is good for your spouse to know your history, because then they can avoid especially painful spots in the future and maybe help you to heal some of those old wounds. But it is also good for you to separate what pain has been caused by your partner, and what pain was already there that has just been reactivated. (This process will help with the anger, too. Much of the anger might have been directed at wrongdoing that your partner is not truly responsible for.)

Also, be clear about what is *actually* lost. You may feel as though you have lost your partner's love, but that may not be true. You might be afraid you have, or believe you have, thinking, "They could never have done this if they loved me." But it might be that they are still in this with you, willing to work it out, because the love is still there. You'll waste a lot of your energy for healing, and you'll drastically slow the repair process in the relationship, if you continue to mourn something that isn't really gone, and so can't be given back.

It's tough, but your partner is the place where you can find these lost things again, if you both are willing. But no matter how repentant and trustworthy your partner is, they can't help you heal the hurts and retrieve what has been lost if your heart is closed and locked against them. Adopt a posture (in your heart and with your body) of a willingness to receive. It might not be a willingness to receive sex just yet, but be open to experiencing moments of comfort, joy, and pleasure. This paves the way to being open to receive and rebuild trust and security.

Forgiveness Might Be Hard Because of *Disgust*

> Ugh. I can't believe how many women he's been with—it's disgusting. What if he has some kind of disease now?

> She is a nasty tramp with no self-control.

> Adultery is morally repugnant—how can I be with someone like that?

Disgust is a hugely important emotion, the primary purpose of which is to help us avoid contact with things that might make us sick (e.g., spoiled milk or decaying bodies). Disgust has a very interesting relationship with sex;

they don't go very well together, and that makes sense. We are vulnerable to disease and infection when we do things like exchange fluids with another person (even from breathing when someone coughs nearby, but all the more during sex). In fact, the list of things that people find disgusting almost always includes things like saliva, sweat, and body odors and fluids near the top.[8] It's a wonder that we're able to have sex considering how gross we think it is, but that is where the magic comes in. God built our bodies with this wonderful ability to recognize things that might be unhealthy for us, but he also built in a mechanism for getting over it in order to be intimate—when we are sexually aroused, our assessment of disgust becomes less sensitive.[9] But the opposite happens, too. When we are feeling high levels of disgust, it is much more difficult to feel aroused.

This is important to our discussion about forgiveness in the area of sex in two ways. The first is rather obvious: if we are disgusted with our partners in the traditional way (i.e., fear of disease), we will be strongly motivated to avoid them. If we are avoiding, we are not drawing near enough to our partner to be able to work on forgiveness. If this is an issue, do what needs to be done to alleviate the worry (e.g., get tested for STIs, agree to limit sexual behavior that one partner finds disgusting).

Probably the more problematic issue is one of *contempt*. Contempt is a hefty emotion that we feel when we combine disgust with our moral judgments of another person.[10] Just like regular disgust leads us to avoid *things* that might make us sick, contempt leads us to cut ourselves off from *people* because we believe they are morally unsound or "disgusting." Contempt has a fair dose of anger in it, too—when we are feeling contempt we are convinced it is the whole person who is bad or wrong, and we tend to think it is irreparable. We nurse angry and disrespectful thoughts because we've begun to think that this person is "less than." We respond to our partners with distance, sarcasm, eye-rolling, name-calling, and the like. This obviously makes entertaining the work of forgiveness exceptionally hard, and it is the single best predictor of divorce.[11] When we get mired in self-contempt, we have a strong feeling that we aren't good enough and don't deserve forgiveness, and that gets in the way of the relationship process, too.

Contempt, or person-disgust, is the antithesis of how we are instructed by the Lord to treat each other. There is no room for building empathy in either direction if we are living in contempt. The answer to contempt is

---

8. Rozin et al., "Borders of the Self," 318.
9. Borg and Jong, "Feelings of Disgust," e44111.
10. Ivan, "On Disgust and Moral Judgments," 25.
11. Gottman, *Seven Principles for Making Marriage Work*.

remembering that your partner, regardless of what they have done, is made in God's image (Gene 1:27), that we are all one in Christ Jesus (Gal 3:28), and that Christ died for each of us, the ungodly (Rom 5:6). The same goes if the contempt is self-contempt. Though the other emotions aren't sinful in and of themselves (and the Bible is clear that we can have strong emotions and *not sin*, e.g., Eph 4:26), if you find yourself nursing contempt for your partner or yourself, you almost certainly have some repenting to do before you will be able to move forward.

But Forgiveness Is Mostly Hard Because of *Fear*

What did she have that I don't have?

Will he do it again? How can I make him stay?

What if we can't get through this?

At bottom, we are all afraid of the same things because we all have the same needs. This applies to biological needs, surely—that's why we're all afraid of sharks and huge storms and famine, but pretty much no one is afraid of bunnies or sunshine or a tree bursting with fruit. We also have needs for safety, acceptance, dignity, significance, support, approval, belonging, etc. that can only be satisfied in relationships. In the marriage relationship, with trust betrayals in something as intimate as sex, our fears ignite into very powerful motivators to run, to fix, to seize back love, or to build a wall to stay safe. These are a few of our most common fears:

> *I am not in control.* You didn't know what your significant other was doing. You couldn't have prevented it. You can't prevent it if they do it again, or something else. You can't make them stay with you if they want to leave. If you could just make sure, somehow, that they will stay with you, love you perfectly and forever, that you'll never lose them for any reason, even death, you would feel so much safer. But alas, there is virtually nothing outside of our own experiences and choices that we can control. That means we might not get our needs met.

> *The world isn't safe.* Early in our lives, we depend on parents to be our shelters and providers. In adulthood, we give that role over to another, chosen adult: our spouse. You expected this person to be your "rock," steadfast and committed through anything. If they have disappointed you, anyone can disappoint you. The world is fundamentally unreliable. Now who can you count on?

I am not good enough. This is the fear that gets us the most. It isn't only that your spouse looks at porn; it's the belief that "if I were pretty enough, sexy enough, etc., he wouldn't want to look at porn." It's not just that your fiancée slept with another guy right before the wedding; it's the fear that "he must have something I don't have or she wouldn't have cheated." These are all variations on the theme that "I am not good enough."

All fears boil down to not having our needs met. We need these needs met. We need it so badly that we will try to control what we cannot control in a world that can't be relied upon to provide for us consistently. When faced with the terror of not being able to control the environment (including other people) in a way that meets all of our needs, we will blame not getting our need met on our "inadequacy"—because if all I must do is be prettier, or smarter, or better, or *enough*, then I have a chance at being able to control things after all.

We've also been holding on to these fears for a long time, so it's very hard for us to entertain anything contradictory, even if it's true. For example, your partner might really be among the more trustworthy people around, despite this one very prominent example of their fallenness. Their infidelity might actually have been about them, not you. They may be willing and able to love you tremendously well, even though we've been taught that relational breaches around sex are always disastrous.

These fears get us so worked up that they get in the way of being able to interact effectively at all, much less engage in the process of forgiving our partner. Also, these fears are deep down and they're sneaky, so it takes some time to find them. They're usually hidden under things like anger and disgust. However, if you are practicing listening openly with your significant other, you are almost sure to hear the echo of your fears in their story. This is the place where building empathy is easiest and richest, so do the work to get there. You *will* find some common ground.

In previous sections, we've gone through the process of evaluating whether these kinds of thoughts really are true. We won't do that here . . . they are true. They've sadly been true since we were cast out from the garden. Our hearts yearn for a love that is perfect and eternal; for bodies, minds, and spirits that are free from sin and separateness; for a world that is completely safe and a partner who will never fail us. Your real, fallen, human partner will never be able to fix these for you. Only God can assure you. Turn to him with your fear and let him meet your needs, assuage your fears. It's not your partner's responsibility, and if you try to make it so, you doom your spouse to continual failure and yourself to perpetual anxiety. Instead, let these common fears connect you and reach out to God together.

So what can you do? What can help you forgive?

First, *rely on God*. Whatever your needs are that haven't been met, whatever your fears are that haven't been allayed, talk to God about those first. Asking another fallen human person to meet all of your needs, to relieve fears that they can't possibly allay, isn't fair. But God can do that. It's a wonderful gift that Christians have in marriages, and we should avail ourselves of it.

If you are in the position of needing forgiveness, *ask God's forgiveness for yourself* and receive it fully. This may be because you are the "perpetrator" of the sexual sin in this case, or you may need forgiveness from the sin of unforgiveness, or anything in between. It may be a process in itself.

Remember you don't always have to be perfectly comfortable. When you committed to get married, it was commitment *for* the difficult times—not for when everything is happy and easy, but when we're angry, scared, and hurt. Just because things don't feel comfortable right now doesn't mean they won't feel comfortable in the future. Also, you don't need to have worked out all of your feelings before you begin the process of forgiving.

You do need to talk about it. Talk; don't scream, blame, or rage about it. The conversation needs to happen, but it doesn't help if the conversation is led by disgust, fear, or anger. The point of the conversation is to be able to work through it, so that needs to be the goal. So before you try talking about it, do a few things: First, figure out what your feelings are and if they're warranted. If they are, own your part in the situation, including your potentially judgmental attitude. Then, be ready to actually listen. If you find you aren't able to talk about it in a way that's constructive, ask for help with that. It's a very challenging thing, and a counselor, pastor, or trusted friend may be able to help that conversation go more smoothly.

Pray for your partner and don't do it like a Pharisee. Commit to praying for your partner's well-being every day. There may be an urge to pray in a way that rehearses all the bad things your partner has done and all the bad feelings you have. The more you do that, the more you grow the divide between you. You seem to get holier and they seem to get worse, and that breeds more dissatisfaction and even contempt. If need be, commit to praying every day for your partner in a way that doesn't touch the sexual sin at all.

Forgive seventy times seven—so, at least 490 times (Luke 17:4). That should probably cover all the wrongs you've been able to think of so far. Really, a more effective way to do this is to adopt an attitude of lovingkindness—toward them and yourself. Being hurt and angry doesn't mean you have to cease being loving or gentle, and building up a habit of lovingkindness will go a long way toward your ability to forgive them (and yourself). *Practice forgiveness.*

Don't dwell. Reorient yourself at least 490 times, too. When a thought pops into your head—an image of the other woman, a fear that you aren't good enough, any kind of reminder—don't indulge it. Rumination makes us much more likely to want to seek revenge than to practice forgiveness.[12] You should absolutely give all of your internal experiences the time they need—in conversation with your partner, in your journal, with your therapist. Designate a time and place for that, so that you know you will give all your concerns their due. Then, when the nagging thoughts pop up, you can just gently dismiss them for later or tomorrow, rather than either letting them fill your mind and heart with unpleasantness or trying to forcefully push them away.

Banish everyone from the bed but the two of you. This includes actual ex-lovers and imaginary ex-lovers, as well as romance novel heroes and porn stars. Allowing them to come to mind, especially when you are being intimate with your partner, just brings all of the negative thoughts and feelings rushing back. You'll never be able to measure up in your own mind to those people, which means you won't be able to accept the actual, real, present adoration and love of your partner. While you're at it, banish your parents and Sunday school teachers from the bed, too. Allow your bed to be a place where no one is judging you.

Is discretion the better part of valor? *Tell the truth in wisdom and love.* If you are terror stricken and guilt ridden with your own sin, it's going to be a problem in the bed no matter what. If you have gotten right with the Lord, though, then consider your motivation to tell your spouse. Often one spouse will "confess their sin" to their partner, but it's really because they are tired of carrying the guilt and want to release their own burden. Recognize that when you disclose anything in this realm, you are going to take away a lot of lovely things from your partner (e.g., safety, trust, comfort) and stir up many unlovely things (e.g., fear, anger, disgust) that will be a lot to work through. If you are going to do that, be willing to do your own work and *help them* through the process. Likewise, consider whether you want to disclose your full sexual histories to each other. If you know that you are free from transmissible infections, have a predisclosure conversation with your partner about whether a full disclosure will be helpful or hinder. It takes a lot of work to get those images out of your head once they are in there.

Remember that you aren't perfect and neither is your partner. *Don't make perfection a requirement for love.* Adopt a model of acceptance and change in your relationship. What this means is that each of you takes on two jobs: accepting the other person completely as they are and changing yourself in ways that you can and that make sense. This doesn't work without empathy. But the magic is that when you both do it, you take responsibility

---

12. McCullough et al., "Interpersonal Forgiving in Close Relationships," 1586.

for what you can actually control and you avoid all of the things that make a hard situation even more difficult. You each end up with a safe place to do the work that needs to be done and you're more effective at doing it.

Know your limits. Only God can forgive sin, and when we commit sexual sin, we sin against the Lord and our own bodies (1 Cor 6:18). You can only forgive the wrong done to *you*. Trust God to forgive your sin or your partner's sin. Remember that your partner needs to forgive himself or herself as well. Additionally, this might not be enough. There are other reasons that forgiveness might be hard, and a Christian counselor, or possibly a pastor or trusted friend, may be able to help. Even when you have it all figured out in your head, it can still be difficult to translate that into your actions and your heart.

Bibliography

Borg, Charmaine, and Peter J. de Jong. "Feelings of Disgust and Disgust-Induced Avoidance Weaken Following Induced Sexual Arousal in Women." *PLOS ONE* 7.9 (September 12, 2012) e44111.

Ekman, Paul. "An Argument for Basic Emotions." *Cognition and Emotion* 6.3–4 (May 1, 1992) 169–200.

Gottman, John. *The Seven Principles for Making Marriage Work*. New York: Harmony, 2015.

Gottman, John M. "A Theory of Marital Dissolution and Stability." *Journal of Family Psychology* 7.1 (1993) 57–75.

Greenberg, Leslie S., and Sandra C. Paivio. *Working with Emotions in Psychotherapy*. New York: Guilford, 2003.

Ivan, Cristina-Elena. "On Disgust and Moral Judgments: A Review." *Journal of European Psychology Students* 6.1 (April 30, 2015).

McCullough, Michael E., K. Chris, Steven J. Sandage, Everett L. Worthington Jr., Susan Wade Brown, and Terry L. Hight. "Interpersonal Forgiving in Close Relationships: II. Theoretical Elaboration and Measurement." *Journal of Personality and Social Psychology* 75.6 (1998) 1586–1603.

Rogers, Carl. *On Becoming a Person*. Boston: Little, Brown, 2011.

Rozin, Paul, Carol Nemeroff, Matthew Horowitz, Bonnie Gordon, and Wendy Voet. "The Borders of the Self: Contamination Sensitivity and Potency of the Body Apertures and Other Body Parts." *Journal of Research in Personality* 29.3 (September 1, 1995) 318–40.

16

Leavening the Dough of Sexual Purity ... by the Spirit

Jay Thomas

A robustly biblical-theological vision of sexuality is essential. It should be intellectually and emotionally captivating when understood. But God's perfection and beauty should be morally captivating as well. In other words, the triad of truth, goodness, and beauty should most certainly jointly manifest as the believer reckons with sexuality and sex. Biblical wisdom is by its nature practical. And so God's wisdom regarding one of our most important defining traits—that of being sexual—must translate into the practical fiber of Christian discipleship, not least in the community where that discipleship is most manifest and powerful: the local church.

The others chapters in this book have assumed as much, and now it is my role to be one of the voices that helps shape our understanding of how to move forward on these matters toward shaping the moral life of God's people. Among the many functions served by a pastor is to be a theological practitioner. This chapter is about how, in very hands-on ways, to put into practice in the local church the theological reflection of this volume.

As the title suggests, I want to discuss what is entailed in the act of discipling, or leavening, sexual purity in believers. I want to draw attention to the key ingredient in that leavening process, namely, the presence and power of God the Spirit. As part of that, we must discuss how the Spirit normally or ordinarily works sanctification in the believer. Two bedrock realities that produce a life of wisdom are the reality of the Holy Spirit and the centrality of the church.

The first reality is so often readily assumed that we can forget to talk about it much. I fear in that forgetfulness we then create a disconnect between ethical belief and ethical formation. I want to be explicit. The second reality, the church, is less assumed. So let me explain now why I am going to focus on the local church as a critical environment for moral formation.

Other environments are not unimportant, not least the family. When I coauthored *Sex, Dating, and Relationships*[1] with Gerald Hiestand, my prayer was that parents would be equipped by the book to disciple their children in this crucial part of spiritual maturity. I also had an eye on young adults, not least collegians, whom I shepherded at the time the book was being formulated. Indeed, campus ministries like Cru or Intervarsity are wonderful places to teach on these matters, as they often do. My church is situated right between the University of North Carolina Chapel Hill and Duke University (which makes for an interesting mix in our church), so I have been able to address this topic several times in parachurch campus ministries on both campuses, to good effect I hope.

While these ministries are crucial to the spiritual and moral lives of our students, I do believe the local church is the "pivot foot" (if you will) of sexual ethics teaching. The centrality of the local church is really about the question of where does God unleash his Spirit and in what sphere does his Word set the course? It is the church. Indeed, the local church is the fountainhead and sustaining force behind theological reflection and character formation, which in turn strengthens the family and parachurch ministries, including Christian educational institutions.

Put another way, if the church is addressing sexual ethics issues well, the other parts of God's kingdom, where virtues are also formed, will be strengthened in turn. Admittedly I say this as a pastor, but more than that I say this as a Christian who believes ecclesiology and moral formation are inextricably tied. Why? Because I believe the Scriptures teach that the church is a central means the Spirit of God uses to form God's people into worshipful servants. Our hope for a solidly biblical vision of sexuality to take root is for people to find truth and power in the Spirit's use of the Christian community, local and faithful.

That stated, what exactly are we looking for in a church that functions in this way? The discipleship test of fruitfulness in a church is whether its members meaningfully "own" a particular doctrine or ethic. Are members living out the value and able to articulate it, and are new attendees made aware of the value fairly quickly upon arrival? Are the members yielding to the Spirit in his role to renew and redeem?

---

1. Hiestand and Thomas, *Sex, Dating, and Relationships*.

Now, sexual ethics is not like the mission statement of a church. You're not likely to find a church's beliefs regarding sex and sexuality on the road sign—I hope not, at least. You may not hear much about it in membership classes, and I would not make it into a blurb or mantra that every member must memorize. But I do think a subject like sexual ethics can and should make its way into the culture of the church, and not simply by means of white papers on highly cultural and political topics like homosexuality.

So, the question is: *how does one begin to teach and lead a church in such a way that the Lord can leaven the dough of sexual purity into one of the most influential spaces and communities in the world, the church?* Put another way, *how do we unleash the Spirit to do his work of sexual sanctification?* And please do not read this as an address for pastors only! I am speaking to any and all who are followers of Jesus, who love the church, and who want sexual purity to be embraced and lived among God's people for the joy of God's people and the glory of God's name. Some of what I say will be more directly for pastors, and when this happens your role is to support, partner, pray, and reinforce what your pastor teaches on these matters. Much if not most of what I say, though, will involve your direct influence.

So, the Spirit and the church are foundational to sexual sanctification. Saying that, however, remains rather broad. We need to break it down a bit. Let me lay out our path. I want to augment the cases made by the other contributors that sexuality is shaped by the gospel itself. The gospel needs to be at the heart of a discipleship vision. Perhaps it would be helpful to envision a cascading progress of ministry spheres that will enable Christian communities to cultivate sexual virtues. We begin with the pulpit, which tends to be the epicenter of Christian formation in Bible-driven churches. From there we will explore the place of Christian education and its constituent parts, and then the community life of the church, often organized around small groups. We will next look at the vital importance of one-on-one discipleship. And, finally, I will address church leaders and their employment of formal ministry training.

As we begin this practical guide to sexual purity discipleship, I cannot stress enough the need for good thinking on these matters and leavening the dough of real human hearts. The editors of this volume were motivated by real students with authentic questions and angst and grief in practical sexual choices and struggles. Sexuality is core to our humanity. It is sacred. And so I pray we are burdened with the need to disciple our people back into their Christward humanity. And I pray we don't see only places like the classroom and dinner table as hubs of formation, but not least the beautiful bride of Christ. The church, practicing a strong, thoughtful, beauty-emphasizing discipleship mission, reveals that sexual purity is not an act of mere self-will, but rather the miraculous work of God's Spirit within us in light of the gospel.

Let us begin with that gospel.

Make It All About the Gospel!

Young people are good at pressing us to the mat regarding the foundational reasons behind a boundary marker, a rule, a value, or a virtue. They ask: *Why? Why is it so? Could it not be otherwise?* I have been struck by how important it is to know how to connect the realities of the gospel to the issue of homosexuality in particular. It is foreign for many millennials to feel an aversive moral posture toward homosexuality because of the ethos they have grown up with in the greater culture. This makes it imperative to reveal a strong foundation for commands that seem otherwise arbitrary.

This is one of the many reasons that churches need to be gospel oriented in all they do. I often use the image of a person falling into a pit of plastic balls, like the ones they used to have at McDonald's playhouses. Remember those? Everywhere you moved, colored plastic balls were in your face. You could push them aside, and more would fill in the gap. The gospel should fill churches like that. People should realize that our churches are obsessed with and driven by the gospel, at every level, for every ministry, and not just for evangelism and global missions.

In Titus 3:7, Paul is summing up his argument that Titus is to disciple his new church plant in ancient Crete by reminding them to live a godly life (3:1–3), which includes both actual behaviors and repentance. In 3:4–7, he bases this moral transformation in the gospel: "But when the goodness and loving kindness of God our Savior appeared, he saved us, not because of works done by us in righteousness, but according to his own mercy, by the washing of regeneration and renewal of the Holy Spirit, whom he poured out on us richly through Jesus Christ our Savior, so that being justified by his grace we might become heirs according to the hope of eternal life" (ESV). Interestingly, Paul does not describe the gospel merely as justification by grace. He connects justification by grace with the regeneration and renewal of the Holy Spirit. Paul clearly taught the power of the Spirit to enact the reality of the gospel in the believer's life. How crucial it is for churches to be focused on the gospel—a gospel both in terms of justification by grace and also transformation by the Spirit.

Our young people are living within rival narratives of salvation all around them. They are offered truths and power sources that try to supplant the real gospel. We cannot just out-argue the culture; we have to out-feel it, out-joy it, out-narrate it (as Tim Keller often suggests), *and* we have to out-power it. The full gospel is the only way to do that. If a church lacks a gospel ethos, and all of a sudden we stake a flag on premarital sex and dating boundaries and homosexuality, the incongruity can strain credulity and can harden an otherwise receptive heart and mind. But, rather, staking those flags in the context of treasuring the gospel can organically lead to unpacking their underlying reasons in a way that will seem natural, consistent, and trustworthy. This can help unleash the Spirit of God to begin to empower new desires and affections for victorious living. I have found this to be the case not just in terms of sexuality but in many other areas of controversial doctrines or ethical categories.

Let me also make mention of particular ways the gospel connects to sexuality. The other chapters in this volume, along with many other very good articles and book-length treatments, can aid in navigating important nuances sure to arise. Young people are thinkers and we want to be able to go with them when they start probing the depths of biblical wisdom and the world they live in and with.

Therefore, local churches need to be gospel-centric. Their teaching on the gospel needs to include the language and realities of the Spirit's power. Churches need to think through the nuances and navigate the implications of the gospel and how those shape sexual purity and identity. And churches need to consistently connect those dots. Let's see how this works out in specific ways.

The Pulpit

The pulpit is the rudder of the church's ship, not least the expository pulpit. Even if one tries to exalt other areas of a church—community, music, children's ministry, etc.—the preaching ministry powerfully sets the tone of teaching and shapes the culture in a church. The proclamation of the gospel from Scripture is something God has written into the fabric of his world. With the Word comes the power of the Spirit, so we need to wrestle with this and accept it as a major consideration for discipling young people in their vision of sexuality.

How does a pastor teach on these matters without making it an awkward hobbyhorse or bailiwick? Obviously, faithful preaching must address a plethora of topics of spirituality and godliness beyond those of sexuality. Still, though, I submit that expository preaching remains the best model for making teaching on sexuality more credible and potent, and here is why: expository preaching forces the preacher to submit to the message of a text in its context, and doing so, rather than just sharing his own opinions, establishes his trustworthiness.

Young people pay attention to these things. Faithful expository preaching makes compatible genuine, earnest curiosity, on one hand, and respect for the witness and authority of God's Word, on the other. An expository ministry makes the pulpit a mail delivery service rather than a weekly op-ed piece.

Pastors should consider an expository ministry if sound and powerful teaching on sexuality is a goal. Their moral capital will be strong, their integrity on the issue will have a firm basis, and their intended audience will more likely receive hard sayings as trustworthy and true more often than not. Good preaching exegetes both Scripture and culture. At this cultural moment, authority is a big issue for millennials. They are wary of human authority; indeed, they take pride in anti-authoritarianism. The more pastors can make this about God's Word and will, the better the chance of speaking to them persuasively.

A healthy pulpit forms a healthy church. So, based on a healthy preaching vision, let's now consider the Christian education sphere of a church and how it presents this gospel-derived vision, not least with the children and youth ministry but also in college, young professional, and older adult learning venues.

Christian Education and Formation

The pulpit is a vital tool in the Spirit's hands, but it is not enough. Biblical sexuality must be discipled through the Christian education ministry of a church, both large and small. The same Word accompanying the Spirit at the pulpit will also have great effect as it is taught in smaller learning environments.

Children's Ministry

Though we must be careful how we begin to teach young children about sexuality, attention to Bible stories and the overall plot line of the Scriptures can give teachers opportunity to introduce key ideas—like what it means for God to have created male and female. Teachers can trace themes of how God has used, and how man has misused, our roles as men and women in creation and in community. It furnishes opportunities to talk about how God cares for marriages and that God cares that we live pure lives that reflect his character—lives made possible by God's enabling grace. With tact and sensitivity, biblical teaching can accentuate God's design for human living, departure from which results in needless and atrocious consequences. Sunday school teachers, modeling care for such themes, sow seeds that will germinate and produce fruit for years to come.

Youth Ministry

In the next step, youth ministry, biblical teaching can more directly address issues of sex and sexuality. Indeed, it would be a misstep not to begin to address these issues, because young people are inundated by alternative sexual narratives at school, in culture, and perhaps even at home. It is also vital for youth workers to include the parents, especially if those parents are believers and attend the same church. Youth work must be sensitive to developmental issues. Methods for addressing this should differ between junior high and senior high. Even within those spheres, radical differences exist between a sixth-grader and an eighth-grader, or between a high school freshman and senior. Youth ministry featuring small groups as part of its structure affords ways to take large group teaching and maximize discussion in smaller groups. The more sensitive and explicit a topic is, the more important same-gender groups become. I might suggest that large group teaching can often be coed, but smaller group settings should be same gender, led by a same-gender adult leader.

As to how often to address sexuality, and to what degree, this depends on a few factors: one's sense of judgment and the structures of the overall church. It's wise to try making it regular and high quality, and, again, to consider various ways to involve the parents. The goal is to reinforce good teaching taught at home, not the other way around.

Unfortunately, of course, youth workers may end up being the most prominent resource for their youth on biblical sexuality. In those cases, it's appropriate to do one's best to disciple the family as a whole. Unbelieving parents may introduce an evangelism opportunity.

At a former church of mine, both the junior high and senior high ministries ran a yearly teaching unit on biblical sexuality. It became expected and it was valued. Beyond those structured lessons, though, youth workers should be vigilant to take opportunities that arise as they teach through the Bible to share practical biblical injunctions, wisdom, and insight on sex. Volunteer leaders must also be adequately equipped to teach on such topics.

College Ministry

Churches near a college campus should consider how to disciple attending students, and this opportunity needs to be critical in your discipleship mapping. At this stage in life, these young men and women are beginning to settle on their views about sexuality. But there is still time. In light of the presence of collegians, it might even be worth talking with the preaching pastor about integrating application points or books of the Bible with sexuality themes in mind in his preaching planning.

In my experience, I have observed some common recurring features of a millennial worldview: sex is viewed as a more casual expression than ever before; many Christian youth are not only exploring sexually but are unapologetic about it; and same-sex behaviors are largely accepted as permissible. We used to have visceral responses on our side; cultural momentum aided our cause. Sometimes, regrettably, this led to dogmatism and ungodly responses, but still, the cultural context was one that helped us make our case. That hour is over. Today, we can expect that many Christian millennials will be filled with sympathy and compassion that easily translates to a rejection of, if not indignation toward, classical Christian sexual ethics. This makes it crucial that we think and pray hard about how to disciple our collegians with the truths and gospel power of the Spirit we have discussed in this chapter.

One effective way of discipling our children, youth, and young adults in the truth and lifestyle of sexual purity is by various ministry leaders sitting down with each other and the other leaders of the church, to get on the same theological page and to map out a consistent discipleship plan. The ministry of Christian education in a church should feature a collective sense of handing off the gospel from one generation to another.

Once more, this process should include the parents. As we set about to plan a teaching series or discipleship plan, we can invite parents to a meeting and glean from them what they would like to be taught, what their kids are wrestling with, where the obstacles are, and how the church can equip the parents to lead the way in leavening sexual purity in their children.

Some churches follow a centralized and programmatized approach. Other churches will be more organic and informal. There is no one-size-fits-all approach. Biblical sexuality must be addressed thoughtfully, consistently, and with age-sensitive pedagogy in mind. Most churches do far too little with this topic. Many Christian college students reach university with almost nothing in their theological and discipleship tool belt. An encouraging reminder is that the Spirit can accomplish great work with very little.

I am a testament to this. I grew up in unhealthy, theologically vague churches, and yet God discipled me powerfully on the topic of sexuality by the direct work of his Spirit through Scripture and godly mentors. What if we gave our youth a robust gospel-centered education and formation ministry? Think about what the Spirit could accomplish for their wholeness.

Adult Learning

Last but not least, adults. Many churches are de-emphasizing traditional Sunday morning adult Sunday school classes, due to space needs and modern attendance challenges. Still, most churches retain learning environments like occasional seminars, conferences, or other discipleship outreaches. Such venues offer a chance for some gospel-centered teaching on sexuality.

It is admittedly daunting to teach these things to people who are midstream, so to speak. But the vision of God's beautiful design for sexuality exerts a significant impact on marriage health, marriage holiness, and gender identity. Parents also need to know what the Bible teaches on these matters so they can effectively inculcate those lessons and timeless truths at home. Adults also need to grow in their own sexual purity, which we forget to our peril.

It is tempting and all too easy to allow this topic be the domain of young people, and to confine our thinking to the realm of politics and public life. Right now, for example, the issue of homosexuality is culturally and politically critical. Often older evangelicals direct their attention to policy and religious liberty issues without first thinking about the theological issues—not to mention their own sexual purity. The former are important issues for believers to engage, but policy, legal response, and institutional positioning will be far better informed once the biblical vision for heterosexual monogamy is apprehended, appreciated, and appropriated. So, rather than adult learning environments neglecting this topic, they should accentuate the need for the Holy Spirit to be at work in the life of the whole congregation, shaping them into sexually whole people. Offering a class on sex may also be a good way to launch a new discipleship track or an inaugural seminar in a series aimed at adult theological learning.

Whether we are teaching five-year-olds or ninety-year-olds, God's wondrous design for sexuality is not just a truth to behold but a life to live. Let's design our Christian education ministry to form hearts, not just minds. Help our churches to taste the goodness of God on these matters, not just pay loose lip service to them. Education for the church optimally functions as nothing less than a matter of formation by the power of the Spirit.

One on One

Personal Discipleship

In some ways the ministry of a local church is a bookend. While Christian education is a powerful means of spiritual formation, perhaps even more powerful is one-on-one ministry. The pulpit and one-on-one ministry are like two pillars, holding the bulwark of the Spirit and the Word together.

If the leaders and disciple-makers of a church are equipped to answer questions about and to nurture sexual purity, in personal and relational ministry, they can do powerful ministry. Again, this is about the work of God's Spirit, and one must always seek how the work of God the Spirit can be unleashed.

In my experience, the moment for shaping hearts and minds comes when a young person asks to meet and talk about an issue or question pertaining to sexuality. Leaders should be ready for something not just theoretical, but something profoundly personal and practical. Often damage has already been done. Prepared leaders will engage with love, look into the person's eyes, open a Bible, take their time, and won't try to either teach or conclude everything in one setting.

Let me be specific. I have found that most young people's minds and hearts have been shaped by the Spirit most dramatically not under the pulpit, but across the table at the coffee shop or cross-legged on a couch. The pulpit often grabs the attention, clears the brush, and offers larger categories, but hearts often turn and yield to God in personal encounters where the infinitely beautiful gospel is held out to them and sexual truth is connected to their fullest humanity.

The Pastor's Office

Pastors, I am going to round the corner and begin to address you personally, as my fellow brothers in this fight for hearts, minds, and lives. Like personal discipleship, you have one of your greatest opportunities in your one-on-one counseling ministry. You may have one or more people you are personally discipling right now, and sexuality may come up from time to time. More often than not, your people will ask for an appointment to talk about the issue and the implications of sexual purity as a one-off counseling moment. So, your study needs to be a place of both truth and safety.

A story that haunts me to this day was told to me by one of my elders. His daughter was struggling with same-sex attraction, and was being pursued by another woman who was open about her homosexuality. The elder's daughter wanted to be a fully devoted Christian. The other woman was not a believer. She and this woman were attending a large and vibrant evangelical church in an inner-city context. Though his daughter was reconsidering many of the ideas she was raised with in a theologically and culturally conservative home and church, her current church attracted her because it was so committed to the biblical gospel and yet also to the racial and economic needs of that city.

Because of her struggles with homoerotic feelings and the actual presence of this other woman, she felt like she needed to talk with the pastor about her situation and what the Bible taught about homosexuality. She and this other woman made an appointment and met with this pastor, who happens to be a great pastor and someone I respect from afar. But, without thinking about it, after some small talk in which he learned that this young woman was working with a government-sponsored initiative known for having many gay people in its organization, he mentioned something about that, quite flippantly, assuming these young women were solidly situated in orthodoxy. He meant nothing by it, but without knowing it he broke her heart. She continued to make small talk and never brought up her questions and personal struggle with same-sex attraction. The other woman—who, remember, was not a believer—had her image of a Christian pastor shattered. This elder's daughter headed down the path of acceptance and now is married to that other woman. Both now affirm faith in Christ but abandoned evangelical commitments for a liberal version of Christianity and now believe discipleship to be compatible with homosexual marriage.

We can't stop people from mistaking us or misinterpreting us. People can use us as excuses, and they do and they will. But we have to be so very careful about how we conduct ourselves in our counseling sessions. Our office needs to be known for safety, even when we have to deliver unwelcome truth. My simple admonition is this: never be flippant, always be earnest, and be ready for anyone to come in your door for any reason. If you are reading this book, I take it you care about developing a nuanced understanding of sexual purity. If you take anything from this chapter, may it be that you respond rightly and warmly to young people struggling with the theology, and the necessary self-denial, that they need to live sexually free lives with gospel love and the promise of the Spirit's power. Before they listen to your counsel and teaching, they need to know you love them as they are, with all their questions—even the dumb ones—and with all the ways they have already allowed Satan to twist their humanity. You are a powerful presence and symbol. Let God use that for his glory and the good of your flock.

Training Leaders

Let me end with a quick word on training. Pastors, this again is mostly for you, especially if you have (or plan on having) ministry training as part of your church's discipleship mission.

Please consider making biblical sexuality a portion of your content and spiritual formation training. Future lay leaders, interns, pastoral residents, and your younger staff will be the culture-shapers at your church and, one day, in other churches or mission fields God places them in. There are a myriad options and plans you can shape—from seminars, full classes, conferences, to reading lists—but please incorporate gospel-centered instruction on a theological vision of sexual purity.

Always remember that the character of your leaders is a key ingredient in your training efforts. The health of a church starts with its leaders' health. The Spirit of God is wont to pull his power away from places of ungodly leadership, and many a Bible story reminds us of this. But when the leadership is faithful and full of the Spirit and the gospel, God does great things in those communities.

So, make sure you are shaping the hearts of your leaders in training. Pray for them. Exhort them to surrender their sexual choices and lives to Christ on a daily basis. Show them both the truth and joy in sexual purity. Make sure they are putting themselves in safe places. Be sensitive to their station as collegians, young singles, young marrieds, young parents, etc., and give them wisdom for each stage. Train men and women to lead the charge. The fruit of a chapter like this, within a book like this, is that the truth found herein can be passed from one generation to another.

Think about the ripple effects you can have if you train future leaders to surrender themselves and lead others in sexual purity—the great dividends of a local church faithful in the fight for sexual joy in Christ. Consider and aim by God's grace to achieve the apologetic, evangelistic, and culture-shaping force of such a community!

Conclusion

Theologically accurate thinking on sexual purity is essential. But the affections must be stirred and the will must be conquered. We cannot do this on our own. We are fallen and our flesh wars against holiness, but the truth of the gospel and the power of the Spirit are ours to have. The gospel and Spirit reign everywhere Jesus is presented as Lord, but the local church—your local church—is God's favorite place to bestow these twin truths. From pulpit to dinner table, we should be intentional, be earnest, have open Bibles, and take our time. With those ingredients, the Spirit of God will do great things to fashion his people into sexually whole and joyful worshipers.

Bibliography

Hiestand, Gerald, and Jay S. Thomas. *Sex, Dating, and Relationships: A Fresh Approach.* Wheaton, IL: Crossway, 2012.

Index

abortion, 104, 126n19, 132
Abraham, 3n1, 204
abstinence, 95
accepting the other person, 238–39
actions, 141, 143
Adam, 11, 12, 37–38
adelphopoiesis rites, 216
adult learning, teaching sexuality and, 248
adultery
    condemned in the New Testament, 109
    failing to denote Christ's single-minded fidelity to his bride, 118n22
    in the heart, 227
    as wrong and remaining illegal in twenty-one states, 126n19
adults, needing to grow in sexual purity, 248
adventure, of marriage, 60–61
Aelred of Rievaulx, 204, 205
aesthetic beauty, of a wedding, 60
affirmations, starting with, 187
Affirmative Consent Project, 126n17
"All of Me" (Legend), 153n6
All Saints Presbyterian, in Austin, Texas, 195n1

Allen and Gorski study, on homosexual men, 213
"(Almost) Everyone's Doing It," 107
alms, giving for the sake of charity, 141
aloneness, relieving Adam's, 11
St. Ambrose, 118
American culture. *See* culture
American evangelicalism, flavor of, 71
amor amicitiae, compared to *amor concupiscentiae*, 144
ancient world, more to marriage than sex, 116n20
angels, forbidden sexual relations, 170n47
anger
    condemned by Jesus, 141
    making forgiveness difficult, 229–31
    working through, 232
animals, none fulfilling the "like-opposite" test, 11
anti-authoritarianism, of millennials, 245
anti-gay bias, church removing, 193
anxious, prohibition against feeling, 141
apostolic fathers, taught extensively from the OT, 4
appreciation, 145
Aquinas, Thomas, 143–44, 146, 204, 205

argument from nature, on sexual orientation as innate, 212
Aristotle, 204, 205
atheism, implications of, xxi
attitudes, sea change in moral, xx
attraction, as a complex concept, 202
attributes, resulting from both creation and the fall, 189
Augustine
    dualistic and Platonic aspects of thought, 36
    on God bidding us to do what we cannot, 98
    role in a negative and prudish view of sexuality, 35
    on struggles against sins of the flesh, 147–48
    on timing of nuptial blessing, 38n12
    understanding Christian eschatological hope, 36
authority
    as a big issue for millennials, 245
    loss of moral, 67–68
    loss of Scripture's, 68–69
    loss of the community's, 71–72
    loss of tradition's, 69–71
    question and location of, 67
    showing the beauty of, 77
autoeroticism, failing to make us generous, 161
"automatic" behaviors, 191
avoidance, caused by disgust, 234

babies
    sex making, 142
    sex without worrying about making, 131–35
"bad" shame, arising from pornography, 166
Bailey and Pillard study, 212–13
bank account passwords, sharing, 136
Barth, Karl, on Song of Solomon, 14
Bath Sheba, 3n1
"Be perfect," 140n2–41n2
behaviors, occurring on autopilot, 191
Benedictines, on work and prayer, 199
Bernard of Clairvaux, 117n21
betrothal, in the ancient world, 116n20

"Beware Elvis Presley," xix
Beyonce, 73
Bible
    celebrating the delight of human sexuality, 25–26
    as completely trustworthy and infallible, 68
    condemning homosexual relations, 193
    contextualizing sex within marriage, 43
    emphasizing storytelling and recollections of the faithfulness of God, 90
    on God's plan for sex to be within marriage, 193
    as a means of understanding Christ and the gospel, 114
    not condemning issues of orientation or desire, 188
    not the final word for progressives, 32
    opening chapters presenting narratives of creation and human sin, 4
    perspective on premarital sex, 19–24
    revealing God's will, 31
    ruling out marriage to another man, 206
    story of sex in beginning, 37–41
    telling us we are not actually born as we were meant to be, 179
    understanding of, 187
Bible Belt, a high rate of marriage dissolution, 125
The Bible Made Impossible (Smith), 114
biblical faith, 13, 93–94
biblical ignorance, 69
biblical marks of gender identity, versus cultural ones, 44n38
biblical sexual ethics
    in a compelling way, 75
    as deeply counterintuitive, 103
    overemphasizing the boundaries of, 79
biblical sexuality, training on, 246, 247, 251
biblical teaching, accentuating God's design, 246

biblical texts, reinterpretations of relevant, 218
Bieber, Justin, 73
Bill Porter, 178n4
Biola (Christian college), 65
biological arguments, not meant to minimize God's power, 192
biological contributions to sexual orientation, ignoring and minimizing, 193
biological determinism, 180–83
biological fatalism, 180–83, 189
biological inheritance, not the sole cause of behavior, 181
biological predisposition, 182, 188
biological purpose, 74
biological transformation, of marriage, 49–61
biologists, viewing behaviors as phenotypes, 181
biology, limitations of, 181
birth control pill, 74
Blamires, Harry, 93
bodies
  as a gift that has been tainted, 37
  movement of as a sort of voice of the soul, 118
  not detachable from "who we really are," 23
  redeeming, 35–37
  as temples of the Holy Spirit, 82, 123n7
  training for ecstasy, 160–61
  training to crave the reward of others' admiration, 158n23
  trusting God with, 79–91
bodily ecstasy, theology of, 161–62
bodily practices, leaving room for God, 82–83
bodily union, metaphor of, 116
Body, Soul, and Human Life (Green), 154n9
bond, between the man and woman, 13
bond of intimacy, as focus of the serpent's ire, 16
Book of Common Prayer (BCP)
  ceremony, 54–56, 58, 61
  on marriage, 49, 51, 56, 60
  on the union of husband and wife, 38n11
  vows, 55
books, on premarital sex, 31
born in sin, 180, 189
"born this way" hypothesis, siding with, 66
"Born This Way" (Lady Gaga), 175
"born this way" rhetoric, 72
"Born This Way" theology
  as an apologetic, 183
  on biblical sexual ethics, 182
  correct in naming God as Creator, 179
  homosexuality and, 175–94
  ignoring the fall, 179
  improper presuppositions, 178
  mistaken in construing innate attributes, 188
  not a Christian narrative, 179
  not accounting for the fall, 184
  refuting with truth and love, 178
  rejecting, 193
  sounding Christian, 178
  as well-intentioned, 176–77
Boswell, John, 216
boundaries
  pushing, 230
  for sex, 79
  against temporary and partial pleasures, 26
bowels, as the center of emotion, 157n22
brain, rewiring by using pornography, 167
brain structure and function, behavior and trauma altering, 214
"breath of life," possession of, 10, 11
bride, entrance of, 52
British royal weddings, pageantry and tradition of, 52
brother-making rites, medieval versions of, 216
"buffered selves," 77
Burr, Chandler, 175–76, 180
Butterfield, Rosaria Champagne, 98

call from God. *See* vocation
call-and-response, of the *BCP* ceremony, 56–57
calling, to marriage or celibacy, 198–203
campus ministries, 241
campus sexual assaults, 127n23
Canaanites, sexually exploitative behavior of, 9
capacities, exaggerating, 96
casual sex, 121, 136
Catechism of the Catholic Church, 20, 124n12
Catholic priests, molesting young boys, 67
celibacy
    calling to, 198–203
    celebrating, 76
    gift of, 190n14
    increasing one's capacity to serve, 110
    sense of being called to, 206
    state of, 22
ceremony, as a microcosm of values, 51
Chambers, Alan, 200, 201
changing, yourself, 238–39
chaos, trying to destroy order, 6
character, of leaders, 251
charity, 159
Charles, Tyler, 107
chastity
    Christian rule of, xx
    connecting one's body to the spiritual, 85–86
    as continuity with other ways God asks us to trust him, 83–84
    definitions of, 154n10
    fixing us on openness, 170
    focusing energies on relationships, 163
    as fruitful, 85
    as a joke, 95
    proving for a daughter, 108
    requirements of, 164
    role in seeking and trust, 88
    rules for premarital relationships, 109
    as a single woman, 82
    trusting God about, 87
chemistry, development of, 136

childbearing, not a word in Genesis 2 about, 14
childrearing, challenges, 90
children
    as a burden, 133
    consumer mentality towards, 135
    doing better in married, two-parent families, 131, 131n28
children of promise, 102
children's ministry, teaching sexuality and, 245–46
Christ. *See also* Jesus
    as the "bridegroom," 115
    identification with and participation in the work of, 45
    lived as the fully Human One, 152
    living in us, 82
    relationship with the church, 117
    words about choosing to give up marriage, 199
Christian dating site (Christian Mingle), 123
Christian education, place of, 242
Christian education ministry, 245–48
Christian emphasis, of the *BCP* ceremony, 54
Christian heterosexuals, treating Christian homosexuals with compassion, 191
Christian identity, 44
Christian leaders, discovered to be inconsistent or hypocritical, 67
Christian Left, injunctions against premarital sex, 123n12
Christian Mingle (dating site), 123
Christian morality, xxi, xxii
Christian scholars, consensus regarding homosexuality, 214–18
Christian story, beauty and goodness of, xxii
Christian theology, of sex, 34–47
Christian view, of marriage and relationships, 126
Christian worldview, evidential force of, 92–93
Christianity
    making a difference in ordinary life, 151

promoting a morality of celebration, xxii
as a system, xxi
Christians
    avoiding situations inflaming temptation to sin, 192
    born unmarried, 201
    disagreeing about masturbation's link to lust, 155
    fostering communities, 205–6
    not choosing celibacy as a ministry to God, 190n14
    premarital sex for, 18–33
    reading the Old Testament through the lens of the New Testament, 21
    regarding biblically based moral norms about sex as optional, 124
    with same-sex attraction, 188
    struggling to live faithfully in the present time, 45
    tolerating sex as a biological necessity, xxii
    understanding sexual intercourse as deeply intimate, 122
    violating their own persons, 23
Christlikeness, growing in, 153
christocentric reading, of sex, 114–18
Christosis, requiring cruciformity, 45
church(es)
    attendees having the lowest divorce rates, 125
    as the "bride" of Christ, 115
    buildings as special places, 60
    cooking for, 89–90
    decorations limiting to crosses, 81
    discovered to be inconsistent or hypocritical, 67
    as essential, 44
    as hopelessly infected, 31
    as the last places on matters of sex, 68
    ministry training for leaders, 242
    needing to be gospel oriented in all they do, 243
    not simply accepting sexual confusion as reality, 75
    offering gospel-centered teaching on sexuality, 248
    plunking us down in a "worship" service, 80
    pushing against the me-centric tendencies of consumerism, 77
    recommendations for on sexual ethics, 75–77
    regular attendance, 90–91
    relating to Christ as a wife relates to her husband, 115
    revealing that sexual purity is the miraculous work of God's Spirit, 242–43
    Spirit of God using to form God's people, 241
    tacit approval of same-sex relations, 215–16
Cicero, 204
classical marriage ceremony
    anticipating the couple's future, 52
    highlighting the values of marriage, 53
    honoring both the past and the future, 59–60
"classical style," of wedding ceremony, 51–52
cloistering, practice of, 108, 109
coffee, years of choosing and enjoying, 180n6
cohabitation, message of, 53
cohabiting couples, moving towards marriage to have a child, 135
college ministry, teaching sexuality and, 247–48
"Colorado Statement on Biblical Sexual Morality," 111n13
Commentary and Homilies on the Song of Songs (Origen), 117n21
commercials, coming loaded with sexual imagery, 35
commitment
    caution against frivolous, 54
    enabling a marriage to go the distance, 128–29
    marriage as, 237
    possible for the marrying couple, 55
    sexual partner willing to make, 137
commitment-to-be-committed, as not the same as commitment-in-fact, 130

committed romantic relationships and marriages, 228
common ground, finding, 236
Communication and Critical/Cultural Studies, 72
Communion ritual, 59
community
    celebrating during a marriage ceremony, 56
    Christians fostering, 205–6
    God forming us through, 90
    living in, 89
    loss of authority of, 71–72
community life of the church, 242
community support, need for, 57
compassion, for those who feel same-sex attraction, 189–93
concerns, giving their due, 238
concordant twins, 212–13
conflating, love and approval, 177–78
congregation, involving in the *BCP* proceedings, 56
consent, as the only relevant boundary, 127
consent framework for relationships, 130
consent mentality, 126–31
consent standard, asking too little, 128
"consenting adults" paradigm, 126
consequentialism, 35
conservative Christians, 195–96
consumer attitude, towards children, 135
consumerism, 71, 77
consumptive behavior, of pornography, 168
consumptiveness, 170
contemporary rituals, severing from morality, 155n13
contempt, 234–35
"contextualized" interpretation, of the Bible, 123
contraception, 131, 132, 133
contraceptives, laws restricting the sale of, 126n19
control, loss of, 235
cooking, for the church, 89–90

cooperative imagination, required for complying, 27
cooperative intention of created husband-wife relations, devolving into a power struggle, 38
Corinthian Christians, 22
counseling sessions, pastors conducting, 250
covenant, 13, 205, 205n31
Covenant Eyes, filtering software, 149
covenantal commitment
    rooted in the character of God, 41
    on the wedding day, 50
covenantal nature, of marriage, 41n27
covenantal relationship, analogous to a marriage, 152
covetousness, rejecting, 158
creation
    accounts of in Genesis 1 and 2, 37
    depicting the union of man and woman, 20
    distinct narratives about, 10
    with no fall, no redemption, 178–79
    potential for disorder, 6
    story of the seven days of, 5
    theology of, xxii
creator God, having neither male nor female consort, 7
Crispin, Jessa, 73
cultural landscape, faulty narratives about sex, 125
cultural roots, of sexual pluralism, 218–21
culture. *See also* gay culture; "hookup culture"; pop culture; purity culture
    affecting one's diet and exercise regimens, 181
    ancient, 4, 42n29
    Christian purity, 34
    moving away from traditional Christian sexual ethics, 19
    pornification of, 220
    providing opportunities for training for greedy taking, 170
    saturated with sex, 121
    sexuality in Western, 44

sexualized, 124–25
treating sexual fulfillment and romance as essential, 208
youth, 74
cyberporn, 169
Cyrus, Miley, 74

daily faithfulness, severing eating from, 155n12
"dating," meaning of, 19
dating apps, putting casual sex at our fingertips, 121
"dating relationships," in the first century, 113n15
David and Jonathan, swore a covenant with each other, 205
decisions, agonizing over, 206
Declaration on Sexual Rights (IPPF), 127
Degeneres, Ellen, 73
demand, lowering, 96
demon of lust, killing, 98–100
desire
　for the other, 43
　sin and, 184–86
desiring and being desired, 143
Desiring the Kingdom (Smith), 80
deterministic thinking, sexual pluralists appealing to, 214
disability, concealing a vocation, 197
disappointment, sadness taking the form of, 231–32
discipleship plan, mapping out a consistent, 247
disclosure, of the past to your partner, 238
disembodied future state, overlooking God-givenness of our bodies, 36
disembodied theology, 80
disgust, 233–35
disorder, 6, 142
diversions, 163
divine creational intention, 72
divine relations, existed before human relations, 39
divorce
　among married couples over fifty, 123n8

in ancient Israelite culture, 42n29
　clarity on emphasized alongside clarity on homosexuality, 75
　failing to denote Christ's single-minded fidelity to his bride, 118n22
　grounds for, 227
　Jesus on, 158n26
　no-fault, 68
　rates among self-professed Christians, 125
Dobson, James, 155
dogmatism, of sexual pluralism, 220
dominion, of humanity over the rest of creation, 6
Donne, John, 46–47
Door to Door (movie), 178n4
Dreher, Rod, 206
"dry f*cking," 27
dualist understanding, of persons as immaterial souls and material bodies, 154n9
Dufault-Hunter, Erin, 149–50
Dunham, Lena, 74

eating, for the sake of pleasure, 143
ecclesiology, tied with moral formation, 241
ecstasy, training our bodies for, 160–61
Eden
　meaning "ecstasy" of an erotic kind, 11
　related to Hebrew words for "pleasure," "delight," and "delicacies," 25
eikons, made in the image of God, 118
"Elvis the Pelvis" nickname, xix
embarrassment, about sex, 34
embodiment, celebrating the dignity of beyond sexualization, 76–77
embrace, of the other, 41n27
emotional responses, to sexual sin in marriages, 229
empathy
　as about "thinking with," 228
　building, 231, 236
　cultivating for your partner, 232

ensouled bodies, all different from one another, 165
entitlements, related to sexuality, 127
epithumeô, 185
erectile dysfunction, porn-induced, 167–68
eros, 40, 43, 146
erotic dysfunction, philosophy as tortured, 92
erotic life, 166
erotic love, celebration of, 46–47
erotic stimulation, 162
"erotica," compared to porn, 164n30
Esther, 3n1
ethical relativism, 219
ethics, understanding Christian, 102
"etiologies," 14
evangelical clergy, counsel on setting boundaries, 106
Evangelical Lutheran Church in America (ELCA), social statement on "Human Sexuality," 123n12–24n12
evangelical megachurch pastors, in adulterous affairs, 67
evangelical sexual ethics, 107
evangelical theology, emphasizing conversion and salvation, 36
evangelicalism
  Christian tradition in much of contemporary, 70
  "personal relationship with Jesus" flavor of, 71
  premarital sexual ethic of, 119
Eve, 25, 38
evil things, coming from within, 122n6
ex-gay beliefs, 200n17
ex-gay ministries, 199–200
ex-gay movement, 199, 201
existing opinion, justifying, 69
Exodus International, 199, 200
exploitation, of others for selfish ends, 130
expository ministry, 245
expository preaching, 244
extramarital sex, as acceptable, 14–15
eyes, enabling scandalous looking and taking, 158

faith
  biblical, 93–94
  experiencing as a divine encounter, 77
  without works seeming dead, 86
faithful marriage, pointing to a faithful God, 42
faithfulness
  actively remembering God's, 90
  required for Israel, 41
  unto death, 55
fall, failure to recognize and account for, 178n4
fallen creatures, 180
fallen human persons, called to marriage with sinners, 230
fallen world, essence of a, 45
false goods, humans pursuing, 204
false narratives, about sex, 125
familial relations, in ancient pagan Greek culture, 112n14
families, God setting the lonely in, 89
"family," definitions of, 126n19
family life, challenges, 90
family relations, forms of affection in, 111
fasting, 83, 85, 88–89
fasting and praying, 84, 89
fatalism, 181, 182
Father. *See also* God
  telling us "no" in love, 33
Father-Son-Spirit relation, 40
fearful takers, becoming, 153
fears
  difficult to cordon off to a single corner of life, 134
  listing of common, 235–36
  making forgiveness difficult, 235–39
feelings, 141, 142
female homosexuality, compared to male, 183n10–84n10
female promiscuity, generally condemned, 108n8
female sexuality, notion of unrestrained, 74
fidelity
  as the central value in the *BCP* vows, 55

longing and physical oneness
grounded in, 41
necessity of, 41n27
pledging, 50
Fifty Shades of Grey (novel), 73
Fifty Shades of Grey series, 131
film industry, porn mainstreamed into, 220
flesh
pointing to the solidarity of kinship, 13
warring against holiness, 251
Focus on the Family, 155
followers of Jesus, as new creatures, 37
forced celibacy, as an unbearable burden, 200
forgiveness, 228–29
achieving, 237–39
asking God for, 237
as difficult, 228
difficult because of anger, 229–31
difficult because of disgust, 233–35
difficult because of fear, 235–39
difficult because of sadness, 231–33
of God, 31
as an important part of thriving, healthy, holy relationship, 227
as less equivocal, 227
in the marriage bed, 227–39
formal affirmation, 51
formal pact, followed by faithful allegiance, 12
fornication, 20, 109, 122
Fragile Families & Child Wellbeing Study, 132n30
"fraternization," 216
freedom, to not explain oneself or one's choices, 72
friends
with benefits, 53
in Christ, 205
friendship
ability to form, 145
based on shared interests or pursuits, 205
developing with someone of the opposite sex, 202
importance in the Bible, 203–4

importance of in the Christian tradition, 208
Jesus' sacrifice of himself as an act of, 204
recovering a Christian understanding of, 203–6
fruitfulness in a church, discipleship test of, 241
full disclosure, degree required or recommended, 227

Gaga. *See* Lady Gaga
Gallup survey, on premarital sex, 123
Gardner, Christine, 72
gay and lesbian people, desires of, 29
gay Christians
God's calling cannot be reduced to marital status, 206
same-sex attraction and, 192
gay culture, 192, 193
gay hookup spots, 192
gay liberation movement, 199n16, 205
gay or lesbian sexual relationships, 198
gay pride parades, 199n16
gay rights, 195
gay students, at Christian colleges, 72
Geisler, Norman, 155
gender(s), 6, 66
gender identities, 44n38, 196n5
Generation Unbound: Drifting into Sex and Parenthood without Marriage (Sawhill), 132
generosity, masturbation and, 162–66, 169–70
generous receivers, 170
Genesis 1, on sex and human identity, 5–10
Genesis 1–3, sketching the OT approach to sex, 5
Genesis 2, sex and human intimacy, 10–15
Genesis 3, Eros under the shadow, 15–16
genetic and neuroanatomic studies, inconclusiveness of, 218
geneticists, viewing behaviors as phenotypes, 181

genitalia
    lie that God cares only about, 82
    touching of done with the left hand, 158n25
Gideon, creating a religious icon, 8
gift
    of another person, 130
    of celibacy, 190n14
    of self, 116
Gift-love, 39
gifts and the calling of God, as irrevocable, 198
Girls (HBO show), 74
Glee (television show), 74
global church consensus, about sexual ethics, 217
global church majority, taking seriously, 218
Gnosticism, putting mind above material, 80
God. *See also* Father
    acknowledging as our Creator, 124
    addressing ritual prescriptions vis-à-vis involuntary activities, 151
    as an angry, never-satisfied Ogre spewing "noes," 24
    of anti-pleasure, 25
    appealing to for help, 96
    asking to shape us, 96
    as the author of different sexualities, 175
    as the author of pleasure, 25
    beyond all categories of gender or sexuality, 9–10
    calling all sinners to repentance and gives them gifts, 197
    caring for marriages, 245
    caring that we live pure lives, 245
    characterization as a jealous God, 152n3
    chose to work through the brokenness, 179
    connection with morality, xxi
    created all that there is and our very selves, 179
    created sex, 187
    creating a male ("dirt creature") first, 10
    creation of the body by, 35
    deserving primacy, 149
    desiring what is best for us, 97
    discipling powerfully on the topic of sexuality, 248
    doubting the goodness of, 79
    doubting the love of, 101
    enduring faithfulness of, 42
    eternal and perfect love of, 101
    extending forgiveness and redemption, 97
    fidelity of, 152
    first and last will for pleasure, 26
    focusing on the greatness of, 148
    forgiveness of, 31
    forgiving our sins, 149
    forming us through community, 90
    giving every Christian gifts, 198
    glorifying in your body, 82
    grace of, 28
    healing us from our pride, 100
    honoring with sexual integrity, 137
    identified only one tree in Eden as forbidden, 25
    imbued human beings with value, 102
    interacting with humankind, 153n7
    lacking any sex-related detail in Genesis 1, 7
    law of, 28
    love for us, 40, 82, 177
    manifesting both male and female features, 102
    on marriage, 50, 196
    never portrayed as an actual man, 7
    as not a man or women, 165n31–66n31
    not engaging in sex, 163n28
    ordained sex and marriage, 118
    out of sight in the "public square" of our culture, xxi
    as perfect in love, 97
    pleasure of seeing the face of, 26
    portraying as the God of "no," 25
    as the primary source of refuge, 232
    relying on, 237
    reputation and character of, 79
    responding to the call of, 206–8

revealing himself to those who seek, 86
role as a problem solver, 124
spoke to Moses as a man speaks to his friend, 204
steadfast love of, 25
thanking for life's blessings, 54
triune nature overflowing with gifts, 152
trusting about an outcome or resolution far in the future, 87
trusting and becoming sensitive to his guidance day to day, 207
trusting to forgive your sin or your partner's sin, 239
trusting with our bodies, 81
turning to with fears, 236
upholding standards because he knows what's best for us, 97
vows said in the presence of, 55
wanting what is best for us, 101
will of, 26
as a witness to the marital promises of non-Christian couples, 55
God and the Gay Christians (Vines), 200n19
"God made me this way" Christian spin, 72
Gomer, 41, 42
Good Christian Sex (McCleneghan), 123n12
Good Christian Sex: Why Chastity Isn't the Only Option, 31
good life, 169–70
goodness of sex, grounded in someone, 41
gospel, 243–44
gospel-centered instruction, 251
grace
    appealing to, 28
    forgiven by through faith, 96
    of God and masturbation, 162–66
gray divorce, 123n8
The Great Divorce (Lewis), 99
Great Philosophers Who Failed at Love (Shaffer), 92
Greco-Roman world, sexual mores of, 108

greed, corresponding with lust, 157
Green, Joel, 154n9
Gregory of Nyssa, 162n27
groom, relishing the body of his bride, 42
Gushee, David, 70
gut (*kardia*), grabbing by means of our body and its senses, 80

habits of heart, for a fulfilling sexual relationship and a happy marriage, 121–37
habitual behavior, feeling innate, 191
hands, enabling scandalous looking and taking, 158
happiness, as a consequence of pregnancy, 133n34
happiness and holiness, convergence of, 100
happiness and joy, moral faith consistent with, 94
hard determinism, 214
Hare, John, 96
harem, of imaginary brides, 145, 150
Harris, Sam, 93
"having sex," not lifting anyone out of loneliness, 30
Hays, Richard, 69
"healing," promise of for gays and lesbians, 200
health, possible by God's grace, 98
health of a church, 251
healthy, being, 149
heart(s)
    as the center directing actions or intentions, 157
    toxic habits of, 125
    yearning for a love that is perfect and eternal, 236
heterosexual desire
    as no guarantee of long-term marital stability, 202
    as not always sin, 184–85
heterosexual evangelicals, failing sexually, 94
heterosexual marriage, sexual activity outside of, 23

heterosexual monogamy, biblical vision for, 248
heterosexual relations, not always holy, 193
heterosexual single persons, sex drive of, 182
heterosexual sins, winked at for generations, xxiii
heterosexuality, righteous in and of itself, 190n14
heterosexuals, feeling repulsed by homosexual thoughts, 190
historical grounds, to be skeptical about sexual pluralism, 217
history, good for your spouse to know your, 233
holiness, 98, 148
"Holiness Code," in Leviticus, 9
Hollywood celebrities, jubilant world of, 73
Holy Communion, in the *BCP* ceremony, 59
holy life, resources for, 97
Holy Spirit
    profoundly grieved by sexual sin, 22–23
    transforming us, 29
    working in the life of the whole congregation, 248
homoerotic feelings, struggles with, 250
homosexual acts
    Bible condemning, 183
    God disapproving of, 177
    heavily emphasized by sexual pluralists, 211
    in the story of Sodom and Gomorrah, 196n4
    as viewed as normal and permissible, 108
homosexual desire
    Bible not condemning, 183
    compared to homosexual sex, 184
    as no more a sin than heterosexual desire, 193
homosexual equivalent, to heterosexual marriage ceremonies, 216
homosexual orientation, biological basis for, 212
homosexual relations, 186–87, 188
homosexual relationships, Christian response putting love front and center, 186–89
homosexual unions, opinions on, 68–69
homosexuality
    acceptance of, 65–66
    Bible not condemning the multidimensional concept of, 183
    Christian response to, 175–94
    condemned in the New Testament, 109
    as culturally and politically critical, 248
    divisions about, 195
    failing to denote the union of the masculine and the feminine, 118n22
    as a natural human variation, 176n3
    positive attitudes toward across the denominational spectrum, 66
    questions surrounding, xxiii
    as sin, 183
homosexuals
    alleviating the personal history portion of the choice, 180n6
    not marrying their same-sex partner as not inequitable deprivation, 190n14
    straying in ways that seem deliberate, but are in fact habitual, 191
    struggle compared to a heterosexual person's struggle, 185–86
    tolerance of, 219–20
honor, compared to shame, 13–14
"hookup culture," 121
hookups, message of, 53
"horniness," not fixating on, 163
Hosea
    on God's people experiencing birth pangs, 97
    life of as overarching image for God's relationship with Israel, 8
    marriage to the prostitute Gomer, 41
    remained faithful to Gomer, 42
"Hound Dog" (song), xix

housing arrangements, fostering connection, 89
human(s)
    acting to gain what they perceive to be good, 204
    as creatures of habit, 150
    doing best in long-term relationships, 53
    as embodied beings, 112–13
    as God's representatives, 6
    having inherent dignity and value, 129
    needing to find their way back into a relationship with God, 16
    struggling with temptation and sin, 197
    as a unity, 142
human creature, in-between state of, 170n47
human discourse, linguistic flexibility in, 23
human identity
    in Genesis 1, 5–10
    as male and female, 7
human intimacy, in Genesis 2, 10–15
Human One, 152n4, 152n5
human race, as a local pocket of evil, 94
human reality, yielding itself to a kindness of touch, 169
human sexuality. *See also* sexuality
    as a complex thing, 201
    in a paradoxical position in Genesis 1, 9–10
    as strictly binary (male and female), 6
humanity
    being "male and female," 7
    creation of as "very good!" 5
humility, expressed by involving the community in marriage, 57
hurts and losses, considering all, 232
husband(s)
    abusing wives, 45
    seeking to control his wife, 38
husband and wife
    in a covenantal relationship, 55
    formally pledging to care for each other, 59
    giving their bodies as gifts to one another, 43
    tensions in the relation of, 38
hypocrisy, amplifying existing suspicions, 68
hypothalamus cells, more numerous in heterosexual men, 213

"I am not good enough," theme of, 236
identical (monozygotic) twins, studies of, 212
identity
    changing, 30
    sin of creating our own, 46
illicit desires, effects of, 142
imago-Dei, instantiating, 117
immanent present, taking precedence, 70
immortality, temptation to, 22
impulses, leading one to masturbate, 147–49
"in Christ" identity, embracing, 46
"inaugurated eschatology," 37
incense, rejecting, 81
incest
    failing to portray the union of dissimilar natures, 118n22
    laws against, 126n19
    role of, 213
inconsistencies, amplifying suspicions among young Christians, 68
incontinence, starting from a state of, 153
incontinent person, more likely to compel his spouse to have sex, 147
individual convictions, now weighted above the consensus of one's community, 71
individualism, 44, 71, 72
injustice, anger is about, 229
innate drives, not necessarily good, 189
innate things, as not sinful, 179–80
innateness, 189, 193
"intercourse," versus copulation, 15

intercourse-then-marriage scenario, not endorsed as God's holy preference, 21
intergenerational living experience, sense of family through, 89
International Planned Parenthood Federation (IPPF), 127, 127n20
Internet, exponential surge of porn on, 220
interpretation, problem of, 68
intimacy
    as a depicting the love of God for Israel, 26
    in marriage relationships bringing dangers, 228
    between men and women about much more than "sexy," 17
Isaiah, 201, 203
Israel, unfaithfulness to her covenant with YHWH, 41
Israelites, "played the harlot," 8
"It's choice" answer, trivializing sexuality, 180

Jacob, 3n1
James, New Testament book of on faith, 86
Jenner, Caitlyn, 73, 74
Jesus. *See also* Christ
    addressing those who look at another's wife, 157
    on the core vision of the Old Testament, 21
    on depth of commitment required for marriage, 201
    on divorce, 22, 42
    on future rewards, 203
    identifying "fornication," 122
    insisting he has not come to abolish Torah, 156
    internal motivation of, 152n4
    at the Last Supper calling the Twelve his friends, 204
    on lust, 159
    on the OT, 4
    on performing the letter of Torah without the spirit, 159
    prohibiting deliberate harboring of desire for an illicit relationship, 185
    reiteration of the law regarding lust, adultery, and commands to cut off body parts, 155
    responding to two schools of thought about divorce, 158n26
    as single, 76
    on speaking truthfully and keeping vows, 158
    on storing up treasures, 158n24
    underscoring men's culpability, 158
Jesus and the Disinherited (Thurman), 87n5
Jewish context, of the New Testament, 36
John of the Cross, 117n21
John Paul II (Pope), 116, 199
Jonathan, David and, 205
Joseph, 3n1
Joseph and Mary, story of pointing to the marriage-before-intercourse sequence, 21–22
journal, writing about hurts, 232
joy, possible only in relationship with God, 97
Judeo-Christian sexual ethic, holding fast to the historic, 221
judgment, predicated on the act, 183
just society, vision of, 9
justice, belonging to the Lord, 231

Kallmann, Franz, 212
Kant, Immanuel, 93, 98, 212
Kantian moral faith, 93–95
Kardashian, Kim, 73
Kavanaugh, John, 207
King, Martin Luther, Jr., 87n5
King and McDonald study, 213
kingdom allegiance, as primary, 43
kingdom life, framing all else, 44
kingdom of God, 37
kissing, 112
Knot Yet Report, 132n30
knowledge of God's law, substituting for doing, 28

Knust, Jennifer Wright, 80
Küng, Hans, 214

la petit mort ("the little death"), as a euphemism for orgasm, 161
labels, piling guilt or anxiety on gay friends, 192
Lady Gaga, 175, 180
law of God, meditation on, 148
leaders
    ready for something profoundly personal and practical, 249
    training, 251
"leaving," depicting something public, 20
"legalism," logic of, 28–29
lesbian or gay Christians, not pressuring into marriage, 203
letter of the law, obeying, 28
LeVay, Simon, 213, 213n8
Levitical purity codes, of the Old Testament, 109
Leviticus, "Holiness Code," 9
Lewis, C. S., xx, 94, 145, 146, 197
LGBT (lesbian, gay, bisexual, and transgender), 196n5
    characters on television, 219
    Christians, "texts of terror," 188
    community, 187, 192
    movement, questions surrounding, xxiii
    relationships with, 66
    sexuality increasingly normalized, 70
    students appealing to essentialism and utilizing "God created me this way" rhetoric, 72
    suffering in the eyes of, 71
liar, predisposed to become a thief, 142
life, accepting all as good, 135
life of wisdom, realities producing, 240
"like-opposite" test, 11
limits, knowing your, 239
listening, training spiritual hearing, 85
literature, replete with the futility of choosing darkness over light, 101
living alone, 89

living together (unmarried), 18
lizard, transforming into a mighty stallion, 103
Lloyd-Jones, Martyn, 69
local churches, 241, 244, 251
logic, of Torah crucial for discussions of sex, 155
loneliness, "not good," 37
Lord, distrusting, 136–37
Lord's Supper, 81
loss, 231, 233
love
    ability to, 145
    Christian definition of, 39
    Christians starting with, 186–87
    as deeper and wider than sexuality, 76
    as the Divine energy, 39
    entailing loss or denials, 161
    harvesting from the Bible as a slogan, 32
    obligating us to respect one another, 159
    as who God is, 101
"love commands," as mandatory, 32
Love in Action ministry, 199
"love of desire," 144
"love of friendship," focused on another person, 144
love of God
    doubts about, 97
    more important than any human love, 45n39
love of God (or others), conflating with the approval of God (or others), 177–78
"love your neighbor as yourself," 83
lover, desiring the Beloved herself, 40
loving Creator, lovingly made us, 33
lovingkindness, adopting an attitude of, 237
lust
    deliverance from, 98
    denoting wrongful desiring, 157
    dynamics and danger of, 154–60
    look motivated by, 185
    meaning in the context of the Sermon on the Mount, 155

lustful feelings, leading to lustful actions, 142
Luther, Martin, 98

Macy, William H., 178n4
"making out," as a sin, 108
male and female, created in God's image, 37
male and female bodies, union as a form of personal communion, 116
male/female difference, basic to humanity, 7
man
    as a body, 116
    forming a radical and profound attachment to the woman, 12
    offering himself to the woman as a gift, 117
    wanting sex more often than his wife, 188
man and woman, nakedness of, 13
Man and Woman He Created Them: A Theology of the Body (John Paul II), 116
manipulation of others, resulting from ignoring desires or repressing them, 164
Marcion (heretic), denied the OT, 4
Marin, Peter, 169
marital sex, not all godly, 190n14
marital unions, as unbreakable, 42
marriage
    adventure of, 60–61
    as an alternative to sexual immorality, 22
    biological transformation of, 49–61
    as a bulwark against sexual temptation, 110
    calling to, 198–203
    as a ceremony celebrating transparent sex, 56
    as commitment for the difficult times, 237
    as comprehensive union of two souls, 56
    concerns regarding sexual behavior and, 227
    as a covenant, 13, 41
    different roads to, 202
    foreshadowing God's unbreakable covenant faithfulness, 42
    invented by God, 50
    involving a real metaphysical change, 50
    as irrelevant, 31
    as less compelling, 66
    losing as a real loss, 30
    as a momentous decision, 201
    as a momentous status change, 53
    mutual self-giving in sex, 83
    never happening, 29–30
    not always godly, 190n14
    not bringing happiness or deep satisfaction to millions, 30
    not the answer to sexual shortfalling, 97
    as the only legitimate context for satisfying one's sexual passions, 110
    as the only legitimate venue for sexual intimacy, 22
    as the only viable form of love, 200
    original plan for, 38
    as permanent, 53
    place of forgiveness in, 227–39
    as a public occasion, 56
    reasons for, 60
    refraining from as better, 201
    as the regular expectation for Jesus's disciples, 22
    requiring a great deal of self-sacrificial love, 146
    as sacramental, 50
    as a secondary priority, 43
    as a special relationship, 49
    taking place in the absence of ceremony, 51
    trust betrayals igniting powerful fears, 235
    understood through a typological framework, 116n19
marriage bed, banishing everyone else from, 238
Marriage Supper of the Lamb, 14
married couples

dealing with some sexual
  frustration, 83
different in kind (or ontology) from
  the unmarried couple, 49
exchanging vows, 130n27
justifying degrading sexual activities
  or dishonoring commitments,
  130
rekindling attraction, 202
as second-class Christians, 198
married sexuality, versus unmarried
  sexuality, 53
married young women, fear of newly
  pregnant, 134
marrying couple(s)
  announcing a change in their status,
  53
  as both inheritors and creators, 52
  exclusivity of, 57
  fidelity of, 55
  not needing a *BCP* ceremony, 61
  strengthening marriages in their
  community, 57–58
masturbation
  as an addictive feedback loop, 150
  affecting feelings for the worse, 146
  as an autoerotic activity, 160
  as chastity's helping hand, 151–70
  as a check on our consumption, 164
  checking our envy or covetousness,
  165
  concerned with no other person but
  oneself, 145
  continence, character, and the
  morality of, 140–50
  defined, 143, 151n1
  directly addressed in the Bible,
  141n3
  disciplining for generosity and
  opening to God's grace, 162–66
  disordering the passions, 140, 147
  done for the sake of physical
  pleasure, 143
  entering into with prayer, 165
  forming us for chastity's generosity,
  169–70
  forming us for generosity toward
  others, 163
  habituating us into being takers, 160
  impeding the pursuit of the life of
  Christian perfection, 142
  impulses leading to, 147–49
  as lament, 165
  love of friendship and, 144
  lust and, 155
  moral importance of, 151, 154
  as morally wrong, 140
  in a nonlustful way, 149
  not necessitating *porneia*, 164n30
  as an opportunity to reflect deeply
  on our sexuality, 156
  practiced to move us toward
  chastity, 154
  practicing as lament, 164
  reinforcing a grasping, acquisitive
  disposition toward others, 160
  releasing tensions, 163
  relieving sexual urges, 147
  reticence to talk candidly about, 165
  reward of orgasm, 160
  role of, xxiii
  serving virtue, 151–70
  supporting generosity, 161
  unveiling of soul, 165
material world, renewed emphasis on
  the importance of, 36
McCleneghan, Bromleigh, 123n12
"me and Jesus" rituals, 69
meaning of sex, 130
meditatio ("meditation"), on the law, 148
Melton, Glennon Doyle, 71–72
men
  abandoned natural relations with
  women, 183
  committing shameful acts with
  other men, 183
  divorcing women "for any cause,"
  158n26
  "peculiar proficiency" for relaying
  visual cues for sexual arousal,
  167
men and women, making new, 97
Menger hotel, 27
Mere Christianity (Lewis), xx
Merritt, Jonathan, 103
Midgley, Mary, 181

Mihalko, Reid, 93
millennials
    anti-authoritarianism of, 245
    Christians more accepting of homosexuality, 65–66
    having sex to "see if they have a connection," 136
    on premarital sex, 121–22
    rejection of classical Christian sexual ethics, 247
    views about sex, 65
    worldview of, 247
mind-body, retraining to identify triggers, 168
mindset, trust taking a different, 82–83
ministry leaders, mapping out a consistent discipleship plan, 247
Mize, Krystal, 181
Modern Family, 74
"modesty," as retrograde, 66
modesty, rule of, xx
Mohler, Al, 199n15
Moltmann, Jürgen, 214
monozygotic pairs, discordance for sexual orientation in, 213
moral attitudes, sea change in, xx
moral authority, loss of, 67–68
moral demand, 96
moral faith, 92–105
    involving two convictions, 94
    Kantian, 93–95
    needed in regard to sex, 105
    parts of, 94
    in regard to sexuality, 94
moral life
    as commanded by Christ, 140–41
    as possible, 94
moral question, ultimate irrelevance of studies to, 218
moral thesis, sexual pluralism as, 214
moral transformation, basing in the gospel, 243
moral values, deriving from cultural preferences, 219
moral vision
    of the Bible, 9
    friends and family help shaping, 71

Moralistic Therapeutic Deism, 69, 124, 124n13
morality, xxii, 94, 101
Mormons, 123n11
"morning after" feelings, survey of, 128
Mother Teresa, on clarity, 207
motherhood, fearful of the demands of, 134
movies, sex between unmarried characters, 19
multigenerational (mixed life-stage) groups, participating in, 90
multiple partners, effects of, 136
multisensory experiences, as more fun, 80
mundane, significance of, 152
murder, preventing, 141
mutual consent, 131
mutual self-giving and joyful receiving, of the husband and wife, 116
My Exodus (Chambers), 200n18
myth, that only married people are normal, 44

nakedness, as a shared quality, 13
National Campaign to Prevent Teen and Unwanted Pregnancy, 107
National Marriage Project, *Knot Yet Report*, 132n30
natural predisposition, as due to God's direct action, 176
neural paths, becoming wider with each exposure to pornography, 167n39
neuroanatomic factors, as potential biological bases for homosexuality, 213
neuroscience, implications for theology, 154n9
new creatures, becoming, 46–47
"new orthodoxy," at odds with traditional moral teachings, 69
New Perspectives on Christian Purity, 31
New Testament (NT)
    expecting communal mutuality embodied in the life of the church, 43

many references to the church as the "bride" of Christ, 115
premarital sexual ethic, 108–13
sexual ethic not apart from Old Testament sexual ethics, 21
Nietzsche, Friedrich, xx–xxii, 92
no-constraints individualism, 72
"noes," of God, 26, 33
no-guilt sexuality, world of, 73
non-Christians, not seeing a homosexual lifestyle as immoral at all, 191n16
nonmarital sex, acceptance of, 121n4
nonsexual activities, 111
Not Afraid to Change (Paulk), 200n17
"not yet," of life in this body, 164
nudity, on film and in television, 73

oaths, practical impact of, 55–56
objectifying others, as a sin, 160
Old and New Testaments, prohibiting homosexual acts, 196
Old Testament (OT)
　approach to sex, 5
　clear statement on male and female, 7
　as an eclectic anthology, 3
　emphasizing storytelling and recollections of the faithfulness of God, 90
　inspired by God and profitable on every level, 4
　Israelites struggled to serve a God who could not be touched or seen, 81
　meaning of purity, 163n28
　relevance for Christian ethics, 21
　as second-rank scripture, 3–4
　on sex, 3–17
　singling out sexual sin, 8
　studying responsibly, 4
　understanding of sexuality, 102
Onan, 155, 155n14
one flesh, becoming, 13, 20, 37, 50–51, 115, 116, 130n27
one-flesh union, of marital sexuality reflecting commitment, 126

one-night stand, as the "worst sex" ever, 136
one-on-one counseling ministry, by pastors, 249–50
one-on-one discipleship, importance of, 242
online pornography, amplified gnostic views of sex, 67
ontological difference, between the married and the unmarried couple, 50
"open" marriages, 126n18
opposite-sex marriage, as an option for some same-sex attracted Christians, 208
orgasm
　achieving without removing articles of clothing, 27
　demands for endless, 162
　training our bodies for ecstasy, 160–61
orientation change, proved for many to be a false hope, 200
Origen, 117n21
Osteen, Joel, 179
OT. *See* Old Testament (OT)
other person, using for self-gratification, 131
ought, implying can, 96, 212
over-eating, under-exercising, as a learned problem, 191
overgeneralizations, damaging and causing harm, 193
Ovid, poems of, 109n8

pagans, on the true good, 204
pain
　expressing without blame, 232
　felt through sexual brokenness, 188
　required for transformation, 100
painful situations, people in, 29
Paratarelli, Marc, 181
parents, 24, 97, 247
partner, praying for your everyday, 237
partnership, of men and women, 8
passionate kissing, 112
Passover lamb, sacrifice of, 117

INDEX

pastors
  becoming theological practitioners, 240
  evangelical megachurch, 67
  lack of consensus on premarital sexual activity, 108
  one-on-one counseling by, 249–50
  people mistaking or misinterpreting, 250
  sending a confusing and mixed message on premarital sexual ethics, 107
  single, 199n15
path toward perfection, action putting a person on, 142
pathways, choosing between two potentially good, 206
patience, necessary for intimacy with another human being, 167n39
patriarchy, perpetuating, 73
Patriarchy Purity Complex, 74
Paul (apostle)
  on the body, 82
  on celibacy and marriage, 109–10
  christocentric reading of sex, 115, 117
  connecting justification by grace with the Holy Spirit, 243
  on doing things we hate to do, 230
  on Gentiles given up to sinful desires of their hearts, 142
  on humans knowing certain things about God, 204
  on husbands, loving their wives, 126
  on love in 1 Corinthians, 122
  on "making out," 106–19
  on marriage, 201
  on marrying rather than burning with passion, 163n29
  meditation on spiritual gifts, 197–98
  naming notorious lifestyles, 30
  on the new creation lifestyle for those "in Christ," 103
  on the relational dynamics of Christian marriage, 115
  on sexual sins, 22, 101–2, 118–19
  as single, 76
  on sinners, 197
  on Titus discipling his new church, 243
  view of sex and marriage, 117
  warning against sexual immorality, 122–23
  wishing that all could remain single, 199
  worried that marriage would bring unnecessary anxiety, 203
Paulk, John, 200, 200n17
people. *See also* young people
  all as worthwhile and lovable, 176
  desires of gay and lesbian, 29
  as discardable, 145
  having inalienable dignity, 130
  proud, feeling entitled to do what they want, 100
perfect family, letting go of dreams of, 135
perfect life, involving doing God's will, 141
perfection, not making a requirement for love, 238
perichoresis, doctrine of, 39
permission, to use someone else for my personal pleasure, 126–31
permissive sexual ethics, toxic assumptions underlying, 125
permissive stance, towards premarital sex, 123n12
personal discipleship, 249
personal happiness and fulfillment, taking precedence, 44
personal mistress or a slave, for sexual gratification, 108
personal openness, receiving as a gift, 117
personal relationship, with the Lord, 129
person-disgust. *See* contempt
persons. *See* people
Peter, 149
Pharisees, 4
phenotypes, 181
philosophers, romantic failures of, 92
physical activity, determining the sexual nature of, 111
physical attraction, timing of, 202
physical body, redeeming, 35–37

physical hunger, serving a spiritual purpose, 89
physical indwelling, pointing to a personal entanglement and intertwining, 41
physical losses, from not being sexually intimate, 232
physicial affection, before marriage, xxiii
"pivot foot," of sexual ethics teaching, 241
Plato, 6, 35–36
pleasure, 142, 143, 161, 162
Plotinus, 36
polyamorous relationships, 126n18
polyamory, 126n19
polygamy
    condemned in the New Testament, 109
    lacking consent, 126
    laws against, 126n19
    in the Old Testament, 3n1
Ponce, Phil, 179
pop culture
    as a causal impetus, 219
    changes during, xix–xx
"Porn Again" (Dufault-Hunter), 169n45
"Porn and the Threat to Virility" (Luscombe), 167n40
porneia
    as a catch-all term to forbid extramarital sexual activity, 109
    commonly interpreted to mean fornication, 123
    covering all the varieties of sexual activity outside marriage, 23
    masturbation not necessitating, 164n30
    variously translated, 227
    women engaging in, 168n42
pornification, of American culture, 220
pornographic images, on every digital medium, 35
pornographic materials, exposure to, 220
pornography
    becoming a reinforced neurological habit, 167
    chemical and neurological effects of, 168n43
    Christian men addicted to, 220
    defined, 164n30
    effects on our culture, 168n43
    husband pressuring his wife to watch, 130
    influence on the sexual landscape of the West, 166
    as liberating or morally neutral, 166
    link to anxiety and depression, 167n38
    now a $13 billion yearly industry in the US, 220
    overtaking our embodied spirit, 168
    regularly used for masturbation, 167
    rise of sexual pluralism coincident with, 220
    shifting content of, 168n41
    from a theological perspective, 169n45
    as training in taking, 166–69
positive vocation, for same-sex-attracted Christian, 197
postmodernist perspective, undermining confidence in reason, 219
power relationship, between man and woman, 16
power struggle, of husband and wife, 38
powerlessness, 181
practical approaches, to pursuing the virtue of chastity, 149
"practicing homosexuality," 183
prayer, accompanying fasting, 83
preachers, attacking orientation or feelings of same-sex attraction, 187
preaching ministry, 244
pre-AIDS gay liberation movement, 205
predisclosure conversation, with your partner, 238
pregnancy
    as a disaster, 133–34
    women's receptivity to, 133n34
preliminary passions, learning how to handle, 148
premarital boundaries, 107

premarital relationships
  as completely nonsexual, 108
  legitimizing sexual forms of kissing in, 112
premarital sex
  among adults as not wrong at all, 122n4
  for Christians, 18–33
  as contrary to God's will, 23–24
  increasing percent of adults approving, 122n5
  as morally wrong, 122
  negative consequences of focusing on pregnancy, 134n36
  no single Greek word referring to, 23
  not attaching a shame-based stigma to, 66
  pastoral and ministry leaders sending a mixed message about, 113
  thinking constructively about within the christocentric framework, 118
  views on, xxiii
premarital sexual ethics
  in the New Testament, 108–13
  question of, 106
premarital sexual relationships
  antipathy towards getting pregnant, 133
  between a man and another man's virgin daughter, 108
premeditatio ("prerehearsal"), of possible future events, 148
Presley, Elvis, xix
pride, as the root of all sin, 100
primary human bond, as the company of disciples, 43
The Problem of Pain (Lewis), 94
problematic scientific argument, for sexual pluralism, 212–14
procreation
  connection with sex now severed, 131
  by husband and wife, 38
  problem of separating sex from, 134n34

progressive Christians, mentioning the Bible, 32
progressive groups, working transnationally to codify the concept of sexual rights, 127n20
progressive views, questioning, 32
"Progressives," focusing on justice, 31
pro-LGBT movement, 189
pro-LGBT slant, in media, 219
propassiones ("preliminary passions"), 148
propriety, rule of, xx
prosperous life, emotional and relational tools of, 53
prostitution
  condemned in the New Testament, 109
  failing to denote Christ's single-minded fidelity to his bride, 118n22
  lacking consent, 126
  laws against, 126n19
  viewed as legitimate, 108
Protestant Reformers, 199
Protestants, 198
psycho-social-biological-spiritual entities, 154
public health literature, discouraging unwed childbearing, 133n34
public occasion, marriage as, 56
pulpit
  as epicenter of Christian formation in Bible-driven churches, 242
  grabbing the attention but hearts turn and yield to God in personal encounters, 249
  as the rudder of the church's ship, 244–45
purification, rituals of, 152n2
purity, narrowing to sexual concerns, 163n28
purity culture
  described, 34
  pushing back against, 72–74
  viewed with suspicion, 66

queer sexuality, normalizing of, 74

radical individualism, tune of, 44
Rahab (harlot), 3n1
rape, as profoundly damaging, 23
recordare ("remembering"), the greatness of God and the virtues of Christ, 148
redemption, 16, 46
referre ("referring"), to the metaphysical hierarchy, 149
Reformation Project, 200n19
relational foundation, disposing both partners to put forth effort, 228
relational intimacy, thriving beyond sexuality, 76
relationships
  as disposable, 145
  measuring the "costs" and "benefits" of, 128
relative, not marrying a close, 187
respect, for the other's dignity before God, 129
resurrection
  of the body, 35, 36
  bringing life from death, 46
  came as a surprise in the middle, 102
  focusing on, 148
Revelation, referring to the wedding supper of the Lamb, 116
revenge, 229, 231
revolutionary developments, throughout history, 218
rewards or goods, pursuing "internal," 153
right hand, causing you to sin, 157
right side, reserved for "clean" activities, 158n25
"righteous indignation," feeling, 229
righteousness, 97, 159
ring exchange, 58, 59
risk, involved in trusting God, 86
role, that God has for us, 208
Roman Catholics, focusing on priestly and religious callings, 199
rules
  as arbitrary impositions, 101
  against sex, 100

ruling and creating, as divine prorogatives, 38
rumination, 238

Sabbath, 83, 84–85, 155n12
sacrifices, needed in married life, 128
sacrificial heart, 128–29
sadness, making forgiveness difficult, 231–33
sadomasochism, engaging in, 131
"safe sex," 104
safety
  loss of, 235
  sense of, 232
salvation, xxii
salvation process, God bringing us through, 177
same-gender groups, importance of, 246
"same-sex attracted," but denying the label "gay," 193
same-sex attraction
  bringing to fullest expression, 182
  calling of God and, 195–209
same-sex behaviors, largely accepted as permissible, 247
same-sex marriage
  reconciling with Christian teaching, 196
  strengthened argument for, 200
same-sex sexual activity, condemned until the late twentieth century, 214
Same-Sex Unions in Premodern Europe (Boswell), 216
same-sex-attracted Christians, pastoral care of, 198
same-sex-attracted men and women, reflections on opposite-sex marriages, 202n21
sanctification
  Christian embarking upon a life of, 177
  seeking while celebrating the gift of sexuality, xxiv
Sawhill, Isabel, 132–33
scientific grounds, for sexual pluralism as spurious, 218

Screwtape Letters (Lewis), 95
scriptural framing, of innate attributes and sin, 189
Scripture
    clear in prohibiting no-fault divorce, 68
    condemning homosexual relations (and lust) as sin, 184
    interpreting in light of our experiences, 69
    loss of authority of, 68–69
    not directly addressing masturbation, 155
    permissivist interpretations of, 219n19
    teaching on premarital sex, 20–23
"secondary anger," covering up sadness or another emotion, 230
secondary emotion, anger as, 231
"second-class" single members, 76
The Secret Thoughts of an Unlikely Convert (Butterfield), 98
secular liturgies, after our hearts through our bodies, 80
secular script, as the cultural message filling our ears incessantly, 95
secular view of sex, 93
self-absorbed sexuality, temptation of, 83
self-consumption, God healing us from, 100
self-contempt, 234, 235
self-denial, 81
self-forgetfulness, 162
selfish habits, 128
selfishness, 134
"self-realization," 45
self-sacrifice, ethic of, 83
self-stimulation, 154, 160, 163
Sergius and Bacchus, 216
Sermon on the Mount, on being perfect, 140
serpent
    channeling the voice of, 25
    as "crafty" or "shrewd," 15
    created as a potential companion to Adam, 15
    deceiving Eve and subsequently Adam, 38
    first words to Eve, 25
    getting behind the lie of, 26
    hostility against the woman, 16
    rejected by Adam as his consort, 15
service, 83, 85
seventy times seven, forgiving, 237
sex
    abstaining from until marriage, 57
    as an act embedded in the social matrix, 14
    acting as a sign of the redemptive love of God, 46
    became sexuality, 74
    bonding men and women together, 135
    celebrating God's gift to husbands and wives, 46
    celebration of in the Song of Solomon, 14
    Christian theology of, 34–47
    Christian understanding of, 102
    Christian view of, xxiii
    Christocentric reading of, 114–18
    as a created and redeemed good, 37
    culture saturated with, 121
    damage caused by misuse of, 118
    as deeper than pleasure, 135
    desiring with someone, 150
    detonating a series of sins, 122
    disgust and, 233–34
    emptied of generosity, 169
    enacting what the covenantal relationship signifies, 42
    "feeling good" whether married or not, 35
    freely chosen and mutually pleasurable as holy, just, and good, 31
    as fundamentally about Christ and the gospel, 115
    in Genesis 1, 5–10
    in Genesis 2, 10–15
    as a gift of God, 93
    as good or bad, 170
    involving the union of two into one, 41
    as joy or temptation, 37
    making babies, 131

making the desire for "idolatrous," 73
meaning of, 130
meant to be beautiful and heavenly, 104
normalized transactional view of, 126n17
not at odds with seeking sanctification, xxii
not supposed to be safe, 104
as now a transcendent reality and divine right, 74
Old Testament on, 3–17
oriented toward another person, 143
outside of marriage as never moral, 111n13
outside the marriage covenant, 136, 190
overly legalistic approaches to as unhelpful, 66
as pleasurable, 142
as procreative, 142
purpose as self-expression and personal fulfillment, 65
questions about as about love and desire, 39
reflecting the realities of the kind of love within the godhead, 46
relational dynamics of, 116
as a social act, 20
as the solution to passionate burning, 110
story of in the Bible, 37–41
taking seriously again, 135
as a thing of shame in many churches, 68
as a totalizing and sacred avenue for understanding identity, 67
traditional boundaries broken down, xx
typological reading of, 117n21
as unitive, 142
viewed as a more casual expression, 247
vulnerability in, 228
within the confines of male-female marriages as the divine ideal, 45
without covenantal commitment as sex without love, 41
without worrying about making babies, 131–35
as a wonderful gift from God, 122
Sex, Dating, and Relationships (Hiestand and Thomas), 241
"sex, drugs, and rock 'n roll," hedonist trinity of, xxii
sex and sexuality, sanctifying us, 45
sex difference, basic to creation, 7
"Sex Geek," 93
sex-shame connection, 165n31–66n31
sexual actions, as always something one can choose, 185
sexual activity
    to be reserved for the marriage relationship, 119
    defining, 111
    difficult to justify any amount of, 118
    losing as a real loss, 30
    meant to be relational, 135
    as noncoercive, mutually respectful, and tastefully private, 19
    popular culture accepting, affirming, and even promoting, 24
    reserved for the marriage relationship, 108, 113n15
sexual anxieties, mapping onto biblical concerns for purity, 152n2
sexual assaults, on college campuses increasing, 126n17
sexual attitudes, prevailing casual, 94
sexual attraction to a person of the same sex, as a temptation and a result of the fall, 198
sexual autonomy, 127n20
sexual behavior
    Jesus reaffirmed the traditional Jewish standards of, 103
    of professing Christians, 94
    rules of, xx
sexual bondage, engaging in, 131
sexual boundaries
    appropriate, 106
    in Leviticus, 9
    traditional Christian, 74

sexual brokenness, 75, 188
sexual confusion, not stigmatizing and not perpetuating, 75
sexual connection, in marriage, 56
sexual consent, explicit, 126n17
sexual consumerism, Jesus's fierce warnings about, 159
sexual crimes, lacking consent, 126
sexual decision-making, authentic, 128
sexual delight, in Genesis 2, 14
sexual desire(s)
    indulging, 100
    indulging, ignoring, or repressing, 150
    masturbating in order to rid oneself of, 149
    misusing, 122
    as a sign of something deeper, 40
    as sin itself, 36
sexual dispositions, not just personal, 160
sexual ecstasy, taking us "outside ourselves," 161
sexual energies, requiring direction, 164
sexual energy, 164, 168
sexual enterprise, possessing the danger to possess and control another, 38–39
sexual entitlements, idea of, 127n23
sexual eros, as a sign or symbol, 40
sexual ethics
    improvising, 32
    Jesus seized upon Genesis 2:24, 21
    making its way into the culture of the church, 242
    recommendations for the church on, 75–77
    reduced to "getting consent," 126
    as a thundering "no" that denies pleasure, 24
    viewed by many young people as arbitrary, 67
    young Christians wincing at old-school, 65–77
sexual experience
    fiancée having prior, 230
    before marriage, 227
sexual fidelity
    of the marrying couple, 53
    public pledge of, 60
    recognized by the community, 57
sexual foreplay, door open to, 107
sexual fulfillment
    desire for not sin, 185
    outside of marriage, 227
    as a subsidiary good, 45n39
sexual greediness, starving our, 165
sexual healing, possible by God's grace, 98
sexual holiness, as possible with God's help, 105
sexual identity, 44, 74, 75–76
sexual imagery, in commercials, 35
sexual immorality
    biblical passages teaching against, 123
    ever-present temptation toward, 110
    fleeing from, 123n7
    as less than clear, 227
    "running" from, 23
sexual indulgence, cannot be directed by our whims, 160
sexual integrity
    as possible, 94
    standing as the image of faithfulness, 9
sexual intercourse
    according to Augustine passed sin from parent to child, 36
    as an image of the combination of perichoretic union and other-serving, 40
    occurring within the context of a covenantally committed relationship, 41
    reserved for marriage, 106
    as a sensory pleasure occurring within one's own body, 40
sexual intimacy
    as central to human nature, 9
    cooperative imagination necessary to protect, 28
    described as much more than sex, 17
    existing in a total weave of life, 14

lacking the marital relationship
  developing a built-in reluctance towards new life, 133
  lines Christians should draw before marriage, 27
  with someone else during marriage, 227
sexual life, 160
sexual love, 135
sexual loyalty, pledging, 53
sexual misconduct, range of terms denoting, 109n9
"Sexual Morality," in *Mere Christianity* (Lewis), xx
sexual morality, unanimity of opinion on, 217
sexual mores, freedom from traditional, 31
sexual oneness, of human marriage referring to Christ and the church, 115
sexual orientation
  categories of, 45
  as fixed, 66
  lesbian, gay, and bisexual dealing with, 196n5
  as a recent innovation in history, 76
sexual partners, lifetime number of, 123
sexual permissiveness, trend toward greater, 122n4
sexual pleasures, individuals entitled to, 127
sexual pluralism
  cultural roots of, 218–21
  lack of Christian theologians defending throughout church history, 215
  as moral thesis, 214
  move toward, 211
  not driven by rational argument, 211
  problematic scientific argument for, 212–14
sexual pluralist revolution
  being skeptical about, 211–21
  not a consequence of rational argument, 221
  as not fundamentally rational, 218

sexual pluralist thesis, potential repercussions of affirming, 215
sexual powers, using intelligently, 154n10
sexual predation, as the ultimate interpersonal abuse of power, 9
sexual purity
  beyond our reach, 95
  Bible's prescription for, 98
  in the church, 242
  developing a nuanced understanding of, 250
  discipling in believers, 240
  failure regarding, 30
  as a patriarchal notion, 73
  showing leaders both the truth and joy in, 251
  as unmarried people, 22
sexual purity discipleship, practical guide to, 242
sexual relations, 9, 109, 110, 115
sexual restraint, mandatory for all, 103
sexual revolution
  failure to deliver on its promises, 169
  of the sixties and seventies, xix
sexual rights, 127, 127n20
Sexual Rights: An IPPF Declaration, 127n20
Sexual Rights Initiative, 127n20
sexual sanctification, 242
sexual satisfaction, life remaining devoid of, 15
sexual sin
  emphasis on appearing selective, 10
  holding center stage pointing to the essence of apostasy, 9
  imagery of, 8
  not recreational sex gone overboard, 98
  as peculiarly serious, 22
  as predatory, 98
  root of functioning at the base of a myriad of sins, 100
sexual standards, of Christian singles, 106
sexual stimulation, as a serious matter, 160

sexual targets, list of prohibited, 9
sexual temptation, avoiding stimuli
	provoking, 149
sexual tensions, releasing, 163
sexual union
	mere desire for not legitimating
		such union, 143
	as a protected privilege, 20
	as a type of Christ's spiritual union
		with the church, 114–18
sexuality. *See also* human sexuality
	bound up with questions of identity,
		72
	Catholic teachings on, 124n12
	core to our humanity, 242
	described, 74
	discarding the traditional orthodox
		view of, 215
	integrating more fully into Christian
		identity, 129
	Jesus' standards regarding, 141–42
	of a married couple compared to an
		unmarried couple, 56
	not the basis for defining a persons'
		identity, 45n39
	pointing to God's own rich
		personhood, 8
	positive view of, xxii
	questions and issues surrounding,
		xxii
	recovering the truth and beauty of,
		135
	shaped by the gospel itself, 242
	as strictly a feature of the created
		order in the Bible, 7
	submitting to God, 124
	understanding in relation to the core
		identity God has given us, 102
	using in a premarital relationship,
		118
Sexuality in the New Testament
	(Loader), 157n19
sexualized culture, impact on
	Christians, 124–25
sexually holy, being, 95–98
"sexy," testifying to emptiness, 16
shalom, 155, 166n35
shame
	absence of, 13
	associated with sexuality in Western
		Christianity, 34
	breeding, 73
	compared to honor, 13–14
	ending in ritual suicide, 14
	hiding before God, 16
	in place of openness, 38
	resisting Christ's promise to address,
		166
	strong links with sexuality, 165
	turning us back toward God, 166
shamelessness, signaling sexual union,
	14
shared goals, friendship taking shape
	from, 205
significant others, expectations for as
	higher, 228
silence, in the Christian life, 84
sin
	corrupting the very image of God, 8
	damages of, 39
	every Christian struggling with, 208
	as innate, 189
	letting go, 99
	lurking in the vicinity of lust, 100
	we are born in, 179
sinful acts, repenting of, 184
sinful nature, acts of, 123n7
single chastity, as obedience to God, 85
single friends, constantly battling
	temptations, 29
single pastors, Protestant skepticism
	about, 199n15
Single Techno-Sex, 167–68
singleness, 76, 83
singles, including in every aspect of
	church life, 76
skepticism, toward sexual pluralism, 221
sleep
	allowing more time for, 84
	heightening spiritual sight, 85
small groups, youth ministry featuring,
	246
Smith, Christian, 114, 124
Smith, James K. A., 80
social media, with superficial
	"friendships," 145

Sodom, 100
Sodom and Gomorrah, 196n4
sodomy, laws prohibiting, 126n19
"Son of Man," 152n4
Song of Solomon
    biblical crescendo relating to sex, 42
    celebrating the sheer delight of sexual intimacy, 14
    erotically charged, 93
    no mention of children or procreation, 43n33
    nothing prudish about, 43
    qualifying as erotic but not pornographic, 164n30
    reflections on, 162n27
    sex celebrated in, 122
Soul Searching (Smith and Denton), 124n13
souls, inextricably linked to our flesh, 154
Southern Baptists, on homosexuality, 66
"sowing wild oats," 24
Spirit of God, 161, 242, 244
spiritual condescension, as a precarious condition, 95
spiritual existence "in heaven," overlooking God-givenness of our bodies, 36
spiritual formation, taking seriously, 97
Spiritual Friendship blog, 202n21, 203
spousal love, "referring to Christ and the church," 117
spouse(s)
    cheated, 230
    "confessing their sin" to their partner, 238
    doing everything for the sake of the other, 146
    as a "rock," 235
    telling overtly of perceived wrongs, 231
Stewart, Kristen, 74
Stonewall Inn, gay bar in Greenwich Village, 199n16
Stonewall Riots, 199, 199n16
strangers, trusting without reason, 136
strategies
    to develop trust, 86–91
    of scaring young people into not having sex, 35
Struthers, William, 167
student leaders, living together and sexually active, 19
subjective freedom, of the individual celebrated, 71
Swift, Taylor, 73
Symposium (Plato), 6

talking, about the situation needing forgiveness, 237
Tamar, 155
teachers, introducing key ideas to children, 245
"technical virginity," not being satisfied with, 28
telos, 160
temporary threesomes, 126n18
temptation
    accepting humbly, 150
    to define our own identity, 46
    every Christian struggling with, 208
    proving insidiously effective, 101
    resisting as a way of growing in virtue, 150
    resulting in sin, 184
Ten Commandments, nine of cast as prohibitions, 24
terror, of not being able to control the environment, 236
theft, types of, 23
theological anthropology, virtue assuming, 154
theological inconsistency, amplifying existing suspicions, 68
theological practitioners, pastors becoming, 240
theological resources, redeeming sexuality, 39
theology
    of bodily ecstasy, 161–62
    of grace, 28–29
    of sex, 34–47
therapeutic deism, 124
Three-in-One, as love, 153
tithing, 83, 84, 85, 88

Titus, 243
tohorah (sacred, clean, or pure), states of, 152n2
tolerance, 219, 220
Torah, 154–55
touch, importance to our mental and physical well-being, 232
toxic atmosphere, in society, 94
tradition, loss of authority of, 69–71
traditional views, questioning, 32
training, leaders, 251
transcendent authority, submitting to, 77
transcendent scriptural truths or moral norms, 70
Transparent, 74
Trinity, doctrine of, 39
"triple-A engine" (accessibility, affordability, and anonymity), 166
triune God, not needing us, 153
true friendship, found among those who pursued virtue and contemplation, 205
True Love Waits-style purity, churches pushing, 68
true righteousness, 159
The True Story of the Whole World (Bartholomew and Goheen), 87
trust
    changing your approach, 83–86
    involving our bodies, 81
    loss of, 232
    raising the question of, 136
    required in responding to God's call, 207
    requiring us to put our bodies on the line, 81
    strategies to develop, 86–91
    taking a different mindset, 82–83
trusting, in God, 208
truth
    determining, 32
    telling in wisdom and love, 238
tum'ah (everyday, unclean, impure), states of, 152n2
typological interpretation, of the marriage relationship, 116n19

unanimity, about premarital sex as wrong, 19–20
unchecked autonomy, burden of, 71
unforgiveness, needing forgiveness from, 237
unfulfilled sexual desire, as a "burning," 110
unhealthy bodies, leading to grouchy attitudes and a decrease in willpower, 149
"unintended pregnancies," majority as "mistimed," 133n34
unintended response, as not Jesus's worry, 159
union, of man and wife as a divine analogy, 187
unjust anger, doing away with, 141
unmarried couples, likely to split up, 132
unmarried persons, finding it difficult to remain sexually inactive, 22
unmarried sex, as never consequence free, 134n36
Unprotected Texts (Knust), 80

Vanauken, Sheldon, 197
vice
    moving away from, 153
    stepping away from, 159
vicious, moving toward continence, 153
Vines, Matthew, 184, 190n14, 200, 201
virginity, prized in unwed women, 109
virgins
    in the ancient world, 108
    portrayed as dysfunctional, abnormal, and emotionally deprived, 19
virtue
    accommodating the blessing and burdens of incarnate temporality, 153
    connecting moral concerns to an overarching, ordering narrative, 151
    enabling Christians to discern the right use of masturbation, 170
    meaning maturing before God, 165
    providing a gracious context for learning chastity, 153

traditionally associated with tending to our erotic life called "chastity," 154
virtue theorists, on masturbation, 168
vocation
    friendship and, 203–6
    of No, 197
    in the pre-Reformation Catholic Church, 198
vow exchange
    central to the classical ceremony, 52
    importance of, 53–54
vows
    emotionally and physically binding, 50
    prescribed for the couple in the *BCP* service, 54–55
    witnessed by the community, 13

Walsh, Matt, 96
Wambach, Abby, 72
Washed and Waiting (Hill), 192
websites, percentage porn sites, 220
wedding artistry, 60
wedding ceremony
    involving the community, 56
    purposes of, 51–52
wedding motif, in Christ's parables, 115–16
wedding rituals, acknowledging responsibilities, 58
weight management, as problematic, 191
Western Christians, operating with an ethic grounded in pragmatism or consequentialism, 35
Western culture, treating sexuality as a matter defining identity, 44
What the Bible Says-and Doesn't Say-About Homosexuality (White), 176n3
wholly sanctified, being, 98
willingness
    to question everything leading to Jesus of Nazareth, 32–33
    to receive, 233

Wired for Intimacy (Struthers), 167n38, 167n39, 168n43, 168n44
wish fulfillment, as an inherent right, 71
witnesses, presence at the marriage ceremony, 57
wives
    degrading husbands, 130–31
    desiring to control husbands, 38
    withholding themselves, 45
woman
    also meaning "wife," 157
    in the body of a man never affirmed in the OT, 7
    "built" from living human tissue, 12
    created to eliminate the loneliness of the man, 37
    creation of, 12
    finding her joy in yielding herself to another, 117
    giving herself as a gift, 117
    looking at with lust, 156–57
    wanting sex less often than her husband, 188
women
    all becoming potential porn stars, 167n39
    often vulnerable in that culture, 158
    ovulating or pregnant often having heightened libidos, 163
    relationship to mainstream porn, 168n42
works, lukewarm, 124n15
world
    as fallen, 102
    as marred, 179
    sin of creating our own, 46
    as unreliable, 235
worldly perspectives, shaping views about Christian teaching and doctrine, 95
worldview, undergirding all the diverse treatments of sex, 5
worship, taking little more than eyes and ears, 82
Wright, N. T., 103, 113n15

"Yes Means Yes" campaign, 126n17
YHWH. *See* God
yoke of Christ, as easy, 100
"You Weren't Born That Way"
    condemning homosexuality in its entirety, 184
    degrading the Christian story, 180
    leaving out sin, the fall, and redemption, 183–86
    not using, 189–93
    from the pulpit, 187
    reinforcing erroneous premises of "Born This Way," 186
    rejecting, 193
    seeming uninclusive, 178
young Christians, not embarrassed by sexuality, 74
young people. *See also* people
    inundated by alternative sexual narratives, 246
    minds and hearts shaped by the Spirit, 249
    offered truths and power sources trying to supplant the real gospel, 243–44
    paying attention to expository preaching, 245
younger American Christians, trends regarding sexual ethics, 66–67
younger Christians
    conditioned to see everything as sexual, 67
    views on traditional Christian sexual ethics, 65
youth culture, setting itself against the patriarchy, 74
youth ministry, teaching sexuality and, 246
youth workers, 246

www.ingramcontent.com/pod-product-compliance
Lightning Source LLC
Chambersburg PA
CBHW032051220426
43664CB00008B/957